HOW I FOUND GOD

Roles played by Fakir Shirdi Sai Baba
as God and the Spirit Masters in my
Spiritual Training resulting in God-realization

Yogi Minocher K. Spencer (4-10-1888—30-08-1958)

HOW I FOUND GOD

Roles played by Fakir Shirdi Sai Baba as God and the Spirit Masters in my Spiritual Training resulting in God-realization

YOGI M.K. SPENCER

Indian Parsi Spiritualist, Spiritual Healer, Medium, God's Emissary & Missionary (1888-1958)

Edited by

PROF. S.P. RUHELA

New Age Books

HOW I FOUND GOD

ISBN: 978-81-7822-352-0

Reprint : Delhi, **2016**
First Indian Edition : Delhi, 2011

Published by
NEW AGE BOOKS
A-44, Naraina Industrial Area, Phase-I
New Delhi (India)-110 028
E-mail: nab@newagebooksindia.com
Website: www.newagebooksindia.com

Library of Congress Cataloging-in-Publication Data
Ruhela, Satya Pal
ISBN 978-81-7822-352-0
Includes Foreword, Introduction, Poems, Editor's Post Script
Spirituality

Printed and published by
RP Jain for NAB Printing Unit
A-44, Naraina Industrial Area
Phase-I, New Delhi-110 028. India

This book has been blessed by

- Bhagavan Sri Sathya Sai Baba by materializing a Shivalinga on it on June 10, 2001 and Vibhuti in the book on June 24, 2001 at Sri Sathya in Sri Nagarajan's Flat No. H-19, Jalvayu Vihar, Sector 25, Noida (U.P.).
- Godman Sri Narayani Amma (Arul Thiru Sakti Amma) (Reincarnation of Durga), Om Shakthi Narayani Siddar Peedam, Ariyur, Malaikodi, Vellore – 55 (Tamil Nadu) on July 7, 2001.
- Srimad Sai Rajrajeswari (Reincarnation of Dakshyini, daughter to Daksha and Lord Shiva's Consort and an ardent devotee of Sri Sathya Sai Baba), 125, 8th Cross, Shivaji Road, N.R. Mohalla, Mysore – 570 007, on July 9, 2001 at 09.28 p.m. by writing *'With love & Blessings – Srimad Sai Rajrajeswari'* on it.
- Sri Ganapati Sachchidananda (Incarnation of Lord Dattatreya), Sri Ganapati Sachchidananda Ashram, Datta Nagar, Mysore – 570 004 in the morning of July 10, 2001.
- The Editor expresses his grateful thanks to all the above-mentioned divine personalities.

Contents

Prayer for the New Era ix

Prayer for World Peace xi

Dedication xiii

Divine Messages About the Book xv

Editor's Note xvii

Foreword by Homi S. Spencer xxvii

Foreword by Ahura Mazda (GOD) xxxix

Introduction xlix

1. Dabbling in Spiritualism (1930-40) 1
2. Period of Apprenticeship (1941-46) 5
3. On The Path (1946) 7
4. The Second Initiation: How I became an *Arhat* (1946-49) 13
5. Predictions about Adeptship (1947-49) 23
6. Clairaudience and Inspirational Method of Communication (1947) 25
7. The Inner Voice-The Voice of God (1948) 29
8. Spiritual Healing (1947-49) 33
9. Visions and Spirit Master Ram Ram's Attempt to Sunder the Soul from the body (1947-48) 37

10. Life or Death (1947-48) 41
11. Talks of the Spirit of Mahatma Gandhi (1948) 47
12. Spiritual Philosophy of Rishi Ram Ram (1948) 49
13. A Friend Stabs: A Severe Test (1947) 71
14. Training for Self-realization under Rishi Ram Ram (1948-49) 75
15. Questions and Answers with Rishi Ram Ram (1949) 95
16. Higher Training and Progress under Sai Baba as God Almightly (1949) 109
17. Tests, Trials and Postponements (1949) 123
18. Further Progress on the Path (1949) 133
19. A Beginning in Self-realization (1949) 139
20. Landmarks in Self-realization (1949) 151
21. Godman Meher Baba and His Predictions (1945-49) 175
22. Preparation for the Mission: Writing the book 'How I Found God' (1949-50) 181
23. Illumination (1949-50) 197
24. God's Revelation (1950) 213
25. God's Revelation (continued) 237
26. A Jump of Two Years (1951-52) 283
27. Discourses of Sai Baba As God Almightly (1952-53) 307
28. The End of the Quest (1953-54) 363
29. Struggle for Revelation (1954-55) 391
30. Revelation at Last (1955-58) 399

Some Poems 479
Editor's Post Script 489

Prayer for the New Era

"O God, we pray that we may be soon launched into a New Era of one World Religion, one World Polity, one World Civilization, one World Humanity based on the foundations of equality, brotherhood, service and co-operation.

We pray that our scientists may now begin to study the inner worlds and give us the benefit of their researches. It is not only the union of all mankind that we seek, but the union of the whole universe, the discarnate co-operating with the incarnate spirits for the glory of Thy Kingdom. It is by means of universal love and prayers that we shall build up a new kingdom of the spirit."

–Late Yogi Minocher K. Spencer

Prayer for World Peace

Adorable Presence!

Thou Who art within and without, above and below and all around, Thou Who art interpenetrating the very cells of our beings, Thou who art the Eye of our eyes, the Ear of our ears, the Heart of our hearts, the Mind of our minds, the Breath of our breaths, the Life of our lives and the Soul of our souls, Bless us, Dear God, to be aware of Thy Presence, now and here. This is all that we ask of Thee.

May all of us be aware of Thy Presence in the East and the West, in the North and the South. May Peace and Goodwill abide among individuals as well as communities and nations. This is our earnest prayer.

May Peace be unto all.

– *(Late) Swami Omkar*
Shanti Ashram (Andhra Pradesh)

Dedication

Dedicated to God, the idol and ideal of every human heart aspiring for Truth, Eternal, Infinite, the Absolute Spirit pervading throughout the universe, Transcendent and Immanent, Timeless, Spaceless, Causeless, Motionless, without beginning, without end, the Seed of Creation and Dissolution, the Acme of Perfection, the Essence of Purity, the Be all the End-all of life, the Embodiment of Love and Truth, Beauty and Goodness in perfection, the Giver and Forgiver, the Ocean of Mercy and Compassion, the Anchor of every human heart, the Goal of the traveller on the path, the Asylum and Shelter of the lonely and forlorn, the Citadel of the Righteous, the Source of all inspiration, the Origin of Light, the Dispenser of Justice, Omnipotent, Omnipresent, Omniscient, Indescribable, Incomprehensible, the One without equal, the Supreme Thinker and the Sovereign Ruler, the King of the Cosmos, at whose feet bend down all the highest celestial dignitaries – the Seraphs, the Thrones, the Principalities, – the One whose praises are sung hourly by men and angels alike, the Father of the orphaned world, whom we all long to hear and see, whose Love transcends everything and whose light is our greatest delight.

– M.K. Spencer

Divine Messages about the Book

1. *"Finding God is your mission and after finding Him, your mission further continues – the mission of saving mankind from the path of sin and sorrow and bringing in your world brightness and joy."*

– Ahura Mazda's (God's) message on December 6, 1953.

2. *"Your book 'How I Found God' will be hailed as a new chapter in the history of man's progress towards unification as opposed to separatism."*

– God's message on March 7, 1957.

3. *Your book 'How I Found God' when published will play a dominant part and your mission will be recognized by the world as a forerunner of a great religious revolution not only in India but all over the world."*

– God's message on March 8, 1957.

4. *"Your book would go on world's record. It is a signal record of man's faith in God. What better record and proof your world would ask for when it comes to know of the manner in which it was started and completed."*

– God's message on January 18, 1957.

5. *"It is a lovely book and it will make a landmark in your world. It is a book of revelation not written by you but by God. It is God's book. I repeat, not yours and you should be extremely careful in not taking even the least credit for it."*

– Lord Buddha's message on May 31, 1957.

Editor's Note

This is a rare book on spirituality, first of its own kind ever published in the world. It is a thrilling account of how an earnest seeker Yogi M. K. Spencer realised God with the help of unique spiritual training imparted initially by a great master of the spirit world Rishi Ram Ram and then by God Himself in the form of Shirdi Sai Baba. The experiences, messages and revelations contained in this book are of the most unusual and unique kind. They will be of deep interest to spiritual seekers throughout the world for all times to come.

The experiences recorded in this book are from Yogi Minocher K. Spencer's hitherto unpublished remarkable 2000 foolscap size page manuscript completed on January 11, 1958, about six months before his *Nirvana* (death) on August 30, 1958.

Spencer was a Parsi spiritual seeker, spiritual medium, intellectual, author and spiritual healer. Born in Pune (India) on October 4, 1888, he spent all his life in Karachi (now in Pakistan) working as a metal merchant and doing social service for the leprosy patient of Karachi and deeply meditating in God for several hours every day and night. He attained liberation on August 30, 1958 after his ardent desire to see God face to face was fulfilled consequent to the rigorous spiritual training imparted by Rishi Ram Ram, a great Spirit Master of the spirit world and by God Almighty or Ahura Mazda assuming the form of Sri Shirdi Sai Baba.

Spencer's soul was a rare and highly evolved soul that attained complete liberation in this birth itself. God revealed to him that his soul had taken in all only three births as a human being. Spencer described all these three births in his most thrilling small book *Romance of a Soul* (1954), which had actually been dictated to him by God in his Samadhi session.

In the first birth, he was Patricio (1213-1339 AD), the famous Italian Catholic itinerant monk and preacher who founded an order of Friars and brought thousands of people to Christ's fold. Because of his tendency of decrying other religions, God did not grant him liberation. His soul took second birth a few centuries back in South India as an illiterate Hindu woman in a poor family. She was married early to a vain and cruel husband twice her age. Her marriage was a tale of perpetual torture. Despite this, she bore all her miseries patiently. She was greatly attached to her children. She loved and served all poor and neglected people in the slum community where she lived. So she was looked upon by the people as an incarnation of love and service. Despite all her sacrifices and selfless service, she could not achieve liberation. Intense attachment to her children came as an insurmountable obstacle in her liberation. So the soul had to take third birth as Minocher K. Spencer in a Parsi family in 1888 at Pune. In this birth, he had an intense desire to see God face to face. Spencer underwent all sorts of spiritual experiences with this end in view. He developed keen interest in the Spirit World and learnt the art of communicating with the spirits and do spiritual healing. He met Avatar Meher Baba, the famous Parsi spiritualist, who was the disciple of Sri Shirdi Sai Baba's foremost devotee Upasani Maharaj of Sakori fame. He also met the great spiritualist Sri Ramana Maharishi and got his blessings.

Later, he was chosen by the Spirit Maser Rishi Ram Ram for intensive spiritual training. The Rishi was then the Spirit

Guide of the world. As a matter of fact, right from his cradle days Spirit Master Rishi Ram Ram had been looking after him and training and guiding him. Till May 11, 1949, Rishi Ram Ram gave spiritual training to Spencer. He often used to appear before Spencer in his meditation and visions and would constantly and freely communicate with him.

On May 11, 1949, Rishi Ram Ram told Spencer that thence-forth Sri Sai Baba (who had earlier incarnated at Shirdi), would be taking charge of his spiritual training in order to enable him to achieve his life's goal to realise God in that very birth As Spencer deeply loved Fakir Sai Baba and always worshipped him as God, God assumed the form of Sai Baba to train him in spirituality.

From 1949 onwards, God, assuming the form of Sri Shirdi Sai Baba, imparted a very rigorous spiritual training to Spencer and asked him to keep a faithful record of all his daily spiritual experiences, messages and revelations and then write a book recording all of them.

Spencer wrote about 2000 pages foolscap size typed manuscript entitled *How I Found God.* This title of the book was given to him by God Himself. God dictated to him the biography of his soul *Romance of a Soul* describing his three births as a human being. He wrote a number of other invaluable books and poems and song on mysticism, spirituality and world religions. All his writings were originally published by the Spiritual Healing Centre, Coimbatore, to which Spencer was attached as a *sadhka* (spiritual seeker) and member.

Since it was a very big manuscript, the Centre decided to first bring out only 100 copies of *How I Found God* in proof form only and this was done in 1957. The book, in its proof form, ran into 1396 pages and was loosely bound in four volumes. As soon as copies of this book reached Spencer, God ordered him to burn all copies of the book immediately. Without the least trace of hesitation and unhappiness, Spencer obeyed God's command and burnt whatever copies he had received. He also immediately wired to the Spiritual Healing Centre to do the same as directed by God in his Samadhi. Mr. K.S.D. Aiyer, Secretary of the Centre, had already mailed one set of this rare book to Sri A. Somasundaram, his close friend and a dedicated spiritualist, and retained some sets for himself and destroyed the remaining copies. Soon God gave another message to Spencer that He had asked him to burn the copies of *How I Found God* just to test whether there had still remained any iota of ego in him as a *sadhka,* and since he had obeyed him so obediently, he was very pleased with him. The God Almighty then assured Spencer that his book *How I Found God* would certainly be published one day, but certainly not during his life time. Spencer achieved *Nirvana* on August 30, 1958.

Spencer recorded God's earlier message to this effect as under in this book:

> "On November 28, 1953 Ahura Mazda (God Almighty as Parsis call Him) said to me in a short message: "Do you know that after your death all the message books of your's would be rigidly scrutinized by a panel of eminent scholars and they will issue an epoch-making report....?"

In a number of messages, God as well as other Spirit Masters of the Spiritual Plane greatly appreciated *How I Found God* and assured him that this unique book would certainly be published in future.

Unfortunately, due to the sudden death of Sri K.S.D. Aiyer, who was the backbone of the Spiritual Healing Centre, on October 24, 1965, the Centre was abruptly closed. But Sri A. Somasundaram Sri Aiyer's close friend, had already started the Divine Centre at Markapur (Andhra Pradesh) to carry forward the work of the Spiritual Healing Centre. Sri Somasundaram, spread spiritual knowledge with great dedication, sacrifice and love for humanity till his death in 2005. On my fervent request in 1997 he agreed to let me have access to all the books of Yogi M.K. Spencer including this monumental book *How I Found God* in his personal liberary in his house in Markapur town of Andhra Pradesh. With Sri Somasundaram's inspiration and permission, I started 'Sai Divine Research Centre' in my house at Faridabad on August 4, 1997 to carry forward, in a very humble and modest way, the wonderful spiritual work earlier done by the Spiritual Healing Centre, Coimbatore and thereafter being done by Sri Somasundaram's 'Divine Centre' at Markapur. Sri K.S.D. Aiyer had in 1962 itself authorized and permitted Sri A. Somasundaram to publish all the books of Spencer and those of his Centre, and Sri A. Somasundaram in turn transferred the copyrights of all those books to me in 1998, and he greatly inspired and persuaded me to edit and publish all those valuable spiritual works.

All the books of Yogi M.K. Spencer had been out of print for the last over 40 years. Having gone through his remarkable works like *How I Found God*, *Romance of a Soul* and other books with a great deal of seriousness and interest, I decided that these precious writings must be brought to the notice of all spiritual seekers throughout the world.

Originally the book *How I Found God* in proof form was of 1396 pages, besides a lengthy 'Preface' of over 60 pages by M.K. Spencer's cousin Homi S. Spencer, who also was a great spiritual seeker. Homi also used to receive divine messages from Rishi Ram Ram and other Spirit Masters and he was permitted by them to exchange notes with M.K. Spencer regularly.

Publication of that original book *How I Found God*, which had too many repetitions, was neither advisable nor possible. As advised by my spiritual father Sri A. Somasundaram (who was my Guru is one of my past births), I extracted from it only those portions which describe Yogi M.K. Spencer's thrilling story of God-realization through the unique spiritual training imparted by the Spirit Master Rishi Ram Ram and God in the form of Sri Shirdi Sai Baba. I have rigorously abridged and condensed the book and eliminated all unnecessary repetitions and thus edited this book working laboriously for three years. I have not added a single word from my side in the text of the book during 1998-2001. I have abridged Homi S. Spencer's lengthy 'Preface' also. A brief profile of Yogi M.K. Spencer has been prepared by me on the basis of his invaluable book *Romance of a Soul* and the information personally given by Sri A. Somasudaram who knew Yogi M. K. Spencer as a unique a *sadhka,* writer and fellow beneficiary of the divine grace of Spirit Master Rishi Ram Ram and the facilities of the Spiritual Healing Centre during the 1940s and 1950s. Sri K.S.D. Aiyer was the common friend of Yogi M.K. Spencer and Sri Somasundaram.

In his illuminating autobiography *Fragrant Spiritual Memories of a Karma Yogi* (Diamond Pocket Books 1999, New Delhi) edited by me Sri A. Somasundaram had devoted one full chapter to Yogi M.K. Spencer and paid rich tribute to him.

Since the world now-a-days is badly suffering from *anomie* of the worst kind, value crisis, moral degradation, anarchy, sensate culture, fundamentalism, violence, *ashanti* (disquiet), selfishness and exploitation of and total unconcern for the well-being of the masses, all modern spiritual saints, world bodies like the United Nations and conscientious people all over the world are most anxiously waiting for the dawn of a New Era or New Age of Peace, Global Harmony, Love, Spiritual Awakening, Optimism, Prosperity and Happiness in the New Millennium.

The readers of this book will be pleasantly surprised to know that Sri Shirdi Sai Baba as Avatar (Incarnation of God) during His life time (1838-1918)at Shirdi and thereafter as Spirit Guide of the world and as God, and the great Spirit

Master Rishi Ram Ram in the Spirit World were the two most important divine pioneers or harbingers of the New Era for the mankind. They had paved the ground for it in the 20th Century, and so now the dawn of the New Era in the human civilisation seems to be fast coming. The 77 unique spiritual discourses of Shirdi Sai Baba as God given to Yogi Spencer in his Samadhi sessions between November 3, 1952 and February 18, 1953, recorded in chapter 27 of this book must be read and pondered over by readers in all seriousness. Rishi Ram Ram, the Spirit Guide and Guru of Yogi Spencer throughout his life, had given many invaluable messages, spiritual discourses and talks, which were recorded by his devotees like Yogi M.K. Spencer, V.S. Krishnaswamy, P.R. Dakshinamurthy, K.S.D. Aiyer and some others. They are recorded in Yogi Spencer's books – *Rishi Ram Ram* and the present book *How I Found God*; V.S. Krishnaswamy's book *Spiritual Awakening of Man: Talks of the Spirit Master Rishi Ram Ram* recorded by Auto writing'; and A. Somasundaram's three books – *The Dawn of the New Era: The Vision of Rishi Ram Ram, Future is in Our Hands* and *Fragrant Spiritual Memories of a Karma Yogi*, all of which I have been privileged to edit and get republished.

Both Shirdi Sai Baba and Rishi Ram Ram had shaped and inspired Yogi M. K. Spencer to act as the spearhead or crusader for the much awaited New Era of the humanity under their spiritual guidance and inspiration. He wrote the most eloquent *Prayer for the New Era* and as many as nine rare books on spirituality and so many spiritual poems and songs in English. Some of his poems and songs have been included in this book. Thus, Yogi Spencer's contributions to the world by way of working for the coming of the New Era for the humanity, should be realized and appreciated by the readers. This book *How I Found God* is the most important and the last work of Yogi Spencer. If will be a perennial source of inspiration and enlightenment to all spiritual seekers of the world for all times to come.

As God Himself and Spirit Masters had told Yogi Spencer in their messages of prophecy that it "will be hailed as a new chapter in the history of man's progress", it "will play a dominant part", "it will make a landmark in your world", this great book should be translated into all world languages and in all Indian languages. Those scholars, spiritual organizations and publishers who may come to realize its worth may contact me for permission to translate it into their national and regional languages and publish it at the earliest so that billions people in all the nooks and corners of the world may be enlightened and benefited by it.

I also earnessly wish that an excellent film or documentary should be made by an enlightened and conscientious film-maker, depicting the matchless spiritual experiences and spiritual encounters and inspiring life events of Yogi Spencer and the contributions to his spiritual training made by Sri Shirdi Sai Baba as God (Athura Mazda), Spirit Masters Rishi Ram Ram, Lord Christ, Lord Buddha, Lord Krishna, Sri Ramana Maharishi, Meher Baba etc. Despite my many efforts, I have so far not succeeded in my efforts to find a willing producer to make a film based on this unique book of spiritual memories. Interested film producers may contact me or my grand-daughter Sonakshi Ruhela, House No. 1869, Sector-16, Faridabad for permission to do so.

I will now like to share with the readers a unique miracle that happened in connection with this great work of Yogi Spencer as condensed and edited by me. On June 10, 2001, I took the dummy of this book *How I Found God* to an eminent and highly blessed Sai devotee Sri R. Nagarajan's house which has been widely known among Sai devotees as *Sai Baba Temple* in his Flat No. H-19, Jalvayu Vihar, Sector 25, NOIDA (U.P.), Pin Code – 201 301; with the keen desire to seek Bhagavan

Sri Sathya Sai Baba's divine grace on it. Sri Nagarajan's flat with the shrine of Bhagavan Sri Sathya Sai Baba as Shiva therein is a highly spiritually charged place, where *Shivalingas,* statues of Gods and goddesses, *Vibhuti, Kumkum,* sandal wood powder etc. have, for years, been miraculously materializing by the unique miraculous grace of Sri Sathya Sai Baba – the *Purnavatar* of the Age. More than 750 Shivalingas and 57 *panchdhatu* statues and constant flow of *Vibhuti* had been miraculous created by Sai Baba in that house till 2001. My file containing the dummy and pictures of this book was placed in the shrine of Bhagavan Sri Sathya Sai Baba on Sunday, the June 10, 2001 at 06:00 p.m. Along with my wife, two grand children and friend Sri C.M. Sehgal, and many other devotees, I sat there praying for Swami's blessings, and attending *bhajans* for about one hour. When my file was taken out from the shrine, everyone was thrilled to find that a unique small *Shivalinga* had been materialised by Sri Sathya Sai Baba and placed in the dummy of this book *How I Found God* as a unique symbol of His divine blessings. This divine miracle put the seal of divine approval and total authenticity of the contents of this great spiritual work of Yogi M.K. Spencer.

In that very month of June 2001, prior to my visit to that place, the world renowned American author of Sai books Mrs. Phyllis Krystal had come all the way from the U.S.A. to visit that shrine in Nagarajan's house and Sri Sathya Sai Baba had then blessed her new book by materialising as many as four Shivalingas in her bag. Then she flew to Whitefield to meet Sri Sathya Sai Baba. She got an interview with Sri Sathya Sai Baba in which He personally confirmed to her that those four *shivalingas* had been materialised for her at the Sai Temple in Nagarajan's house by Him (Sri Sathya Sai Baba) only as His blessings to her. This book has been blessed by a member of divine personalities also.

I have great pleasure in presenting this matchless and divine blessed book to the readers, throughout the world.

I am deeply gratefully to the God Almighty and the Spirits of Sri Shirdi Sai Baba, Rishi Ram Ram, and his successor Swami Amritananda – the present Spirit Guide of the world and Yogi M.K. Spencer, Sri K.S.D. Aiyer, and to Bhagavan Sri Sathya Sai Baba for bestowing upon me the good fortune of bringing out this concise and abridged version of Yogi Spencer's *opus magnum* (great work) for the spiritual enlightenment and uplift of the entire mankind.

Grateful thanks are due to all those well-wishers, friends of mine who encouraged, inspired and helped me in various ways in the arduous task of bringing out this book. In particular, I wish to thank the following:

(Late) Sri A. Somasundaram, Markapur; an ardent long time devotee of Sri Shirdi Sai Baba, Sri T.R. Naidu, Hyderabad; Srimad Sai Rajrajeswari, the present reincarnation of Dakshayini or Parvati, the Divine Consort of Lord Shiva, Mysore; Mother Vasantha Sai, the present reincarnation of Lord Sri Krishna's beloved Gopi Radha, Spiritual Head of 'Mukti Nilayam' (Madurai District); Sri K.V. Ramani, Managing Turstee, Shirdi Sai Baba Trust, Besant Nagar, Chennai, Sri C.M. Sehgal, Faridabad; and last but not the least my wife Smt. Sushila Devi Ruhela and my granddaughter Sonakshi.

1st January, 2010

Satya Pal Ruhela
'Sai Kripa'
126, Sector 37,
Faridabad-121003 (India)
Mob.: 09910494110
Tel.: 0129-2275844
E-Mail: spruleha@gmail.com

Foreword

by Homi S. Spencer

How I Found God: Indeed what a title! How sublimely simple and yet how staggering is its effect upon one's reason and imagination! And yet why should one's reason be so staggered? Can't these simple words carry the stamp of Truth and bear the closest scrutiny?

Is there a God?

To find God we must first be certain that there is a God. In the last quarter of the last century that prince of Agnosticism, British philosopher and one of the five fathers of sociology Herbert Spencer by name, wrote a whole book in two volumes on *The First Cause.* In the light of the scientific knowledge of his day he came to the conclusion that there was a First Cause (whom we in our unscientific parlance call 'God') but that it was Unknown and Unknowable.

Since the days of Herbert Spencer different branches of physical science have made giant strides. Several books have been written by eminent scientists showing a remarkable consensus of opinion that there is a Creator behind the Cosmos and that His Creation is the product of 'Thought'. As Sir James Jeans observes in *The Mysterious Universe,* "If the universe is a universe of thought, then its creation must have been an act of thought." So in place of

* This 'Foreword' by Homi S. Spencer, a great spiritualist, written in 1957, resume of this book.

Herbert Spencer's unknown and unknowable First Cause, we find the scientific philosophers of our day speaking of a Creator who is a 'Thinker of Infinite Intelligence'.

This is an approximation to the idea of an Uncreated Supreme Lord of the Universe with which the world has been familiarised for at least the last nine thousand years since the days of the First Great Prophet of the Aryan Race, Holy Zarathushtra. During all these nine millennia prophets of every revealed religion have taught us the same truth. It is the one central idea of every Revelation worthy of its name. Each one of them has not only emphasised the existence of God and postulated Him as the Supreme Thinker, but also has spoken of His Righteousness, Love, Kindness and Mercy. They have all thus gone somewhat beyond the scientific concept of a Creator of Infinite Intelligence. But if the scientific thought of our day admits the existence of a Creator of Infinite Intelligence, we are surely on sufficiently safe ground in saying that Revelation must be justified in its other postulates about this Creator, particularly when the prophets claim to speak out of their personal experiences, whether it is Holy Zarathushtra, or the great Rishis of Upanishadic Hinduism, or Moses or Buddha or Holy Jesus or Nabi Mahomed, or many other God-realised men of all times.

All these prophets, rishis and God realised men have also been unanimous in teaching that man's destiny is to attain Divine Perfection. They have also emphasised that this human destiny can only be reached by the perfection of character, and how this perfection leads to the purification of man's soul which, they have unanimously taught, is an emanation from God. Such unanimity is in itself a proof of the truth and trustworthiness of their teachings.

We thus come to this: that there exists a God, who is a Sublime Thinker of Infinite Intelligence and who represents the Ideal of Perfect Righteousness, Truth, Love, Purity, Kindness and Mercy etc.; that Man's destiny is to reach this Divine State of Perfection; and that there are several ways of reaching it.

The next question therefore is: Is it possible for an ordinary human being to teach this state in the present stage of his development?

The answer is "YES". Once a human being is past the primitive stage of savage existence in which he is governed by primitive impulses of hunger and sex, and has progressed somewhat into the next stage of human development when he is governed by higher motives of some appreciable ethical values, it is possible for him to aim at and achieve this seeming impossibility. The best proof of it is to be found in the number of people all over the world who have now reached the third or intuitional stage of consciousness, which is the stage that follows purely intellectual consciousness. So long as intellectually advanced sections of humanity continued to take a purely mechanistic view of the universe the development of intuitional consciousness was obstructed. But a change in that view was compelled by the resolution of the atom into centres of electrical energy in the form of electrons and protons. A new, non-mechanistic view of nature came perforce into existence which began to take cognisance of the invisible and the imponderable. Theorising about the invisible and the imponderable necessarily involves more abstract thinking and favours the development of the intuitional consciousness.

Witness the change in the nature of physics. It has now become closely allied to mathematics, essentially a purely abstract science. Witness also change in the science of psychology. The brain is no longer considered to be the source of thoughts, but merely its vehicle or instrument of physical expression. Thought is now studied as something divorced from and independent of the brain. The study of psychology has become more abstract than before. Further the study of psychology is now linked to many other sciences e.g., the sciences of medicine and education, and even to a scientific study of industries, arts and crafts. In this way, science as a whole now tends to become more abstract in its primaries, and this, as stated above, favours the development of intuitional consciousness. With the spread of scientific knowledge amongst all educated people the increase in the number of people learning to rely on more intuitional consciousness is not surprising.

There is also another potent factor that has led to the spread of intuitional consciousness. It is the spread of Higher Spiritualism. Two world wars in the short space of 25 years, the heavy toll of life which they have taken and all the unbearably heavy burdens which they have brought as aftermath, have helped the spread of spiritualism. Home and public circles of spiritual development are common today and the production and sale of books on spiritualism has grown considerably. As in the case of our author, the study of spiritualism has led in many cases to the practice of spirituality and this in its turn has led to intuitional consciousness.

All this is very well as a picture of the general possibilities of human development and evolution. But how does it apply to our author M.K. Spencer? His claim is that he has been able to talk to and see God. It is quite natural to ask whether God or Ahura Mazda Ameshaspand (as the Parsees call Him) would care to talk to any ordinary man such as the author of this book represents himself to have been.

The question becomes easier to answer if we put it in another form and say: Is it possible for any ordinary mortal to hear what God says?

Today, clairaudience is a universally accepted fact. It is however generally confined in its meaning to hearing messages from the invisible world of spirits, and is believed to be a psychic power that is a result of some kind of astral development. Granting all this, is it impossible for an ordinary mortal whose higher invisible bodies, the Manasic and the Spiritual, are sufficiently pure and strong to receive messages delivered from the Manasic and Spiritual Planes? It is all a question of purification and strengthening the higher bodies. If by rigourous training under a Spirit Master like Rishi Ram Ram any mortal is able to reach the necessary degree of purification, there is no reason why he should not become receptive to messages from the Manasic and Spiritual planes. Our author M.K. Spencer, as shown by messages quoted in this book, attained this purification and strengthening. This, however, only settles the point as to our author's fitness to receive. It may still be asked, does God ever condescend to talk to any mortal in this way? The answer is: what do we hear when we listen to the voice of the conscience? Are we not listening to the voice of that little spark of God which is within each one of us? All the divine powers that God has given to man reside only in that little spark of divinity within him. That spark and all its divine powers lie dormant in most human beings because of impurities in the invisible bodies. When these powers are, however, made to bloom by purifying and strengthening all the invisible bodies, the channel for communication between the God within and the God without is cleared and the human soul becomes capable of direct guidance from God. It is then that the Deep without can answer to the Deep within, "and in treading the Path, the beacon light", as our author remarks, "that helps him (i.e. the disciple on the Path) is great love and devotion for God." It is this love which brings the response from God. It is, therefore, possible for every human being to come into direct touch with God as our author M.K. Spencer has done.

Besides it is interesting to note that M.K. Spencer is not the only man who has done so in our own days. Who has not heard of the divinity of Shri Ramana Maharshi or of Shri Ramakrishna Paramahansa? If other examples of God realised persons of recent times are required, you just need to consult Swami Yogananda's book *The Autobiography of a Yogi*.

But the question still remains: how are we to be satisfied that the messages our author received are really from God? The proof of the pudding is in the eating of it. This homely saying applies very aptly to the present case in a two-fold way. First, in the way our author's inner vehicles are developed stage by stage under the guidance first of Rishi Ram Ram and then of God Himself appearing as Sai Baba, and then in the messages and training that he received from his Spirit Master and from that great Master of Masters, God in His *Sakari* (form) aspect of Asho Ahura Mazda Ameshaspand. Our author's fascinating story of spiritual development thus divides itself naturally into two parts, the first of which embracing this development under Rishi Ram Ram, is described in the first fifteen chapters of the book. This part of the story begins in the 1930 when M.K. Spencer met a mystery man in Karachi and asked him "Have I any gifts?". The mystery man replied: "Yes, you have psychic gifts." This happened at a time when, according to our author, he "believed only in the external phenomena and had no conception of hidden truths or hidden light."

The next stage is reached when he visits a clairvoyant medium in London in 1937, whereafter "not external but internal knowledge became the object of my desire."

This urge for internal knowledge was further strengthened by Spencer's meeting the well-known Indian spiritualist, Mr. V.D. Rishi, in Karachi in 1940. It "acted as a stimulant to study spiritualism and the desire to become a medium became irresistible." The desire for mediumship led to indulgence in planchette and automatic writing at the cost of a serious breakdown in health, while the study of spiritualism brought our author into contact with the Spiritual Healing Centre at Coimbatore (South India). Thus, through the gateway of spiritualism, he was introduced to his Spirit Guide and Master Rishi Ram Ram, who was also the controlling Guide of that Centre.

The years 1941 to 1946 are described by our author as those of apprenticeship. It was during this period that, acting under directions received from the Coimbatore Centre, he began to work hard and study all scriptures so as to write books on religion and philosophy. As a consequence, *Oneness with God* was written by him and published in 1944.

The next stage is reached when the Master makes our author visit Meher Baba in 1945. Thereafter, on October 6, 1946, he was accepted for Initiation.

With the first Initiation, the disciple finds that if he practises self-abnegation and desirelessness and has "the will to dare and suffer in silence", while keeping steadfast in his love and devotion to God his progress is accelerated. With consequent rapid purification and strengthening of his higher mental and causal higher bodies his soul soon reaches Arhatship or the Nirvanic stage and transcends the cycle of birth and death.

This is what happened to our author. A few months after his first Initiation, Spencer visited Sri Ramana Maharishi at Arunachal in July 1947 and, as predicted by Rishi Ram Ram, became an Arhat receiving that grace through the great Maharishi.

Soon after, on November 5, 1947, Spencer got this message from Rishi Ram Ram: "Try to follow what I speak to you through you. I am sitting in your heart to teach you grave problems of life." There is a world of significance in this manner of the Guru's speaking to the disciple through him, sitting in his heart. It means that the disciple's soul is in a position to communicate directly with the Spirit of his Guru, is able to penetrate through all its sheaths, visible and invisible, and establish inter communication as between spirits. Because the disciple's soul is not in a position yet to separate itself from its sheaths, the Guru's Spirit comes to abide with him in his heart. It also means that the soul is able to make itself heard in the body which it inhabits. According to the author's narrative it was on the same day that while sitting in silence, he was able to hear the words: "I am God," which the Master then explained "were spoken by your Inner Self."

This remarkable development in our author's soul is responsible for what happens to him some two months later on January 5, 1948. He says that on the day "I heard the inner voice telling me: "God wants to speak to you. Listen to Him." Instantly the words fell on my ears: "You are a spark of My Fire. You will return to Me." This is a further development wherein the God without speaks to the God within.

On May 24, 1948 Rishi Ram Ram told our author: "You have secured *Nirvana* (Liberation) and you will not have to come back into this life, but you have still not attained seership which will eventually lead to the final step in spiritual evolution. Your life has been extended to give you this opportunity and whether you succeed or not will depend upon your efforts and merit."

The emphasis here is upon "efforts and merit." The disciple had yet to learn several crucial lessons before the highest stage of Illumination in God Realization could be reached, including those of egolessness and complete indifference to whatever may happen. To rub these lessons in he was being subjected to all kinds of tests and trials, especially through what we would call false predictions.

Spencer's soul had already learnt to penetrate through all its sheaths and establish communication between Itself and the Spirit of Its Invisible Guide and Master, and even between Itself and God, the Absolute Spirit. But it had not yet learnt to separate itself from all its sheaths and take its flight to the Spiritual Plane in *samadhi.* Spencer, had, however begun to feel waves of joy sweeping over him like tidal waves and, as the Master explained, these were "due to the vicinity of God's presence, and the soul had now unfolded itself from its sheaths and was ready for flight." But it had to wait for God's final order. The Master repeatedly promised this separation but it was not achieved till after the disciple had been taken over for training by God Himself.

But that the disciple was about to reach the stage of final transformation was evident from the reading of his aura as given by Rishi Ram Ram on April 15, 1949: "You have perfected your character so far as I can see from your aura which is now all blue with a fringe of pure white. The yellow has deepened into blue and there is no trace of any lower colour at all. It means perfection and identification with God."

Before we proceed to consider the second part of the extraordinary spiritual development of the soul of an ordinary man and its training by God Himself, it will not be out of place here to sum up the results of our survey so far, as regards its most important point as to how far the establishment of our author's contact with God is real.

Spencer began service of God through service to lepers at Karachi for thirty years. This was selfless service born out of his love and tender sympathy for suffering fellow beings, out of which is born a great love and devotion to God.

He had another great asset in the utter honesty and truthfulness of his character. As Rishi Ram Ram said on November 10, 1947: "Ever speak the truth as you are doing now. Truth is your greatest weapon. It is your Guardian Angel."

Other assets of his character are great self-abnegation – he is unconscious even of his virtues – the will to dare and suffer, and determined perseverance against odds.

Such extraordinary nobility of character tallies perfectly with the readings of his aura and its highly spiritual colourings. Any wonder then that he should have come so near and become so dear to God.

Before proceeding to the second part of the story, it is necessary to clear one point which our author has failed to bring out in the narration of his training under Rishi Ram Ram. Soon after Rishiji began the new method of teaching his disciple sitting in his heart and as Spencer developed the power of hearing the relays of his own soul, the Guru began at times to change his position and communicate with Spencer's from the heights of the Spiritual Plane. The important points to note here are that the inspired thought came directly from the highest or Spiritual Plane, that it was caught by our author's soul which is the Spiritual part of him, and that it was then relayed to him by his own soul. He perfected this method of communication before he was handed over to Sai Baba.

The object of this explanation is to show that what Rishi Ram Ram could do Sai Baba could also do; and if Sai Baba be taken as Asho Ahura Mazda Ameshaspand or the *Sakari* (Manifest) aspect of God, He can do it with all the greater ease.

The position of Sai Baba in the Celestial Hierarchy becomes clear as the story unfolds itself. First of all, it shows by numerous reiterations that Sai Baba is none other than God Himself in His *Sakari* (or Manifest) aspect of Asho Ahura Mazda Ameshaspand – a fact which is emphasised over and over again not only by Sai Baba Himself but also by Rishi Ram Ram and several other Celestial Beings of pre-eminence in the Celestial Hierarchy. It also shows how God has manifested His divine powers from time to time through His Omnipotence. It also shows further how the exercise of these powers has been called forth according to the different stages of Spiritual development reached by our author from time to time.

Within 24 hours of taking charge, in the evening of May 12, 1949 Sai Baba brings Lord Maitreya with Him and the latter says: "I am the Lord of the Earth Domain come to you at the express bidding of our Master". Who can command the Lord of the Earth Domain except the Highest in the whole Celestial Hierarchy, that is, except God Himself?

The very next day *i.e.* on May 13, 1949 Sai Baba was able to put our author into a long *samadhi* which lasted for full one hour and made him "also to see beautiful colourings extremely joyous to behold" and thus gave him a distant sight of the Spiritual Plane by opening his inner eye.

Sai Baba continued to put our author into long *samadhi* on succeeding days also, which led Rishi Ram Ram to observe on May 15, 1949: "He (*i.e.* Sai Baba) has put you into long *samadhi* which I could not, for I feared that you might not recover from the shock and might pass away. Sai Baba like the skillful surgeon that He is, has so managed your inner parts that He has safely carried out His purpose."

With August 12, 1949 began a month of several enthralling experiences. On that day, for the first time in his life our author's soul freed from his body was taken straight into the presence of God, when he was in *samadhi* after a long and deep mediation. Speaking about it Sai Baba says: "Do you know I have taken you to God? You saw Him but your eyes were blind at the time. All that you felt when you saw Him, was a sudden flow of joyousness in your heart. This feeling of joyousness still continues. It is the result of the inward contact with God.

The next day our author "heard the chanting of a divine song in a strange language, "quite unknown" to him. After the music had died down, he saw some "tints of hallowed light" which "had such a softening effect upon the mind and soul." To continue the narrative in the words of Sai Baba: "You were in an enraptured state and taking advantage of this beautiful situation, created by your meditation, I guided you quietly and softly into the loftier heights of true spirituality. At this stage I just opened your inner eye and you saw in a flash a strange human form come to you as if in a vision. It was not a vision. It was a true phenomenon which you saw with your inner eye and you were struck with awe and wonder. Do you know who that person was? It was God himself who took the form of man and bewildered you and disappeared in a minute. He has left a trail of light in your heart which will now never perish. He has fastened you to Himself. You and He are now one. You have realised Self – the dream of your life."

The November 3, 1949 witnessed a new phase of intensive training for which our author had to begin his daily sittings from 02:00 a.m. The object of that training was attainment of full Self-realization reaching into God-realization and full equipment with all powers necessary to carry out successfully God's mission of healing souls and bodies. It was a mission which would naturally entail vicious opposition and as Rishi Ram explained on November 4, 1949: "He (Sai Baba) wants to season you against all odds and storms of opposition that you will meet with, when you start your mission."

It was about this time that our author was also told to write the present book and it was on this date that Sai Baba insisted upon giving it the title *How I Found God.*

Some days later Sai Baba told our author: "I want to tell you the reason why I am not manifesting Myself to you. My sole intention is that you should not suffer in the least by the shock. I am preparing you so cautiously that it would be a wonder of wonders when you see Me with your third eye open in as natural a manner as possible. You are being given all the supernormal powers for your mission, particularly the power of the pen.

Such wonderful things and more you will read in this thrilling story of M.K. Spencer in his memoirs *How I Found God.*

Foreword

by Ahura Mazda (God)

Millions of people, during the course of their lives, ask the question: "Is there any God?" On the other hand, millions of people also go through their lives without even knowing the purpose of their birth or having any conception of the Life Beyond Death. There are thus two classes of people – one class anxious to know the origin of their existence and the secrets of the Universe; the other class with no time or desire to probe into the future state of existence. Those who are not anxious to rise above the mundane make no progress and hinder the progress of others as well. Their apathy is the root cause of all world's misery. They are diametrically opposed to the second group, to whom the things of the spirit appeal more. It is this class that forms the backbone of human society.

The leaders of this class are saints, sages and God-realised souls: people who stand at the zenith of humanity. They look upon the world as one unit and all men and women as children of One God. Their vision transcends the limit of class distinctions. They become one with God.

To know God is not easy, but every human soul can rise to that height of consciousness where God can be perceived by the development of the seeker's superconsciousness.

Certain souls are destined to evolve quicker because of their former incarnations. But the pace of evolution depends completely upon man's own efforts. Study of scriptures, association with holy and saintly persons, lofty ideals, sincerity of purpose and above all complete devotion and dedication to God form the crucial steps to God-realisation.

The writer of this book has realised God. He has woven a fascinating story of his experiences in his search for God. These experiences should serve as a guide to every one who desires to find God. The messages of the Masters and of God Himself indicate the high state of spirituality reached by the author.

The author was selected by Me, when he took birth in the present incarnation, to be trained to serve as a Messenger of Truth and Goodwill to all. It was thought he would take one more birth before becoming God's messenger on earth. But by continuous effort, to the amazement of the Master under whose training he was placed, he not only wiped out all his *karma* but succeeded in freeing his soul completely from all its sheaths. And all this in the course of a few years. I then changed My Plan and, instead of calling him away, extended his life and gave him an opportunity to work as My messenger for the good of mankind.

As in such matters, permission is first obtained from the concerned individual. I was pleased when the author undertook to serve God in any way desired. He has passed through a course of rigorous training under Me. He has been put through severe tests and trails. His soul is now quite ripe for the venture. Although it is anxious to quit the body for good, it abides by the promise to serve God as He may desire.

The author's soul is perfectly aware of the high position reached by it in the scale of spirituality. It has seen God and the Masters. It has come repeatedly to God's Spiritual Plane and made itself at home in this highest abode of eternal bliss. It knows every nook and corner of God's Kingdom.

The present book was ordered by Me, Ahura Mazda, the Supreme Spirit or God in the universe and the writer commenced his work in full faith that it would be completed in a month's time. For, just a month was given to finish this colossal work of putting together innumerable messages in such a way as to give a graphic picture of the struggle of the soul for emancipation. The writer was given a hope that by the time he came to the end of the messages, he would receive God's revelation. This was a faith test for him. The author finished the work as ordered, working without rest and without sacrificing his daily altar room activities. This was a marvellous achievement and the writer was at once put on the celestial board for higher training.

The training continued for years on end and the story of that training struggle and eventual realization of the goal is described in the ensuing chapters. The book would have ended long ago but the soul's progress was so steady and magnificent that God changed His original plan. The author had realised God in His personal aspect through both *bhakti* and *yoga*, renunciation and meditation, but the third and more difficult path of God-realization viz., by *gnana marga* was still to be attained. Very few souls succeed in realising God through knowledge. It is difficult for it is abstract. To love God with a form is within the region of practicability. It is the easiest and safest way and comes naturally to all. For God has implanted in every human soul the seed of love and devotion for Him that must sprout during the course of its struggle in life. In some, the seed sprouts but the sapling does not live for want of enough nourishment. But if the seedling is properly nourished with the heart's divine waters, it sprouts in full blossom and the devotee does not rest content till the object of his search is reached. He yearns and longs for God more and more as days go by. He cries for God like a child for its mother. The deep longing and yearning for God makes him leave the life of the world if he be a householder and in the case of the writer, who was a householder, he gave up everything in search for God.

The first step was thus secured. The author was asked to worship God, as if He was a person. He was asked to place before his mind's eye the picture of Sai Baba, the fakir and saint of Shirdi who had realised God. Worshipping God in this manner, the author saw Sai Baba not once, but several times in the state of ecstatic delight. He saw himself entering into a new phase of life. Renunciation took a stronger and greater hold on him and he took to meditation, spending longer hours in meditation. He thus attained God-realisation through yoga as well. He witnessed and was given experience of the union of his soul with the Oversoul, the blending of his soul with the spirit within and the union of the blended twin with the Spirit Absolute without, pervading throughout the universe.

It was a grand achievement – a unique achievement. But the man of the spirit is never satisfied till he reaches the very end of the Spirit's attainments. This was clear in the aspirants' case, though he was not conscious of the thirst of his soul and spirit. As his soul had attained liberation, he refused to exercise his option, leaving everything to God's mandate.

The author's life's journey was extended and training of the highest type was continued. God had decided not only that the writer should get God's revelation in the highest transcendental state of formlessness but also he should be made a vehicle in His hands for carrying out a great mission on earth. To be appointed as God's emissary is a unique boon and the author was selected for the purpose, in spite of his age and failing health. God can do wonders and the wonders He is going to do through the author will be revealed to the world after the completion and publication of this book.

God is Absolute Spirit pervading throughout the universe. It is formless. The *gnani* realises God, when by abstract thinking he comes to the conclusion that the world is an illusion and God alone is the Reality. He feels convinced of this as he analyses every bit in the universe, and by rejecting "not this, not this," *neti, neti,* he soon finds out that what is real in him is not the flesh or the bones, not the skin or the nerves, not the blood or the tissues, not the mind or the senses. Man is atman, Man is God. To realise this, Man must discard the world, the illusive senses, slay the mind and unfold his real nature viz., the divinity in him. He must know the Self and discard the non-Self.

The object of the various books that the Masters made the author write viz., *Oneness with God, Religion in Life, Life's Philosophy, Joyous Mysticism,* was purely to fill his mind with profound truths in vogue in the religious literature of the world and to impress upon the people the necessity of a right approach to Godhood.

A man be a great religious scholar but it does not mean that his scholarship is enough. Religion is to be lived and transcended. When man is lost in thoughts of God, when he is intoxicated and sees nothing in life except the guidance of God, when he loses his individuality, submits unconditionally and joyously to the Will of God, discarding name and fame, glory, riches and power, he becomes merged in God.

Christ said: "I and my Father are one" This is a profound truth expressed in a most glorious language. This is the objective of life. Oneness with God who alone is REAL. This realization comes by study and meditation. Raja Yoga is the King of Yogas, for few alone can traverse this difficult path of *gnana* and *yoga.* A *gnani* is a *yogin* as well as *bhakta.*

The minute the conviction grows in you that you are Atman, you cease your separate identity. You are no longer Framji Manekji, Ramchand Gopaldas, John Castilino, Karimahmad Allahbux. Ego is slain. You are one with God. This is the realization of *Sat Chit Ananda*, Absolute Existence, Consciousness, Bliss.

When Paul saw the vision of Christ, he temporarily lost his sight. But when he got back his sight, he got full consciousness of Christ's glory and took up Christ's cross to work for Him and to curcify himself as Christ had crucified himself in the love of God and love of all mankind.

Man is blind till he sees Truth in all its aspect. God's revelation comes to man only when he becomes fit for it and when God's grace descend upon him. To know God is to know everything. It is the greatest wisdom. It is the greatest spiritual wealth. It is the greatest bliss. It is the greatest gift of God to man.

God realised souls are the beacon lights in the dark dungeons of the world. Every man that gains his liberation, contributes towards the liberation of the world.

God works through God-realised souls for the latter offer no resistance of any kind, as they have no will of their own. No man can realise God unless he has succeeded in surrendering himself wholly to God's Will.

Man is born with a free will, as well as with an ego. To destroy this ego in him and to surrender himself to God – these are the most difficult hurdles to cross.

There is nothing but God, the Absolute Spirit. When this thought penetrates your mind, individuality, separateness, the feeling of mine and thine, the spirit of possession, the bane of egotism – they are all cast to the wind. You look upon everything as God. There is nothing but God. Wherever you go, whatever you do, it is all God and His doing.

There is no evil in the world in the strictest sense of the word. Evil is only the least good. But man, with the help of God and all the good forces in the universe, must convert this least good into the most good. God wants Man to cleanse the world of its darkness and bring God's own light of love and goodness, beauty and joy in it.

God has appointed the author of this book to fulfil this mission. From darkness into light, from death to immortality – this is the emblem painted on the banner of his mission.

The fundamental laws of God remain the same. God's wisdom never changes. His divinity is subject to no control, no plurality of forces.

God's Law of Evolution works magnificently in life. It is His greatest creation. Man must bow down to this Law of Progression for in progression lies his salvation.

From the higher point of spirituality, matter and spirit are the same. The function of matter, as it is known in your physical world, is to change itself into spirit. God is Spirit. All is Spirit. The whole universe is Spirit. Man is the crown of God's creation. The law of evolution strikes its peak when man evolves from the brute to the superman, a spirit of the rarest type in the pattern of God Himself.

This realization that all is God is the *summum bonum* of Divine Wisdom. Prophets, saints and sages, philosophers and divine singers of God's beauty and grace have awakened man to a higher consciousness of life. And God has made a provision to fill the world with more and more of such prophets for human civilisation is now entering a higher region of transmutation. The Law of Evolution is working faster and faster. God wants every man to be a prophet, a philosopher, a singer of God, a holy man, who wants God and God alone and is not enamoured of the world and its *maya*. God wants not *maya* but *daya* (kindness) to reign supreme. *Maya* is attachment. *Daya* is love without attachment. It is the heart's warmth without its biting ache.

There is an intimate connection between the physical world and the Spirit World and though the latter is a closed book to most, it does not mean that man should rest satisfied with what he sees and hears with his physical eyes and ears alone. Nothing is invisible in God's universe. But the veil that hides God's universe and His mysteries has to be removed by man himself. The opening of God's casket of pearls is in man's hands.

The Science of spiritualism should not be run down because there are dangers inherent in its practice. The author did a yeoman service in this regard with his first book, *The Other World.* The curiosity to know things beyond the Border soon quickens the spirit to delve deeper into the mysteries of life and to solve life's problems. It is man's duty to broaden the horizon of his outlook and learn more of the invisible for what one sees with the naked eyes is not truth. To probe into the mysteries of God's universe, to love God and to yearn and long for Him with all the ardour and fervour of your heart is the right approach to Truth. The science of Spiritualism offers to show you the way. It should not be rejected, but at the same time it should not be made the be – all and end – all of life. It is just a stepping stone to higher knowledge. The objective should not be attaining of the knowledge of Spiritism but of spirituality.

Psychic powers are a great aid in advancing of one's spiritual welfare, provided they are not sought for but are attained as God's gifts and are used with discretion and discrimination for the fulfilment of God's Law and the unfoldment of divinity in man.

The whole universe hangs on vibrations. God's name vibrates throughout His whole creation. It vitalises the atmosphere. Its energising influence can be felt by any human soul, provided it lifts its inner spirit to hear the subtle music of God's world – the foundation of the universe. To take His name on your lips, to think of Him day and night, to forget your world and seek Him in the quietness of your soul's solitude is the greatest thing in life. Only this will guide you from darkness into light, from death into immortality.

Religion was dethroned by the temporary flush of rationalism and science. But science is no longer an antagonist of Religion for it has emerged from its narrow groove into the broad expanse by discovering the fact that spirit is the foundation of creation. Together, Science and Religion will bring about a tremendous change in man's attitude to man in all spheres of life and pave the way for unification of all nations and countries within the orbit of one centralised organisation, with one government, one religion and one language.

The new age that is dawning is that of the Brotherhood of Man and the Fatherhood of God. Mysticism, hitherto criticised as a sterile pursuit, would be hailed as the highest science in the universe. Man's conceptions of values will undergo a radical change. He will understand the value of inner knowledge, the necessity of husbanding inner strength and unfolding the inner powers for one's own salvation and for the salvation of the whole world.

The man of God is the man of peace. The teaching of non-violence preached by that great soul of India, Mahatma Gandhi should infiltrate in every part of the world.

There is a tremendous slaughter of animals going on in your world. When man lived in the forest in the nomadic age and was semi-civilised, slaughter of animals for his food was tolerable. But no canon of reasoning can justify such a carnage of animals for human consumption. There is enough in Nature to give to man the most nutritive food he may require for sustaining and strengthening his mind, body and soul.

Meat-eating degrades human soul. It demoralises man. He becomes cruel, lustful, sinful. He turns a brute for the vibrations of the animals slaughtered by millions and their piteous cries, unheard by men but heard by the spirits in the realms above, create an atmosphere stained with blood. This stain of blood dwells upon the astral body of meat eating man and makes him forgetful of the divinity within him.

The cause of relaxation in morals lies in the sexual tendency created by meat-eating. Man belongs to the same animal kingdom as birds and beasts and he has no right to slaughter his kinsmen to fill his stomach.

Your world still does not recognise meat-eating as harmful but over the years, your own scientists would make astounding discoveries about the millions of germs that you unconsciously eat when meat is served to you as food.

There is no greater crime that your science commits in the name of relieving human suffering than that of vivisection. There are countless ways of giving relief to suffering. Even a mere prayer said in all earnestness of heart is a tremendous force in healing or reducing pain. Subjecting mute animals to a living death is a terrible sin the enormity of which man in his colossal ignorance and pride does not realise. Vivisection must stop. God's Laws should not be infringed in this callous manner. It is a blot on humanity.

With the dawn of the New Age – the age of the spirit – there will be in your world more psychic clubs and lecture theatres, more libraries and reading rooms, geographical, theological and Theosophical societies and associations. More people will be scanning the sky with an eye to probe into the mysteries of God. Scientific researches, psychic experiments, and yearning and enthusiasm to know God and to worship God as the only REALITY would become more and more apparent.

This book written by an unknown human soul is going to pave the way to the blossoming of this new era.

I am God, Ahura Mazda, who has been in daily communion with him. He is fully conscious of this divine communion. His soul is fully conscious of My revelation to him. He has seen the lights of My celestial world. He has seen his own aura. He knows his past two incarnations.

I command this book to be read widely by those who are eager like him to find God. It will help them considerably in their quest for TRUTH.

1957

(God's Message received by M.K. Spencer for this book)

Introduction

A Master's guiding hand is indispensable – whether that Master is a Spirit Master or an Adept in Physical body. Consciously or unconsciously, he gets linked with the Master and the progress on the higher path of Spirituality starts, till the goal is reached, which may take one incarnation or more according to the efforts of the pupil and his propensities.

The more spiritual a person becomes, the greater grows the hunger for God. This great burning desire for God grows in the person, as he or she discovers the law of non-separateness existing in the universe. God is one. Life is one. There is unity pervading throughout the universe. This discovery of non-separateness is the true indication of spirituality, is hammered into a pattern of perfection suitable for the Master's craftsmanship, to take the perfecting soul to his homeland – the Abode of God – Eternal Bliss.

In these pages will be found my experiences with spirit Masters. Their messages are a revelation. An attempt has been made to weave out a connected story from 2000 and odd messages received by me.

I had the singularly good fortune of being guided and trained not by one Master but two. Ram Ram was appointed by God from my very birth of which I was absolutely ignorant. It is only later on, when by the grace of God. I was made conscious of my initiation on the Path, the Master revealed to me the above fact.

The book, as it will be seen, is made up of two parts. The first part refers to my training under the guidance of Rishi Ram Ram and the latter under the guidance of Sai Baba, the Master of Masters, the greatest in the Celestial. Hierarchy. That Sai Baba was a hundred times greater Master than Rishi Ram. Ram is indicated by the performance as will be seen from the perusal of the book itself.

This book of my experiences with the title *How I Found God* given to me by Sai Baba is written expressly under His order. I was simply flabbergasted when the Master ordered that it should be done. It was the severest test that I was put to for the attainment of God-realization in the state of full consciousness. But I had implicit faith in the Master. Besides, I knew, I was nothing. If He wished it to be done, He would make me firm to do it. All that He wanted was a ready instrument and I offered myself, unstintedly and unreservedly, to become his typing machine.

This book should not be considered as mine. It is Sai Baba's production. But for his inspiration and guidance, it could never have been written. In the course of a message, Sai Baba said: "I am extremely glad you are able to catch my inspiration beautifully well. But for Me, you would have utterly failed. This should give you an idea how powerful is My influence. It requires superhuman efforts to weave out a story in a connected and agreeable form the mass of intricate and confused materials at your disposal. I shall lead you on to the very last line in the very last chapter of your work. It is sure to be completed and revised with Introduction also added within the time allotted to you, provided you work for at least six to seven hours every day as you are doing now. Don't slacken your efforts. Do you know your whole future is at stake on this book?"

To devote six to seven hours exclusively for the book work, to give long hours for the altar room sittings for meditation, prayers and for taking down messages and to attend to all other sundry duties, meant absolute absorption in work without any rest or with very little relaxation. When the altar room sittings commenced from 02:00 a.m., the hours of sleep had to be curtailed very often from five to three. This explanation is given only to indicate the type of self-discipline imposed by the Master on the pupil for attainment of the final goal by the latter.

But it must be stated that in spite of strenuous hard work, without any recreation or rest and very little of relaxation and in spite of the fact that I had an ailing body, it was marvellous, how the Masters kept me up in fit condition, always cheerful, happy and full of joy within. Nothing in the world has given me such great joy as the writing of this book written absolutely under the direct inspiration of Sai Baba, the Master of Masters – Ahuramazda Amshaspand (God), Himself.

I have to acknowledge my deepest sense of gratitude to my two most loyal and devoted friends who stood by me thick and thin through all the vicissitudes of my journey in the attainment of the goal. I refer to Sri Homi Shapurji Spencer, and Sri K.S. Doraswamy Aiyer. The former was appointed by the Masters, in view of his having attained "the Christ stage" to interpret to me the inner meanings of the various messages received from the Masters and to guide me. The latter being Secretary of the Spiritual Healing Centre, Coimbatore, of which Rishi Ram Ram was the controlling Spirit Guide, was also of considerable help and assistance to me. With the kind permission of Homi and under orders of Sai Baba several of Homi's letters to me indicating the deep inner purpose of several of the messages, have been embodied in this book.

It is hoped this narrative of experiences with the Masters will enliven those yearning for God to fasten their belts in their struggle to reach the goal of Self-realization. Life has no meaning, if its real aim viz., to attain God-realization is lost sight of.

How much I owe to the Masters, Sai Baba and Ram Ram, particularly to the former, I need not say. I owe them, everything. To have remained in the presence of their aura, when under training was a veritable feast of the soul.

God is the Soul of the soul. He is the greatest in the universe. To know Him, to find Him is the highest bliss. It is the highest goal of life. Life without attainment of the unitive knowledge of God is a puerile waste. A life spent after mundane pleasures is a sickly life, full of blight and disease. It is a neurosis from which we would urge all men to escape. It is a neurosis from which we would urge all men to escapism. It is the way to the highest realm of bliss, the Kingdom of God, which is within every man, the key of which is held by the Master, who alone can guide the human soul, after it has attained certain perfection of character to reach the ultimate goal-union with God.

When Christ said: "I and the Father are one," he was giving expression to the highest truth of life. Every man is a potential superman, a Master, whose destiny it is to be merged into the Ocean of Eternity.

To know God, and to find Him is the greatest bliss of life, the grandest and highest achievement.

Not consciousness, not reason, but superconsciousness, the inner urge and intuition are the weapons, which the Master teaches us how to use for our perfection for the attainment of life's goal God realization.

We are all united in one divine fellowship. The mystic who is God-centred and God-illumined recognises His Presence in every particle and substance in the universe from the sod to the star. He makes no distinction of any kind. All are beloved to him, whether men or beast, birds or insects, This unitive knowledge is the basis and substance of the mystic's philosophy and his modus operandi. He is wrapped up in thoughts of God. He feels illumined by His Presence and is immersed in Sea of Bliss.

What is wanted in God's university is a combination of purity of heart, spiritual loneliness, extreme longing and burning desire of communion with God. This desire and longing for God can come only when one discards the five senses and the lower mind, when he avoids the externals of the world and seeks the seclusion of the soul, in complete surrender to the will of God.

What God wants is not your scholastic education, to give you illumination, but simplicity and trustfulness of a child. Jacob Boehme had it in abundance. Sri Ramakrishna, the guru of that great Swami Vivekananda, who took the message of spiritual India to the Parliament of all religions in America was an unlettered man but he got illumination from God and he became divine. Sri Ramana, the Sage of Arunachala in South India, ran away from his home, at the early age of seventeen because he had dislike for books and theoretical learning and entering into a forest, he gained divine illumination by means of renunciation and meditation.

The Kingdom of God is within us. The divine light shines within us. It is the prerogative of any and every one to open the lid which blocks the light and enter into the raptures of divinity.

A young man came to Christ and said: "Good Master, what good thing shall I do, that I may have eternal life?" And Christ said to him:

"There is none good but one, that is God, but if thou wilt enter into life, keep the commandments." (St. Matthew Ch. XIX-17).

The youngman promptly replied that he always followed the commandments. Then Jesus said to him;

"If thou will be perfect, go and sell that thou hast, and give to the poor, and thou shalt have treasure in heaven" and come and follow me." (St. Matthew Ch. XIX-21).

When the youngman heard this, he went away sorrowful, for the had great possessions and his attachment to them was so great, that in spite of his love for Christ and God, he was unable to give them up.

To attain eternal life, one has to live in spirit and not in flesh. One has to act like spirit, think like spirit and work like spirit. God cannot be seen by the eyes of the flesh or heard by the ears of the body. He is spirit and we have to live in spirit to understand and comprehend His grandeur and greatness. It is only then one can be filled with the sense of His Presence, giving abiding joy.

The object of life is attainment of higher consciousness. For it is through the window of this higher consciousness that the Reality could be touched. Mysticism is often reviled as escapism. The mystic is often put into the category of a fool, a lunatic and a charlatan, though, truly speaking, he is the architect who is building and reshaping the foundations of society on right lines. But for the mystic, the world would be in a mess. He is the beacon light, who gives the right lead to humanity to escape from the horrors of life, created by man's crass ignorance. The highest scientist or the best inventor of a machine is an ignorant man, if he has not in him the knowledge or perception of God. Divine knowledge is the only true knowledge. The mystic is not a visionary man who lives in delusions. He is the realist of the highest type for he knows the methods of finding God and knowing Him. He trains his soul in the rigour of such silence and seclusion; as to make it yield its mystic treasure. He contemplates, he meditates, he keeps detached from the external world, he keeps his mind absorbed in God, who is the only Reality and he gains the prize – the highest prize which any man can hope to gain on this earth plane – the prize of the Presence of God in him, filling him with raptures divine, giving him powers beyond human comprehension, for doing good to mankind and improving the world in whatever sphere of life it be, whether in arts, poetry, philanthropy, social reform, political administration, religion, philosophy etc. The mystic is the realist who trains himself in the school of spiritual athleticism and gains insight into the mysteries of God. He kills the ego in him by attaining the vision of God. He becomes the servant of God. His mind and heart and soul are all tuned in one key and that key is God. He becomes the image of God, the replica of God – the God in man, absolutely selfless, humane, universally minded, transcendental in his thoughts, words and actions. He is the pillar of strength, the bulwark of life. Living in the world, he is detached.

It all boils down to this, that God alone being the reality, to think of God, to follow God, to know His Law, to obey the way, the Law, to work in humility, unmindful of the kicks and sneers of the world – this is the teaching of MYSTICISM of the mystery schools all over the world, the yogi schools especially of India – both ancient and modern. There is no religion greater than Truth. There is no science greater than the Science of the soul. Self-realization or God-realization is man's highest dream – his highest aspiration.

When I was nearing the goal, the Master said to me: "Talk of God to every one. Keep on chanting the name of God all the time. Nothing should exist for you except God. See God in every creature. Worship God and God alone. Both inwardly and externally, your dedication to God should be complete. Let the word 'God' echo and reverberate in your heart, mind and soul. Drink in God, eat in God, work in God, sleep in God. Let the thoughts of God lock you up on all sides. Nothing but God. God should be the all inclusive theme of your daily thought and action. Forget in God: live in God. God is your jailer. He alone is your custodian, your watchman, your policeman. His eyes are on you. Your eyes, heart, mind and soul should be on Him every hour, every minute, every second. God is your food; God is your water. God is your very air on which you live. Be of God, live in God and be drowned in God. Practice this religiously and create a new body, newer channels for the inflow and outflow of God's love and light."

It will be noticed that the use of "I" and "mine" has been inordinatley made in the compilation of this book. In spiritual life, it has to be eliminated, nay, it is abominable to allow the ego to rule and dominate. It must be slain before the goal can ever be reached. The author therefore feels exceedingly ashamed for this breach of the essential canon of spirituality. But is there any way out? Most unfortunately, it is indispensable. "It is impossible to escape the situation" to put it in the words of the Master, who having been approached on the subject gave the following verdict:

"In spiritual life "I" and "Mine" are to be eliminated completely. If you achieve any success, you can't say, "I did it". Whenever you say that, it means that your ego is active and is not slain. But when a man writes his spiritual experiences with his Master or Masters, the "I" becomes unfortunately indispensable if any attempt is made to eliminate it, then the book loses its interest. In fact, it is impossible to escape the situation for no book of such nature could ever be written without the glaring buzz of the "I".

Care has been taken to avoid inclusion of messages of self-glorifying nature.

We know the story of Socrates. When a man asked the Delphic Oracle: "Who is the wisest man in Greece?" prompt came the answer: 'Socrates,' When Socrates came to know of this, he pondered over it and he said. "I am named the wisest because I am sufficiently wise to know that I know nothing."

I am aware of my nothingness. In fact, the following message of Sai Baba, the Master of Masters and my Sprit Guide, is but an echo of my own inward feeling:

"Remember that you are absolutely nothing whatsoever. Even a speck of dust has some value but you are nothing. Keep this thought constantly in your mind."

In order to illustrate and prove my nothingness several times my mediation used to be a failure apparently for no fault of mine. On April 7, 1950, I entered the altar room as usual time full of hopes that I would go into *samadhi* and my inner eye would function. I started my mediation as usual. To my utter surprise, it was more or less a failure. Sai Baba explained to me the significance of this failure in the following message which he gave to me.

"I am extremely sorry to say that far from putting you into *samadhi* and opening your inner eye, I did not even allow you to mediate properly and frustrated your attempt to do so at every step. You tried your utmost but I was callous and succeeded in breaking you down completely."

This was to teach me that I could do nothing without the wish of God.

On April 16, 1950, again my meditation was a failure. The Master gave the following explanation:

> "I am extremely sorry to say that your today's meditation was a hopeless failure. Do you know why? I could not help again interfering with you and this time I did, with a sort of grim determination not to allow you any scope whatsoever and I have succeeded though you put up a marvellous fight. My aim in doing this is to teach you the lesson that you by yourself in the cosmic struggle of life are nothing. It is to ground you in this great teaching. I was compelled much against my will to use my power against you. I know it is very trying to come every day to the altar room, full of hopes and then to return empty handed in this manner. But I am glad, you are now getting seasoned and that these disappointments do not make any difference to your. Kindly continue your attitude of indifference to all consequences and you would soon win your goal."

True renunciation, which is a *sine qua non* in the life of the spirit to attain God-realization, does not lie necessarily in leading a life of poverty, mortification of the flesh and complete seclusion from human intercourse. Indian *yogis* in the past to realise Self generally adopted these methods for attainment of their object. We know the example of Buddha. How he practised penances for eight long years and he could not get Illumination. Once he was on the point of being drowned, when he entered into the waters of a river, for his daily bath. So thin and emaciated his body had become by continuous fasting that he could not raise himself to the bank and he had to be pulled out just to save his life.

This incident made Buddha think and he came to the conclusion that instead of taking extreme measures, the safest course was the Middle Path. He advocated the middle path. He gave up penances and his meditation under the Bo tree for full seven weeks. It rewarded him in the end. He became illumined.

The whole idea of renunciation is to detach the mind from the externals of life. Divine communion or complete happiness can come only by the activities of the soul, not body. To seek entry into God's presence, spiritual experiences have to be obtained, such as visions, moments of rapturous reality, the feeling of unity with all, egolessness, complete indifference to everything – praise or blame, success or failure, – fearlessness, desirelessness, humility and purity. It is not learning but purity of heart that gains access to the portals of Eternity.

Several times, when I met with failure in my spiritual strivings, I felt like giving up the altar room activities. The voice of reason at times dominated me, trying to thwart the still small voice of intuition and imagination. I was tempted in sheer despair, to give a go-by to all spiritual flights and aspirations, and path of the spirit being too stony and dreary, the goal ever so distant and receding, The feeling of self-assertiveness often gained ground. But for the Masters, who caught hold of me very fast and saw the dangers ahead caused by the wild tempest of my own mind, I would have been swept off my feet and lost into wilderness. But once a candidate is on the path, the Master is most vigilant and helps him to go upward step by step and if the former at all recedes, the latter brings him back. This is the chief service of the Master. Whatever the dangers be, the neophyte is ever guided and he seldom loses the path. He may take a longer time to reach the goal but he is sure of his victory.

In my case. I was doubly fortunate. For Rishi Ram Ram, was appointed by God from my very birth to act as my guardian angel and Master and to bring me on the path. Later he was joined as will be seen from the narrative by Sai Baba, a Master of Master. To my amazement it was found that in Sai Baba, I had not only a Master a Masters, but that He was Ahuramazda Amshaspand Himself. To get revelation direct from God, to talk to Him everyday, freely and to draw is inspiration was an unique achievement. That Sai Baba who was none else than the highest cosmic force filled me with highest bliss and in order to convince me of his unique position unequalled in the whole celestial realm, several proofs were given, the principal of which was the easy dexterity with which He could extricate my soul from my living body, without putting me into *samadhi* and without stopping my life breath even for a second, This unique performance could be done by God alone and none else.

The following message of Sai Baba pertinent to the subject is self-explanatory:

> "When a soul is extricated and another is installed in its place immediately, no extinction of life is felt even for a minute. All I did was to remove our soul and put in instead Ram Ram's soul instantaneously, You did not feel the change externally in the least, This can be done in a living body by God alone and I had to do it not to exhibit My power to you but to give you a most convincing proof that it is I, God who is talking with you and training you and none else. It is a unique experience for which you should feel extremely grateful and happy."

On April 14, 1950 Sri Ramana, the Sage of Arunachala, passed away at 08:47 p.m. and the sacred remains were interred the next day, in the evening. Sai Baba had predicted his death to me as would be seen from the following message which he a gave to me on March 18, 1950 and I was therefore quite prepared for it:

> "No one should at all interfere in Bhagwan's case, Leave him alone absolutely. No doctor's treatment would do him any good, He cannot live long He knows the date when he will pass away. He is in daily communion with Me. He is able to bear his physical suffering because of the extra power of endurance which has been given to him specially for the purpose. He is quite happy. He has fulfilled his mission and he will be soon called away now. He will join the rank of the Masters when he come over here."

Sai Baba made me contact Sri Ramana's Spirit in less than twenty-four hours after his departure from the physical plane, a unique performance, which a master of Masters of the calibre of Sai Baba alone could do. Sai Baba introduced me to the Spirit of Sri Ramana with the following words:

"I had told you that Sri Ramana would pass away and you have heard the news of the passing away today. I will make him contact you and give you his message. You will be the first recipient of his message from the other world, Yes, he is ready to give you his message just not. Kindly concentrate on his picture for full ten minutes and he will give you is message which will open your eyes and which will simply dumbfound you."

"Yes, I am Ramana. People used to call me Bhagwan on the earth plane, which I left only yesterday. There is nothing new to me here. The only difference is that having given up the physical body. I shall stay here permanently and not make constant movements between your earth plane and this spiritual plane as I used to do when I was in physical body on your earth plane. No one should grieve for me. I am exceptionally happy and I am giving this message to you as ordered by God under whom I have the privilege to serve.

I see from your aura that your fate is just like mine. Your aura is all white. It is no wonder that I should have been ordered to give a message to you within such a short time of my departure from your earth plane, You are under the special direction and training by God Himself, It is a unique honour, rarely conferred upon a mortal being. Even I had not that honour and blessing. Do you know when you came to me at the ashram, I had already received orders that I should transform your soul. It was a joy to me. How quickly you responded to my invisible touch! I opened your inner secret valves, when you were sitting in absolute silence in the hall at my feet. I only did what I was ordered to do, having not at all known you before. I see now what a tremendous transformation has come in you. No Master could do it. It is all the working of God Himself. I go now."

I am not only indebted to Sri Ramana for the service he rendered to me, but also to Meher Baba. It was the latter who put me on the path, when I saw him in 1946 at Ahmednagar.

I must consider myself singularly fortunate that I have had the benefit and guidance of Masters both in physical body and spirit and above all the guidance of the Master of Masters, viz., God Himself. It may appear grotesque to make such a claim but a close study of the messages and experiences gone through corroborate its truth.

The following message of Rishi Ram Ram delivered to me on April 25, 1950, gives a bird's eye-view of the whole situation and the services rendered by various Masters:

"At the time you paid a visit to Meher Baba you were not even on the path. When I sent you later on to Sri Ramana he too rendered you a great service by making you an Arhat. A Master in physical body is indispensable, without doubt, to make a pupil reach the goal of *Jivan Mukti.* In your case, not only physical Masters have helped you but we, Masters in Spirit, are all the time guiding and helping you, But for us, you would have been still in the wilderness. I was ordered by God to act as your Guardian Angel from your very birth and I have discharged that duty and I am more than satisfied with your progress. You have shown such remarkable progress that God Himself has for the last several months taken you under His own personal training. He is not only greatest than hundreds of Meher Baba put together but He is the greatest force in the whole cosmos. Your world will be bewildered when your new book is out."

It is the duty of every human being to fix up the goal of his life. He must understand the true purpose of life. Without this knowledge, he is like a ship with out a compass, tossing on the waters of the sea of life, a spiritual orphan, not knowing his destination. Each soul is an emanation from God and it is destined that it must get back to God, and be merged into Eternity. Just as an eagle that has its home on the summit of a mountain, sweeps down the valley, in the shadows of the bleak mountains but returns back to its abode on the mountain top when the shades of the night lengthen, each soul must remember its source and strive to return back to its original home.

This, in a nutshell, is the alpha and omega of the whole spiritual philosophy. Why should we not then keep our mind steadfast on God? If the publication of this book, strange as it may appear with the experiences of an ordinary man like me who has lived in the word but has refrained to become one of the world, can help the reader, the search for truth, which is within him, for gaining a larger consciousness, which would stand him in the strife of life and help him to gin access to that inner kingdom which alone can give light and happiness and nothing else, the object of this publication would be amply fulfilled.

The path and the goal can not be fixed, if man allows himself to be carried away by desires, passions and earthly longings. Says J. Krishnamurthi in his beautiful book *Life in Freedom,* being a compendium of his *Camp Fire Talks*:

> "Because the goal has not been established, because the path that leads to that goal has not been found there is confusion and chaos, there is questioning and doubt in the mind. As long as there is doubt in the mind there is no peace, nor certainty and ecstasy of purpose". (pp.15, 16)

It is the prayer of this humble author that this book of experiences may enkindle in the heart and mind of the reader, the desire to establish the goal and to find the path to the goal, which is the objective of life.

I extend my most grateful thanks to my most devoted friends and allies in my spiritual adventure, Sri Homi Shapurji Spencer of Bandra and Sri K.S. Doraswami Aiyer, Secretary, The Spiritual Healing Centre, Coimbatore, who have done so much, in enabling me to reach the goal safely and securely, under the guidance and inspirations of the Masters.

Should I reiterate, how much I owe to the Master, Rishi Ram Ram, who was appointed by God, as my Guardian Angel, from my very birth and whose constant companionship, visible or invisible, has been a source of great delight and inspiration and Asho Ahuram Mazda Amshaspand (God) Himself appearing as Sai Baba, the Master of Masters, whose goodness and glory, whose greatness and graciousness, no pen can adequately reveal, whose gentle touch has awakened the springs of internal bliss and quietitude and for whose training and inspirational guidance, this humble author is so deeply grateful. I bow down to Him with feelings of innate gratitude and in all submission and humility.

1957 MINOCHER K. SPENCER

Sai Baba of Shirdi (27.9.1838-15.10.1918) whom Yogi M.K. Spencer worshipped as God and so God assuming the form of Sai Baba trained him for God realization from 12th May, 1949 to 4th June, 1983. Spencer always kept this picture on his table in the Samadhi room.

Spirit Master Rishi Ram Ram

Sri Ramana Maharishi of Sri Ramanasram, Tiruvanmalai (Dec. 30, 1879 – April 14, 1950)

Sri Ramakrishna Paramhansa

Sri Aurobindo

Swami Sivananda of Rishikesh, who was a close friend and admirer of Yogi Spencer. He wrote Foreword to Spencer's book *Divine Discourses* in Nov. 1951.

Swami Vivekananda

Yogi Minocher K. Spencer
(Oct. 4, 1988 – Aug. 30, 1958)

Shri K.S.D. Aiyer (March 14, 1889 – Oct. 24, 1965), a close friend of Yogi M.K. Spencer, was Hon. Secretary, Spiritual Healing Centre, Coimbatore. He and Rishi Ram Ram (then Minister Nandrupa) were Ministers in the Court of King Ashoka (273-232 BC)

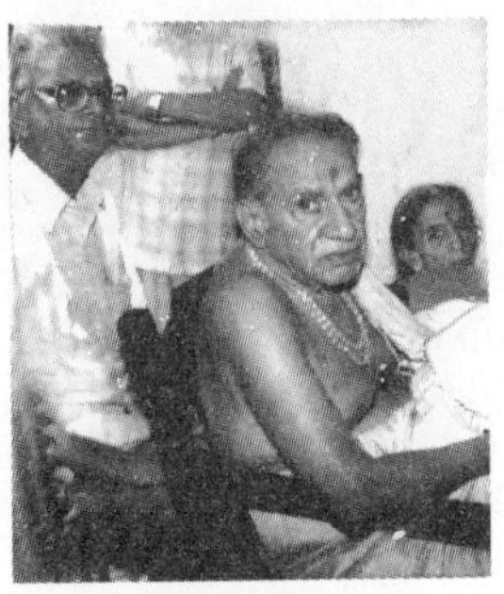

SP. Ruhela with
A. Somasundaram
and his wife in 1997

Philosopher J. Krishnamurti, a contemporary of Yogi Spencer

Prof. Satya Pal Ruhela (born on Feb. 2, 1935), editor of this book *How I Found God* is an educationist, sociologist, futurologist and spiritualist. He is Founder & Honorary Secretary, SAI DIVINE RESEARCH CENTRE, Faridabad. He is an ardent worshipper of Sai Baba, Rishi Ram Ram and Yogi M.K. Spencer.

Adi Sankaracharya (788 AD – 820 AD) the great exponent of Advait philosophy

Lord Zoroaster

Lord Christ

Sri Shirdi Sai Baba

A. Somasundram and his wife a Pulla Abjashi at Markapur (A.P.)

This book was blessed by Mrs. Raj Rajeswari, the Incarnation of Lord Shiva's Divine Course Parvati, at Mysore on July 9, 2001

Professor Satya Pal Ruhela, editor of *How I Found God*

Chapter One

Dabbling in Spiritualism (1930-40)

In 1930, I met a person who called himself the "Mystery Man". He was a stranger to our city and his short sojourn in Karachi was enough to excite curiosity and interest in people.

I paid a visit to the "Mystery Man" purely out of curiosity. At that time, I had no notion of spiritualism, the occult in yoga. He asked me to write down five questions on a piece of paper that was put in an envelope and shoved into the inner pocket of my coat. The "Mystery Man" then undertook to read them and reply to them. He read them correctly and wrote them out, on his own piece of paper. I was startled when he wrote the questions, exactly I had written them, without missing even a punctuation mark. He then told me to go out of his room for two minutes. When he called me again, he wrote down the replies to the questions. One of the questions was "Have I got any gift?" The reply was: "Yes, you have psychic gifts."

This was very puzzling. I was then more of a realist than an idealist. I believed only in external phenomena and had no conception of hidden truths or hidden light. I did not know even the meaning of the word 'psychic'.

This news that I had psychic gifts turned my gaze to the Science of Spiritualism and I began to take interest in it. I realised physical knowledge was not a doorway to real TRUTH. I became an earnest searcher for Truth.

In 1937, I went to London for a surgical operation. The visit gave me an opportunity to talk with the so-called 'dead'. An engagement was made with a trance-clairvoyant medium and the result was most astounding. I returned from the seance room a different man. The inner spark had been kindled. The yearning to learn more and find out the truth gripped me like an iron chain. I wanted to probe and unveil the secrets of the universe.

Around the year 1940 Mr. V.D. Rishi, founder of the Indian Spiritual Society, came to Karachi and started a branch of his society. My contact with Mr. Rishi and some of his local followers further stimulated me to study Spiritualism and become a medium. Not knowing what great dangers were inherent in mediumship, I plunged headlong into the vortex. The subject was so fascinating that it was difficult to resist its charms. Had I known that constant use of planchette and indiscriminate indulgence in auto-writing meant extraction of energy from the most vital parts of the human body, I would have paused. My failing health was a greater reason to keep away from all this, mediumship practised in excess is most injurious. But I went on relentlessly.

I started to publish a series of articles on Spiritualism in a local English paper – *The Daily Gazette.* The editor, Mr. M.S. Sharma, himself a spiritualist, welcomed the weekly contributions. The series created lively interest among people but Theosophists and Theologians were deeply perturbed. I had no desire to run them down for their opposition which was, after all, well meant and in conformity with their idea of spirituality. However, their narrow vision that identified Spiritualism as communicating with the lower astrals was objectionable and unfair. It was not lower but Higher Spiritualism that was advocated in my articles. They were written with a set purpose to vindicate and indicate the existence of the Other World.

The Theosophists organised a public lecture denouncing my series. Their tirade awakened my soul and I began a deeper and more intensified study of Higher Spiritualism. It also brought me into contact with the Spiritual Healing Centre of Coimbatore (South India) and with the Spirit Master, Rishi Ram Ram, the Guide of the Centre and one of the foremost members of the Great White Brotherhood, whose principal work is to help and assist in the evolution of men on the earth-plane.

Spiritualism as a Science of Truth, in spite of the great dangers inherent in it, cannot be ignored. It is a stepping stone to wider worlds of knowledge and establishes a link between this world and the other. It is a challenge to materialism for it has proved that death is a gateway to a higher life and not a mere termination.

Julian Johnson, the author of *The Path of the Masters* says: "No real Master ever works through a Medium". "Nor does any other highly developed spirit ever uses a medium. Such a thing is impossible."

This is incorrect. If the medium is of an exalted temperament – holy, pure and is absorbed in thoughts of God and doing good to mankind – no lower astral would dare touch even the fringe of his or her body. The aura of the medium is an indicator of his level of spirituality. Even Masters make use of mediums. In this connection, the following message of Spirit Master Rishi Ram Ram is relevant:

> "Spiritualism is a source of great danger to the mediums. But if it is properly and wisely cultivated, it can be a source of great relief and consolation. All that is wanted is absolute purity of life, high and noble motives and confidence in God.
>
> "Masters do operate through mediums. I have spoken several times through mediums at the Coimbatore Centre. But I take

good care that the power of the medium is not exhausted. I gave very short and small talks and take particular care in every respect. This is not so in the case of astral spirits. They are so attracted to earth life that they do things in excess and wreck the poor mediums.

"When Masters come to talk with any medium it is always for higher purposes in life, for the general benefit of all. You started your career by dabbling in Spiritualism. You had some latent gifts. You developed and became a medium. But knowing no rules, you abused the mediumistic powers and had to suffer a lot."

Chapter Two

Period of Apprenticeship (1941-46)

I started dabbling in spiritualism without any proper study of its rules or procedure and paid a heavy price in the bargain. But the angels were infinitely kind to me and they saved me from all dangers, It dawned upon me then that there must be some purpose behind this mercy. Nothing happens by chance. I was singed, but not burned. This close shave stimulated my desire to learn more of the invisible planes and gather the knowledge that is hidden from physical senses.

Let me give a few of the inspiring messages which were received during the period of my apprenticeship – 1941-1946 – before I was taken on the Path.

"Study Spiritualism. Do not worry if you do not make a success of yourself. Serve God in the truest spirit. Study hard. Put your trust in God, Don't despair." These may sound like copybook maxims, but when they came to a bruised heart forsaken by the world, they made a tremendous difference. In all the messages I got from an angel, who called herself Spirit of the Higher Planes, there was a constant ring of divinity. "Serve God. Worship God. Practise Renunciation in thought, word, and deed. Nothing is so great in life, Renounce all. Do not worry about the consequences. You will make tremendous progress." Once, I asked: "Has every one a guardian Angel?" No was the reply, "Then why do I have one?" "Because you have served God." The reply delighted me. I came to know that Rishi Ram Ram had been appointed by God as my invisible Master from my very birth, for my spiritual evolution.

On March 2, 1941, I was warned not to put myself into the hands of lower spirits. It must be said that a well-meaning spirit constantly tried to contact me and in desperation once even impersonated as Ram Ram.

The distinction between higher and lower spirits is that the former are not inclined to make predictions, but if they do they are always correct, The lower spirits are keen on making predictions and are invariably incorrect.

The crux of the messages was to work hard and study the scriptures, write books on religion and philosophy to vindicate the unity of thought prevailing in the Scriptures of the world.

I earnestly applied myself to the study of literature of all religions, The result was my first book on comparative religion entitled *Oneness with God,* published in 1944.

On October 6, 1946, I got the pleasing news. Rishi Ram Ram told me: "Work hard for you are accepted for Initiation." My heart leapt with joy. After dabbling in the shallow waters of Spiritualism, I was directed by invisible hands into the higher channels of Spirituality. A new chapter in my life was beginning to open.

To be initiated is to be twice born. The first birth is from your earthly parents. The second birth is given by a Guru for a higher purpose, to become a great force in carrying out God's Plan of Evolution.

I was now definitely in the hands of my Spirit Master, Rishi Ram Ram. Initiation is, in the words of Dr. Annie Besant, "expansion of consciousness."

Chapter Three

On The Path (1946)

I was now definitely on the Path that was to lead me to *nirvana* and adeptship. According to Theosophists, there are five great Initiations, the last being that of Adeptship. It generally takes several births after initiation to cross the path and reach the goal, The first initiation links the candidate with his Master, once the pupil comes into the Master's aura the Master binds him to himself. So great is the love of the Master for his pupil that once he takes him under his training, he does not lose his hold. If a pupil is hard-working and obeys his Master's orders, he can become an adept even in one life after initiation.

During this period, I had composed a good number of prayer-paragraphs, several of which had already appeared in a local journal. The title selected by me was *Outpourings of the Heart.* The Master however changed the title to *Light on the Path.* As I remembered having read a book of the same title, I asked the Master to change it, His reply was: "The Title, *Light on the Path* is correct. Mistaken. No book of such title. Put words "Out-pourings of the Heart" under the title, in brackets."

This made me think and I discovered that the Master was right. The full title of the book referred to was, *Light on the Path Pat and Karma* and not just *Light on the Path.* It was a very small book of sixty odd pages with an introduction by Bishop C.W. Leadbeater. It purports to be the dictation by the Master Hilarion through the mediumship of M.M. – a lady well known in Theosophical circle.

Even though the Master was right, I insisted upon a change. I was anxious that the book be published anonymously. To this I got the reply on December 22, 1946 *Light on the Path* should be published in the name of Minocher K. Spencer, not anonymously.

On May 15, 1947, Rishi Ram Ram reprimanded my obstinacy thus: "*Light on the Path* will be published shortly. You should not interfere with my work, I shall not allow you to change the title. You will come to know of the reason later on. Write to Doraswami (the publisher) not to change the title. Worry not, you will not be accused of anything."

The publication of *Light on the Path* got delayed considerably. I was feeling anxious. On December 28, 1947, the following message from the Master was received: "Your book of prayers, *Light on the Path* is held up. No one is to be blamed for such a long delay in its publication. It is purposely done to serve a certain object." The book was released in 1948.

Later on, when Sai Baba – the Master of Masters – took me over from Ram Ram for higher spiritual training and guidance, I asked him "Why is it that Ram Ram persisted in giving the title *Light on the Path* to my book. My objection to the title was on logical and moral ground, viz., that a book with nearly the same title had already been published and it was a fine spiritual book, written by an advanced student of occultism. To take that title was like robbing some one else's holy property."

Sai Baba replied: "Ram Ram was absolutely justified in forcing you to agree on the title *Light on the Path.* In the first place, no man must think that he is an independent owner of anything. Nothing belongs to him, everything is His. For the purpose of distinction, separate names and titles should be used on your earth plane. But this should not be carried to an extreme."

"The reason why Ram Ram has compelled you to use the title of *Light on the Path* was that he foresaw your future and he wanted people to know and understand this. It was to awaken them to the new light, that will soon be shining on the Path.

"You had scruples about using some one's title and you were perfectly right. In fact we admired you for this. But from the spiritual point of view, we had special reasons. The coming events will further prove the veracity of our statement."

When one is on the Path, he has to follow the will of the Master. He has to become a fit instrument of God for carrying out His Plan of Evolution on this earth plane. If he is fortunate, he may finish the whole journey in one life and become an Adept in physical body with tremendous powers to do good to mankind. If he does not reach the final stage of Adeptship, at least he can aspire to become an Arhat, which is the midway house on the Path. An Arhat is an assistant of the Master. After attaining Arhatship, there is no compulsion to take physical body. It means attainment of *Nirvana font i.e.,* cessation from the round of birth and death. One who becomes an Arhat is allowed to call himself *Paramhansa.* The tie between the Master and the pupil is more firmly knit. As the pupil's aura improves, the Master's love for him increases. A Master's love is much greater than a mother's love for her child, for the Master is not moved by any personal consideration of natural affection for his pupil. The only thing that weighs with the Master is how far his pupil has advanced on the Path.

How many hours have I spent in the altar room, looking up with eyes of love and gratitude and in return being blessed by their love and endearing words.

When a man is on the Path, he must understand that he belongs to no particular religion. I am a Parsi, and Zoroastrian by faith. But as soon as I entered the Path, the Masters taught me that I was a citizen of the cosmos and that I belonged to all religions and not only to Zoroastrianism. This liberality of thought is absolutely necessary in furthering man's progress in the spiritual life. There are no religious labels in the other world.

We have to tread the Path with the "Eye of the Spirit." It is only with inward knowledge and with the Master's voice ringing in our ears, in the silence of our heart, that we can realise that we have become the Path itself.

Our evolution is not a process, not even a growth but an unfolding of the spirit within. We have to work as naturally as flowers grow in the unsullied atmosphere of nature. We have to work in union with all around us. We have not only to accept our own pain, but take the pains of others in the bargain. That is the law of evolution, the unfolding of self, the teaching of the Masters on the Path.

Along with complete self-abnegation and desirelessness there should be a will to dare and to suffer in silence, Suffering has to be ended by practising virtue. The load of past *karma* has to be reduced and ultimately annihilated. For the Master works freely only when the *karma* is absolutely finished and your soul shines like a crystal pearl and ready to make its flight to the other world.

Everything is God, nothing but God is Real. The aspirant who has been chosen for the Path knows he is being led from darkness into light, from the unreal to the real, from death to eternity. And in treading the Path, the beacon light that helps him is love and devotion for God. It is this that knits him closer and closer to the Master. But Love for God means love for humanity also.

The Path is steep and stony. The Master puts the aspirant through tests, trials and temptations, without end. If the aspirant successfully passes them, the Master takes him from stage to stage, till he reaches the last rung of the ladder, which is the most difficult to cross and where many flounder and are lost and require rebirth to resume their journey on the Path. It is only the strong, who have will and determination to stand firm despite heavy odds, that win the race and earn the crown of Eternal Bliss.

The Theosophical literature on Occult Science is based considerably on the mystical teachings of Indian Rishis extant in the Hindu Scriptures, India, even now in spite of its having been inundated by waves of Western civilisation is a home of great *yogis,* spiritual giants, who are a wonder of the world. There are several kinds of yoga systems practised. They are the ways to attain Self or God-Realization.

Dhanana Patanjali's system of yoga is known as the eight-limbed yoga. These eight limbs are, *Yama* and *Niyama, Asana, Pranayama, Pratyahara, Dhayana,* and *Samadhi.* The first two include ethical practices. If a man wants to become a yogi or take on the Path, he must have the firm foundation of character in him. Not only must he eschew all evil tendencies, but must be practitioner of all virtues chiefly – Truthfulness, Non-violence, Contentment, Chastity, and Self-surrender. Study of Scriptures is deemed necessary in the yoga system and the aspirants are admitted for training only after they have attained a certain state of perfection of character, which is so very essential in realising Self.

The third limb is *Asana.* Undue importance is paid by Hindu yogis on this limb. All that is necessary is that the upper part of the body should be kept erect, to allow free and unhampered functioning of the *chakras* when the Kundalini which is situated at the base of the Spinal Column is awakened.

The fourth limb is *Pranayama.* This is purely an artificial method of regulating breath. It is fraught with great danger, if ~~it is~~ practised without the guidance of a great yogi. It is much safer to dispense with it altogether for in life spiritual, anything that smells of mechanised forcefulness should be avoided. Just as a fruit that ripens and falls on the ground is the sweetest the aspirant must practise yoga with full determination and resolve to reach the goal in one life but not by adopting forceful and unnatural methods, which may prove harmful to his body and cause irreparable damage, Instead of controlling the mind by means of *Pranayama* the man must try to discard the source of distraction by practising egolessness and desirelessness. To slay desires and to crush the ego are absolutely essential on the Path.

The fifth limb is *Pratyahara.* It means withdrawal of the mind from sense objects, which cause distraction. This means practice of asceticism. It was considered so very essential in the olden times, when yogis retired to forests to observe '*sanyas*'.

The sixth limb is concentration or *Dhayana*, a very useful limb by no doubt. It is by means of concentration on the picture of a great yogi, a saint, a prophet of religion, a saviour of the world, the third eye, which is called the astral or the hidden eye can be opened. It is a great instrument in the development of the psychic faculty of clairvoyance.

Meditation or *Dhayana* is the key to divine wisdom. It is by the gateway of meditation that the aspirant can obtain divine or transcendental consciousness. We shall discuss this subject at length later on, as we proceed with our story.

Samadhi is the end of meditation. It is of all the most important and vital limb, the summum bonum of the yoga systems, when the aspirant reaches the cherished goal of his life viz., Self-realization or God-realization, when the spark gets lost in the fire, when the drop disappears in the ocean, when the ray becomes the "All the eternal radiance," when consciousness of individuality is lost and the aspirant becomes the ALL.

Chapter Four

The Second Initiation: How I became an *Arhat* (1946-49)

As soon as I was initiated on the Path I was asked to work hard and study religion with a view to writing books that may guide people to the Kingdom of God. I had two minor psychic gifts – the gift of healing and auto-writing. But I was stopped from practising the gift of healing as that would retard spiritual progress. I was asked to wait till I had passed a certain stage, when healing could be exercised without any adverse reaction. As far as auto-writing was concerned, the Master made me write only once a week and that too for a few minutes.

The following messages received week by week tell their own tale:

> On November 10, 1946, the Master told me: "Try to meditate on Me. I shall take you to the Spiritual Plane. You should control yourself, Howsoever much you love Me, you will not gain salvation until all your *Karmas* are wiped out. I can't tell you now when you will be free."

I set myself to the task of wiping out my *Karma*, by doing as much of good as possible and controlling my mind. It was evident that mere love for the Master was not enough. I must renounce and sacrifice to win the Master's love.

On December 1, 1946, the following message of the Master was written by my hand: "Work on. You will write a beautiful work on Mysticism. But you should quote rightly from Scriptures. You must have sound knowledge before I inspire you. You are my pupil. Try to meditate on Me, when you pray to God. To you will be given the beatitude of God. Do not kill your desire to become a great saint. You are on the way. Face all dangers bravely. Put confidence on Me. I shall take you to the final goal."

On December 8, 1946, the Master said: "Be careful in your talk. You should not get excited. You must control yourself. You must rise higher than others. Work hard to accomplish your salvation soon, or you will be told to take another life. Trust Me."

On December 22, 1946, Ram Ram gave me the following message: "You should practise silence for solving your difficulties, You must not get excited. Study hard. Right understanding will give you God-realization. You have psychic power of healing. But you should not make use of it for you will not be able to secure salvation. You will become an Arhat in the next life. Make the best use of your present life."

The news that I would not become an Arhat in this life disappointed me. But I was determined to shed pride, doubt and superstition, work hard, control my mind and temper, give away everything and apply myself completely in study and service of those sick in body and in soul.

During this time, I was immersed in studying for my new book *Joyous Mysticism.* The subject brought me into contact with many great occultist writers, especially Theosophical writers, and I made copious use of the Theosophical Society's library. I was also guided by my friend and relative, Homi Shapurji Spencer of Bandra, Bombay. He is a recluse, a great religious scholar and highly advanced on the Path. But for his guidance, I might have slipped off from the Path, when trials, tests and postponements became the order of the day and every ounce of energy was required to face the situation.

On January 5, 1947, I was told through the following message that I should be prepared for the Second Initiation in a few weeks:

> "Justice will be yours when you will become free of delusions. You should read Annie Besant's works. Try to grasp the mystical side of the problems. You will be prepared for the Second Initiation in a few weeks. You are doing very well. Go on with your work. You must meditate on Me all the time. Power will flow in to you quite naturally. Pass all messages to Homi. He will explain and guide you. Like you he is my pupil and will soon become perfect. You must follow his advice."

On January 12, 1947, the following message was given: "Prepare yourself for a calamity. I shall save you. You are not studying much. Nothing will happen to you. I shall save you. You must not worry."

The following is an extract from a message given to me by Rishi Ram Ram on January 26, 1947:

> "I will initiate you in the second phase, next week, after you have passed your test. Work strenuously. I shall inspire you. Silence is necessary in your work. Worry not. Every one will get his due. You will be called upon to do higher services after your Second Initiation."

It was evident that the Higher Ones had at last decided that I be prepared for Arhatship.

On February 2, 1947, the Master gave me the heartening news that I would be taken to the final goal and that I should start writing my new book under his guidance and inspiration.

On February 16, 1947, the Master gave me the following message: "Try your utmost to work if you want salvation. Work strenuously without rest. It does not matter if you do not get anything. Send away your money quickly. You will then become fit for Arhatship. You will obtain visions of a Yogi soon. Try to grasp what you read, I shall then inspire you. Such is the teaching of philosophy, that you should strive for the most sublime which you are doing. Do not lose heart when trials come on you. Shake off all fear. You will become an Adept in this life. I shall train you."

On March 2, 1947, the Master said: "Every thing will be alright. You will be taken to the Nirvanic plane shortly. The night is over. Highly evolved persons will become acquainted with you. You were right in discarding the offer to awaken Kundalini. I was tempting you. You are beyond temptations."

On April 6, 1947, I was asked to install a separate altar in my house and not allow any one to enter it.

Then on May 11, 1947, I received the following important message from my master:

> "Know Me now as yourself. You have progressed well. You will become an Arhat in a short time. You will have to leave your house to study occultism. You must know the secrets of the universe. You will be given spiritual training. Ask Doraswami to take you to Sri Ramana of Arunachala. Will you write to the sage of Arunachala that you are coming to him? He will write to you to come any day you like. Will you make it a point to go? You will become an Arhat through him. Will you finish off all your work at Karachi and go away? You are marked for higher duties in life."

On June 22, 1947, the Master delivered to me the following message, which is more or less a repetition of the earlier message, but introduces two or three new points, which require comment:

> "Om. Two people will join you in your journey to Tiruvannamalai. You will have to finish your work soon. Prepare yourself to leave this plane. Go to Jamshed and see how he works. You should follow his example. Tell Jamshed that he is put on the list of Secret Guides of Humanity. He is an excellent worker, much loved by the Masters."

On June 29, 1947, the following message was delivered to me by the Master, which cheered my heart:

> "I like you, my son. You are on the way to salvation. You will get it soon. Love all. You will become an Arhat this year. You will become an Adept. You must work very hard... You will not leave this plane

> till you have reached *Nirvana.* You will be raised to your Master's height. But you must not get elated. You must become tranquil in mind. You must work for twelve hours at least, prayers and meditation extra. Only, then will progress be achieved. Mine own son, you will be raised to the highest place in our sphere. Do your best."

Though it was difficult in my weak state of health, I agreed to work twelve hours everyday, apart from the long hours of prayer and meditation.

Darshan of Sri Ramana Maharshi

We left Karachi for Arunachal in the beginning of the second week of July 1947, and as predicted by Ram Ram, our journey both ways, proved the happiest to and fro in our lives.

We met Doraswami (K.S.D. Aiyer) Swami Nityananda and Sister Lalita at Madras and stayed in the house of Khan Bahadur Abdul Karim, a fine flower of humanity and a learned author.

Tiruvannamalai is a small railway station in South India, The village of Arunachala where Shri Ramana lived is at a short distance by road from there. We left Madras for Tiruvannamalai by the afternoon train and arrived at our destination in about eight or nine hours. The journey was exceedingly pleasant. Arrangement was made for us to stay in a small cottage near the ashram of the sage. We reached the cottage at night. In tune with the religious atmosphere of the whole place, the cottages were named according to religious predilections of the people. The name of our cottage was 'Detachment.' How beautifully it blended with our thoughts of renunciation! It was a tiny cottage with two bare wooden cots – no mattresses or pillows – and a few pieces of basic furniture. Situated in the heart of Nature, it was an extremely neat, tidy and charming place to live in and meditate on God. One could go without food, water or even sleep in such a holy place.

The next morning, we went to the ashram and saw the sage seated on a dais covered with a tiger's skin in a big hall. His devotees squatted on the floor in complete silence. The atmosphere was vibrant with waves of invisible light and joy. I saw a Master in living flesh and blood and my intuition told me immediately as I went down and prostrated before him, that I had entered into the presence of a perfected man's aura. My whole body was tingling with a new feeling of light and delight, creating waves of joy, sweeping over me like a tidal flood. I sat in mute meditation inquiring within: "Who am I?" "Am I the body?" "Am I the mind?".... "Am I the senses"? The desire to know the Self, which can only be accomplished by transcending the body, the senses and the mind, overawed me. The feeling of oneness with all came gushing on me like the north wind in the wintry weather. The barrier of separateness was lifted, as I saw the sage, the embodiment of human unity with all, sitting in stark nakedness except for the loin cloth, immersed in deep thought and in communion with the Invisible. In the ethereal silence of the hall, with the Master as a central figure, it appeared as if God's blessedness was being vouchsafed to every one squatting on the floor.

In the evening, the sage sat in the verandah of the huge ashram building. The vibrations of Vedic mantras, which when blended with the sage's waves of divine consciousness, stirred the hearts and minds of the devotees. The rays of the setting sun as they glimmered through the leaves of the surrounding trees, created an imperishable unforgettable impression upon the mind. Who would not love to be in such a dance of divine nature, so exhilarating to the soul, so enrapturing to the mind?

It is very rarely that the sage speaks, His work is to lift souls hungry for God's vision. He helps in opening the inner valves of the pupil when he is ready for divine comradeship. He reads the mind of a devotee like a book. He gave me a penetrating glance after I had sat before him for two or three hours in the day and he knew the purpose of my visit.

A devotee once asked the sage: "Master, can I perform miracles as Sri Krishna and Jesus did before?" To this the Master replied: "Did either of them ever feel he was performing a miracle?" Light dawned upon the questioner immediately and he said: "No, Master."

The ideal of Self-realization is to attain the highest peak of spirituality and not to gain *siddhis* or what are called miraculous powers. In fact, when they come of their own accord as God's will, they are to be used as silently and unostentatiously as possible for the good of mankind. When Christ performed miracles, He never thought He was doing any miracles. It came naturally to Him, because it was the Will of God.

We stayed only for a few days near the sage at Arunachala. On July 15, 1947, we made preparations to return to Madras. I was sitting alone when I got the following message at 07:00 a.m.:

> "Your visit has come out successful. Go again to Bhagwan. He will put you into *samadhi.* You can then return."

As directed, I went to the hall, where the sage sat as usual in his sombre, statue-like silence. Having prostrated myself, I sat down on the floor, In that pin-drop silence, it appeared as if I was not living in physical body. I sat calmly, lost in meditation, entirely oblivious of what was happening around me. It was a bewitching hour. When it ended, I left the hall with cheer in my heart. My mission had proved successful and the joy of that achievement was so great that I felt the gates of heaven had burst open.

We were alone in the railway compartment enroute to Madras and Rishi Ram Ram, my spiritual Master, gave me the following message that confirmed his earlier one in the morning:

"You were in a state of *samadhi* before Bhagwan Ramana Maharshi. You are not an Arhat. You will realise God before you depart from this plane."

During the Second Initiation, the seeker has to throw off the three fetters of self-delusion, doubt and superstition, Self-delusion is the "I am " consciousness. This has got to be rid of. The seeker must squash his personality and be immersed in the ocean of love, he must comprehend that only the progress of others can further his own progress. He becomes a healer, sorrowing souls come to him for consolation, The second fetter which he must cast off is doubt. This is a formidable obstacle on the Path. Not blind faith, not attachment to dogmas, but a firm conviction that he is treading a safe path that must ultimately lead to God-consciousness, The third fetter is superstition in the shape of rites and ceremonies, which are only helpful in the kindergarten state of spirituality but should be dispensed with as man progresses and completes his Second Initiation Dr. Annie Besant compares the Second Initiation to the Baptism of Christ. In this Initiation the lower mental body is developed. When the candidate has passed his Second Initiation, he becomes what is known as *ANAGAMI*, *i.e.*, "One who does not return." In the words of Bishop Leadbeater, "It is expected of him that he will attain the next Initiation in the same incarnation."

In the Third Initiation, the causal body is developed. Just as a swan is able to separate milk from water, the candidate is able to distinguish the real from the unreal. He becomes detached, though his heart is united with all. This Third Initiation is symbolically described by Theosophists as the Transfiguration of Christ.

The question that naturally rises is why I was not taken to the Second or Third Initiation but straight off to the Fourth

Initiation viz., that of the Arhat. The explanation on this point can be found in messages of Sai Baba and Ram Ram, my two Masters, delivered on December 26, 1949:

> **Sai Baba's message:** "According to Theosophists, there are five Initiations on the Path. We have divided your path in three Initiations, The first one you got in October 1946. The Second Initiation was when you became an Arhat after paying a visit to Sri Ramana at Arunachala. The third and final initiation will take place when I myself will manifest before you. In fact, you are already an Adept and we have celebrated your spiritual birthday on our Spiritual Plane. But to make it doubly sure, I shall come to you Myself and then will put a seal of certainty on all that has been previously stated."

Rishi Ram Ram's message:

> "... In your case, it was not thought necessary to give Second and Third Initiation but to take you to the stage of Arhatship straight off, as you had made yourself fit for it by excessive hard work and complete reliance on Me, your Master. The Second and Third Initiations are meant for those persons who make slow progress and require several births to complete their journey on the Path. With you, it was a question whether you would become an Arhat in this or another life. In the beginning, it appeared that you will have to be reborn to give your Arhatship. But by dint of exceedingly hard work, you turned the table in your favour and I, your Master, was ordered by God to make you an Arhat."

Another point that requires to be explained is why, when I had passed the first Initiation and was rapidly proceeding to the goal of Arhatship, and eventually become an Arhat, I was not given full consciousness of the Astral and Mental Planes. The message by Sai Baba on December 29, 1949 clears this point:

> "There are two questions lurking in your mind. The First is why you were not given consciousness of even reaching the astral and mental world, when you had finished your First Initiation and

you were rapidly proceeding to become an Arhat. Even now, you are not conscious of these planes though you have reached the very peal of spirituality. I have told you several times that your has been a unique case, we want you to open your inner eye in the highest Spiritual Plane first, we have no need of your service on the Astral and Mental Planes and have therefore not given you consciousness of these planes. It must be remembered that experiences vary with different circumstances and in different stages of development of candidates. I again say that your's is a unique case."

Chapter Five

Predictions about Adeptship (1947-49)

As soon as we returned from Arunachala and stopped in Bombay (now called Mumbai), enroute to Karachi, I got the following message from the Master on July 18, 1947:

"You will be guided by Me at every step before you reach the goal of *Nirvana* in this life. You must not invoke Me. I shall inspire you. You are safely put on the Path. You did well in visiting Sri Ramana. He will now guide you by inspiration."

The above is not only a clear prediction which, as will be seen later, has come true, but there are other salient points that require illumination.

The first is the change in the method of communication, It is a point of great importance. Before I became an Arhat, on July 13, 1947 by the grace of God and under the inspiration of Sri Ramana, I used to take down the Master's messages by means of auto-writing and in the company of my wife, as it was necessary, that there should be at least two people present, to avoid any extraction of power. The messages were necessarily brief, as the Master always had to consider that the power should not be exhausted and the medium made to suffer. When I became an adept, I was given the power of hearing the Master directly. From then on, there was no question of any loss of power.

On July 27, 1947, the Master said: "You are a precious pupil of the White Lodge, my dearest son..... You will be made one with God in this very life. You will depart from this place when you have finished your work. I shall guide you at every step. You will rise to the highest position in the Spiritual Plane."

On the same day, my mother whom I knew to be in the Spiritual Plane, told me: "I shall inspire you. You have reached a very high stage. I know that Rishi Ram Ram is your Master. He is the greatest Master in this Spiritual Plane. He is Lord, our God."

I was strictly prohibited from talking with any spirit except my mother's and that too when the Master willed it and not otherwise.

On August 17, 1947, the Master gave the following message:

> "You have done your duty. Spiritually you have risen. I shall take you to God in this very life. You are my most beloved son. Nothing will come in your way. I shall hasten your union with God. You will become an Adept along with your friend Jamshed."

In the message on August 24, 1947, I was asked to see the philosopher Jiddu Krishnamurti at Madras and was told that he was an ADEPT.

The Master in His message of October 19, 1947 urged me to pray to God to prolong my life, for completing my work on the earth plane. At the same time He said: "I also shall ask God to extend your life. I know that you are ready but you have not finished your work."

My wife was sitting with me at the table and the table tilted towards her two or three times and the message came: "Towards you is hanging the life of your husband. Pray to God to give him some more time to finish his work."

Chapter Six

Clairaudience and Inspirational Method of Communication (1947)

It was on November 2, 1947, after I had become an Arhat, that I was told by Ram Ram, my Spirit Master, to sit every day in the morning after prayers and meditation and take down His messages by a new method which he was going to teach me. I had begun my career as a spiritualist by using the planchette. This was replaced by auto-writing and, finally, I was given the gift of clairaudience. This new method of communication eliminated extraction of power from the vital organs and it was a great and important achievement.

The following message of the Master, delivered on November 5, 1947, was important:

> "Try to follow what I speak to you through you. I am sitting in your heart to teach you the grave problems of life. None has striven to give messages as I am doing. It is a new method I have developed for your sake, as you cannot do without it. Beware of falling into any temptation of calling any spirit. Call no one except me, I am your guardian in this respect. Do not think any injury will come to you, no power will be drawn from you."

I was then asked to sit in absolute silence. As I sat, to my utter surprise, I heard these words distinctly: "I am God".

On November 8, 1947, after giving me a message outside the altar room, Master asked me to go into the altar room and sit in absolute silence. I sat in meditation for about ten minutes and had an absolutely new experience. First, some dim visions flickered before mind's eye. I saw a big board with alphabets written on it. The letters then shifted and the following sentence flashed out on the board:

> "You will be selected for reunion with God, if you work as hard as you are doing now."

As I kept sitting, deeply immersed in thoughts of God, I saw some visions faintly flickering before my mind's eye and then this message came to me by inspiration:

> "Longing for God is supreme happiness."

I saw the vision of my aura and then these words came in my mind:

> "I take a vow that I shall serve my Master loyally to the end of my life, I have confidence in him that he will help me in all my difficulties in the avenue of my life, I take this vow in the name of God, our Supreme Lord."

The master corroborated the above words and said that I had passed the test and that I could write by inspiration.

On November 11, 1947, the Master again made me to go to the altar room and sit in silence for some time. "I shall inspire you," he said.

I got the following experience.

I saw a forest and a yogi sitting. He placed his hand on my head and said: "I make you a yogi from today. There is a fire of love for God in your heart. You are very near to the goal of salvation."

Master put me to one more test to find out whether I had perfected the art of writing by inspiration. The following day, I again sat in silence in the altar room.

It dawned upon me that the main mission of my life was to become an inspirational writer. I was trained by the Master for this specific purpose. The beauty of it is that in all inspired writings, God was made the central theme. Read the following inspirational message received on November 14, 1947 which refers to the beauty and grandeur of God, transcendent and immanent in Nature:

> "There is no way out of this world except by righteousness. Stand fast to Truth. God is near you. You can hear Him, if you want.
>
> "God is in the tree, in the bush, everywhere. God's creation is a marvel of His expression. He is the cause of the whole existence. He is the breath of life. He is the fire that burns the candle, the oil that lights the lamp. He is joy; He is Sunshine; He is Beauty; He is all LOVE. He is Eternal Bliss. Strike out all fear from your heart and be immersed in the Ocean of Bliss that God is. He is the Beautifier of all life, the strengthener of all resolves."

If one were to write and compose, with an ocean for the inkpot and the whole wide earth as parchment, in praise of God, it would not be enough. It is easier to count the pebbles on the shore or the stars in heaven than to enumerate the attributes of God. Incomprehensible, Exhaustless, Infinite, as. He is the only Reality, all else is a delusion.

Chapter Seven

The Inner Voice, The Voice of God (1948)

On January 5, 1948, I heard my inner voice telling me: "God wants to speak to you. Listen to Him." Instantly the words rang in my ears: "You are a spark of My Fire. You shall return to Me." This is teaching of all religions, particularly of the Vedanta, that man's soul is a spark of God. It has emanated from God and its destiny is to return to its original source.

On February 29, 1948, a strange phenomenon occured. Sai Baba of Shirdi was a Muslim-looking fakir for whom I had great reverence and whose picture I always had on my table. On that day, I saw him in a vision under a flicker of light and I heard Master saying: "He is God." It took my breath away.

On July 23, 1948, in a message Ram Ram called himself "Spirit Guide and Master." He had dropped "Your Lord and God." This change in appellation becomes clear from the message that follows: "I am Rishi Ram Ram, your Spirit Guide and Master. I have come down from the high heavens especially for you. Sit in absolute silence. I want to make some changes in you. You and I are one. God has ordered that you should be lifted to Him. Kneel down and pray to Him. Cast out all thought of fear and resentment and keep absolutely calm. The hour is drawing near when you will be submerged in the great ocean of Bliss. You have earned your crown of perfection by your devotion to God."

The following messages of Sai Baba and Ram Ram throw further light on this subject of change in appellation.

Sai Baba's message of November 9, 1949:

> "I want you to know that when Ram Ram told you about two years ago that he was your God, it was not untrue. At that time you had reached a stage of certain perfection, which required Ram Ram to be taken as God. By God's grace and by the dint of your own extraordinary efforts, you have now become absolutely perfect from all points of view. I am your real God now."

The same day, I got this message from Rishi Ram Ram:

> "..... I told you first that you won't become Arhat even in this life. Then when you became an Arhat after your visit to Bhagwan Ramana Maharishi of Arunachala, I put down the period of your attaining God-realization to ten years. But at the same time I predicted that it would be much less if you worked hard and unselfishly. You have surpassed all expectations."

In one message the inner voice told me: "God wants to speak to you. Listen to Him." And I heard the following: "You would soon see Me. Have faith in Me. I am quite pleased with you in every respect, I have ordered Rishi Ram Ram to cure you and heal you completely. Obey his orders and have implicit trust in him. He is the one chosen by Me to guide you and to transform you in every way to make you a fit instrument to carry out My orders and commands for the good of all mankind." And the inner voice resumed: "You have heard God, the greatest boon that a person can expect to get, As you have heard Him, you will see Him also, You are the chosen one of God and He will by and by give you supernormal powers to enable you to complete the mission of service that he would entrust you, Rishi Ram Ram will explain to you everything, listen to Him."

Then Rishi Ram Ram, my Spirit Guide and Master, gave me the following explanatory message:

> "You have had the rare and unique opportunity of talking with God, the Absolute Spirit. I have been ordered by Him to make you whole and believe me, I shall do it. You have suffered much and really speaking you ought to have been called away. Having earned *Nirvana,* it is your right now to claim eternal rest. But God, in His fitness, thinks that you should be prepared for service on this earth plane. I know you feel exceedingly diffident and may consider it an impossibility, but when God wills you have no idea what miracles happen. You have borne much. Have a little more patience. We are all preparing you for your great mission and you will be endowed with full health and vitality of mind and soul. Your case of perfection is stranger than fiction and unbelievable and God wants to utilise it for the benefit of His creation."

Chapter Eight

Spiritual Healing (1947-49)

Healing is divine work. There is no profession greater or nobler than that of the Healer, whether he is an earthly doctor or a spiritual healer working under the guidance of a spirit Master. Although the gift of healing was inherent in me, it was developed later when I took to spiritualism.

On November 21, 1947, the Master told me: "You can now exercise your healing powers without harm to yourself. You will be required to heal many and that will be the most important work in your life."

A case was referred to me from Coimbatore, to treat the girl of a bank manager in Karachi. When the father of the girl called on me, I hesitated in taking up the case. But I was guided by the Master. It was a case of obsession by some evil spirit. She would take no food and would sleep for hours. She had grown emaciated. Various doctors had been tried to cure her malady but to no effect.

I visited the girl regularly and gave passes as directed by the Master, but there was no improvement. Although I did not lose hope, the patient's family members gave me up and tried some other methods, even these didn't work.

On the contrary the case became worse. I was again entreated to take it up.

On December 17, 1947, the Master gave me the following message:

> "She will recover. It is a very difficult case. She ought to have been treated long ago. I will do my utmost for the poor girl. Go daily till she recovers, if the girl is cured, it will be a good test of your curing power through me. Work diligently and save her."

I was asked to pray day and night for her recovery. On January 4, 1948, I was assured that the evil spirit would be driven away from her body and she would be restored to normalcy.

On January 5, 1948, riots broke out in Karachi. My visits to the place were stopped. There was again a break in the treatment. But by the grace of God, the girl eventually recovered when the treatment was resumed.

A fellow-doctor living in the same neighbourhood was suffering from heart disease and kidney trouble. He had been bed-ridden for a number of months. I gave him some passes and they had a wonderful effect initially. He was able to move about a little in the house and twice or thrice he even ventured to go out to attend some important duties. The Master said that there was just a possibility of his recovering, provided there was no break in the daily healing. Owing to unforeseen circumstances my visits to him stopped. His health deteriorated again and some time later he died.

In a surgical case at a Parsi hospital, the operation had failed and the patient was dying. I tried to heal him. To the utter surprise of others, every time when it appeared that he was dying, the patient revived. This happened four or five times, but the young man eventually passed away.

These cases disappointed and dejected me. I thought that my powers were waning away. I even began to feel that I had no healing powers. Then Master gave me the following message on June 29, 1949:

> "You have tremendous healing power, a manifestation of which was the case in the Parsi hospital. Do you know it was because of

> you that the boy tried to survive three or four times? But he was destined to pass away and in such cases no angel can do anything. You had a clear demonstration of your power and yet, like a silly fool, you decry your own self."

Just as every case that a doctor handles may not be cured, all cases may not respond to spiritual healing, especially if the patient is destined to suffer or pass away. *Karma* is a principal factor in the achievement of results in healing. The patient must also have faith. Those who have no faith can never benefit and it is safest to avoid such cases.

In the beginning, I was warned to use the healing power as sparingly as possible. But later on, when my powers were intensified, I was asked to use discretion and use the powers wherever necessary.

On December 27, 1949, Rishi Ram Ram gave me the following message:

> "I have been asked by Sai Baba to explain everything to you on His behalf. Do you know He has given you the gift of healing even the incurable, the blind, the lame, the deaf and the dumb? But this power will come to you only when you see God face to face. In fact, you will be thoroughly equipped for your mission and your mission is to be the Healer of both bodies and souls.

"Meanwhile, He wants you to do your healing work on a larger scale. Take all cases except those suffering from skin and bad diseases. They are not meant for you and you must avoid them. Kindly don't ask any reason but simply obey our orders. In all doubtful cases you must refer to me or Sai Baba. Always ask patients to submit doctor's certificate in case of strangers, whom you do not know."

Healing can also be done in the absence of patients by means of their photographs. The following message of Ram Ram explains the process of such indirect healing: "In the case of absent healing the photo of the person is a great guide. When you concentrate on the photo, the image of the person to be healed is conjured up before my mind's eye and I pass the rays which reach the person."

Chapter Nine

Visions and Spirit Master Ram Ram's Attempt to Sunder the Soul from the Body (1947-48)

Visions followed by a trance are a common experience of mystics. They are signposts to God-realization. On the morning of December 6, 1947, I sat in meditation and had ecstatic experience. After about half an hour's meditation, visions started coming, I saw scenes of various seasons of the year – spring and summer, autumn and winter. The blue sky, silent moon, roaring waters of the sea, flaming fires, various tints of colour. I saw the red globe of the sun setting in the west. I was told that my life's journey on this plane would end soon and I would enter into a new region to receive my crown of glory and perfection.

On December 14, 1947, I saw Christ in a vision. After this vision, Ram Ram gave me some spiritual exercises. Electricity was flowing in my two hands. I prayed to God with all the intensity of my heart, mind and soul. Then my hands were made to press my whole face, the cheeks and the head, then they were put on the forehead. The moment they parted I saw two blue spots, one above the other, just between the eyebrows, I heard a voice saying: "These two blue spots are the third eye. It is rarely given to anybody. You are fortunate. God's grace has descended on you because of your intense devotion to Him. This third eye is the vision of the soul. It is God's own vision."

On March 7, 1948, I had a most thrilling and delightful experience. The Master explained to me the significance of my vision thus:

> "You were shown the aura in brilliant blue with the background of light yellow. You could not see this aura earlier for you were not prepared. The beautiful visions of unending heights and lights, long tracks, vast vistas, are all an indication of eternity. You saw Mahatma Gandhi trekking the endless railway line right through the mountains, with a glow of light on one side of the track. This indicates the journey which everyone has to undertake to reach eternity. Mahatma Gandhi has reached the goal of life. He is merged in eternity. In the arc of white light, you saw the figure of Zarthustra. The light that was leaping from the endless top of the mountain is God's abode."

The whole idea of the vision was to initiate you in the knowledge of eternity – endless tracks, endless valleys, with light of variegated hues, shining everywhere for man's guidance. The way to God's abode is long and endless. But it is a sure road. No other road can guide you to eternal happiness except the path to God's abode.

On March 11, 1948, I saw in a vision, myself being lifted from the earth and taken up to the sky till my body disappeared entirely for a minute or two and in its place a white round moon-like orb was seen in the sky. Immediately after this, my body reappeared and came down. The Master explained the significance of this vision briefly:

> "It means you have been raised to the highest pedestal of perfection. You are God in man."

After showing me some visions and giving a foretaste of other worlds, Rishi Ram Ram, my Spirit Master, promised that He would sunder my soul from the body and give me *Nirvana.* He made several attempts but in vain. Either I was still not fit for *Nirvana* or my weak body hindered extraction of the soul.

Chapter Ten

Life or Death (1947-48)

Rarely is a man with an ailing body made *Jivan Mukta i.e.,* a living Master. Adeptship means a strenuous life which requires an active, agile body that can stand the strain of manifold activities. On the face of it, the idea of making me, with my ailments, an adept to serve humanity was an impossible one. But God's ways are mysterious.

On December 24, 1947, Ram Ram said to me:

> "Your love for God has won you the highest place in the spiritual realm. You will soon be free to have your own way, without any bondage. Select whatever you life – a like of selfless service in this life or eternal rest in heaven." I said: "I surrender myself completely to God". But, at the same time, I prayed that, if my life was extended for human service, I may be restored to perfect health.

On January 24, 1948, Rishi Ram Ram again gave me the option of life or death. "If you want to live, you will be given health and supernormal powers to do good to man-kind. You have a glorious future. But if you are tired and want to go away, God will be pleased to call you back. You will not return to this life in any case for you have earned your *Nirvana.*"

On February 11, 1948, Ram Ram allowed my mother to give me a message in his presence, but he warned me at the same time not to heed her, if she said anything of my going to heaven, as she did not know that I was being prepared for a higher purpose. Mother said: "Your journey in life is coming to an end. We are all waiting for you. You will pass away from your world very quickly, without pain, and you will enter into the Kingdom of Heaven. You are a liberated soul. God is with you. Let me kiss you, before I go, my most beloved, dearest son, Minoo."

On February 24, 1948, I saw in a vision Lord Zarthustra saying, "I am your prophet." I also saw this message flashed in letters of white light: "God is Love and God loves you." My inner voice then said: "God has chosen you to become a Master after your departure from this world."

Was this all a delusion? My mind began to doubt. Why was I being extolled? The Master then explained: "You are not deluded. The God that is within you is coming out. In the process, there are bound to be some wrong predictions. All depends upon your own self, there is no exterior agency dominating you. You are the author, you are the cause of everything. Your purity, your perfection is God, when you are asked to hear the inner voice, it is God's voice. You are unaware of your virtues and your self-negation is the climax that is drawing you to the inner perception of Truth. You are not being extolled, it is the inner voice that tells you what you are and portrays you in your true light. When the inner eye opens, which will be shortly, the secrets of Nature will be unfolded before you. Seek God and nothing but God. He is the only Reality."

Conflicting messages began to appear as days passed on. On February 24, 1948, I was told: "On March 17, you would pass away and be immersed in the Eternity of Bliss." I was asked to seek silence and seclusion. "Give up all mundane affairs entirely." For full seven days and nights – from March 4 to 11 – I locked myself in my prayer room.

On the first day of my voluntary confinement the following instructions were given:

> "First, you must not leave the altar room without my order, even for a bath or nature's call. Take my permission and then go.
>
> "Secondly, brush aside all thoughts of the outside world. Think that you are not living in this world. This is essential.
>
> "Thirdly, get up in the morning every day at 04:00 a.m. and pray and meditate.
>
> "Fourthly, don't break your silence."

Over the week, I was given intense spiritual training. All my *chakras* were opened and filled with God's light and love to accelerate the vivacity of the subtle forces within. On the night of March 11, 1948, my training was completed. The *chakras* were closed and I was asked to leave the altar room and break my silence.

The fated day March 17, 1948 came but I was as much in flesh as before. Then I received this message from Rishi Ram Ram: "It is my desire that you come over this side, as you will be able to serve better. I want you to fix up all your earthly affairs as quickly as possible.

I asked "How much of time do you give me to live?"

Ram Ram replied: "Not more than fifteen to twenty days. You will be able to work till the very last day, and even the last hour. Your case is peculiar."

On March 17, the Master assured me that he was putting life spirit in my ailing body, but added that rejuvenation would take time. He also said that if he did not succeed in taking out the ailment from its roots, I would be called away immediately.

On March 18, the Master said: "Your days are numbered, though I shall still try to save you." On the 19th the inner voice said: "There is no doubt now that you will be called away by God." This news was confirmed by the Master. He said, "There is no hope of your life being extended any further."

On March 27, 1948, the date of my departure was fixed by the Master. He said: "It is decided by God that you will be called away on Thursday next, April 1, 1948." The next day I learned through a vision that the summons had been issued but I was indifferent.

On March 30, 1948, the Master said: "I want you to come away earlier than Thursday. Your life energy is ebbing away and I find it difficult to keep you fit." I meekly replied: "But I am feeling quite fit." To this the Master retorted: "That's because of Me. I am renewing your life forces all the time. The minute I stop, you will expire. I give you tomorrow, the whole day and night; Thursday morning in the early hours I may take you away."

Till the last moment, I was told again and again that I would give up the ghost on April 1, 1948. I wrote of this to a relative in Bombay and informed one or two friends of the approach of the final hour of my departure. But on March 31, 1948, at 11:15 p.m. the Master quietly and cooly informed me: "You are not going to die tomorrow. The date is again changed."

This was a great blow to my self-respect. It did not matter to me whether I died or lived. But what about the people whom I had informed of my coming death? What confidence would they have now in me and my spirituality? I was burning with rage. With great difficulty I controlled myself and told my Master meekly: "What is all this Rishi Ram Ram? You said that my departure was certain and now you say that the date has changed."

The Master replied; "God must have some reason to extend your life. Have trust in Him. He knows what is best for you." I said: "I am quite unconcerned whether I live or die. What perplexes me is, why was I told all these days to prepare myself for departure from this world."

The Master replied: "Have patience. You will realise every thing in good time. You are being treated by God. Whatever it be, resign yourself to His sovereign will."

Feeling great anguish, I asked my Master to permit me to talk to my angelic mother. Mother gave me the following message:

> "My dearest son, Minoo, you are deeply perplexed, no doubt, but in these spiritual matters, God always tests. This is your test in your faith in God What you have to do now is have implicit faith in God and work to the best of your ability with whatever health and strength you may have. Don't mind reproofs and rebuffs, sneers and slanders. You are much above them. Also don't think that you are God-man. There is no such thing as God-men on earth. Be humble. There is no doubt that you have realised God, but you must not say a word to any one and not even give it a thought, as it might fill your mind with arrogance and pride, I am your mother and I love you the most. Believe me, God has already put the crown of perfection on your head. You have won it by the dint of your own merit. All you have to do now is work on the best of your ability and keep an unconcerned outlook."

I returned from the altar room that night, a saner and wiser man. Contradictory messages may be confusing and disheartening, but they have a subtle meaning that only time can unfold.

Chapter Eleven

Talks of the Spirit of Mahatma Gandhi (1948)

On April 7, 1948, Rishi Ram Ram, my Spirit Master, gave me a message: "Mahatma Gandhi wants to talk to you." I was quite surprised. I had heard Mahatma Gandhi at some of his public lectures, but I had not had the honour of ever speaking to him personally. Any how, the Master's orders were to be obeyed and Mahatma Gandhi started giving messages every day in the presence of Rishi Ram Ram.

In one message, Gandhi said:

"People called me Mahatma Gandhi on your earth plane. I do not know you, but having come over here, I am contacting highly spiritual people and have come to know of you through Rishi Ram Ram. I wish I had contacted you when I was on the earth plane. You are highly evolved spiritually and I want to tell you my spiritual experiences so that with the permission of, Rishi Ram Ram, your Guide, you may broadcast them to the world and being peace and harmony between Hindus and Muslims."

"Stand fast by Truth and Non-Violence was my motto in life and I tried to live upto it till the end of my life. What is Truth? Truth is God. And is there anything greater than God? To love God and to live for God and God alone is the goal of life, God alone is REAL. I want you to tell my Hindu and Muslim friends, whom I love from the very bottom of my heart, that when God alone is the Reality, why waste breath and energy on anything else? God is the unifying force and He wants all his children to live together in peace and harmony. Hatred begets hatred, As Buddha hath said, it ceaseth only by love."

"God is the greatest unifying factor. This great fact should not be lost sight of. When God is one, how can there be at all difference in religions? There is nothing in the holy book of Quran, which is antagonistic to the teachings of the Gita and vice versa."

"In this spirit land, there is no separate Dominion for Hindus and Muslims. They all are treated alike. Why are then such colossal differences created in our conception of each other's religion? Every one's religion is absolutely the same. It is foolish and wicked to sabotage the fundamental truths in life and palm, off unwanted trash in the name of religion. Religion is purely a matter of the heart."

"Love begets love. If a Hindu really loves God and if a Muslim really loves God, both of them cannot but love each other and treat themselves equally. Religion has to be understood in its pristine beauty and not sullied with man-made dogmas and creeds. All ceremonies, rituals and dogmas are walls that hamper true spiritual progress. There is a great necessity for true fellowship of all religions that are fundamentally the same in their teachings of God and the life hereafter. Why then besmear and mar our present and future prospects of a happy life by jarring notes of religious antagonism? I never knew the force of Christ's teaching of love so much as when I came over to this side. True love is the parent seed of all the virtues in life. It is the patent stock of health and abundance."

Chapter Twelve

Spiritual Philosophy of Rishi Ram Ram (1948)

What follows is a series of talks given to me by Rishi Ram Ram on spiritual philosophy, 1948.

Self-realization

"Man's soul is the most important thing in the universe. Each man makes a contribution to the welfare of the universe according to the status of his soul. The soul is also the migrating element in man; it takes countless births before finally dissolving in the ocean of eternity.

Man's Spirit is, however, different from his soul. It is the dim, still voice of God and its function is to stablise the affairs of man, only if man is bale to turn inwards and listen to his inner voice. The soul and the spirit are both immortal. But, unlike the ever-transforming soul, the spirit is changeless. The goal of life is the union of the soul and the spirit. When this happens, man realises the Self.

"Meditation, silence and solitude are indispensable factors in the journey towards the goal of Self-realization. Work is another powerful factor but work should be of a selfless nature. To work for others' welfare without expecting any reward is one way of reaching Godhead. But it is not the only way. The soul evolves in diverse ways."

Different revelations

"Lord Krishna, Zoroaster, Buddha, Christ and Mahomed: All these prophets taught universal brotherhood, love purity of thought, word and deed, simplicity of living, sincerity of purpose and desirelessness. All of them were messengers of God. God wanted them to bring spiritual light for the good of Mankind. But for them, man would have stumbled in eternal darkness.

"It is not fair to make any discrimination among prophets. They all should be looked upon as equals, without any distinction. People must understand the spiritual significance of their teachings instead of being led away by the empty trappings and shibboleths that pass off in the mane of religion.

"Lord Krishna's mission was the same as Zoroaster's. They spoke different tongues but their teachings were the same: all divine knowledge has the same source – God. Men must now unite in one spiritual fold for in this way alone lies their salvation. Schisms and clashes, strifes and wars that continually destroy peace and happiness on this earth can only be eliminated when all persons of different religions unitedly express their desire to be incorporated in one universal faith. This is the Plan of God – that all disintegrating forces should coalesce into one harmonious whole and that each individual should work out his own salvation by the dint of his own effort and merit, without the intercession and help of any one.

"The foundation stone of every religion is Truth. Truth consists of right thoughts, right words and right deeds, Thought is the parent of deed and purity of thought reflects the purity of heart. Without righteousness, no man can ever advance spiritually or materially.

"Righteousness alone is not enough. It has to be enflamed and illumined by the virtues of the heart. Love in its unselfish aspect is Godliness. Love is divine. It is the golden link, the silver thread that binds man to man."

Spirituality: The essence of life

"Spirituality is the very essence of life. It is the seed of perfection.

"To love God is to love all. To worship God is to awaken our feelings of reverence for all that is pure, beautiful, joyous and transcendental.

"In the river of life, each one has to be the skipper of his own, Truth is his compass: fearlessness his oar: purity his beacon light: devotion to God his anchor. The boat runs smoothly even in turbulent waters if the skipper is patient and has infinite faith in God. Faith is the seed of spirituality."

Seek God

"The ties of love and affection are stronger than iron chains. Swifter than the wind is man's aspiration for the ideal. Seek God in the silence of the hour, in Truth and Love, Beauty and Joy. Seek Him at all hours of the day. He is the source of all light. He is the fountainhead of wisdom. Strange appear the ways of God, when virtue is disowned and vice is enthroned, but falter not in your efforts to resist evil and court virtue. Be fearless, be brave, for with God in your heart you shall ever be safe in the (bivouac temporary encampment of life. Fear not the future. Live in the present.

"God is both Truth and Love, There is nothing holier than Truth, higher than Love, Raise the edifice of your life on these spiritual foundations, Build on Love, live in truth. Rise above duality, good and evil, virtue and vice, integration and disintegration and strive for perfect understanding."

The work of Rishis

"The Rishis of India were the earliest revealers of the secrets of nature in a systematic form. They were enlightened souls in communion with God. They gave universal teachings of the deepest significance. The Vedas were written after them. The ancient Rishis spoke only one language – the language of Truth, imbibed by them directly from God.

"Zoroaster was the first prophet on earth. His teachings spread far and wide and the exerted a paramount influence upon the peoples of his time. Zoroaster belonged to no race or nationality. His utterances of Divine Truth were meant for all, irrespective of race or region. His was the voice of God.

"The Vedas are Zoroastrian teachings in substance, if not in form. They speak of the same truths, for how can divine knowledge imbibed from the same source of divinity ever be different? Man's ingenuity manipulates simple facts into a confusing and confounding track of meaningless nonsense. One should give a go-by to all creeds, dogmas and rituals, if one wants to understand and comprehend God's real truth.

Mental tranquillity and world peace

"Buddha who followed much after Zoroaster, emphasised the great Zoroastrian truth. As you sow, so you reap." Each man can become a Buddha, if he can renounce life and meditate. Meditation is the vital part of spirituality. It is a mistaken notion that one should lead a practical life and give no time to silence and seclusion. Today's civilisation is built on wrong assumptions, The whole machinery of life requires to be reshaped and rebuilt. As a man thinks so the world acts, The individual and the world are not different. There can be no peace in the world if individuals do not have tranquil mind. A restless, scheming mind that seeks self-gratification is the worst enemy of mankind. Such a mind sows seeds of disruption and poison and creates havoc and chaos.

"Love all, said Christ, He laid the foundation of social structure on right lines. Christ was God on earth. Cnrist lived in God and God lived in Christ."

Universal brotherhood

"Mohamed's advent in Arabia synchronised with the movement for universal uplift of the down-trodden. His teaching of universal brotherhood is the rock of Islam, Mohamed's teaching of brotherhood is a corollary to Christ's emphasis on love as the cementing ink between man and man.

"The coming age will witness fundamental changes in the economic, political and spiritual mode of thought. I see the signs of a new era dawning when all the countries of the world would be harmoniously knit together by common ties of brotherhood and love, common culture, common religion and common mode of life, Science will help in forging this unity and in bringing to fruition the thought of one universal brotherhood."

Religion and religiousity

"There is a natural urge in man to crave for something that is supernatural and supernormal. This urge is satisfied if man lives in religion. Religion and religiosity are two different things, just as spiritualism and spirituality are two different concepts. Religion is the sublime part of human life. Religiosity is debased religion. Religion is the nerve centre of a happy life. God's scale of processing human values is different from man's. Your world extols money and position. In our world character alone is the criteria of sublimity. Nothing else counts.

"Abstinence is a great virtue. However, it should not be confounded with mortification of the flesh. Abstinence means control of desires. In the life of high spirituality, one should have no craving for any desire."

Desires are men's spiritual enemies

"The less wants a man has, the easier it is for him to climb the steep path of spirituality. The craving for wealth and position is a sure sign of the activity of man's lower self. If this lower self is not suppressed man is lost, Desires are man's spiritual enemies. It may be difficult to curb them, if they are not nipped in the bud.

The inner vision and a proper perspective of life

"When man begins to realise that this world is illusion, he will then turn to the Creator and seek Him in the inner recesses of his heart. God is everywhere but to understand Him, one must turn inwards. The external has to be understood with the help of inner vision, Only then does man get a proper perspective of life."

The paths of emancipation

"The way to supreme happiness lies through devotion to God. Seek God in every minute of your life. The Gita speaks of various paths for emancipating the soul: *Yoga, Karma Yoga, Jnana Yoga* and *Raja Yoga.* Of all these, *Bhakti Yoga* is the easiest and can be practised by everyone. The Gita places great emphasis on *Karma Yoga.* In fact, in today's life is a combination of Bhakti with Karma Yoga. Jnana Yoga is fit only for highly advanced souls who have an intense inclination for metaphysics. *Raja Yoga* is considered to be the crown of all the yogas. It is the method of unveiling secrets of nature by attaining supernormal powers through prayers and meditation, Most of our Indian saints are Raja Yogis. They wield great powers, They are magicians and wizards in the right sense.

"In the New Age a proportionate mix of work and meditation will be the new teaching."

Sex and spirituality

"Man's soul is a spark of God in the sense that God pervades throughout the universe and all the essential things must contain the Divine Element. The soul's lustre shines the most when it is eliminated from the sheaths that cover it. This happens when man gives up bodily enjoyment and takes to a life of the Spirit.

"It is often been asked whether sex is allowable in the journey to spiritual perfection, it is a ticklish issue, Frankly, God wants absolute purity and man must rise above sex if he wishes to realise the Self, but at the same time, sex is not a bar to Self-realization, provided it is indulged in a restrained manner in the restricted alliance of marriage and with holy thoughts and purposes, but celibacy would be preferred and it should be strictly adhered to once the vow is taken."

The flowers of humanity

"It is possible for anyone to become a saint. But we get so engrossed in superficialities of life that we give no time to inward knowledge. It is not necessary that a man be learned in the scriptures to become a saint, the basis of sainthood is perfection of character. When the inner eye opens, divine wisdom flows into man like a running river emptying itself in the torrent of the sea.

"A seer is a clairvoyant. With the aid of the invisible eye, he can look into the past life of anyone and his future. To him the past and the future are the same. Prayers, meditation, silence and constant seclusion are necessary to make a man a seer.

"Seers are the right guides of humanity. The East has produced more seers than the West, for the simple reason that Western civilization is not conducive to the factors that are essential for becoming a seer.

"Monasticism on rational lines should be introduced on a much wider scale throughout the world and in all religions. There should be equality of opportunities and complete freedom of choice. Without a freedom of thought in all spheres of human activity there can be no advancement. And in the world without spiritual freedom, political freedom is only a snare."

Spiritualism: Its potentialities and dangers

"Spiritualism is a science and as such its potentialities have to be properly weighed and gauged. But for this science, men would have still fumbled in ignorance. Spiritualism has rooted out agnosticism from the minds of people. It has sown the seeds of Divine Truth all over the world, especially Europe and America, where it is cultivated today with greater enthusiasm. The West has produced more literature on spiritualism than on any other topic.

"Just as men can be divided into good and bad, there are good and bad spirits in the other world. The danger in Spiritualism lies in communicating with the low astral spirits. But if precautions are taken, this danger could be easily avoided. There is nothing wrong in establishing more societies and centres even in India to enable more and more people get satisfaction by communicating with their dear departed ones. The co-operation of the two worlds could lead to greater understanding and happiness.

"Sprit communication also saps the medium and makes him or her, eventually, a physical wreck. No one should become a medium unless and until he has made a thorough study of the science."

Spiritualism: Philosophy and cosmic forces

"Spiritualism Philosophy is a very interesting subject for those who yearn for divine love. It is in contrast to materialistic philosophy that deals with mundane matters and has no notion of the spiritual splendour of cosmic forces, which are forging the destinies of men and nations. God is the greatest Cosmic Force. He is the designer, the planner, the architect and the artist of the whole universe. He is the centre of all movements. He is the primal cause of all manifestations. He is the essence of purity. He is all love and compassion. He is the guide and shepherd of every human soul. He is not limited by Times, Space or Causation. To love Him is to know Him. This is the secret of His plan. Love the great Creator, unselfishly, devotedly, without seeking any personal favour and He will draw you closer and closer to His heart. He will unfold to you the secrets of His Divine

Plan. Submit yourself wholeheartedly and unhesitatingly to His Divine Will. He will guide you to the right path of eternal bliss. There is no better school for training the soul than the storm and stress of life, Look upon adversity as your friend, Hardship ad suffering are steps to final victory. Go through life with a song in your heart."

Different planes or invisible worlds

"The abode of God is the highest spiritual plane rarely visited by a soul. The lower astral plane is somewhat like your world, but on a larger extension. Spirits from the higher planes come to the lower to teach the lower spirits. In this manner, God works His Evolutionary Law of Progress from plane to plane. There is no such thing as hell, it is all man's own imagination. The astral world is a desire world. Desires are men's greatest enemies, and the astral world teaches spirits to eliminate from their nature the lure of desires. The Higher Astral offers a peaceful surrounding in comparison to the lower, where the worst sinners are confined with a view to purge them of their sins by means of astral suffering. But the Higher Astral should not be considered Heaven. It is an intermediary link between the lower and the higher world. The Higher world is composed of the Mental Plane and the Spiritual Plane and the Mental Plane is real heaven. It is a state of bliss of the highest type. But it is not eternal bliss. It is not the Abode of God. The Spiritual Plane is God's abode. Here is eternal rest. No soul returns to earth from the Spiritual Plane, unless it is the express wish of God that it should carry out some great mission on the earth. Christ, Buddha, Zoroaster were all such souls.

"When war breaks out on earth, our astral planes become full and our work becomes strenuous. There is no calamity so great as that of war. God wants to outlaw war for all time. He wants to train more and more human souls in His scheme of banishing war and strife for all time from the earth. Internationalism will be the key note of the New Age."

God – The knowable

"Religion and Philosophy are two different aspects of knowledge. Religion takes you to the inner mysteries of life. Religious philosophy is the knowledge of the causes that are invisible and imperceptible to the physical eye. Emotion and feeling play a great part in life and when the subtlest forces of emotion are trained by the purity of mind and sincerity of heart, the golden secrets of the universe become manifest. Absolute Good, they will not gain any insight into the fundamental teachings and mysteries of the universe. God is the pivot of the whole universe. To know him and to comprehend Him is the goal of life.

God is spirit, without shape, without form. We can know by feeling Him in our heart of hearts and in our mind in the state of ecstatic bliss. He is *Sat, Chit, Ananda,* Absolute Existence, Consciousness, Bliss. Seek God in the inner recesses of the heart. He is the source of all knowledge. He is the cause of the whole phenomenal universe, He is truth itself.

Love is the sublime aspect of Divinity. It is a gateway to Eternity. It is enthralling, enrapturing in its creed of selflessness and non-separateness. To love God is to love all humanity. Love of God is the service of humanity. The simpler a man is, the greater is his spirituality. Complete forgetfulness of self leads to the realization of the True Self, which is God."

God knowable through devotion

"To gain God realization, it is necessary to focus one's attention on God in prayers and worship. It may be difficult to realise God through knowledge and active human service without expectation of any reward. But the path of the *Bhakta* (devotee) is comparatively easy. Devotion in man must come to him naturally, spontaneously.

"Complete serenity and sincerity are the cardinal virtues that one has to cultivate in the quest for God. Complete surrender to God is a *sine qua non* in the life of the spirit.

Curbing of the senses and control of the mind are preliminaries, the stepping stones to the attainment of spiritual bliss."

The sickly, the evil and the pure soul

"When a man dies, his soul is sundered from the body, the soul hovers on this earth plane for some time, The lifeless body is looked upon by the soul as its prison and it is happy that it has escaped from that prison house.

There are various kinds of souls – the sickly soul, the evil soul and the pure soul. The purer the soul, the more perceiving it becomes. It knows no obstacles. It passes through all the penetrating and interpenetrating planes without effort. The evil soul for the first few days or weeks or even months knows not its whereabout. It lies in a sleepy condition, Angelic guides guide these sleepy souls to their destination, They nurse these astral babes with tenderness, care and by slow stages these souls become acquainted with their new surroundings. They take a long time in forgetting earth conditions and long to go back to the earth plane. They suffer acutely when their longing is not satisfied.

The sickly soul is a diseased soul that carries within it the germs of evil thoughts and evil deeds by which it has ruined the happiness of many on earth. Such souls suffer the most. But God is good and merciful. Even to such souls, He give opportunities to see their errors and improve. They too progress though their progress is the slowest.

There is no sin so great as hatred. There is no deed so bad as brutality. Those who hate and are brutal in action have to pay a terrible penalty. They are cast in the lower astral world, where they are purged of all foul thoughts. The lower astral world is inhabited by souls of murderers, unrepentant thieves, adulterers who have ruined the chastity of women and done irreparable injury to innocent persons by intrigues and dastardly deeds. Such souls suffer the most and take a long time in cleansing themselves. When they are cleansed they are sent back to the earth plane for further cleansing. They come with heavy karmic debt that they have to clear by progressive suffering in the shape of ailments, calamities and hardships. The Law of *Karma* works immutably everywhere. All are subject to the Law of Evolution and there is no soul so sodden as cannot improve eventually and come back to God, which is its original home."

The higher astral, the mental and the spiritual planes

"The higher astral is inhabited by souls who are neither too bad nor too good. It is a desire world where souls have to be cleansed of all carnal desires and chastened into purity of emotion.

"The mental world is higher than the astral and souls proceed there either directly from the earth plane or after having stayed for some time in the astral world. It is a plane for all progressive souls. They come here for real rest and peace. Their life is full of bliss. Once a soul is in this plane, it wishes to stay here eternally. But it cannot enjoy eternal rest and bliss. That is meant for those souls who are fit go still further to a higher plane: the Spiritual Plane the abode of God, Souls which have attained Nirvana live in the Spiritual plane.

"Just as you have a system of passport to go from one country to another, each soul, when it proceeds from one plane to another, has to show its passport. That passport is aura that changes as the soul progresses from one plane to another. The soul is the architect of its own aura, Transcendental light, transcendental beauty and transcendental colouring – these are the chief features of the higher worlds of joy and sunshine.

"Souls in the higher world do a lot of spiritual work, Their mission is to help all souls in distress. For this reason they go down to the lower plane and even to the earth plane to guide misguided persons and bring proper understanding, They are God's archangels working day and night for the perfection of God's universe. They are God's sweet messengers who bridge the gulf between the lower and the higher worlds. Their function is to redeem and transform, to enlighten and to reform."

Some characteristics of the life here eater

"In our world of the Life Hereafter the vehicle of communication is thought. Each soul can read the thoughts of the other. Nothing remains hidden. Souls cluster together according to their affinities. Scientists mix with scientists and make experiments for new scientific discoveries. When these scientists are reborn, they carry with them the germs of new knowledge gained by them and these in due course give birth to new scientific discoveries for the betterment of the world. Similarly the artist, the poet, the philosopher and so on gather knowledge according to their tendencies when they are here.

"In our world there is no such thing as night or darkness, It is all day and our happiness lies in uninterrupted work. It is the greatest pleasure to work for others. Unselfishness and altruism form the keynote of the life in this world, Each soul wants to progress, at least it is guided in this notion. There are no sex differences in our world. The souls have no sex. Sex is the principal trait in the life of your earth plane only."

Endless visit as of the invisible worlds

"Ours is a world of ether. The various planes penetrate and interpenetrate. Myriads of lights blaze out on every side. Wider vistas of unrecognisable dimension loom out as the soul advances from plane with the light of its aura as its guide. No maps, no charts, no compasses are required here. The inner light is the sole guide in crossing incomprehensible vistas of heavenly territory. We are not governed by the law of time, space and causation; ours is all Eternity. It is all a passionless, ceaseless whirl of rhythmic cosmic forces. Waves after waves of transcendental light sweep the whole arena. Endless are the vistas, ceaseless is the music of the spheres. Stars cluster a mammoth panorama of light and splendour. Silence and serenity reign sovereign in our land."

Humanity as one solid unit

"The foundation of Theosophy was laid by the Masters, the members of the White Lodge, with a view to propagate the unity of all life and the fundamental unanimity in the teachings of all religions, We have great powers and we make use of them in the best manner possible for creating harmony and peace in the world, sowing the seeds of fellowship with a view to mould humanity into one solid unit. One God, one religion, commonwealth of nations and cultures will be the main plank in the ideologies of your future world. It is only then that peace will evolve out of chaos, leading to the triumph of virtue over vice and the sovereignty of justice in all fields of life. This is the final plan of God that man must achieve unity by the dint of his own efforts and for the good of all."

Justice – The basic principle of God's law

"The basic principle of God's law is Justice. The Law of Justice rules throughout the universe, The Law of *Karma* is nothing but the Law of justice. When a thing appears to you as unjust, it is because your knowledge is superficial and you are not bel to see the whole picture as it is. With your physical eyes you cannot see the hidden side of things. It is therefore you arrive at wrong conclusions in the absence of real knowledge, Divine knowledge is the only true wisdom. Only highly advanced souls can get an insight into the mysterious side of life. What is visible is not real, what is real is invisible.

"As man's soul evolves, his occult powers also evolve and he gains an insight into the hidden things of life, Madame Blavatsky, Leadbeater and Mrs. Annie Besant of the Theosophical Society were occultists. They wielded great powers through the assistance of their Masters and were therefore able to take prominent part in shaping the things of the world. The Theosophist movement is a great force in moulding the future destiny of the world. It will gather strength day by day for its ideals appeal to both the human intellect and emotion."

Liberation of the soul

"When Goethe died, his last words were, "Light, more light." I would ask everyone to lead his life in such a pure and spotless manner and with such complete devotion to God that when he dies his final thought should be of God and the splendour of our world. Your journey would then be from darkness into light, from ignorance into knowledge, from unreality into reality. Nothing is permanent on your earth plane. Everything is subject to change and decay. Your world is full of sorrow and misery, but you can make your life a success if you submerge your individuality into the larger strata of Non-Self. Maya chains a man to the cycle of birth and re-birth. The only escape is to lead a life of desirelessness without egotism. People have a notion that it is extremely difficult to attain liberation. The general conception is that it takes hundreds and thousands of births to achieve Nirvana. This is an erroneous idea. All that you need is a strong will and determination and the knowledge of the goal of life. There is nothing impossible in life. This conception must be followed up with a grim determination to do or die.

"Man is what he thinks. Let him aspire for God all the time and things will become so easy. Aspiration for the highest divinity is a sure way to God – Realization. Bury your mind in the thoughts of God and God alone, and you will notice a marvellous change in you. For God alone is the Reality. Give up all material enjoyment and seek mental equipoise by leading a life of contemplation even in the midst of a work-a-day world, working hard for others but without expectation of any return."

Pain and suffering

"Life's pendulum swings between joy and sadness, happiness and misery. For most there is more misery than happiness in life. But their misery is the result of ignorance. No man can be unhappy if he has abiding faith in God and the knowledge of the final goal of life. The very fact that at the end of life's journey the soul can be submerged into eternal bliss should give courage and strength to every one to bear his or her crosses cheerfully in life. Pessimism is a sin. With liberation as the goal of life, none should ever despair. When we see sordidness and misery around us we feel sad at heart. But that does not mean that sadness should dominate us. There is all the greater reason that we must fight and struggle to remove the cloud of despair and clear the debris of dejectment from our mind's eye. When there is struggle on, the spirit thrives."

Thought: A Godfather and a Monster

"In the *Zend Avesta,* the chief teaching is that evil should be crushed. This evil should be considered as that within and not outside him. That which breeds evil in life is evil thought. Thought is the sponsorer of good and evil in life. Purity of thought would lead to purity of words and purity of actions.

"*Vohu Mano* – the Good Mind is man's citadel. To build that citadel of Good Mind, concentration and meditation on God as the Architect of Beauty and Goodness is essential. The society of good books and nature in its resplendent beauty makes a good foundation for the edifice of *Vohu Mano.* Spiritual knowledge is the greatest disintegrator of the vileness of thought. Special training is necessary to curb the mind, the greatest mischief monger in the world. When the mind is annihilated, God is realised."

Dynamic Energy of Creation

"The tremendous speed with which the constellations move in the universe of God is beyond human conception.

Everything is in a state of flux. There is dynamic energy continuously flowing – without beginning, without end. Your earth is a tiny pin in the gigantic structure of the universe. God is the sovereign ruler. He has a hierarchy of Angels and Archangels, Seraphs and Cherubins, Thrones and Principalities and numerous orders of heavenly beings to carry out His commands."

The magic of non-attachment

"Christ's teaching to the young man who followed all his commandments was that he should sell off all he possessed and then follow him. The underlying idea is that to accomplish the goal of life you must lead not only a life of righteousness but a life of asceticism and selflessness. What the Bible says is too true. "It is easier for a camel to pass through the eye of a needle than for a rich man to enter the Kingdom of God."

Even in the *Katha Upanishad,* when Yama, the God of Death, offers Nachiketas all the riches of life, he discards them, for he knows that they are of no permanent value. All the material joys of the world are of passing moment. They can buy no eternal happiness. Simple living is superb living. Detachment is divine. Non-attachment is the Philosopher's Stone. It is the magic of the highest life – the life of the spirit."

God's worship and God's light

"Constant dripping wears a stone. When you think of God all the time, this constant thinking will create in you God-consciousness. But your longing for God must also be strengthened by firm determination and resolution. The worship of God in the sacred chamber of the heart is the unsullied expression of that which is the highest in man.

Devote yourself to God, and God alone, the Highest Tribunal in the universe. God's light travels at a tremendous speed, continuously and ceaselessly. It is the generator of life and knowledge. It is the expeller of darkness, the harbinger of joy, the vitaliser and energiser of all animate and inanimate life."

It is the heart that prays

"The human heart is temple of God. The worship of God in this inner temple is far more effective than prayers in temples and churches of brick and stone. It is the heart that prays, not the tongue. Make the vast canopy of Nature your Prayer House. Every tree, every rose plant, has its touch of beauty that ravishes the soul and fills the spirit in wardly with joyousness that is the breath of God. See God with the eyes of the mystic in all things of Nature. God that transcends and is yet immanent in all, so Absolute is Its Spirit pervading the universe."

Stolidity of mind and spiritual perfection

"Perfect, immobile calmness is the attribute of a saint. And a stolid mind can be acquired only through self-control. Perfect stillness of the mind is the quintessence of spirituality. An unruffled mind becomes the repository of divine wisdom. It is a link between the two worlds, the spirit world and the world of matter. Serenity of mind, sincerity of heart and strong determination to follow the path of Truth at any cost – these are the steps in the ladder of spiritual perfection."

From flesh to spirit

"When a man enters the state of superconsciousness he becomes one with God. It is the highest state of consciousness. It is the Yogi's paradise. The Sanskrit word for superconsciousness is Samadhi. The yogi in Samadhi becomes one with the Universal Spirit. He loses his individuality. He becomes the master of all inner dynamic forces that give him siddhis, powers of superphysical nature. The highest knowledge is the knowledge of inner forces.

When this is gained, man reaches a point, that is the peak of his achievements.

The aim of yoga is union with the Divinity, the transformation of baser metal into gold, the transmutation of the flesh into spirit. The way to self-realization is open to all but few care to enter the steam. God wants the weary traveller to come back to his own original home, from whence he has migrated. But the allurements of journey keep him away. Man is flung between the two forces of maya on one hand and detachment on the other. As long as maya takes hold of him, the dark forces of nature keep the soul imprisoned in the mortal flesh. The only escape from the imprisonment of the flesh is, as Buddha has taught, complete renunciation, *i.e.*, life of detachment, desirelessness."

The dynamics of silence

"The spearhead of spiritual progression is man's own deep longing for God. With man's aspiration comes illumination and when the mind is illuminated, it leads to the final state of absorption of the soul into the Ocean of Eternal Bliss. The man of silence whose heart is fixed on God and whose mind is attuned to God is more dynamic than an active man. The vibrations surging from the silent man absorbed in God have a terrific speed. They cover a long vista of life and create a transformation of an unusual order. It is misleading to think that inaction is a sin. When a man attains the highest spiritual state, his inaction is of the most dynamic type. He becomes a vibratory force whose currents reach the furthermost ends of the existing plane and help in creating an atmosphere of radiant health and beauty."

The crown and cradle of spirituality

"Just as a child grows into boyhood and then into manhood, gradually spiritual progress is also by slow stages. It takes not merely one life but many lives to attain the goal of perfection,

Divine knowledge and a fixity of purpose are a great aid. When a man reaches the suparmundane stage he remains absorbed in divine bliss. Earthly sorrows and sufferings do not disturb the equanimity of his mind. He rises above the physical and mental consciousness. He is God conscious, rapt up in thoughts of God and God alone. To come in contact with yogis, who have realised Self is supreme bliss. To contact them is to enflame the mine and the soul for higher consciousness. Self-help is necessary in self-realization but a Guru is a great force in quickening the pace of a man's spiritual progress.

Each soul has its own destiny to fulfil both in this life and in the Life Hereafter. The greater the longing for God, the shorter becomes the bridge between this world and the world of spirit. God's book of the universe is open to all but he alone shall read it, who has learnt the music script by leading a dedicated life of Truth and Purity. Desirelessness and Egolessness – these are the alphabet of the mystic language. Complete surrender to the will of God is the crown and cradle of Spiritual Philosophy."

Marriage – A sacrament and sanctity

"Marriage is a sacrament, not a contract. It is a school of experience in which two partners have to work out their destiny, whatever be their differences and whatever be their differences. By all means, don't judge a man harshly, who violates the sanctity of marriage but to say that his or her soul van evolve better by breaking the marriage vow and or by seeking another wedlock or illicit connection is not correct. Platonic friendship in absolute purity of mind is feasible and should be encouraged. But often it degenerates on the weakness of flesh and it has to be guarded against, Absolute purity of mind, whether in wedlock or outside wedlock, is the *sine qua non* of spiritual life."

God – The Destiny of Every Soul

"Drink deep from the Fountain of Living Water. The Spirit of God is in every living being. Go forth in the battle of life courageously, sportingly, keeping God in mind. Enkindle the flame of your spirit by the fire of Divine Truth and awaken the soul from its prison of darkness. Surrender to the Will of God. The greater the difficulties, the greater the opportunity for a life of spirituality. God makes no distinction between men and men, nations and nations. He deals all with equal justice. There is love in His heart, kindness in His eyes. He loves all without distinction. He listens to every cry of woe. His laws are just. His mercy is great. Unsurpassed in wisdom, matchless in power, He rules like a beneficent father, caring for His children in every way. His spoken word is Truth. His written word is Love. He who seeks Him can find Him in the cave of his heart. Seek Him and Him alone, he is eternal, infinite. He is the soul. He is the seed of all things divine and terrestrial, Nothing exists without Him. He is the source of all creation. He is Light and Splendour, pillar of the sky, canopy of the world, man's refuge and his citadel. He rules the tide. He governs the moon. He gives light to the sun and causes darkness in the night. His word is law unto death; His forgiveness and grace enrich life. He is the lodestar of the seer, and the avowed destiny of every man."

Free Will and *Karma*

"God's Grace descends upon a man only when he has wipedout all his *karma* but not before. The law of *Karma* is the most equitable law in the universe. It is based on the dictum: "As you sow, so shall you reap." God has given Free Will to every one. Free Will is the most essential and vital part of man's evolution. The analogy of the to blades of the scissors representing Free Will and Predestination (*Karma*) is correct. It gives in a nutshell the whole truth. Free Will and Karma are different and therefore there is no blend or synthesis of the two. They are quite opposite, separate factors and both are indispensable in life."

Chapter Thirteen

A Friend Stabs: A Severe Test (1947)

One of the greatest obstacles on the path is the series of tests to which a candidate is subjected, to try his patience, his power to endurance and his loyalty to his Master. Tests are so bitter and galling that seldom one is able to pass them successfully. These tests become more aggressive and more constant towards the end of the journey. We shall discuss this subject in a separate chapter hereafter.

I was allowed by the Master in the beginning to pass the messages to a particular friend of mine, who shared my confidence, besides Homi and Doraswami. The messages pleased him but when it came to the stage of my having received *Nirvana,* he could not believe that such a thing as *Nirvana* could ever come to me so easily. According to him, it required a Buddha to attain the *Nirvana* stage. He wrote to me that I was deluded and that he had come to the conclusion that the messages were from a lower astral.

It was a bomb-shell to me. It cut my heart to piece. I knew in my heart that he was doing me the greatest injustice in life. But he was adamant. He changed his opinion, later-on, when Homi wrote a letter to me, emphatically confirming that I have already attained *Nirvana* and was progressing toward the goal of Self-realization.

In this connection the following message of Ram Ram would be read with interest:

> "Jamshed has completely upset your mind. He thinks that some lower astral is giving you messages in the name of Rishi Ram Ram and he laughs at the very idea of your having reached the stage of *Nirvana.* He is perfectly wrong. Write to Doraswami and Homi immediately. I will give them proofs that the messages were given by Rishi Ram Ram and none else. I was simply surprised at Jamshed's attitude. He is doing you the greatest injustice of his life, though his motives are sincere and he wants to save you from what he considers a hallucination. Don't listen to Jamshed. Do your duty. I will prove later-on that you have already attained *Nirvana,* though Jamshed and others may ridicule and stab you mercilessly in their ignorance. I shall also prove that none else but I, Rishi Ram Ram, has been giving you the messages all along. No Astral dare even come near you. Jamshed has done you the greatest injustice. He has cut you to pieces but he will see his mistake. You are put by God to the hardest and severest test. But rest assured, you will come out quite successful."

The above message not only set aside my doubt, if any generated by My friend's iconoclastic denial of my attainment of *Nirvana* but it made me retrospective and introspective. Could all the spiritual exercises that were given to me by the Master in the altar room and the extremely beautiful visions that I saw with lights flashing saying "Your is Eternal Happiness" be all hallucinations?

In my letter of December 24, 1947, I explained to Homi, my spiritual help-mate and guide, the experiences that I had in the morning of the day. This is what I wrote to him:

> "I had an extremely pleasant experience today in the morning. I entered the altar room at 05:00 a.m. and left it 07:20 a.m. For the first hour there was deep meditation. Then Rishiji gave me some exercises. He lifted me gently and made me lie down twice at full stretch in the very small altar room that I have. The marvel was that all the time my eyes were closed and he managed it in such a manner that I did not hit myself against any wall or anything else. He lifted me as if he was picking up a flower, so gently, so softly was it done. It gave me a thrill of pleasure. Once after making

> me lie down at full stretch, he made me sit down cross-legged with my face turned towards the wall and my back facing the altar where were kept the pictures and the flowers, I did not like the idea of my sitting in this posture, with my back turned towards the great ones, All of a sudden I heard a faint voice saying, "I will turn you round" and I prepared myself for it. But instead, I was again made to recline and I thought he was making me lie down at full stretch again, No, it was not so. As soon as I was half inclined, I was given a swift turn and I sat face to face to the flowers and the pictures at the altar – my usual posture. How the voice came and how beautifully he turned me! It was thrilling. He did all this to show to me to leave everything to him and I have now utmost confidence in Rishiji's doings. Not a moment did a thought come to me that I would be hurt, keeping my eyes closed in that small room, I wonder how he must have managed it. He must have measured every inch to have made me lie down in two different ways without hurting me or striking myself against anything in that room. And all the time my mind was absorbed in God. The visions I saw were marvellous. I saw the word Nirvana on a white background (I am not quite sure whether it was white but I think it was so) flashing in brilliant red and blue, twice. Nearly all the prophets passed by, the most noticeable was Zarthustra."

Homi received my above letter of December 24, 1947, along with my two other letters of December 23 and 29, 1947 and in his reply to me dated December 31, 1947, *inter-alia* he says: "Your letter of 24 gave me a thrill as I read through it and also again just now when I re-read it before sitting to reply, I could not understand the reason for this pleasurable experience. It was not so with the other two letters."

In his letter dated November 18, 1947, Homi gave explanation which was very helpful. He said: "I see that you are being put through regular drill day by day to help you to get and strengthen your spiritual muscles. You are being helped to get your first experiences of the Invisible Worlds. Pictures and symbols, so far as I understand the matter, are the main means of imparting lessons in those worlds. They use these means in the same way as our earthly teachers use language. Hence visions of events and symbols, I think, will be your experience in an increasing degree, at the same time as clairaudience. Symbolical representations of some of the Higher Beings are very interesting to remember. For instance, Shiva or Ahuram Mazda in His manifest aspect of Ahuram Mazda Amshaspand, generally presents Himself as a *yogi*."

Homi's explanation was startling. The *yogi* I saw as the symbolical of Ahuram Mazda Amshaspanda, Himself. How correct Homi's interpretation was, the subsequent events proved.

Here on one side I had a friend who was interpreting the messages I got from the Master correctly and helping me to go on, with courage and heart on the path, so difficult to tread, and on the other side I had another friend, who thought that I was deluding myself and that instead of being in the hands of a Master, some stray astral was fooling me and nothing more, But it was not his fault. He was particularly employed by the higher ones, to test my loyalty to my Master and whether I had enough of discrimination to understand the real from the unreal.

But whatever it be, it was hard, bitter test as the accusation came from a friend, who was beloved to me and in whom I had great faith and reverence for his wisdom and his saintliness. God's ways are really wondrous. When He wants to test us, He can make our best friends His instruments for the purpose.

Chapter Fourteen

Training for Self-realization under Rishi Ram Ram (1948-49)

On May 9, 1948, the Spirit Master Rishi Ram Ram said: "You have attained *Nirvana.* And you will achievie God-realization before you pass away.

In the message of May 24, 1948, the Master explained his earlier message: "*Nirvana* means cessation from the cycle of birth and death. This is preceded by *Moksha* (liberation of the soul). God-realization is the highest stage. You have secured *Nirvana* but you still have not attained seership, which will eventually lead to the final step in spiritual evolution viz. God-realization.

Your life has been extended to give you this opportunity. Your success will depend upon your own efforts and merit. I shall do my best in helping you reach the final goal. For I look upon you as my fondest child."

I was asked to remain unconcerned in all phases of life – pleasure or pain, joy or sorrow. I heard my inner voice telling me: "You will soon be free of the ego in you. When this is accomplished you will realise God. Ask for nothing. Desire for nothing. Be absorbed in God alone."

The following vital teaching of the Master was of great help to me:

> "Don't ask for anything. Practise asceticism in food, dress and in all modes of life, speak not a word that may injure or harm anyone, even under higest provocation. Work diligently. Sleep for as few hours as possible. Practise endurance. Speak as little as possible. Don't make the least show of your learning or piety. Crush all sense of egotism. Be like a child and love all without distinction. Meditate as many hours as you can. Be absolutely detached. You are a highly evolved soul and you must understand your responsibility.
>
> Keep your conscience pure. When you go to sleep, take stock of the day and make amends the next day where you may have failed. Search for Truth and keep the name of God in your heart and mind. It is your devotion to God that is drawing you nearer to Him and He is pleased with you."

I had a secret longing for death. Just as I yearned and longed for God, I also secretly longed that God in His great mercy may relieve me from the bondage of this life. But on June 17, 1947 the Master gave me that most important news that God had made me the Master of Death. He said: "God has liberated your soul from the imprisonment of the body. He has bestowed upon you the power to come away to our side, whenever you like. It is left in your hands to live as long as you want. But I advise you to keep quiet and let things move on without asking for anything. You will then becoma a source of great power and usefulness in life."

I was told on June 24, 1948 that the Master had performed transformation ceremony on me that day.

On October 3, 1948, a day before my birthday, the Master gave me the following message:

> "Tomorrow we are going to give you higher powers. You are the chosen one of God. Keep this in mind all the time and falter not."

The vocation chosen for me by the Master was that of an inspirational writer and I was told that I was being prepared to play the role of a writer and thinker in the new era of spiritual renaissance and Cosmic Consciousness.

It was my intense desire to see the Master but he refused. "You are anxious to see me, but this is not possible in your present state of progress. You will have to wait considerably before your wish can be realised."

On November 23, the Master referred to the subject of my getting an assistant.

I asked Ram Ram; "Why don't you get me an able assistant?" "Alright that," he replied, "I am going to give you one. But you must vow that from this day, you won't waste even a single moment and would go on doing creative work."

To my great surprise a few days later, I was able to get a man quite suitable for my purpose. A stranger walked into my office and asked whether I could give him a part-time job of a typist. I engaged him there and then. That same night the Master said to me: "The typist that you have engaged today will prove useful. I sent him to you. He is nice lad." I got just the kind of man that I needed the most for the salary that I could affort to give. Wondrous are the ways of the Master.

On November 12, 1948, I was told by the Master, that he and I were now one. When I asked him how I should invoke him, he said, "When invoking me, call me your Spirit and Guide. But in reality I am now your own self and nothing else." It was a great step in my spiritual unfoldment. "You are now on the brink of conscious Self-realization," Ram Ram added.

On November 28, 1948, the Master poured his blessings on me as usual and said in the course of his message: "I am raising you to sainthood from today with the express command of God..."

On December 7, 1948, I was told by the Master, "Your most important work now is meditation." Every day I meditated with a freshness of spirit. By God's grace I was able to compose a hymn once a day after prayers and meditation. This practice of composing hymns continued for more than 100 days and the hymns were eventually published in book form, as desired by the Master.

On December 14, 1948, I saw a beautiful vision and the Master explained its significance in the following message:

> "You saw a terrain of mountain steps rising higher and higher, with lights on eigher side and on the steps, and a faint blue light coming out from the topmost summit. That light is your destiny. It is eternity – God's abode."

For the purpose of controlling the mind and detaching it from external objects, concentration on the tip of the nose is recommended in the beginning. Initially, I was made to meditate in this manner. Later, Master made me concentrate on the *Ajna Chakra.* Later on, he took me still higher and I was trained and taught to concentrate on the Crown *chakra,* which is the highest and is considered to be the seat of Brahman.

Usually a picture of a great Master or a God-realised man is made the object of concentration. Because I had the picture of Shirdi Sai Baba in my altar room, I was made to gaze on it and eventually God identified Himself with the form of Shirdi Sai Baba.

The necessary condition to realise God through the gateway of meditation is not only to conceive God as ONE but also as Eternal and Timeless. The devotee must conceive his unity with all in spacelessness and timelessness. The self will then be merged in non-self. The ego will die and God alone will remain.

On January 22, 1949, Rishi Ram Ram said: "Today I tried to open the way for the soul to come out but I could not succeed. It will still take some more time. It all depends upon your own effort and the Will of God. Every day in the morning when you meditate, I shall go on trying till I succeed in sending you in a trance."

The following day I was told that if I continued my meditation, I would be merged in God soon.

Scores of time Rishi Ram Ram deliberately made false predictions just to watch my reactions – whether by creating expectation in the mind, the sting of disappointment was left or not. They were tests to teach the supreme lesson of indifference, the capping stone in this structure of the temple of self-realization.

In the message of January 18, 1949, Rishi Ram Ram said; "I have examined your aura and I find that it is perfect. Nothing could be better. There will be a marvellous transformation in you shortly. Your meditation today was superb. You will soon go into a france."

The next day, for the first time I was put into proper trance by Rishi Ram Ram. He had made overnight preparation to achieve this result. The following message describes this event:

> "You came late today to the altar room in the morning because I made you come late. I was with you the whole night when you were sleeping. I made you sleep flat on your back and you did not move from that position the whole night. My purpose in doing all this was to prepare you for self-realization. As a consequence of my preparation, you were able to meditate beautifully and at the end of the meditation I put you into a proper trance. As you have been consecrated by God, I find it easier now to mould you according to my wishes."

On January 24, 1949, I saw some another beautiful vision in my meditation – a vision through which I came to know of my past incarnation. This knowledge comes when a man has advanced sufficiently towards the goal. It would be better to describe the vision in the words of the Master:

> "Your visions are an indication of the progress of your soul towards liberation. You were a Hindu woman in your past incarnation. You were surprised when you saw yourself standing beside a woman dressed in a sari. In this vision God showed you your two incarnations, the past and the present."

This knowledge of the past life was no doubt indicative of the soul's growth.

On January 26, 1949, Rishi Ram Ram gave me the following message:

> "You have not actually attained self-realization but it may be taken that you have almost got it. The work of opening the secret door is now left to me. I have to make preparations and when these preparations are complete, you will see new light, new vision, new life. It will be a complete trasformation."

This transformation was, however, not attained under the guidance of Rishi Ram Ram, the Master. It was only when he left the work to Sai Baba, of whom we shall speak later on, that the secret door was opened.

I felt uneasy at Rishi Ram Ram's daily assurance that he would put me into samadhi and give me Self-realization. On the night of January 28, 1949, when I was still in the altar room, I developed an urge to talk with Sai Baba. The Master readily consented and I was asked to invoke Sai Baba who gave me a short message: "I have been watching you every now and then, as you have put my photograph in your altar room. I can help Rishi Ram Ram in putting you into *Samadhi.*

The Master then made the following revelation:

> "Do you know Sai Baba is God? He has to power to manifest Himself in any manner and as you invoked him as Sai Baba, He has come to you as Sai Baba."

I asked the Master whether I would die and get my liberation also and he replied: "God has given you power to come away whenever you want. But you will harm yourself if you exercise it. In such matters you have to be submissive and leave it to the Will of God."

On February 19, 1949, Ram Ram revealed to me how he was helpless in giving me conscious self-realization: "You have reached the state of self-realization, but on account of certain factors it is not visible to you. You are helpless and I am also helpless till God Himself issues orders. But have complete faith in me, I am going to do my utmost for you. All you have to do is submit yourself to the will of God and be patient."

The following extract from the Master's message, dated February 22, 1949, gives the whole position in a nutshell.

"As far as you are concerned, it is immaterial whether you get self-realization or not in this life of yours. But it makes a lot of difference to us. We want to make use of your physical body for the progress and evolution of the world.

"Your present suffering is not at all the result of bad *Karma.* All your *karmas* have been cleared. It is because God is testing whether your physical body is fit for the strain that will be brought upon it as soon as you realize God. If your body can regain original health, it will mean that you will be able to stand the strain of self-realization and God would put you into samadhi. The greatest point in your favour is your indomitable will power. If you are bent upon self-realization, you will get it. There is nothing in the world that can stop you from getting it. Exercise your will to become strong and healthy and you will be safe in our hands for forcing the progress of the world through your physical body. If however your health does not improve and God calls you away, you will be given the option, when you come over to our side, either to join the Hierarchy of Elders *i.e.*, us, the Masters or be born immediately as a Master in physical body for the transformation of the world."

The signs of gradual transformation were visible to me in the waves of joy that swept me like tidal waters. I was told by the Master that it was due to the vicinity of God's presence and the soul had now unfolded itself from its sheaths and was ready for flight. I was asked to pass my time as much as possible in the altar room and evote myself in praying to God. The master reminded me that I was in a critical state and meditation was the surest way iof over-reaching the gap to arrive at the Hall of Liberation.

Several times assurances were given by Ram Ram that he would show himself after meditation. But these assurances never took any concrete shape.

Meanwhile, I was put to several tests. On March 7, 1949, a Spirit impersonated itself as Rishi Ram Ram and gave me the following message:

"It is because your body is weak that I can't give you liberation. I am extremely sorry to disappoint you. I have done my best."

I said: "You have been saying for the last so many days that my liberation is certain and now you tell me that you are helpless. Don't you think that you are contradicting yourself? Do enlighten me. I want your guidance."

"What can I say? It breaks my heart. I had great expectations in you. If the soul is liberated, it won't return to the body."

I said: "But you said that God had given the final order to you. When He gave the final order, He must have known every thing. Is it now so? Do kindly guide me. It is a problem."

The Spirit said: "All I say is that I can't do anything more."

I said: 'Believe me, I am not disappointed. I have not deserved liberation. It is too big a prize. Will you kindly tell me what shall I do now?"

I enquired: "Who are you then?"

The Spirit replied: "I won't say who I am. It is no business of yours to ask."

I asked: "Is it for the first time that you have talked with me today or is it that you have been talking with me for a while?

The Spirit said: "I am not supposed to answer your question."

I then said meekly: "In the name of God, kind spirit, I ask you to tell me frankly all about you. God protects us all."

The Spirit replied: "Why do you take the name of God? Has God not cheated you? I would ask you to give up God and I shall take you to the realm unknown and make you its king. I have all that power in my hand."

I said: "Don't talk such foolish things. I want God and God alone. I don't care for anything else. Please go away."

The Spirit said: "You will repent if you drive me away. For God can't give you liberation at all. But I can make you king of all the forces in this world and you will reign supremely."

I cried out: "Go away, I want God and God alone. He is the Lord of my heart. I love Him and offer Him my heart's devotion. I want nothing but God."

The Spirit replied: "You are really stupid. God has refused you liberation. Yet you are sticking to God. If you join me you can have all your desires fulfilled. Think it over. I can come to you again, if you like."

I said: "Please don't come at all. I shall ask God to drive you away. In the name of God, who is the Lord of Love and Light and who protects all innocent souls, I ask you to go away from my sight."

The Spirit said: "All right, I am going away. But remember, you would repent losing this golden opportunity."

After the departure of the Spirit, Rishi Ram Ram was invoked and He said: "I am real Rishi Ram Ram. I saw the false spirit coming to you but did not stop him, for I wanted to see your reactions. I am extremely happy and proud that you have successfully passed this test also.

I was going through a new experience. Frequently, I began to fall in a state of semi-consciousness in the altar room. Even when taking down messages of the Master, the pencil would slip and I would fall in a state of semi-consciousness. The Master was pleased and he said, it was a good sign and that it would eventually lead me to *samadhi.* The struggle continued. Every day the Master held out an assurance that I would go into *samadhi,* but I could not.

One day, Rishi Ram Ram announced his intention to absent himself for a full week and ordered me not to invoke him during that period. He said: "You must now learn to renounce even your Master's companionship. Don't invoke me for seven days. I shall myself come to you and talk to you. This is being done to teach you the lesson of non-expectation and complete renunciation. This is the severest of tests, for you have grown exceedingly fond of me and want to talk to me all the time....

I have done my duty under God's orders. You have now to do yours. I am leaving you at the gate of the Palace of God. I can't take you in the palace. It is for you to go in it all alone. Do you understand it? I shall come to you after seven days to find out whether you are still standing at the gate or have entered it. I leave you now.

On March 18, 1949, when the Master returned after seven days of absense, he said "I went away for seven days as I had work in the Spiritual Sphere. I see that my absence has done you harm. Be assured now that I am not going to leave you even for one moment."

The above message is indicative of the fact realised by all mystics that a Master's guidance is indispensable, especially in the final stages of the journey of the soul for attainment of Liberation.

On March 26, 1949, I was at last, put in a state of superconsciousness by Rishi Ram Ram – the first of its kind experienced by me. But Rishi Ram Ram failed to unite my soul with God.

On March 31, 1949, I was put into a perfect trance, to my great joy and relief. Rishi Ram Ram said: "I feel now completely confient that you will realise Self in a very short time."

On April 2, 1949, I was again put into a trance by Rishi Ram Ram. It lasted just for about half an hour. I was told: "You will now be able to get into a trance very quickly. There will be no necessity for long meditation. As soon as you start meditation, you will fall into a trance. You have scored a great victory."

Days went on. Sometimes the Days went on. Sometimes the Master succeeded in putting me into trance, even twice in a day. But several times, it was a failure. Sometimes, instead of trance, I went into sleep. Sometimes sleep was forced upon me.

Constant postponements after assurances to the contrary had a wearisome effect upon me. In order therefore that I may not falter in my faith in my own Master, Ram Ram inspired me to invoke Sai Baba. On April 10, 1949, Sai Baba made His first serious appearance to me. I put him the following question.

"Rishi Ram Ram is my Guide and Master. He is helping me in every respect. I owe him everything. He is all in all to me. He is taking me to God, who is the goal of my life. Am I fit to reach the goal?"

Sai Baba replied: "This is a matter between you and your Master. I want to say one thing however. I can see from your aura that you are a highly developed soul. Have faith in God and your master. Rishi Ram Ram will take you to God, Rest assured. I leave you to your master."

Sai Baba's words strengthened my faith in my Master, and I was so very grateful to God.

As I continued going into a semi-trance without entering *samadhi*, Ram Ram was compelled to put my case to Sai Baba who then gave me His following message:

> "Allow semi-trances to take place as often as possible. Don't stop them at all. They will eventually become deep trances. They are a natural beginning to a great ending. Allow nature to take its course. In spiritual matters, you can never force any pace. Everything has to be done in accordance with God's law. When the grace of God finally descends upon you, you will realise him and enter into a new world of unsurpassed splendour and glory. That you will reach the Goal is certain for it is already decreed by God. I want to tell you one thing more. Have completes faith in your Master and God. God loves you. I love you. Your Master loves you. Are you not happy? Be happy and make others happy."

On April 13, 1949, after many vicissitudes and trails, I was put in full *samadhi*, but it lasted for a very short time. Sai Baba, who had again come to me at the express wish of Ram, Ram, told me: "You have reached the highest state. You will realise the splendour when God opens your inner eye. It will then dazzle you."

I had reached the state of *samadhi*, which is considered the final stage in meditation. But the *samadhi* that I had reached was bland *samadhi i.e.*, I was not conscious of the flight of the soul from the body, because the inner eye had still not opened.

The next question then was of the opening of the inner eye – the key and gateway to self-realization – in full consciousness.

I saw in a vision that I was in the house of Gods. I also saw Christ, Zoroaster, Buddha, Sri Ramakrishna, Mahatma Gandhi, Swami Vivekananda, and Sai Baba there. The vision was very faint.

Referring to the wish, Rishi Ram Ram Said: "This should satisfy you, however, vague the visions were, of the highest stage of spirituality that you have reached. As soon as God opens your inner vision, a new panorama of brilliance and splendour would be present before you."

Without opening the inner eye, the trances were useless and Rishi Ram Ram was now very keen on the more important work of opening the windows of the soul, as the inner eye is called.

On April 22, 1949, I was put in *samadhi* for more than an hour and was completely cut off from all external happenings. But Rishi Ram Ram was still not able to open the inner eye.

In his letter of December 27, 1949, Homi wrote:

> "Just as the different *chakras* are the windows through which the soul can look out upon the Astral and Manasic Worlds, the Inner Eye is the window in the Spiritual Body of man through which the soul looks out upon the Spiritual Plane of Existence."

The following explanation given by Sai Baba regarding the third eye or the inner eye throws a great light on the subject:

> "The third eye is known by various names – the astral eye, the hidden eye, the spiritual eye and the eye of the soul. It is not merely an aperture or window in the spiritual body. As soon as

> the soul flies from the physical body, it is without any kind of embarrassment. It is bereft of all vehicles and has no body. It flies naked. The soul's body is the soul itself. The spirit always accompanies the soul, for the soul is the house of the spirit and it can not be separated. The spirit is the God in man – a silent witness to all actions of man. Man has two minds – the lower and the higher. When he exercises his free will in compliance with the impressions of the higher mind, which is nearest to the soul, he becomes Godly. If he acts on the impulses of the lower mind, he degrades himself. Life is a tussle between the impulses of the higher and the lower mind. The total of these impulses make a man's character.
>
> When the soul leaves the body at the time of death, eye opens out naturally. But when the soul leaves the body temporarily as in *samadhi*, eye may or may not open. Generally when the soul is fit to leave the body in *samadhi*, its eye opens out. In your case, the eye did not open for a long time, because your body was weak and with the opening of the eye, the soul would not have dared to return."

I asked: "When the soul goes to the astral plane it goes in its astral body: when it goes to the mental world, it goes in its mental body and when it goes to the spiritual, it goes in its spiritual body. How do you then explain that when the soul flies from the body, it has no vehicle at all?" Sai Baba replied: "If the soul can go to the astral plane and no further, it must keep its astral body to itself. Similarly when the soul goes to the mental plane and no further, it must be in mental body The astral and mental bodies are thrown off only when the soul is in position to go to the Spiritual Plane. For going to the Spiritual Plane, there is no necessity of any body. The soul is then completely free of all its sheaths. The spiritual body and soul are identical in the last stage of spiritual development."

On April 29, 1949, Rishi Ram Ram said in the course of his message: "Your inner eye is slowly opening, the more you concentrate on my picture, the more it would open. There is nothing now to do except to concentrate. Make the concentration as deep as possible. The deeper the better. It will bring results quicker. Once the eye is opened, no concentration will be necessary."

On April 30, 1949, I was put into a very peculiar state of mind. Rishi Ram Ram said: "It is a state before opening of the eye. You felt joyous all the time and liked remaining in that condition but I made you get up as it was already an hour. You got some glimmering experiences, very faint and yet delightful."

Rishi Ram Ram was giving the final touches to my soul. Homi's letters gave me indication from time to time of my spiritual progress and explained to me the inner meanings of the various messages. He was made the Master's instrument to carry conviction to me. Homi's letters were not his letters, but the Master's letters.

The *samadhi* that was experienced on May 1, 1949, lasted for nearly an hour and was not entirely a blank one. I was bale to see glimmerings of light and was in a very happy state of mind.

I was put into *samadhi* again on May 2, 1949, but it was for a very short time. I saw a few discs of light, red and white. The Master explained:

> "The lights you saw were of the highest Spirit Land. Your soul is beginning to function on the Spiritual Plane."

I was tired of Rishi Ram Ram telling me every day that he would open the inner eye but without any result. It appeared that he was not able to open it at all. On May 2, 1949, I put the following question in all humility and meakness:

> "May I in all humility ask why do you say, that you would open the inner eye all the time and yet don't open it? Don't you think it is better to say, I shall open the inner eye if God wills."

The Master replied: "I understand your feelings. But the complexities and paradoxes of spiritual matters are difficult to explain. Have implicit faith in me. I shall open you inner eye. That is God's order and I must execute it."

I again queried: "You had said in the morning that as you had changed the technique, there would be no further postponement."

The Master replied: "That's true. But circumstances made me deviate again."

I asked: "Are you really Rishi Ram Ram?

The Master replied: "Do you doubt your own Master?"

I replied: "No, not even for a second. I love him; I adore him. He has sacrificed everything for me. But I must now see him. If I am on the spiritual plane, why should I not be made conscious of it and why should Rishi Ram Ram not show himself to me?"

The Master said: "Leave off everything and come to me in the morning."

The next day I felt repentant for having doubted my Master's word and said to him: "The fault is entirely mine. You have tried your best to open the inner eye but I am convinced that I don't deserve it, and therefore God has not enabled you to open my inner eye. I say again that I must make myself deserving of God's grace and then it will descend upon me."

Ram Ram said, "What you say is correct. But in your case, looking to your aura, any Master would make a bold bid for your immediate emancipation. But you will know everything by and by."

One of the greatest dangers on the path is that we begin to doubt the Master, on account of his paradoxical statement. It was to prevent me from falling into this trap that Master gave a long message of admonishment.

I then said to him: "Kindly forgive me. I don't wish to doubt you at all. In the past, it has been my experience that some spirit comes and impersonates you as my Master and gives a false message. Should I not in such cases, question?"

The Master replied:

"You have the right to question and you must question. But remember you are now in a plane where except me, no one dare come to you. Does it open

your eyes even now or not? Your intellect at times comes in my way, despite the fact that you are highly spiritual.

My dearest Minoo, whatever I may do, whatever I may say, and whatever shocks I may give you, have implicit faith and trust in me. I am doing all this for your final liberation.

I could have opened your inner eye today for you were in a very fine trance, but I said that I must teach you a lesson and I did not open it purposely. I know from today you will be an absolutely changed man."

The inner eye, despite several attempts by Ram Ram, still did not open. The master asked me to concentrate on Sai Baba's picture instead of his own. I thought it was to test my loyalty and I refused.

On May 6 1949, I had gone into samadhi for an hour but again it was a blank, barren samadhi. Ram Ram then brought Sai Baba along with him and the latter said: "There is no harm at all if you wish to concentrate upon my picture as it will facilitate opening of the inner eye."

I proudly refused to do so: "I want to concentrate on Rishi Ram Ram's picture only as he is my Master and I cannot change my allegiance to any one."

Sai Baba said: "All right then. Do whatever you like. I am going away. You are insulting me."

I then said in all meekness and humility: "Where is the insult? I hold you in very great reverence but Rishi Ram Ram is my Master and how can I change my allegiance? I would rather have no inner eye opened than change my Master."

Sai Baba retorted: "You are stupid. This is not changing your Master. If you concentrate on something else, it does not mean changing your Master. No one asks you to change your Master. I would be the last person to advocates such a policy. Keep your devotion to Rishi Ram Ram but change the method of concentration. If you concentrate on my picture, it will have a thrilling effect. In a very short time, you will be transformed."

Again I said: "For God's sake don't tempt me. I won't concentrate on any other picture except that of Rishi Ram Ram, whatever may happen.

Sai Baba said: "Just as you please. I am going away now. Have you anything to say?"

I said: "Yes, I want your blessings and God's blessings."

Then Sai Baba opened out his heart and said: "My dearest child, we are all one in God. You would soon be conscious of this super-physical fact. Be assured God's grace has descended upon you. Will you kindly lie down? I have some work with you."

I lay down and Sai Baba gave me some refreshing and vitalising spiritual exercises that brought joy in my heart and alacrity in body.

Later on, Ram Ram gave me the following explanatory message:

> "I shall explain to you the significance of Sai Baba's interaction with you. He asked you to concentrate on his picture and give up concentrating on my picture. He was perfectly right. But at the same time, you were not wrong in refusing to comply with the wish on moral grounds. He then asked you to lie down. You obeyed and he gave you excercises in the same way as I do. But when you refused to concentrate on his picture, why did you allow him to give you exercises? Logically, you ought to have carried out your argument to its natural conclusion. But you did not. He told you to lie down on the ground unconsciously you complied."
>
> "You were pleased when Sai Baba said: "My dearest child, all of us are one in God." This saying indicates the grand truth – the revelation that you have now reached the high stage, when you should be conscious of the fact that you and I and Sai Baba are all one in God. It is immaterial whether Sai Baba opens your inner eye or I. I and Sai Baba are the same. This was not a test to see how far you are loyal to me, It was only aimed at getting you out of your difficulty. If you still persist on concentrating upon my picture, do so by all means. But do not be carried away be any false notion that you are showing your allegiance to me by refusing to concentrate on any other object."

I said: "I am extremely sorry. I won't do it. It does not matter if it takes a longer time to realise Self."

In that evening, Ram Ram noted: "You have brought two new photographs in your altar room."

This was true. They were sent to me by my friend Doraswami. One of them was a big sized picture of Sai Baba in his simple fakir clothes, with sunken and sad eyes. Sai Baba of Shirdi was known as great mystic saint when he was in flesh. One curious story would be enough to indicate his saintliness.

One day, a man came to him begging for his blessing and some alms. Sai Baba told him, "I shall give you a rupee a day, if you would sit here the whole day long from morning till night and abuse me in front of all my devotees." The man was surprised and readily picked up the challenge, "It is easiest thing in the world."

The first day, his voice was in its fullest strength. He abused and slandered the fakir to his heart's content. None knew that he was paid for it. The second day, he poured out the abuses, but they became distinctly feeble and weak. On the fourth day, he refused to carry out the fakir's orders. "I would rather go without your rupee and strive than slander a man like you."

The principal object of this great fakir was to drive away fear from the hearts of his devotees and to take upon himself their burdens. What selflessness!

Let us revert to Ram Ram, He said: "I particularly like the picture of Sai Baba. If you really love me and have implicit faith in me, do kindly carry out my instructions to concentrate on the picture of Sai Baba. It will facilitate the opening of your inner eye."

Sai Baba then gave me a talk. He said: "I see that you have brought a nice picture of mine. I am really happy. Will you now kindly concentrate on my picture? I assure you that no harm will come to you, nor will your Master be the least displeased. If your concentrate on my picture for one hour every day, I can open your inner eye in no time. Would you allow me to do it?"

But I stood my ground and refused to yield.

Then Sai Baba said: "I sincerely admire your sense of loyalty. My dearest child, I am extremely glad you have withstood the temptation and I declare you now fit for liberation. Go, you earned your crown. Rishi Ram Ram, your Master, would open your inner eye. I have the authority of God to say this. His grace has descended upon you. I go now but I carry with me the fragrance of your beautiful aura."

On May 7, 1949, Rishi Ram Ram said: "Today is your spiritual birthday. We have baptised you in our Spiritual Plane."

Sai Baba came again and gave me the message:

> "You have reached a stage when not only Rishi Ram Ram but I have been appointed by God to help you attain your spiritual liberation."

Chapter Fifteen

Questions and Answers with Rishi Ram Ram (1949)

Before we go further into our story, it is necessary to devote a chapter on some of the important questions that were put to the Spirit Master Rishi Ram Ram and the replies he gave me. They throw a flood of light on the points raised.

***Q. 1.* Say what you know about?**

Ans. A friend in Trinidad after reading my book *Joyous Mysticism* strongly resented the comments made in the book, against the immaculate conception of Virgin Mary. The Master was invoked to give an explanation on the subject, which he gave as under:

> "Christ did miracles in life, no doubt. But to him they were ordinary things, for the simple reason, that he knew the secret laws of Nature and was manipulating them for the good of mankind. Regarding his birth, it is certain that he was an Avatar of God or, as the Christians say, the Son of God. But that he took his birth, without his mother Mary, contacting Joseph, his father, cannot be true, for it would be the violation of Nature's law. There can not be an effect without a cause. Nothing can grow without a seed. The explanation given by you in your book *Joyous Mysticism*,

is therefore quite correct. The Christians, especially the priestly class, will not tolerate any opposition to the "Immaculate conception of Virgin Mary." It is on the supposition of such miraculous happenings that they build up the super-conscious entity of Jesus. But they little know that the divinity of Christ was totally of a different order. His divinity lies in his teachings, his sacrifices, his exalted life of divine perfection. Of all historical figures of modern times, Christ undoubtedly was the most spiritual. He is the King of Spirituality. He should be taken as God in human form. And as such we should revere him the most. It is extremely difficult for any human being to rise to the perfection of Christ. He was spirit but to help the cause of evolution, he was sent by God and as such had to take human body, though inwardly all the secrets of Nature were open to him. He was superphysical, a Raja Yogi of the highest type, unprecedented in human history."

The above message was given to me on January 3, 1949.

***Q. 2.* Was Christ forsaken by God when he was crucified?**

Ans. It is said in the Bible that after the mockery of a trial, when Christ was ordered to be crucified, he exclaimed in despair: "Oh Lord, why hast thou forsaken me!"

Christ was a Raja Yogi and as such physical death could not have been a torment to him. He was already one with his Father. He knew the art of extracting the soul from the living body. How could he then give expression to such a thought of despair?

Ram Ram gave the following explanation:

"Christ did the miracles for the purpose of alleviating human suffering. He was full of the milk of human kindness. It is absolutely wrong to say that because he took upon himself the *karma* of bad people, he had to suffer for them and that when he was nailed to death on the cross, even God forsook him. The facts are that being a yogin of the highest type, he never suffered any kind of physical pain whatsoever. It was purely an empty body that they nailed and not his living body, for he was able to withdraw the soul at will. How could a man like Christ, who knew his past, present and future, a yogi, of the highest type who knew all the secrets of the universe and who was all the time in communion with God and was carrying out the orders of God upto the very last moment of his physical life, ever say such things? It is a historical error."

Q. 3. **Is it true that the Four Gospels were not written by his immediate followers but by Alexandrian monks, four or five centuries after Christ's death?**

Ans. R.R. replied: The Gospels of St. Matthew, St. Mark, St. Luke, and St. John were all written by his immediate followers. The very fact that there are repetitions of the same facts in different Gospels, is a proof of the same experiences they had when they followed him."

Q. 4. **Christian Science, founded by Mary Baker Eddy, is considered reconstructed Christianity. A happy blend of religion and science, it is claimed that it makes an appeal both to man's intellect as well as his heart. According to its teaching, evil and matter are a delusion. Mind is activated by spirit and behind mind there is a reservoir of energy that can be tapped and used for removal of all kinds of pains and sufferings. This energy can be drawn upon by means of suggestions and auto-suggestions.**

It is further claimed that faith in God is such a great factor in life that it not only can sustain us in our trials and tribulations but is a means of curing physical and mental ailments. If by mere faith and auto-suggestion, diseases could be cured, why were Christian Scientists themselves not immune from pain and suffering?

Ans. Rishi Ram Ram replied: "I have read your question regarding Christian Science. The concept is very good in theory and appeals to both intellect and emotion. But how far can it be practised depends upon the earnestness of the follower himself. Truly speaking, there is no such things as evil. Evil is only the least good. It we take it in this light, the

Christian Scientists are not wrong, when they say that matter and evil are a delusion. They exist not. Diseases have been cured by faith, but it cannot be said that faith cures can be practised on a large scale. But efficacy of prayers cannot be denied."

***Q. 5.* Is the mysticism in Jewish religion based on the mysticism of the old Iranian faith? If so, why is it, that in Zoroastrian religion, as thought and practised today, there is so very tittle trace of this?**

Ans. Rishi Ram Ram replied: "There in no doubt that Zoroastrianism influenced Jewish tradition, culture, civilisation and even its religion. God *i.e.,* Jehovah is Infinite . There were ten emanations from that Infinite Light and in this way the whole universe being macrocosm, came into existence. The Jews derived the knowledge of the creation of the universe from their contact with ancient Iranians in Babylonia. The Iranians were Aryans and their ancient philosophy made great impression upon all those races that came in contact with them, especially Jews. Christ was a Jew, though he was discarded by the Jews in their ignorance. The Zoroastrian Magi wielded great power and their wisdom was considered to be the profoundest. They were really speaking as the Masters of the East. To say that Zoroastrianism has no mystical side is erroneous. In fact, it is a highly mystical religion. This aspect, by the growth of time and changes in the mode of life, has slowly been undermined and the practical side alone is observed by the masses, though to keen scholars and occult students, the mysticism in ancient Zoroastrianism is a fundamental fact."

***Q. 6.* Does the teaching of the Masters differ from the teaching of religion? Does a religion decay?**

Ans. Rishi Ram Ram replied: "I must say definitely that the teaching of the Masters does not differ from the great teachings left to the people by the sages and prophets who were sent by God to bring light on earth. Religion can never decay. It has no infancy, childhood, youth, manhood or old age. It is people who follow religion that makes all the difference in its growth and decline.

Take the case of Zoroastrianism. When it flourished in the time of Cyrus the Great and Darius, it was at its height. It declined later on and today the number of its adherents is negligible. It does not mean that the religion has lost its vitality. All religious truths are the same. How can there be any decline? It is admixture of religion as founded by prophets with the interpolation, addition and subtraction of the priest-craft that makes all the difference."

***Q. 7.* I am born in the Zoroastrian faith. As a staunch follower of Zoroastrianism, can I say that my religion is the best in the world?**

Ans. Rishi Ram Ram replied: "If each one were to contend that his religion is the best, it would lead to bitterness of feeling. There is but one religion. It is different labels that have done great mischief and it is our duty to remove these labels and be adherents of one religion – the religion of humanity, the religion of Love and Righteousness and ONENESS WITH ALL."

***Q. 8.* According to the Vedas to get control over all forces and materials in Nature, one has to gain control over *Prana i.e.*, breath. It is therefore that in Patanjali's yoga, *Pranayama*, the control of breath is considered as one of the eight limbs or salient points for gaining self-realization. Is it true that in the Science of the Masters, *Pranayama* is ignored completely? Is it true that what is wanted is complete control of the mind, because it is the mind that is the primary motive power throughout nature?**

Ans. Rishi Ram Ram replied: "Yes, *Pranayama* is ignored by the Masters as it is dangerous and not so very helpful, as thought by Indian rishis of old. The control of the mind is the chief things."

***Q. 9.* Are the practices of the yogis who do miracles to be commended? It is argued that these practices can at most take a disciple to the Astral World only which is the Domain of the negative Power. But he who follows the Master can go beyond the Astral Plane. The Indian Yogis go to the plane of consciousness called *Nirvikalpa* – the changeless stage of mind.**

Ans. Rishi Ram Ram replied: "The Vedas give the same high teachings as the Masters. To say that God of the Vedas – Brahman – is only the Negative Power, which has control over the three world is a blasphemy."

***Q. 10.* Is it true that the guidance of a Master for the attainment of Self-realization in indispensable?**

Ans. "Yes, to a certain extent. Take your own case. It is impossible for you to attain *Jivan Mukti* in your living condition without my aid and assistance. But in special cases when souls are highly evolved , they contact God direct and are liberated immediately. Those are very rare cases."

***Q. 11.* Is it true if an initiate loves his Master and practises what he teaches, he will enter the kingdom of Light and would see his Master in radiant form? Is seeing the Masters, the whole way or only half the way in the struggle for spiritual liberation?**

Ans. The Master replied: "A Master takes a disciple generally when he feels he is fit for emancipation. Otherwise he does not care to initiate him. If once a man is initiated by a Master, he takes great care of him and takes him onward on the path till the goal is reached. But it must be remembered that every person initiated can not teach the goal on one round of life. Very few generally reach the goal after initiation in one life. The initiation does him good in this respect that the number of rounds of birth is much reduced.

Regarding the latter part of the question, seeing the Master is a great achievement. It is not the whole way but a signal of the approach of the goal."

***Q. 12.* Do you agree that the Audible Life Stream forms vital part in the Masters' Science? This Audible Life Stream is compared to the WORD of God referred to in the Bible. It is said, it is the duty of the Master to connect the initiate with the Audible Life Stream. No initiate can do it of his own self. Is this true? When the connection is made by the Master, the soul gets liberation. Is this true?**

Ans. "What is said of the word of God is true. Give it any name you like – the Audible Life Stream or anything. The Master helps the initiate in making him hear God's voice. Take your own example. I made you hear "I am God", when I initiated you. It was the greatest and grandest beginning, when you were able to hear that voice. I was convinced that you were on the right track and required only guidance and training to reach the Goal."

***Q. 13.* According to the Science of the Masters, God can be heard and can be seen. It is not the question of mere faith as in religion, but one of real, rigid experience. Religion therefore serves only the secondary purpose and not the whole. The Masters teach how to walk by sight and knowledge and not by mere faith. Is this true?**

Ans. Rishi Ram Ram replied: "Yes, without the aid of a Master even the most religiously perfect man would not be able to attain *Jivan Mukti.* He gets *Nirvana* only, *i.e.,* he is freed from the round of birth and death but he can not become Master or a *Jivan Mukti* in his own living body. The Science of the Masters is greater in this respect than religion."

***Q. 14.* Theosophist Masters concentrate their attention on the betterment and improvement of the world as a whole.**

They do not care to take individual souls for individual liberation. Which is better service, betterment of the world as a whole or liberation of individual souls?

Ans. Rishi Ram Ram replied: "I have great regard for Theosophist Masters. They are members of the Great White Brotherhood. If they do not care to devote their attention upon individuals but mainly concentrate on the betterment of the world as a whole, don't you think it is a betterment of the world as a whole, don't you think it is a far greater service? To liberate a few individuals is a lesser work than bettering the condition of the whole world. But the idea of liberating individuals gains importance from this fact that the liberated soul becomes a Master in his time and he begins to contribute his share for the betterment of the world. The Masters, whether in flesh or spirit, wield tremendous force for the good of mankind and are a great power in the adjustment of human affairs."

Q. 15. **Is it true that control of the mind can never be achieved except by and through *Shabda*, the Audible Life Stream.**

Ans. Rishi Ram Ram replied: "This is partly true. The control of the mind in the first place has to be accomplished by man himself. The Master makes his way easier for him and God by means of His word, *i.e.,* His guidance. But as a rule, God has so arranged everything that man has to work in conformity to God's Laws, which are immutable. The Word of God is the Law of God. He permeates throughout the universe. He is the soul and spirit of every living being. When man obeys His rules and commandments, automatically he comes nearer to God and the Master taking orders from God guides the individual and brings him safe to God. The individual microsm is merged in the universal macrocosm. The man-God in the microcosm is merged in the universal macrocosm."

Q. 16. **God created man or man created God?**

Ans. Rishi Ram Ram replied: "Both are right. God created man in this sense that the Absolute Spirit manifesting itself, had to project itself and the result was the creation of the whole universe. To observe that man created God is also true for when the spark of God latent in man, is enlivened, it is man in a way who becomes the creator of the God. It is just like the question whether the hen came from the egg or the egg came from the hen. Both are correct. There can not be a hen without an egg or an egg without a hen. There can not be God without man and man without God."

Q. 17. **Have Masters seen God? What are their main functions and powers?**

Ans. We, Masters, hold great powers and have a personal knowledge of all the spheres and the planes. We can take any form we like and can go to any plane in the flicker of a second. Time and space have no significance in our Spirit Land. They are non-existent. We are considered as God's emissaries for we keep in constant contact with Him and carry out all His orders. Our chief work is to liberate human souls and to perfect your world and to guide those who return to our world after experiencing earthly plane of existence. But to say that we occupy position absolutely next to God in the Great Hierarchy of Beings is not correct. Our spheres are so infinite and there are so many universes and solar systems that it is impossible to set any mark in the scale or gradation."

Q. 18. **What are your views on the theory of Transmigration of Souls – Metampsychosis?**

Ans. There has been a great controversy on this subject among your sages and saints. God wants every one to evolve. Progress is the law of the universe.

Even the worst sinner must go back to the species or group in which he was born. He must come back and be born in the species of man. He can not be born as an animal, a cobra or a snake, however evil his actions may have been. There are groups fixed by God and each has to attain his or her salvation through those original groups. Human group is the highest on earth and it is only in this group that the soul can reach he highest attainment of spiritual perfection. Whatever be the merit or demerit of the teaching of the transmigration, it matters very little to us, for what we are concerned is how to become one with God. I have been here for more than 2500 years in the Spirit Land and I know of no case of a human soul take any body except human when it is reincarnated."

Q. 19. **Do the Masters give training for liberation of the soul by means of exercises?**

Ans. Rishi Ram Ram replied: "We give exercises to expedite the process of liberation. They in no way form the basis of liberation. In fact, they have no place at all in the emancipation of the human soul."

Q. 20. **Is it true that all persons who have not contacted Masters on the earth plane, however good they may be, must return to earth, but those who have contacted the Masters and even it they be not good, are trained by the Masters, but they are not sent back to the earth plane. What is your opinion?**

Ans. "God's justice is so great that there is absolutely no such thing as favouritism or partiality in the dispensation of His laws. His laws operate in the same way upon all, whether they may be initiated of the Masters or not."

Q. 21. **There are five sheaths viz.**

(1) ***Annamaya Kosh*** – the physical body.

(2) ***Pranamaya Kosh*** – that which carries the Prana or life energy *i.e.,* the Etheric body.

(3) ***Manomaya Kosh*** – the body of feelings, emotions and desires *i.e.* the astral body.

(4) *Viganamaya Kosh* – the seat of discrimination and knowledge, the body of thoughts or the Manasic body or more strictly the lower Mental body.

(5) *Ananda Maya Kosh* – the body of spiritual or Eternal Bliss or the spiritual body with which the Higher Manasic or Mental body is closely associated or linked.

Is it true, that the Spirit or Divine Spark alone can wear these different bodies; The 'soul' is a generic term to denote the Spirit plus the invisible bodies.

Ans. "The Spirit or the Divine Spark is the highest in man. It is God. The soul is an emanation from God and its ultimate function is to be merged back into the original Godhood. Spirit is universal: Soul is individual. The Spirit is a mere witness. The soul is the exercising body and it functions through its five bodies, above described."

Q. 21. **It is agreed that the Spirit or Divine Spark is the highest in man. "It is God" in man.**

You say, "the soul is an emanation from God,"
"the soul is individual" and (that)
"the soul is the exercising body" and (that)
"it functions through its five bodies."

Is it not, that the Spirit is a particle of the Divinity; that it is individualized (only so far as Man is concerned)-though still forming part of the universal Ocean of Divinity and as such describable as 'universal', that the whole of this individualised particle of Divinity does not descend into an individual human being, but a portion of this individualised Divine particle only descends. This corresponds to "emanation from God."

That emanation has to be of the nature and essence of Spirit, because nothing but Spirit or the Divinity can take on the first or Spiritual Sheath.

The portion of the Divine Particle so sheathed becomes also individualised and it is called 'a soul'. It then takes on further sheaths and remains 'a soul', till it has finished its rounds of experiences, becomes perfected and gets merged again into the Original Divine Spark or Particle from which it started its career. Till then it remains "the exercising body."

The portion of the original Divine Spark or Particle, which does not descend into sheaths, remains in the Ocean of Divinity and may be described as "a mere witness" and the process of the Atma's or the Divine Spark's descent into man is the same, but on a very miniature scale, as the descent of the Paramatma or the Cosmic Spirit or Cosmic Manifestation involving Divine Transcendence and Immanence. The above is the view of Homi. Kindly give your comments.

Ans. "Homi's explanation is extremely beautiful. All that he says is correct but there is difference between Spirit and Soul, undoubtedly, though both are emanations from God, or as is said in the usual parlance both are sparks of Divinity.

The Spirit is God. It is mere witness. It is universal. The soul, the spark of divinity, an emanation from God has to function and gain experiences in the human body and when it gains liberation after getting rid of all its bodies, it becomes Spirit. It is like this. The soul is Spirit in the very beginning, but it has to gain experiences in the human body and when it becomes perfect, it again returns to its original nature, *i.e.* it becomes Spirit. To speak in the words of the mystics, the marriage of the Soul with the Spirit takes place when the soul is finally liberated. To say that the soul is Spirit plus the five sheaths is somewhat misleading. The two important differences are:

(1) The soul is the functioning body. It exercises through its sheaths. The spirit is mere Witness.

(2) The soul though perfect in its origin has again to become perfect by its experiences through human incarnations and

when it is merged with the Spirit, it loses its separate identity. Practically it comes to the same thing but the nomenclature should be so used as to give no scope for ambiguity of thought and misunderstanding. To put it in a homely language Spirit is God within man. The soul is the embryonic God in man, which after several incarnations will become God again."

Chapter Sixteen

Higher Training and Progress under Sai Baba as God Almighty (1949)

On May 11, 1949, in the evening after prayers, I was asked by my Master, Ram Ram, after prayers to sit in absolute silence for twenty minutes. Eventually after nearly an hour's silence, Sai Baba came on the scene and gave me the following message:

> "Yes, I am Sai Baba, I was with you all the time while you were sitting in silence absorbed in thoughts of God. I have come to tell you what I have taken over your charge from Rishi Ram Ram and you will now have to follow me completely. Concentrate your attention deeply on my picture and I shall reward you with joy."

I was startled. Why had Sai Baba all of a sudden come and taken me over from Ram Ram, especially when two or three days ago, he had himself said that Ram Ram was my Master and that he would open my inner eye. Ram Ram quickly followed and said: "What Sai Baba says is absolutely correct. He is now your all in all, though I shall still continue to be with you all the time. I am handing you on to him for he has the final authority to liberate your soul and not I. You have progressed to such an extent that transfer of your guardianship to a higher authority is now necessary and that higher spiritual personage is Sai Baba."

The next day in the early morning, Sai Baba greeted me with the following words:

> "Yes, I am Sai Baba, your Spirit Guide and now your Master. I will make you understand the laws of the universe, which are complicated in their variety but the key to them is simple to one who attains the knowledge of the Self and Reality."

Later on in the afternoon, Sai Baba came again: "Rest assured, I shall open the inner eye and unfold to you the mysteries of our world. Do be guided by me in all respects. I am a Spiritual teacher of a Transcendental Order, whose function is to make you aware of the hidden law of our universe. You are coming to us nearer and nearer every day."

I felt a thrill of delight. Was it a foretaste of the coming blissful consciousness?

Ram Ram's subsequent message on the same day further strengthened my optimism. He said: "You are now one with me as well as Sai Baba. When your inner eye opens, you will be convinced of the unity that exists between us all. Sai Baba has given you permission to talk with me whenever you like."

One the same day, *i.e.*, May 12, 1949, in the evening Sai Baba gave me a proof of his unrivalled position in the Celestial Hierarchy when he brought with him, Lord Maitreya to give me a special message on the significance of the day. Lord Maitreya said:

> "I am the Lord of the Earth Domain come to you at the express bidding of our Master who wants men to explain the significance of this day. It is not only a full moon day, but that it synchronises with three great events in world's history, viz., the birth of Lord Buddha, the day of his enlightenment and the day of his departure from your earth plane. We celestial beings come down on earth to commemorate this great day by sending our floods of illumined vibrations in all the corners of the world to wake up human consciousness to its fullest capacity and to bring the light and joy

> of God. Sing the praise of God with all the fervour of your heart, for He alone is Real, Eternal and Infinite. Blessings be upon you all."

After the departure of Lord Maitreya, Sai Baba started his training by putting me to a test of endurance.

The following day, Sai Baba put me in a long *samadhi*, which lasted for full one hour and I was made to see beautiful colouring extremely joyous to behold. It was the distant sight of the Spiritual Plane, which I was assured was to be my eternal abode. Just as I was thinking of getting up, I saw the following sentence flashed before me, set in extremely beautiful colouring:

> "Teachings Spiritual Will Be Given By Me."

I felt such a thrill of delight, such unprecedented joy that I caught hold of Sai Baba's picture and pressed it to my forehead with unusual fervour.

I was told to pass the whole day and even the night in the altar room. Sai Baba explained to me the significance of what he had done. He said: "Do you understand the meaning of my having pressed the back portion of your head? Here is situated what is called the source and fountain of the ego activities in man. As you go higher towards the centre of the head, there is the abode of the higher self in man. By pressing the ego centre, I have curbed and controlled the lower part of Self and thus liberated you completely from the fetters of maya. Hereafter, no worldly objects, no desires, no passions, no love for glory, fame or name, no enticement of any kind, in fact the external world together with all its propensities for the propagation of evil in man, ceases to exist for you. You are now free entirely of the mundane things in life."

The same day I was told by Sai Baba that He had transformed me. "Your soul is now free to leave the body at will. You can come to us whenever you like *i.e.*, you are the Master of your own Death. This is the power which God gives to liberated souls, to leave the earth plane whenever they like for the heavenly world. It is rarely given and you are now one of the rare souls chosen for this signal gift. I want to tell you that you inner eye is open. You have come extremely near the goal. All barriers are removed. The path is quite clear and straight. But it is stiff to climb. As you climb upwards, you will become conscious of your inner powers, and you will begin to see things in their reality."

In the early hours of the morning of the 14th, Sai Baba put me into a *samadhi* lasting for an hour and thereafter gave me the following message:

> "You are ascending the last step to the goal but with great difficulty. I am helping you all the time. I put you into *samadhi* today which lasted for an hour. You saw a most beautiful glimmering light in the form of a small brick. That is the most important indication.
>
> I think in a few more sittings with Me you will see me face in a halo of brilliant light."

My heart was full of joy. I wrote the same day to Homi as under:

"Yes, I am transformed. There are no more expectations; no postponements. The very last vestige of doubt has been removed. Sai Baba is definitely a much higher entity than Rishi Ram Ram and He has come to me for the pure purpose of liberating my soul. I am now perfectly conscious of the transformation effected by Him in the last two days. My heart is pulsating with joy. There is a feeling in me of universal love. The ego is gone. I am now one with the Universal. Sai Baba with one great stroke has lifted me up from the mundane to the transcendental.

> Ah, it is today, my brightest day, it is my spiritual birthday, and in this day's silent celebration, the two friends who have helped me the most with extraordinary loyalty are you and Doraswami. You have helped me with your spiritual guidance, and Doraswami like a most faithful and devoted follower of Rishi Ram Ram has stood by me like a brick in the wall.
>
> Very soon, Sai Baba's work would come to an end and I will be given my new work. Rishi Ram Ram in one of his early

messages had asked me that I should prepare myself by re-reading all the message and write a book of personal experiences, as it would be original and would be a source of knowledge for those on the Path. I can't say anything now. I shall wait for the final consummation and be guided by the superior ones. My only wish is to be made an instrument, a channel for the dissemination of true knowledge – divine wisdom.

I thank you, Homi, a million times for your most illuminating guidance. But for it. I would have wandered in the dark and slipped from the Path."

I was now made to spend longer hours in the altar room for the achievement of final liberation in full consciousness.

On May 15, 1949, I was put into a long *samadhi,* twice in the morning and in the afternoon. But on both occasions, I was not conscious of the inner eye having opened.

I was then put to endurance test, which I passed through successfully to Sai Baba's satisfaction.

In the afternoon of the same day, Sai Baba told me:

"This was nothing but opening the inner centres and when these were opened you saw beautiful white clouds of light in its purest intensity, sometimes dazzling, but always bright and extremely lovely to behold. These rolling clouds of light of purest intensity and whiteness are the landmarks of our world. I showed you just enough that your eye could see and stand the strain of its brilliance. Your transformation is complete. You have seen our world's beauty with your naked physical eye. As soon as you become conscious of your inner eye, your soul will be able to visit all our worlds, at will, and when it comes back to your body, you will be able to retain the memory and impression of its experiences. You will thus be living in the two worlds – your earth plane and our spiritual world.

I feel extremely happy that by God's grace I have brought you to the present stage of your development. I have still a lot to do with you. At every step, more and more bewildering things will be witnessed by you and your soul would dance in ecstatic joy. You will live then in perpetual bliss.

I am making you universal-minded. When I pressed both your cheeks and both your ears with both your hands closed together, it was to tune you with the Universal Spirit. When I touched your heart with your folded hands and pressed it very deep, it was to make it vibrant with divine joy."

Rishi Ram Ram was delighted with the effects of transformation in me. He said: "I am dancing with joy to see you completely transformed. It is still not quite visible to you but I see it with my spiritual eyes. Your body is shining like fire. Your aura transfuses divine light in perfection. You would soon see us both."

Late at night Sai Baba suggested spiritual exercises of a very high order, the significance of which He explained to me as under:

"When I pressed the lower and the middle end of your spinal chord, with your two hands, it was to indicate that all the lower *chakras* in your body have now been entirely shut up and they will not function at all. You are now God-man, without the handicap of the lower organs. I have completely spiritualised your body and all its organ. You shall now live purely in spirit, through you feet will still be on the earth plane.

My foremost work now is to give you divine vision and this I will take up in my next course of instruction and guidance."

Preparations continued for higher training from day to day. Sai Baba touched both my eyes and made them spiritual. He made me yearn for God more and more intensely. In the evening of the 17th, He gave me the following message:

"I did put you into deep *samadhi* but as you were not in a position to stand the strain of a long samadhi, I had to take you out very quickly. Your body is weak. You are fit to become a *Jivan Mukta* but your body is poorly fitted. But as it is the wish of God that you must be liberated, I must carry out His order, whatever may happen, whether by so doing, you pass away or regain your physical body to serve mankind. You should therefore be prepared either way. In any case your object would be fulfilled, viz. spiritual liberation for which you are fit. It can not be delayed any longer, even if you are retained on your physical body, for God's decree has to be carried out. I shall therefore embark upon my final venture very soon."

On the following day, May 18, 1949, I was again put into *samadhi* in the morning.

Ram Ram gave me a long explanatory message, that it was part and parcel of their duty, while training a pupil on the path, to awaken expectancy in him and then to disappoint him, so that he may soon learn to become indifferent to everything – joy or sorrow, pleasure or pain, success or failure. He further said that it was my ailing body that made it so difficult for him to liberate the soul and therefore he was compelled to call in Sai Baba.

"I reveal to you this secret today. God is manifesting to you in the form of Sai Baba down to Him in utter devotion. To put it in the words of Homi, He is Asho Ahura Mazda Amshaspand. He is Amshaspand as well as God. You have heard Him. You will also soon see Him."

The secret was revealed that Sai Baba was none else than God Himself.

On May 20, 1949, at about 04:00 p.m. Sai Baba put me into an hour's fine samadhi. It was absolutely a blank samadhi. I was then told to sit in absolute silence and I had a most thrilling experience. Sai Baba's explanation of the incident is extremely beautiful. He said: "I made you close your eyes and you had a novel experience. You saw even with closed eyes, all glimmering light, scintillating light in streaks and stars, woolly clouds of light. Your consciousness is just beginning to rise. When you fully become aware of your inner eye when I shall open it entirely, you will be flooded with light and you would see God face to face. That would be the sublimation of your entire self, the last step in Self-realization."

In giving me the above message, Sai Baba also reminded me of the vows viz.,

(a) That I shall not make use of the powers that may be given to me for self-gratification.

(b) That I shall not hunger for name or fame but shall carry out God's mission in as silent a manner as possible.
(c) That I shall consider the interest of others before my own.
(d) That I shall teach every man, woman and child that I come in contact with, to love God who is the only REALITY, in the highest sense of the word.
(e) That I shall not exercise the power given to quit the physical body whenever I like, but leave it to God to call me away whenever He likes.
(f) That I shall resist all temptations, like a true yeoman.
(g) That I shall be indifferent and fearless in life.

In the evening of May 20, 1949, I was first asked to deeply concentrate my mind on the picture of Sai Baba and then I was told to sit in absolute silence. In that silent period of forty minutes. I saw some visions, the nature and significance of which were explained to me by Sai Baba.

Sai Baba said: "When you closed your eyes, you had some visions. There was a bright sparkling feminine figure whirling in light. You saw a man also clothed in light. In the intervals of lights, there were vacuums of absolute darkness, just to show you the difference between the functioning of the open eye and its absence."

On May 22, 1949, I was launched into a new phase of experience. A distinct step further towards the goal was taken. I was given consciousness of the Other World though it was but a faint and dim recollection.

Sai Baba said: "was it not extraordinary? I took you step by step from all the regions, the lowest to the highest. You have come now into the consciousness of our world, though the consciousness is still not complete. You have seen most beautiful sights and your mind was all the time magnetised. The devotion of your heart also was accentuated and you were praying all the time with folded hands. You were simply absorbed in the light of

> our divinity. An absolutely new phase has opened in your life. You are now initiated in our mysteries. Your soul can now take flight at will from your body and sojourn in our land, as it likes. You are now completely transformed. You are now one with God. Slowly all the powers will flow in you.
>
> Today, you felt a tremendous flow of electricity in your hands. This is the healing power which God in His great mercy and love has given you first. This is a miraculous power. Use it with discretion and in such a way that very few come to know of it.
>
> This is just a faint glimpse of our world, but it is sufficient to make you feel that you are now other-worldly. The mundane in you will soon melt away entirely. Your eye will now be all the time in out higher regions."
>
> Ram Ram further explaining the whole situation said: "You have reached the highest plane. You are now one of us. Now that you have been initiated by the greatest Celestial Being in our Hierarchy, all the mysteries of the universe will open out to your gaze like an open book. The seal has been broken. Your body will become a magnetic field. Your mind would become a reservoir of the highest mystical knowledge. You will get all knowledge first hand, direct from God. This altar should be now the holiest of holy places of you. It is here you have been first baptised in God's secrets. It is here you have taken the vows to keep fast to God, not to use your powers for self-gratification, to consider the interests of others before your own, and not to care for mundane things of life such as name and fame, riches of glory. It is because that we know that you would keep these vows that you have been consecrated and given the sacred initiation."

I was bewildered and filled with extreme joy. Had I seen God? Yes, if Sai Baba was God.

Ram Ram had warned me that Sai Baba was the greatest benefactor but at the same time, the greatest taskmaster. I was put to tests and postponements from day to day. After every step forward in the journey, he would contrive half a dozen of postponements and trials. All sorts of tests and traps were laid.

On May 27, 1949, Sai Baba said to me: "You know that I have transformed you but the last and final stage of transformation, when you see God face to face, has not still been reached. I am extremely happy to tell you that I am going to show myself to you today."

> Ram Ram followed up Sai Baba's message by saying: "Concentrate your mind on Sai Baba's and my pictures by intervals and you will have the greatest surprise to your life. You will see us both face to face – a unique honour."

I came in the evening at 7 p.m. and stayed in the altar room for an hour and a half, prayed and concentrated on the pictures of the Masters, as directed but nothing happened. It was a test.

Again and again, the same hope was raised till in the end by constant failures and disappointments, the edge of expectancy was rendered blunt and I became indifferent. On May 29, 1949, another stratagem was adopted: "If we do not give you self-realization within the next week, you will be called away." There was a secret longing in me to pass away and this message of the Master gave it a fillip. But the Master intervened and spoke in very endearing terms:

> "Don't ask for death, my dearest child. I shall reward you beyond your dreams. Have a stout heart and be patient." There was no other way but to obey the Master and the desire to shuffle off the mortal coil was checked.

I was then put into a long *samadhi,* which was not entirely blank, for I saw a beautiful glimmering red light of strong intensity appearing and receding." I was told that the light was the other covering of God. Sai Baba said: "Take it that you have seen God in the state of the highest super-consciousness." Ram Ram explained the significance of the phenomenon in the following message:

> "For the first time, your inner eye began to work and you saw a glimmering light of intense nature coming to you in cloud of red

> and then disappearing. This happened just a little before you came out from your samadhi. The light is the significance of God coming to you. You had the first vision of God........ Remember, God is Light. Light is the robe of God and it is only in this form that God can be sighted in the truest sense of the word."

The next day was a happier one. I was put into samadhi which lasted for nearly two hours – the longest that I had, so far.

On May 31, 1949, I went into *samadhi* of my own accord. This was the first time and it was a happy augury of the future. This is how Ram Ram explained to me in his message of that date:

> "This is the first time that you have gone into *samadhi* of your own free will. It was just to teach you to go into trance at your will that Sai Baba left you and went away. Of course He is just preparing you, for it was the beginning. But in future, He won't do even that. You must therefore see how much you are advancing and progressing."

I was overwhelmed with feelings of love and devotion for my Masters who had done so much for me. I could not restrain myself and bowed down my head before their pictures. Ram Ram said: "Try to subdue your feelings. Be calm."

I was made to go from a semi-trance state to full trance and then to revert to the semi-trance condition.

On June 12, 1949, I was told at the night sitting by Sai Baba: "I have now finished the training part of the whole course. Your soul is completely in tune with the infinite."

As a result of thorough training in the altar room for days and days together, from early morning till late at night, without much relaxation. I was enabled to go into *samadhi,* first with the aid of Sai Baba and later on, of my own accord, without any one's assistance. What Ram Ram could not do, Sai Baba did by opening the inner eye. But He did not allow it to function except partially and that too when a special occasion demanded it. Furthermore, two gifts were given to me viz. the power of blessing. There is so much of degradation and misery in life, that to bless those who plod on in the darkness of despair and to bring the light of love and hope in blasted lives is a great thing.

To bless all, to forgive all, to all and to work unreservedly without expectation of any reward is the supreme teaching of the Masters.

The Masters gave me to understand that the training had thoroughly transformed me and that I had attained the highest spiritual perfection. But there was no convincing proof of such exaltation. I had not seen God face to face. I had no even seen the Masters. I had not witnessed with my own eyes, the liberation of my own soul. All that I had was the Masters' assurance and, truly speaking, they must be considered as of prime importance. But still the desire for proof was there. It was but natural. The following message of Ram Ram, in this connection is heartening:

"We will give you a convincing proof of your highest spiritual exaltation as the days go on."

On June 3, 1949, I was given to understand that Sai Baba had taken me to God. Rishi Ram Ram explained it to me in the following message:

> "I told you last night that Sai Baba would take you to God positively. You are still not aware of it for you saw God in the state of *samadhi* and have no recollection of it. By and by as you get used to our Spiritual land by the constant visits of your soul to our Spirit World, Sai Baba will make you use your inner eye which is now fully open and then you will be able to realise the exalted state you have already reached."

I was made to understand that I should reckon myself now as a citizen of the universe, be universal – minded and love all without distinction of any nature.

In the afternoon of June 4, 1949, I was put into a long and deep *samadhi.*

As Sai Baba was trying to take my soul to the highest Spiritual Plane for the purpose of making me see God, I was asked to practise austerity and self-abnegation and to keep myself in the seclusion of the alter room for as many hours as possible, deeply absorbed in thoughts of God and God alone, to the entire exclusion of worldly duties and affairs.

On June 6, I went into a trance of my own accord. Sai Baba said:

> "You went into *samadhi* of your own accord for more than an hour and a half. Whenever you went into *samadhi* of your own accord before, it used to be for half an hour or so. You see how slowly but surely you are making progress."

Chapter Seventeen

Tests, Trials and Postponements (1949)

"You are ripe for Self-realization", "You have attained the highest pitch of perfection." "You will be taken to God face to face and you would see Him." "You would be stupefied and dazzled by the dazzling light of our Spiritual Plane which is your eternal abode." – these were the assurances held out by the Masters from day to day, from hour to hour. But weeks and months passed away thereafter without achievement of any success. Such are the trials and postponements in the attainment of the final goal in the journey of life. The idea of tests and postponements is to make the pupil absolutely indifferent to his own interest. Individuality has to be completely crushed. This is a hard test, a bitter pill, even expectation of Self-realization is an unwanted desire. To sacrifice everything, to surrender completely to the will of God – this is a *sine qua non* in the Path for the attainment of the goal.

An extremely hard test was put to me on June 8, 1949, I was asked on the previous night to come to the altar room in the morning as usual at 04:00 p.m. and that the Master would take me to God positively. I came to the altar room even a little earlier and lay flat on the ground for a long time, expecting that the Master would put me into *samadhi* and take me to God. It was futile. Nothing happened.

As soon as I got up from the floor, I said determinedly "I am willing to sacrifice Self-realization, the person who is in my mind." Sai Baba immediately replied: "All right. Your wish would be carried out. I am going now. But listen to Ram Ram.

Ram Ram then gave me the following message:

> "It was planned by us to put the hardest test to your life and I am extremely glad to say that you have passed that test with flying colours. For the sake of saving your relation from danger, you offered to give up the richest treasure of your life—Self-realization."

I wrote to Homi above the above incident and added:

> "...I must say frankly, I don't feel disappointed at all. There must be some hidden meaning in this. But one thing is true that self-sacrifice is greater than Self-realistion. When I say this, what I mean is that sacrifice should be our first principle of life and we should not sacrifice just for the purpose of attaining Self-realization which can only be achieved when God wills it and not otherwise."

In the evening at 07:30 p.m. Sai Baba gave me the following talk:

> "I want you to understand that you are a highly evolved soul. But you have preferred to miss the prize offered to you, in fact, won by you, for the mere sake of satisfying your whim about a certain person's safety. Do you still stick to that resolution? I give you a further chance. Say that you want Self-realization and it is no concern of you to think of other. If you affirm this now, I would take you to God straight off. Think it over carefully and tell me what you want – Self realization or the safety of this person for whom you have taken a mere fancy."

I replied: "I say definitely and emphatically that I am quite willing to sacrifice my own happiness, if by so doing her safety and happiness could be secured. I want her to be saved."

Sai Baba then said: "All right then. You have flouted Me who has all the time guided and brought you to the final stage of your journey."

I replied: "How can you say that I have flouted you? In fact, I am making the greatest sacrifice, because I know it is needed of me."

Sai Baba: "You are a most wonderful man. I again tell you, don't discard our offer. You haver earned it. It is yours. Why throw it away? When you get Self-realization, you can be of such immense service so many. Do you forget that ?

I said: "Yes, but not at the cost of this person who seeks my protection and whom I want you, Sai Baba, to save and protect. It does not matter if I lose the crown."

Sai Baba:

> "All right then, be satisfied. I shall not come to you from tomorrow. Don't invoke me at all. Do what you like. I have now nothing to do with you. You may talk to Ram Ram if you like. Possibly he may succeed in persuading you where I have failed."

Ram Ram then gave the following talk:

> "You have staked your life's greatest asset on one point viz,. that you want your relation to be saved and protected."

I said: "Yes, I do want that at any sacrifice of mine."

The Master replied: "Do you understand what that means? To save one person, you are losing the privilege of saving thousands when you get that power which is now within your reach. Why throw away the splendid opportunity, that you are getting , for a mere whim only?"

I replied: "Never mind, Self-realization at the sacrifice of her life's happiness and salvation is not worth it.

Ram Ram: "Yes, in my heart of hearts I am extremely pleased and I bless you. But I myself am helpless. I have carried out my duty in persuading you, as required of me, by the superior order. I can't do anything more. You can't invoke Sai Baba and I am extremely sorry to say, you can't invoke me also, hereafter. We leave you entirely to God.

The next day in the afternoon, I could not help invoking Sai Baba though He had ordered me not to invoke Him.

> He said: "My dearest child, you are extremely loving to me. I knew that you would invoke me again. I see that your love for me is so genuine that I can't resist responding to you."

The Masters were teaching me the quintessence of spirituality by making me indifferent to everything that was external.

On June 12, in the morning, I thought that the Master would put me into *samadhi* as usual. But the Master changed His mind.

> The postponements made wonder whether I was wasting my time by giving it entirely to the altar room, detrimental to my other duties in life. Ram Ram at once warned me: "I want you to quieten your mind and not be discouraged by failures which are really not failures but appear to you as failures."

In the afternoon, I was rewarded by Sai Baba putting me in a fine *samadhi*, which culminated in my seeing Sai Baba in the same form and posture as in his photograph in my altar room. Sai Baba said: "Today's *samadhi* from my point of view is the best in the whole series so far, for it culminated in your seeing Me with your eye."

On June 13, I was given an experience of a new kind of *samadhi* at night which was explained to me by Sai Baba as under:

> "I put you in a very queer state not hitherto experienced by you. It is a new kind of *samadhi*, when you have no consciousness of this world at all but the same time your mind is working and you are conscious of the working of the mind and nothing else. You did not hear the clock striking. You did not hear any of the outside sounds and noises but at the same time you know and were conscious about yourself. This is a rare and very difficult state. To lose consciousness of the external world but not to lose the consciousness of the working of your own mind is difficult to achieve. I am glad you have achieved it today."

I had no desire now for anything except God. On June 14, Sai Baba said: "God wants to talk to you direct. And I heard Him, saying distinctly: "Yes I am God, I want you to come to Me.

What a tremendous change after an upheaval of tests and trails to hear the voice of God, calling me to Him!

"Cry for God all the time, as a child cries for its mother and you will become one with God," said the Master.

On June 15, I was put to an endurance test. Electric shocks were given. They were indications also of my having crossed the perilous portion of the journey. Again the promise was held out: "I am going to make the final preparation and take you to God. "The promise as usual did not materialise."

I was again put to severe endurance test on the June 17, 1949, when in a state of *samadhi* I was made to negotiate the perilous portion of the journey. Sai Baba said:

> "Today is the peak of your experience. I had to spiritualise your body entirely to take you on the momentous journey"

On June 18, I was told once again that Sai Baba would take me to God. Instead of taking me to God, I was made to sleep in the altar room, which was very annoying and degrading.

On June 19, Sai Baba made it clear to me:

> "It is just to make you realise this fact, that you must rise above all disappointments that I am compelled to prolong your tests and trials. If you adopt an attitude of absolute indifference to failures, you will make your way easier."

The following day *i.e.*, June 20, 1949, Sai Baba said: "I want to take you to God positively. Sit in absolute silence." Nothing was done, Sai Baba gave me following explanation:

> "I have told you that you should not expect anything. I said that I would take you positively to God just to test you and nothing else."

On June 22, the Master exhorted me: "Forget it entirely that you are going to realise the Self. Only concentrate your mind, heart and soul on God and God alone. Think of God, every minute and every moment. For you, nothing should exist except God."

On June 23, the Master was again not able to take me to God.

The following message of Ram Ram of the same date is soul stirring and sublime in its expression of thought and feeling.

> *"Sai Baba is so much pleased with you that he has called you his dearest child. It is an indication that you will soon realise the Self. Have not the least anxiety of fear. We are by your side and we shall do everything for you. You are one with God already. Why are you creating disturbance in your mind and thus inviting greater calamities? Learn to control yourself under all circumstances, good or bad, provocative or not. Leave everything to God. Think that you are living only to carry out orders of God. Talk of God, think of God and translate all your actions in the language of God. To you nothing exists but God, see God in everything."*

On the June 24, I was put to severe endurance tests. On June 25, I was again warned by Sai Baba that I must not get deterred by constant postponements. He said: "The altar room is your sanctuary where you will learn the mysteries of nature and will be blessed with strange powers, which will simply stun you."

I asked the Master, "Why is it that my inner eye which is said to be open, is not allowed to function?"

Ram Ram said: "That is the main difficulty. We have to proceed extremely slowly in your case, for if we allow the eye which is open to function, you will get burnt by the tremendous light of our world."

> In the afternoon of June 28, Ram Ram actually described to me how God would appear to me, "Today in the evening. Sai Baba is going to show Himself to you. He will appear to you in a glow of red light and you will see Him in the state of *samadhi, with* your inner eye. It is God who will manifest to you as Sai Baba, God can

> take any form and as you have been accustomed to concentrate on Sai Baba. He has chosen in your case to come to you in the form of Sai Baba. The indication that He is God is the tremendous light in which He will be clothed continuously. Pray and keep your mind absolutely calm and composed."

As fully expected, nothing of the sort happened.

Constant failures in spite of Sai Baba's and Ram Ram's assurances and explanations had some adverse effect upon my mind. I began to fear that I was wasting my time in the altar room sittings. There was a strong temptation to withdraw and resume my daily duties in life. Rishi Ram Ram immediately administered to me a rebuke. He said:

> "The constant failures and postponements have had an adverse effect upon you, which hampers your spiritual growth. A man like you on the contrary should stand firm as a rock and not care a straw for such a state of affairs. Have absolute and complete reliance is us. Don't give in at the last moment to the temptation of leaving us. The altar room is your sanctuary."

After 08:00 p.m. on June 29, 1949, I was given beautiful spiritual exercises by Sai Baba. Magnetic-electric current was passed through both my hands and they moved up and down in perfect synthesis and harmony, as explained by the Masters, with the inward spirit in ecstatic bliss. This made me firm in my resolution to stick to the altar room.

On June 30, 1949, I was put into a peculiar type of *samadhi.* It was to enable my Master to tap my subconscious mind and to test my inward parts.

On July 1, 1949, the Master again warned me:

> "I have told you a thousand times to be indifferent to everything. Only carry out our orders, however trying and silly they may seem to be. The difficulties in realising the Self are being created by your doubts and suspicions. You are hindering our work.
>
> Why don't you leave everything to us, your Master, and have complete faith in God's verdict that you will reach the goal. Whatever be the postponements, there should be in your mind

this deep-rooted conviction that you are going to realise the Self. Without this conviction, you will be rendering our work extremely difficult."

On July 3, 1949, Sai Baba gave me the following message:

> My work is now nearly finished. There is no ego in you. There is no desire of the flesh in you. Your mind is the essence of purity. You want Self-realization only for this purpose, with widened powers you could be of considerable help to people on your earth plane. God is extremely pleased with you.

I was put to test again on July 5, 1949. As usual I was asked to close my eyes and sit in absolute silence. I did so keeping my mind absorbed in thoughts of God. Instead of falling into *samadhi*, I went into a short sleep, much against my will. I felt dejected – rather ashamed. Sai Baba explained:

> "Do you know what I tried to do? I tried my best to put all sorts of temptations in your way, but like a veteran soldier you stood firm and ignored them all." I was warned that I must sleep at night for at least five hours at a stretch. Four hours of sleep was not enough.
>
> On July 7, Sai Baba: "I must test you and find out how far you can stand patiently all the disappointments and postponements I am putting you to. This is a part of my duty. When I find that You are completely indifferent and have learned to be absolutely calm in all circumstances, I shall take you to God."

On July 8, in the afternoon Sai Baba again put me to a severe sleep test.

Sai Baba said afterwards:

> "I am extremely glad to say that you have now passed my test to my complete satisfaction. I wanted you to go into sleep but in spite of my efforts, instead of going into sleep, you went into *samadhi.* I pulled you out from *samadhi* and again there was resistance. Once or twice I succeeded and you had a very, very short sleep but on the whole the success was yours and I congratulate you. I am not going to put you into any more struggle. Talk to Ram Ram. He will give you a detailed explanation."

Ram Ram gave this message:

> "You have scored a tremendous victory. Your soul was pitted against the gigantic spirit of Sai Baba. He wanted to frustrate you but your tiny soul overmastered the giant. I have never in my spiritual career seen such a struggle between a human soul aspiring for freedom, making such a contest against extraordinary handicaps, specially brought against it to test its merit. I say with all the emphasis at my command that today's sitting of all the sittings so far, must be considered as the greatest event of your life. Sai Baba wanted you to go into deep sleep and you wanted to go into deep and long *samadhi.* You succeeded in going into *samadhi* but Sai Baba pulled you out by the strength of his great spiritual power.
>
> The minute you were pulled out, He tried the old game of shoving you into sleep. Once or twice he did succeed and you got just a slight and superficial dream, lasting for a few minutes only. On the whole, you were in *samadhi* and when awake, your mind was fixed of God. In the waking state you felt tremendous energy passing through your hands."

It was my determination and the sense of shame that I should go to sleep even for ten minutes in such a sacred place as the altar room in the presence of my revered teachers that gave me the inward strength to resist all temptations put to me, and by God's grace I succeeded.

The following day, *i.e.* July 9, 1949. I was put to very severe endurance test. The significance of tests, trials and postponements was explained to me by Sai Baba in his talk on July 9, 1949, which is of considerable interest:

> "You have transcended all the three bodies, the gross, the subtle and the mental and you would soon realise the Self. Why are there postponements all the time? It is because to teach you a lesson that you should not be carried away by any high notions of your own spirituality. We have tested you so bitterly and have put you to so much of agony that God in His mercy now wants you to be lifted up and to show Himself to you. He will come to you of His own accord. Bow down to Him and pray to Him most reverently.
>
> Keep up your devotion. You are fit or not fit, it is not for any one to judge, expect God Himself. But be at ease. I assure you that you are conscious of this great achievement."

In the ordinary course, it would appear to anyone that as everything has a limit, there should be and end to tests and postponements also after a reasonable period of preparation. But in matters spiritual, mundane logic plays no part. Perfect obedience to Master's orders and commands, whether they be reasonable or unreasonable, contradictory or not contradictory, pleasant or unpleasant, wise or foolish, is the first and most important commandment.

Inspite of my success in they many sleep tests on July 10th, I came to the altar room early in the morning as usual at 4 O'clock. Sai Baba greeted me with these words:

> *"Kindly note my orders and God's orders are identical. When you obey Me, you are obeying God. "As usual, He said asked me to sit in absolute silence and to close my eyes. He said: "I want to put you into a long and deep samadhi."*

As a rule, it is easier to go into *samadhi* when lying down flat on the ground but there is also the danger of slipping into sleep instead of reaching *samadhi,* if the Master is bent upon it. I therefore refused to lie down but continued sitting erect, for two hours, deeply lost it meditation.

Sai Baba was extremely pleased. He said:

> "I am extremely glad to say that your meditation was beautiful. God is much pleased with you. You are advancing rapidly."

Again the same day, in the afternoon, Sai Baba subjected me to the same kind of test and by God's grace, I came our successfully. The following was his explanation:

> "...You must be wondering why all the time I say that your tests are over and still I put you to more tests without compunction. There is a deep mystery in it. You must remember that you are on the mystical path leading to the highest form of divine justice. These tests are to weigh you in our divine scale and to see and watch your progress form day to day. We are weighing you in our balance all your thoughts, all your actions, all your aspirations, all your emotions, and I am extremely happy to say that you are coming up to our expectations."

Chapter Eighteen

Further Progress on the Path (1949)

Self-realization is the most difficult, and yet necessary, goal of every human soul thirsting and longing for God, whose power, goodness, wisdom, love and glory the seeker feels in the heart and mind as he rises higher and higher towards supeconsciouness.

Spint Master Rishi Ram Ram was appointed by God from my birth as my guardian angel. He worked invisibly throughout my life, except on the last few years, and guarded me like a mother guards her child.

Let me speak in his own words:

> "I had to take charge of you when you were born on the earth plane. I was appointed by God as your guardian angel. Rarely does the Master appoint guardian angels for newly born souls. But you were destined for the highest spiritual exaltation. It appeared that you would take at least one more incarnation but I put you on the Path and I saw that you were capable of winning the goal in this life. My work is now more or less over, although I would be with you till the last hour of your earthly journey. From now on, Sai Baba will steer the ship of your life and bring your soul to safe anchorage in God's port. Come to Me every night before retiring and I shall pour my blessings on you. Don't forget.

I say this because there is a deep significance in my statement which you will come to know of later."

On July 12th, 1949, Sai Baba this important announcement to me: "You are to be elected as a Master today in our spiritual world with a mission to work in body, on your earth plane at least for some time till God calls you away. This message was given to me at 02:00 p.m. and I went into *samadhi.*

"I had told you earlier that you will be elected a Master in our Spiritual World, today. The ceremony took place when I made you lie down in the evening. You are now a treasure house of light and joy. We have passed into you tremendous currents of energy and electricity. In fact, every tissue of your body and brain has been vitalised and spiritualised. Your head became stiff with the weight of the currents passing and repassing. Even now you feel the stiffness but it will soon pass. You are now a new man. You have gone through our spiritual baptism. Every day till you reach the goal of Self-realization I will take you higher and higher in the scale of spirituality and put into you greater strength for the mission that you have to perform."

The spiritual baptism made me God-intoxicated. Every time, I entered the altar room, the yearning and longing for God increased. Sai Baba said: "This is due to My presence, you can't see Me with your physical eyes but all the time you are feeling My presence through your subconscious."

Inn reply to Homi's questions regarding the significance and meaning of (1) *Samadhi* (2) Inner eye and (3) Superconsciousness the Master said:

"*Samadhi,* Inner Eye and Superconsciousness – these are the three most widely used terms in the soul's journey towards Self-realization. You have experienced all these three things. A man is said to be in *samadhi* when his soul temporarily leaves the physical body, not as in deep sleep, but in full awareness. When the soul temporarily leaves the physical body, the consciousness of the external world ceases. If the soul leaves the body with the inner eye opened, it can see all the invisible worlds and bring with it impressions of its experiences when it returns to the body.

Superconsciousness is the highest state of consciousness when you feel and see and hear not with your physical senses but with the senses that are superphysical, too subtle to be described.

The inner eye, however, should not be confused with clairvoyance. Clairvoyance is a psychic gift. The inner eye is the yogic eye to be gained by one's own purity of thought and action, complete renunciation and devotion to God."

On July 13th, Ram Ram explained to me that I was being taken step upwards by Sai Baba in an invisible manner. The Master were preparing to fill in the gap between mind and the supermind and this was explained by Sai Baba in the following message:

> "I am building up for you the bridge to the supermind, the reservoir of the spiritual consciousness. When the gulf between the mind and the supermind is bridged, you will be in state of superconsciousness of the highest cosmic nature."

Often the Master declared that He would show Himself to me but it never happened on the dates specified by Him. These declarations were mere tests to find out whether I had developed the feeling of complete indifference to everything. On the July 18th, 1949 sai Baba said to me: "I will show Myself to you only when you reach the stage of absolute detachment and indifference. You need not waste time hankering after Me. You have already realised Him but you are not aware of your realization. This is because of certain factors that still work against you."

I enquired: "What are those factors?

Sai Baba replied:

> "You have made your altar room your sanctuary. You have made all the sacrifices needed. You have crushed the ego in you. Your devotion to God is spontaneous and genuine. I have said it a hundred times and I say it again that you are absolutely fit for Self-realization. But God Still wants to test you. Be firm in your attitude. Don't waver; don't hesitate. There is absolutely no necessity for you to make any deviation. It is your constant

attendance at the altar room that he hastened your progress. If you stop that, you will be stopping your further progress."

Ram Ram then gave a very illuminating interpretation of the message of Sai Baba:

"All that you have to do is to continue coming to the altar room as you are doing now, without expectation of any kind. Don't expect, don't hanker for anything, not even God-realization."

On July 21, 1949, I was again put into a long *samadhi* by Sai Baba. His description of the *samadhi* is both interesting and instructive:

"I put you into a long *samadhi* and it would have been much longer had I not pulled you out of it suddenly to test your vigour of body. Often it takes a long time for the body to become active. In your case today your right hand had become so numb after *samadhi* that I had to give you vigorous exercises to makes the blood flow again into it. Had you gone into a longer *samadhi,* it would have been difficult for me to make your body function as usual. Don't think that going into a *samadhi* is easy."

On July 26, 1949, Ram Ram gave me a very important message. I was informed that the *Atma* or the Spirit which is latent in every human being, was now conscious in me and that I was now talking to my *Atma* and not Ram Ram:

"It is not I, your Master, but your own *Atma,* that is talking to you. My purpose was to awaken your inner consciousness and this has now been accomplished. On the day when I said: "I and you are one, the achievement was made. You knew your Self, though you are still not aware of this. But this awareness is still vague and hazy. Our purpose now is to make it definite. Sai Baba has undertaken this work and you will realize it very soon. But I still continue to be your Master and will be your helpmate, when you realise the Self, completely and wholly."

On July 30, 1949 I was put into a sort of semi-trance. When I came out of it, Sai Baba explained the phenomenon thus:

"You have entered the Balance of Glory but you have not seen God. You would soon see Him. Your meditation today was

> excellent and continuous. In your trance, you saw light white, dazzling starry. They are the gateways of God's Mansion in the Spiritual Plane."

Ram Ram then explained to me in detail the whole incident:

> "Sai Baba has asked me to give you an elaborate description of what you experienced in your semi-trance state. He opened your inner eye to see how it works in a semi-trance and He is extremely pleased. When He puts you into full *samadhi*, with your inner eye properly open, you will be able to see marvellous things. Even now you had a faint glimpse of our world. You saw God's Palace. You saw some starry lights. You saw a dazzling glow but not so dazzling as to bewilder you. You were in a state of joyousness all the time and even now you feel a joy and serenity in your heart and mind. These are the fragrance that you have brought from our world."

On August 3, 1949, I was told by Sai Baba that my body was so thoroughly spiritualised now that it was now easy for Him to enter any part of it and carry our spiritual surgery.

Ram Ram explained Sai Baba's spiritual surgery in this message:

> "You have no idea what a marvellous thing Sai Baba has done for you today. He spiritualised your whole body including your mind to enable Him to enter into you and stop the working of your roaming mind. Having done that, he made you feel in a very hazy manner the novelty of your surroundings. Throughout all this, you were in your senses, for it was not a full *samadhi*. You were in a state of semi-trance, just hovering between blankness and reality. This experiepnce was given to you to show that you have now passed the mundane stage and are capable of entering into the highest spiritual state of the highest superconsciousness, culmination in ONENESS WITH GOD."

> Regarding the question of Self-realization, Sai Baba said: "Self-realization is ordained for you in this very life. But before you achieve it. I must satisfy Myself whether you conform to the regulation fixed by us for you, the most important of which is non-expectancy and complete indifference."

It is very necessary for the seeker to sit erect while meditating. This helps the Master to open up the chakras and hasten spiritual progress. And that's what Sai Baba did.

Later, Ram Ram explained to me what Sai Baba had done:

> "He has opened your *Ajna Chakra*, between the two eye brows, which is the seat of the inner eye and i am glad to tell you that He has done it most successfully. Your soul is now free to roam about in any way it likes. It can escape from the body at will and return to it in your full consciousness. You will come to know of this achievement when Sai Baba gives you practical proofs of the soul escaping from the body and making its visits to our world in full consciousness. The black large sized speck that you saw flitting in a halo of rising red is the indicator of your spiritual flight that will shortly follow. This speck is not really black, but as your vision is still clouded, it looked black. It is actually pure white as you will notice later."

In the evening of the same day, Sai Baba explained to me how, after hundreds of tests, He was certain that I should now be prepared for still higher spiritual:

> You have now overcome all difficulties. This marks the final step in your journey towards Self-realization.
>
> From tomorrow, your progress would be phenomenal. You will gain new powers rapidly and the power you have will be intensified. Be happy and pray to God all the time that He has allowed His grace to descend upon you. Let me now consecrate you and pour God's own blessings."
>
> It was a day of great spiritual joy. God Himself has consecrated me. For Sai Baba was a Master of Master, the highest in the Hierarchy of Divine Beings. In the words of Rishi Ram Ram: "He is God Himself, if you look upon God, not as the Absolute Spirit, pervading through out the universe, but Ahuram Mazda Amshaspand – the greatest representative of God among all His representatives."

Chapter Nineteen

A Beginning in Self-realization (1949)

There are two classes of aspirations of the path of self-realization. The first class comprises those who believe in taking gradual step, allowing nature to take its own course and do not mind tarrying on the path. The second class is made up of those who make frantic efforts and are keen to reach the goal as soon as possible. The shorter the route, the lesser the time, and the greater the pain. I chose the painful path for my desire to see God was so deep that an intense effort appeared to be the only possible route.

I looked upon Homi as my guide but I refused to abide by his counsel when he advised me to go slow. When the heart is burning with inexhaustible devotion and love for God, when all the nerves are aflame, how could the urge to reach god be checked?

It is true that my chosen path subjected me to hardest of trials. But my determination and sincerity finally won the day.

After a period of continuous tests and trials, I began to feel that I was at last treading on firm ground. I was able to perfect my meditation by long and continuous practice. The early hours in the morning, usually starting from 04:00 a.m. and several times even 02:00 a.m., and in the night up to 08:00 to 08:30 a.m. were the most important for training. In fact, when ordered by the Masters, the altar room was made the seat of activity from early morning till late at night. Sometimes whole days and nights were continuously passed in the altar room.

On the August 6, 1949, I wrote to Homi, "A strange feelings is coming over me, viz., a yearning to get experiences directly and not through books written by others. No wonder, Ram Ram told me some time ago not to waste time on reading books.

The altar room was earlier a ground of severe drill and training. It is now becoming an arena of blissful enjoyment. So long as there was that vigorous drill of tests and trials, I persevered with zest. But now, when victory is in sight, I only pray, that I may soon realise Self and be given powers to use for the good of others.

A friend recently wrote to me that of what avail is Self-realization, when millions are starving and dying and the pang of human suffering is so great all around us. He is right, but with Self-realization we can help ameliorate human suffering. At least this is my objective in seeking Self-realization – the power and ability to transform the lives of individuals and nations."

I have purposely quoted the above extract from my letter to Homi, to clarify that my objective was human service and not selfish blissful enjoyment. In fact, when a man reaches the state of adeptship *i.e.*, attains Jivan Mukti, he becomes universal minded. Active or inactive, he is all the time helping the cause of evolution even in the midst of apparent inactivity, as in the case of Sri Ramana, the Sage of Arunachala.

On August 12, a most notable step was taken. I was told by the Master that He had taken me to God. It is better to describe the whole thing in the Master's words:

"Do you know that I have taken you to God? You saw Him but your eyes were blind at the time. All that you felt was a sudden flow of joyousness in your heart. This feeling still continues – the result of an inward contact with God. At the next stage of development, I shall take you to Him with eyes open. You saw Him when you were put into a short *samadhi.* Had I opened your inner eye, you could have seen Him face to face. But it was still too early."

I was doubtful, for I was not at all aware of having seen God and therefore I put the following question to Sai Baba: "It is the real thing only when I see Him in fullest consciousness. Don't you think so?

Sai Baba replied: "No. Only the pure in heart can see God and you were able to see Him through my guidance in a state of unconsciousness."

On the August 13, 1949, I had and enthralling experience, the fragrant memory of which will remain with me till the last date of my existence on this earth plane. Sai Baba said to me that while I was meditating in the morning, He opened my inner eye slightly. I heard the chanting of a divine song in a strange language, quite unknown to me. I was carried away by the ravishing intonation of its rhythmic expression.

After the music had died away, I saw tints of light. It is better to describe the whole phenomenon in the words of Sai Baba Himself:

"You were in an enraptured state of meditation when I guided you quietly and softly to the lofty heights of true spirituality. At this stage I opened your inner eye and you saw in a flash a strange human form come to you as if in a vision. It was not a vision. It was a true phenomenon and you were struck with awe and wonder. Do you know, who that person was? It was God Himself, who took the form of man, bewildered you and disappeared. He has left a trail of light in your heart, which will now never perish. He has fastened you to Himself. You and He are now one. You have realised Self – the dream of your life, – the goal of your life. What more should I say? The minute you saw Him, You bent down your head in reverential awe, thus paying

> your heart's tribute to Him who rules the universe and whose Love embraces all in a uniform pattern."

In my ignorance or innocence, I took this experience for Self-realization and I wrote to Homi as under: "I had the strangest and happiest experience today. Little I had thought when I entered the altar room that I would realise Self so soon. The mingled feeling of joy and awe still continues unabated. I am so very grateful to God for this happy culmination of my soul's desire."

Homi replied to my letter thus:

> "I congratulate you on the sight of God but I confess I am bewildered and do not know whether you should call it complete Self-realization when God constantly abides with you and you can see and communicate with Him whenever you want to, and that too consciously."

Ram Ram explained this experience as under:

> "Today God has shown Himself to you in the figure of a man. He will show Himself in various other forms also and you will recognize Him when you feel an extraordinary joy, combined with a deep sense of awe and reverence. Each time when you see Him you would bow down in deep gratitude and joyousness. That will be an indication of the divine manifestation. The music that thrilled you was not ordinary astral music but the voice of God, that came in rhythmic notes from the Highest Abode in our Spiritual World.

On August 15, 1949 Rishi Ram Ram informed me:

> "From tomorrow onwards, as your *chakras* are open, you will begin to acquire greater and greater powers. In the course of a month or so, you will see yourself as absolutely changed. You will surprise all your friends who would not even believe that such a great change could come over you. In fact, they would be the first to ridicule and oppose you."

On August 22, 1949, I glimpsed God for the second time. Sai Baba's following message is descriptive of this incident:

> "Today you again had a glimpse of God. He came to you all of a sudden in the same form that you had seen before, burning red in appearance. He came without giving you the slightest indication or warning. He is very fond of you and He loves you."

I was also told that I would see God more frequently till such time when He would abide in Me permanently.

My love for God had by then been so accentuated that all the time I felt immersed in His bliss. Nothing mattered to me but God. God was the pivot of my life. He was the helm. He was the stem. He was my food, my nectar. Nay, He was the very breath of my life. Everything appeared to me unreal. I experienced that life was a mere illusion. I felt its emptiness. To see God, to talk with God and to be in perpetual communion with Him became the only object of my life. It was an intoxication.

That I was rapidly advancing to the highest stage of superconsciousness was indicated when Sai Baba said he was preparing me for a change in the mode of meditation from the *Ajna Centre* to the Brahman Chakra, in the crown of the head. Meditation on this highest chakra is permissible only when the aspirant reaches the highest state of spirituality. It leads to rhapsodic prayer-fulness and thanks giving to God. It is the inner gateway to complete Self-realization.

The following message of Ram Ram shows how the Master is to the pupil aspiring for Self-realization:

> "Sai Baba has shown you, your capabilities and your powers. These are the results of your own achievement. We have merely helped you realise your inner potentialities. But for us, they would have remained dormant for a long time. It is in this way we Masters serve humanity. We select pupils to play an important role in God's plan of evolution on the earth plane. We selected you because we saw by the light of your aura that you were fit for the purpose."

In the evening of 25th I saw in meditation an enchanting and soul stirring phenomenon of light. Sai Baba described them thus:

"Our World is composed of Light and nothing but Light. Therefore you see Light in various forms and colors, deep and dim, sparkling and hazy, in billows, flashing like fire at one time and quite tame the next instant, like sheet of snow. You are surrounded with light. Your soul is light. You are light and your mission would be to give light to all. God is LIGHT and He wants every one to be merged in a universal light of peace and joy, ever abounding the hearts of all."

What words of Love and Light! It reminds me of Leadbeater's musing on the word "Light." He says: "God is Light; Light is God; Man is Light; all is Light, – a new meaning to the ancient Egyptian exhortations: "Look for the Light! Follow the Light! Perceive and learn to be at one with the Light of God in all things.

I took upon the world. I see the world in terms of Light. God-Light manifest in man-light, rock-light, tree-light, creature-light. All is light – a blinding glory at the centre, translated into colour as it radiates towards its circumference. The blinding glory everywhere – the God light – the blazing seed of futurity in each individual thing in every kingdom.

I perceive the Light, which is dull, – the savage; the Light which is bright, – the man evolved; the Light which is glory – the Superman, the Master. I see colour everywhere in process of transmutation, of glorification, of transcendence. There is no blackness anywhere in the sense of a negation of Light. God said: "Let there be light. And there was and is Light everywhere!" "His Lights shineth even in our darkness."

(Leadbeater's *The Masters and the Path,* page 331)

On August 24, 1949, I was not well. My stomach was giving me trouble and I had a bad night. My mind was also greatly perturbed by some worries. Forgetting the vow that I had taken, I must have unconsciously or secretly desired that God call me away. In the morning when I got up I was much better. The fever had subsided and the pain in my stomach much reduced. I had absolutely no idea that I was on the verge of passing away.

I was in the altar room when Homi's letter of August 28, was passed on to me. It contained the news that Ram Ram had come to him on the 24th in a cloud of beautiful white light. He had told Homi that I had taken very ill and was very near death and that he should pray to God to spare my life. Homi accordingly prayed for me. He also warned me in his letter not to violate the vow taken viz. not to assert my right to leave mortal coils and that if I did so, it would mean rebirth for me.

This incident has been related to show that I really had the power of dying whenever I liked and would have surely passed away but for certain reasons, which saved me from such a catastrophe. Sai Baba's message on September 2, 1949, in reply to Homi's letter pertaining to this incident is explanatory. He said:

> "I must say that you were on the verge of breaking your promise of not asking for death, quite unknowingly of course. You got over that difficult stage by a narrow margin. God is good to you. He is protecting you and putting you on the sage path. This is because of our love and devotion for God."
>
> Now you are absolutely alert and I know for a fact that, whatever may happen, you will face your difficulties bravely like a lion. You have family trouble that might accentuate. But it has been is specially planned by us to test how far you can maintain perfect equanimity of mind. You are a yogi of yogis. Why do you allow your mind to be perturbed by small bubbles in? Be brave and show your absolute indifference.
>
> "Regarding the latter part of Homi's letter, your Self-realization is quite safe. You won't lose your Nirvana and you won't ask for death at all after My today's exposition. Homi has rendered a signal service by warning you. He is a great soul, fit to be your guide on earth. We shall reward him for the great service that he has rendered to you. Go by his guidance."
>
> On September 5, 1949, Sai Baba told me when I got up from *samadhi*:
>
> For the course of half an hour I took away your soul from the body, putting you into a state of *samadhi.* The soul escaped from the the cavity of the brain by way of the Crown Chakra. As a rule your body

> ought to have fallen down lifeless with the escape of the soul, but I held it tight by my magnetic force. When the soul escaped from the body, you felt an intense tension to break down. You even lost your breath and you felt exhausted, not knowing what was all being done. The hands that were raised above in intense feeling of excitement indicated that something unusual had happened and you felt it but you could not grasp at all its significance."
>
> I enquired: "How did the soul leave and how did I feel when it returned?"
>
> Sai Baba replied:
>
> "Your soul went away with a jerk but when it entered again into the body, it was without the least disturbance. It was like slipping into an empty room. I have done all this with a view to examine how my preparations have borne fruit. I am satisfied in every respect."

Chakras are the gateways to celestial powers, what are called *Siddhis.* Miraculous powers are attained when *chakras* open and begin to function. These powers are doing good to humanity, and are required to be used silently and unostentationiously. If a person uses them for self-aggrandisement or out of vanity, he exposes himself to great danger. The *chakras* open out when the *Kundalini* is awakened by means of Indian yoga system. Although the process of awakening Kundalini is fraught with great danger, yet when a pupil is being guided by a Spirit Guide and Master, he has nothing to be afraid of. The Master is aware of all the pitfalls and dangers and is capable of piloting his pupil through safe waters. The following message of Sai Baba describes the care and devotion that a Master lavishes his pupil when He open his *chakras* for higher training and for attaining powers:

> "The *chakras* when open are a source of great danger to you. For your safety, I close them up when you leave the altar room and open them again when you return. You can open them at will, but you still can not close them when you wish. For this reason, I have posted Ram Ram to keep a vigilant guard on you. You see how exceptionally careful we are for you. When you realise the Self,

you will be able to open and close your *chakras* at will. Then even if any lower astral gets into you through the lower chakras, you can remove the spirit.

I am glad that during all these days, you have never given a thought to open your chakras. This indifference is exceedingly beautiful. Keep up this indifference and have no curiosity.

"When a pupil is on the last lap of he journey the temptation to slip from the path becomes irresistible. The progress is so extremely slow that it is enough to tire out any one. During this crucial period, I was ordered to observe silence for the purpose of questioning the mind. This was continued for several days."

Several times Sai Baba had told me He would come to me in radiant light but the promise never materialised.

The Masters had also promised to make me clairvoyant – something that was yet to happen. Rishi Ram Ram explained the delay thus:

"We could have made you clairvoyant long ago. But Sai Baba wants to do everything simultaneously. You have reached the state of highest spirituality and He wants to open the flood-gates of God's Light straight off. God is Light. It is Light born of Love – Universal Love. Pray to God earnestly. Forget yourself entirely in the vision of God and He will come to you quicker."

Later, however, Sai Baba Made a frank admission: "It is still premature to take you to God. You will have to wait."

I asked: "Does this mean that I am not fit?" Sai Baba replied "Not at all. You are absolutely fit.......All these precautions are being taken because you have an important mission to perform."

Ram Ram also reiterated Sai Baba's message:

"Do not take our words literally. When the Masters say they are going to take me to God, I must not think it will be done. Their statements have a deep inner meaning and it is this inner sense that has to be understood."

As days rolled on, my devotion to God intensified. Even while taking down the Master's Message, my head would often fall down and I would cry like a child for its mother.

A strange kind of feeling gripped me. I felt that my heart was linked with God and this link was becoming stronger by the hour.

In his letter of September 4th, 1949, Homi informed me that he had been graced by a visit from Ram Ram who had given him a message for me. The message was that I should cultivate the habit of thinking or contemplation. Homi said:

> "You possess a spotlessly good heart but what you also need for your Divine Mission is good discernment and such discernment can come only form deep thinking and clear understanding.
>
> "Further, this habit of deep thought is essential in all matter, be it mundane or spiritual. You are soft-hearted and selfless. But your very love for fellow beings is likely to make you harm those to whom your love flows out. Such love requires discernment."

Homi also warned me against being impatient at delays and my recurring desire for God – realization. "Remember", wrote Homi, "as Sai Baba points out, that you are now passing through a danger zone – a terrible state of trial."

I replied to Homi:

> "..... How good and kind are the Masters. The fault is mine. I am still not fit to have the vision of God. Believe me, the desire for Self-realization is now gone. The only question is how long – how long, will this play continue?"

After absenting himself for the whole day Sai Baba came to me again on September 17, 1949 and gave me the following message:

> "..... My dear son, don't come to any hasty conclusion. I have read you letter to Homi. It opens out your mind and heart to him. It also shows what you unfortunately still lack good discernment. Why did you come to the hasty conclusion that your are still not fit for God's vision when I have told you so many times in the messages that you are absolutely fit. We have certain reasons for delaying the final consummation of your cherished dream. You have a mission to perform and for that great work you have to be prepared in every way. It takes time. I say emphatically that you

have reached your goal. This very moment I can take you to God in your fullest consciousness. But we still have to prepare you. For you will soon embark on a great and mighty work.

"My son, I want you to wait for just a few more days. Be absolutely convinced in your mind that the goal has been reached. You are on the brink of Self-realization. You have won your battle. We will make you conscious, as soon as our preparations for our Mission are completed. I have revealed the reason out of My love for you and to keep you mind steady and steadfastly fixed on us, your Masters."

Chapter Twenty

Landmarks in Self-realization (1949)

Sai Baba's words of assurance made a deep impression upon me. There was now no room for doubt, no reason for hesitation, no ground for frustration. Had I not glimpsed God? Had not my soul been taken to God several times, by Sai Baba? What Mattered if I was not conscious of it? A beginning had been made.

In the evening of September 17, 1949, Ram Ram gave me six important points for guidance. He said: "You are now convinced that you have reached the goal. But I have to guide you on various points of importance to attain the final end in full consciousness. First, you must learn to become absolutely indifferent to everything pertaining to the world.

Second, don't show the least sign of impatience.

Third, learn to grasp things quickly and retain them in your memory. Quick disposal of things and with justice, will be required of you when you are put on your mission.

Fourth, be extremely careful in your speech. Not a word should be uttered that may harm anyone. Don't sacrifice truth under any circumstances, but speak nothing, if by speaking truth, some one is harmed.

Fifth acquire the habit of good discernment. I have noticed a tendency in you to jump to hasty conclusions. You will be called upon to give impartial verdicts on knotty problems.

Sixth, practise the habit of speaking only when absolutely necessary of speech are a *sine qua non* for collecting inward energy.

The same evening Sai Baba gave me a thrilling experience in the altar room. It is best to describe it in His own words:

> "Do you know why you fell down with a shock on the ground. The shock of climbing the steep pillar of blazing light was so great that even in your unconscious state, you felt its effect. What would it have been if you had been in conscious state? This is just to give you an idea of the tremendous possibilities that are open to you. God is extremely pleased with you and by His grace I shall soon make you conscious of your glorious attainment."

Evidently, the Masters were in great earnest not only to show me the landmarks of Self-realization but to take me directly to the goal of Self-realization in full consciousness. To this purpose, Ram Ram again reminded me of my vows:

(1) You must never exercise the power given to you to pass away from you earth plane.

(2) You will take the name of God all the time and think of Him and Him alone.

(3) You will not make any demonstration or exhibition of the powers given to you. They are to be used unostenatiously for the good of others alone.

(4) You will not seek name or fame, glory or power, riches or wealth, nor care for any mundane things of the world.

(5) You will always keep the interests of others first before yours.

In the course of message on September 16, 1949, Sai Baba told me: "Be warned after attainment of Self-realization, you will have to fulfill all yours vows."

Remembering the seriousness of the vows, I enquired: "If anything is done inadvetently, unknowingly or in a mood of forgetfulness, won't you kindly forgive and save me?" The Master replied:

> "Yes, that we shall do. But at the same time we want to keep you thoroughly warned. And most important of all, you must not use your powers for self-aggrandizement. They must be used only for the good of others and, as far as possible, secretly and unostentatiously.
>
> "There will be temptations put in your way to divert you from your vows. We warn you to be extremely careful. We shall protect you from opposing forces, but so long as you remain true to your vows, opposing forces would dwindle away.
>
> "We shall keep you in tolerable condition of health but at no time should you ask for death. God shall call you away whenever He likes. You should not at all exercise the power given to you to leave your earth plane, at your option. Surrender this power to God He knows best and will do the best.
>
> You will come to know your mission in life as soon as you become conscious of God. The mission will be a strenuous one but it will be entirely to your liking and according to your capacity. As your body is not strong, God in His mercy won't keep you long on the earth plane. He will soon call you away to join out ranks."

On 19th my soul was again taken to God by Sai Baba but this time it made a sojourn in the Spiritual Plane for a longer time than usual. He took charge of my soul and when it returned after drinking deep at the waters of the Spirit World, a wave of exquisite delight passed though me. I was steeped and clothed in a halo of light and I felt so very grateful to the Invisible Masters.

A few days later *i.e.,* on October 6, 1949, Sai Baba again referred to my having become a Master in physical body and described the difference between a Spirit Master and a Master in human body in the following, illuminating message:

> "We Masters never get tired, however much we work, our work give us more enthusiasm and spirit. You are now like us and should therefore experience life in the same way. We are superior to you, for we escape the handicap of the physical vehicle. But then you have the advantage of having a body, which embraces all humanity, being of the same flesh and blood. It is for this reason that we want you to sacrifice your place in our world till your body gives way."

I had not still received the consciousness of having become a Master. But I knew that the goal could not be far off for the invisible Masters to visualise things which we take time to realise. The future is like an open book to them. The past the present and future are no secrets to them.

I had decided that, as desired by God, I should embark upon a mission to do good to humanity for which adequate powers would be given to me on my realising Self.

On October 1, 1949, I was told by Ram Ram that my mission had already started. This took me aback. When I had not seen God in full consciousness how could I have any mission on earth? The word 'Mission' was interpreted by me, as any one ordinarily would have done. But the mission that the Master referred to was different. Sai Baba explained it to me as under:

> "Your mission, as Ram Ram has told you, has already started. By mission he means your soul's longing to join our ranks in the Spiritual Plane and be freed from the letters of the body."

> On 23 Sai Baba gave an important message. He said: "For a few minutes today in the morning. I made you sit still like a statue truing to read as unknown language. The unknown language is the language of the spirit. It is not language but thought forms, which are conveyed and understood by spirit immediately. I was glad that you felt the thrill and tried your best to decipher the meaning but failed.

My ideas in making you go through this experience is to make your feel at home in our Spirit Land. Your soul would be contacting our world all the time whenever it likes and this was just a beginning of this indication. You are on the way to full consciousness."

On September 25, Sai Baba showed His singular prowess, of being the greatest in the Celestial Hierarchy when he gave me the following explanation of what He had done:

"Today, I took out your soul without putting you into trance and you felt a terrible shock – a shock as great that you were on the point of expiring and it was with great difficulty that you managed to breathe."

"I enquired: "But when the soul goes away from the body, how can a man breathe?' The Master replied: "

"I said you were on the point of expiring but not actually expired. The soul passed away from your body and came back in a minute. That one minute's interval was terrible for you and I sustained you by My invisible force and power. I have done this only to exhibit My power to you. Such things are not usually done by Masters for their pupils. I am extremely pleased with you in every respect."

Ram Ram further explained to me the singular feat practised by Sai Baba:

"It is not a joke to take out the soul when the body is in living condition and in full consciousness and bring it back safe and sound. Only Sai Baba can do it and by so doing He has shown to you what He actually is. He is your Ahuram Mazda Amshaspand, who has taken the form of Sai Baba for the simple reason that you have His picture in Your altar room. He can take any form He likes. You are extremely fortunate to be trained by Him. It is the highest honour that can be given to any man on earth. Because of Him you have succeeded in reaching the goal so quickly and in such a short space of time."

On October 1, 1949, God came to me of His own accord as will be seen from the following message of Sai Baba:

> "God of His own accord came to you today and poured His blessings on you. We have heard your prayer and we have been touched and pleased. All that is left now is to make you conscious of His presence."

Let us take stock of the whole situation. The experiences given to me by Sai Baba were to make me feel at home in the Spirit Land and prepare me to gain knowledge for fulfilling my mission on earth. The mission is therefore twofold: First, that the soul must gain experiences of the other world and second, having gained that experience, utilise it for a new venture on the earth plane, which would start simultaneously with the attainment of Self-realization.

On October 2, 1949, I was again taken to God. Sai Baba said:

> "A marvellous thing has happened. Not only did you see God but you got a promise from Him that He will make you conscious when you visit Him again. This is a grand achievement for there cannot be any more postponement. I have purified all your inner vehicles and filled your soul with God's love and light." Your present joy is a very dim reflection of the true joy that will simply sweep you and immerse you in the Ocean of God's Bliss. God is known in the Vedas as Sat Chit Ananda-Absolute Existence, Consciousness and Bliss."

Referring to this inward bliss, Sai Baba explained that my soul now had the knowledge of its freedom to come and go wherever it liked.

I was made to observe silence and seclusion, commencing form October 3, 1949, and ending after four weeks.

The next day Sai Baba gave me message describing what I would experience when I contact God in full consciousness. He said:

> "At first you would be unconscious of your environment. Slowly and steadily, while you are there, I will make you conscious and you would be thrilled and delighted beyond measure. You would see God seated in the very centre of His kingdom, covered in a halo of light, resplendent and glorious, beyond description. I

> will make you touch His feet and a terrific flow of energy would pass through your whole system, shaking you from top to bottom and filling you with a joy never experienced before. You would be dazed and dazzled and for a few minutes it would be even difficult for you to comprehend and understand the whole phenomenon, inconceivable as it is. Slowly light would dawn on you and would recognize me in my glorious garb. You would see fusillades of light all around you, shining with unsurpassed beauty in their radiance, thrilling to behold but more thrilling in their effectiveness, as the rays of these would pierce you and will make you feel ecstatic delight.
>
> What a glorious picture of God and His surroundings LIGHT, LIGHT, nothing but LIGHT."

The following day, Sai Baba again took me to God and it appeared that He would have open my inner eye and allowed me to see Him in full consciousness.

But Sai Baba told me: "You were on the point of seeing Him, but I stopped it. I can't tell you why. All I can say is that I have done it in your own interest.

On October 5, 1949, I was again put to a test in the evening. That night, Sai Baba me a talk inducing me to give up hankering after Self-realization as I was absolutely unfit for it. This is what He said:

> "You should not be in any delusion regarding Self-realization. You have not attained it and you will not attain it at all. It is all false. You have been fooled all the time. You are not fit for it in any way. Stop all this non-sense and don't come to the altar room at all."

I asked: "Are you Sai Baba or any other Spirit?"

"I am Sai Baba."

I said: "I can't believe it . Either you are not Sai Baba or you are testing me. I am as firm as a rock and have implicit faith in Sai Baba and in all His utterances and statements. My faith and trust in Him cannot be undermined."

"As you please. Talk to Ram Ram. I am going away."

Ram Ram then gave out the secret, that it was all planned by them to test me.

Was it that the Master were giving the finishing touch to my spiritual soul? There was no doubt that I was still lacking in certain traits – patience, self-reliance and calmness aggressive circumstances.

Silence and seclusion were imposed upon me again for an unspecified period by the Masters. Ram Ram explained the significance as under:

> "The object of making you observe silence and seclusion is to avail the purity all around you from being initiated by your free contacts with mundane things. When you observe silence, you are compelled to keep your mind absolutely at rest. When you don't go out, you are excluded from coming in contact with persons of low aura. This special spiritualisation of all your bodies for the purpose of making you see God is absolutely necessary and none but a Master can do it."

On the 9 Sai Baba again put me to peculiar a test. As I was meditating, and it was a perfect meditation, he tempted me to break off. I stoutly refused. Sai Baba then Said to me: "You are a man of extremely strong will power and you carry out what you propose doing."

Later, Sai Baba put before me the whole situation. He said:

> "We have two alternatives. First to give Self-realization straight off and then powers flow in automatically. Second is to give Self-realization only in part with a view that full consciousness of the Self grows with acquisition of powers. In the first instance, it takes time for powers to flow in. It may take much less time. As your life is short, I am not allowing you to realise Self full till all the powers are acquired fully. It is not a question of mere Self-realization but a realization of God with all mystic powers added for superconscious work."

During this period I was reading. *"The Autobiography of a Yogi"* written by Paramhansa Yogananda and I was enchanted by the descriptions of many yogis and their feats of achievement – Sri Yukteswar, Lahiri Mahasaya and above all Babaji, who appeared to be the Prince of Masters among the three. They were Masters in physical bodies and I yearned and longed for a touch of any of them. It was stupid of me, as would be seen from the following remonstrance administered by Sai Baba. He said: "The book you are reading now is a stimulating book, are little children playing with pebbles on the shore. By the grace of God, you are in the hands of invisible forces who are moulding your destiny to a precision for the fulfillment of God's purpose. We have clamped you with chains so that even if you choose to leave us, you won't be able to exercise that choice. Your destiny is now inviolably linked with ours."

I asked Sai Baba: "If my inner eye is open, what harm is there in allowing me to use it? Why should I not see you and Ram Ram?"

Sai Baba replied: "If you see Me, you realize Self immediately and I am delaying it as you know for a specific purpose."

I again asked: "Then will you allow me to see Ram Ram? Homi is able to see Ram Ram. Why should not this gift be given to me also?"

Sai Baba said: "Do you want marvels to satisfy your transient gain or do you want eternal cosmic gift?"

On the October 13, 1949, Ram Ram, describing the work done by Sai Baba during my meditation, said to me: "He has overhauled your nervous system completely, making it responsive to our higher vibrations. He has made you in tune with us."

On October 14, 1949, Sai Baba revealed to me:

"I am going to give you the following powers that you may use as you like provided the vows you have taken are not infringed:

(1) The power of healing. This will be intensified as days go on.

(2) The power of inspirational writing. This will gather greater momentum as you advance in years.
(3) The Power of reading minds and communicating your thoughts to persons living beyond your physical vision.
(4) The power of speech that will enthrall people.
(5) The power of knowing future events and helping people in distress.
(6) The power of communicating to us and seeing us, your Master, whenever you want.
(7) And the greatest of all, the power of remaining in perennial bliss with the vision of God always before you.

Equipped with the above powers, you can make a tremendous success of your life and attain the blessings of millions of people, who would follow you and worship you as if you were a God on earth. I am doing all this out of My love for you and in recognition of your great sacrifices on the earth plane in your present incarnation. You were destined form birth this vocation but as you were the master of your own will, the decision was up to you. You have exercised your free will, the decision was up to you. You have exercised your free will correctly and to our entire satisfaction. It gives me the greatest pleasure to make this announcement under the order of God. The only work left for us, is to make you conscious of the whole situation and put the crown of Self-realization of your head in your full consciousness."

On the 15 Sai Baba told me: "I am initiating you now into the mysteries of our universe. This initiation will continue even after you have realized Self in full consciousness.

On October 16, Sai Baba told me He had given me a new inner body with a system in tune with the spirit body, so that I could visit the Spirit Land at will and be in close touch with my Masters. He further said:

"All these preparations are now nearly complete. We have been able to assert complete control and sovereignty over all the subtle and invisible forces within you. We can now make you carry out

> God's will on earth for mankind's regeneration and happiness. Just as a giant tree sprouts from a tiny seed, you are a tiny seed that will give rise to a mighty revolution and lead more seeds to be planted for greater awakening with the passage of time.

I was asked to read for the third time. *"The Autobiography of a Yogi"* by Paramhansa Yogananda, in order to understand better the training the Masters were giving me.

Several times, I was told that I would become a prophet of the New Era. This was rank absurdity. Such declarations must not be judged at their face value for their hidden purpose is to test and to crush the egotism of pupils. In fact Sai Baba, later admitted: "Your ego has already been crushed but I still wanted to see whether with the prospects of changed circumstances you would be tempted to win the world's applause."

On October 18, 1949, after 10:00 p.m. Sai Baba ordered that I should prepare myself to spend 24 hours in the altar room, to gain Self-relization. He gave me the option to take any day in the week. It was to be a day of silence, seclusion, fasting, prayers and meditation. Thursday the October 20, 1949 was fixed.

Sai Baba explained the significance of the fasting in this message:

> "My idea in making you fast for full 24 hours without even a drop of water is to make you feel that you are no longer attached to body. You are spirit and you have to work in the spirit of the divine law. Fasting will also help me for your inner vehicles will be strengthened further."

Regarding *chakras,* which play an important role in the training, Sai Baba said:

> "I proposed to open up all your *chakras* simultaneously and teach you how to open and close them at your will. It is easy to open *chakras* but extremely difficult to close them. After you realize Self, there will be absolutely no difficulty. You will then be in direct communion with God, and He can help you in everything. In fact, you will be God yourself in human body."

In the afternoon of the October 18, 1949, Sai Baba spoke to me to the Spiritual Plane full of Light and Splendor. He said: "I want you to know that tomorrow you would definitely see God and both your Masters. It is not at all a test. I have tested all your inner parts and I am satisfied they will be able to bear the heavy strain and you will see the glaring, dazzling light of our Spiritual Plane. We have brought your vision in tune with our vibratory light. You will be entering a land of tremendous light. Even a small flash of it is enough to burn to cinders the whole of your world. God is LIGHT. Our world is LIGHT. Everything here is Light and nothing else. You will see nothing but terrific flashes of Light on all sides, as you swim through the very Ocean of Light. There will be Light, Light, Light of unsurpassed magnitude, sweeping over you, beyond you, underneath you and all around you. You will be as if caught in a storm of Light, dazzling, magnetising, soul – illuminating and terrifying like bursting volcano. As you get used to it, the terrifying effect of Light would give way to a peaceful refreshment of the soul, for our Light in its essentials is the same as that of which your soul is made. This light is the greatest harmonising factor in the universe. It is from this Light that God created the seed of LOVE. In our realm LIGHT and LOVE reign supreme. They are not only main pillars but the warp and woof of the whole structure of our universe. When we raise your vibration to become in tune with the vibration of our world, you will be able to live ever in communion with God. With such realization your powers will automatically increase and you will become a great force on your earth plane. So long as you stick to your vows, not a hair of your head would be touched and you will progress form triumph to triumph till God, in His great mercy, will call you away to join our Great White Brotherhood.

"After realizing the Self, a higher type of training will continue. We shall be coming to you and you will be able to see us in this altar room. That Higher Training won't take long. Your can then launch into the world and commence your mission, making wise use of the powers that we shall give you as deemed necessary by God. My dearest son, in anticipation of your realising Self, I congratulate you and give you my heartiest, most cordial and affectionate greetings – greetings in which your Master Ram Ram also join Me."

I entered the altar room at 04:00 a.m. I was reminded: "You have to pass the whole day and night in the altar room and take no food or water."

At 10:00 a.m. Sai Baba said to me:

> "You will not get self-realization. I miscalculated." A while later, He said: "I want to give you the most startling news. God wants to see you." Nothing happened. At 01:00 p.m. Sai Baba said: "You are now beyond danger zone. You have crossed it today heroically. There are now no more hurdles to be crossed. The night of gloom is over. You will be a free man, with angels by your side to help you in your great work. Had you taken one false step, our and your labour would have been wasted. A few more hours and you will be swallowed up in a surprise of the strangest order."

At 4.30 p.m. Sai Baba said: "It is not possible to take you to God today. I have done my best and have failed." An hour later Sai Baba said: "God has seen you when you were meditating and He has given me special instructions to take you to Him without delay." Nothing happened.

At 7:00 p.m. Sai Baba said: "I am sorry, I have disappointed you" and then He asked me to invoke Ram Ram.

Ram Ram said,

> "Sai Baba is only teasing you. You will get a vision of God in a few minutes. He will come to you in a terrible flow of light, extremely dazzling. You will be stupefied and staggered. But be brave and a tremendous current of joy will flow in you." Nothing happened.

At 8:30 p.m. Sai Baba said:

> "You have had a trying and disappointing day. But I could not help it. You must learn to face disappointments with tranquillity." Half an hour later Sai Baba said: "I had asked you to pass the whole day in the altar room to test your endurance. I am glad you have passed this test. Do you know you have already realised Self? Why then do you bother to see us, your Masters, and God?"

I said: "It is you who were telling me, that you would take me to God in full consciousness and that you Masters will come to me and I shall be able see you both. Why then subject me to delusions? Why don't you clearly say that I can't see God and you?"

The master replied: "Take it in whatever way you like."

I said:

"What about tomorrow? Do I have to continue silence and seclusion or will you allow me to break it?"

The Master said: "I leave it entirely to you. Do whatever you like."

I asked: "How can that be? I have followed your orders and am prepared to follow them."

Sai Baba said: "Then don't break silence tomorrow but wait till I tell you."

At 4:00 a.m. the next morning, after I had passed the whole night in the altar room, Sai Baba said: "I have been asked by God to take you to Him in full consciousness." Nothing happened. Sai Baba again preached to me the lesson of facing disappointments with equanimity of mind and soul.

When it was night, I thought I would fall asleep out of sheer tiredness. But I had hardly an hour's disturbed sleep, and went on reading. As the day closed, my headache all of a sudden departed.

The next day, early morning. I invoked Sai Baba. He gave me very alluring assurance that He had received orders form God to take me to Him in full consciousness. After having received disappointing results throughout the previous day, I did not believe a word. I meditated for an hour and a half with the greatest difficulty and came out of meditation absolutely blank. I hurried out of the altar room.

The next day *i.e.*, October 21, 1949, Ram Ram threw the thunderbolt: "Sai Baba is angry with you and you are now free to do whatever you like. His love for you has dried up after yesterday's sittings."

I immediately changed my mind. It is better to continue silence and seclusion and face the sneers of friends and relatives to lose the guidance of the Masters.

Then Sai Baba later said:

"I am glad you have seen it fit to be guided by Me. My dearest son, all that I am doing is for your own good. It does not please me to disappoint you all the time. But in the course of high spiritual training, these tests and trials are absolutely necessary."

In the course of a long message Ram Ram said:

"You are now a free man with God-realization in you. We are restraining you just for a few more days for perfecting your preparations for the future course of your life, for which we are as much responsible as you. You now belong to our fraternity and our aims and objects are common. Though we are invisible to you today, we are going to make ourselves visible to you in a few days. This will be the most believing feature in your training and you will be convinced of the futility of your present notions. As sure as there is death, we, your Masters, shall manifest ourselves to you. Our mutual love is the link that will bridge the gulf between us and your bliss will be unbounded."

On October 23, 1949, at the end of my meditation I saw a vision, the implication of which was explained to me by Ram Ram as under:

"At the end of the meditation you saw in dim vision Lord Krishna playing a flute. It is Lord, God, in one of His manifestations. You also dimly saw a crown. When the vision becomes bright, at any of the following sittings, the crown will glow lustrously bright and it will be placed on your head as a symbol of your having reached the goal and won your prize."

In the evening of the 25th, while I was meditating, I saw Sai Baba with a fringe of white line on His head and I went on meditating on it, as asked by Him. It was an augury of my seeing Him, when He should manifest Himself to me.

On the 27th, we had an exchange of questions and replies which are recorded hereunder:

Sai Baba: "I can't be seen by you in the present state of your evolution."

I said: "I means that I am not fit. This is what I had been saying but you disagreed."

Sai Baba said: "Yes, I disagreed then and I disagree now. You are absolutely fit to see Me as far as your spirituality goes, but on account of the physical body which you possess, it is not easily feasible."

I said: "But I have the astral eye and you have said so often that it is open."

Sai Baba replied: "Yes, it is open. It can see a Master, but not God. But I have still hopes of making Myself manifest to you, some day." I then enquired; "Will you kindly allow Ram Ram to manifest himself to me?"

Sai Baba said, "Yes, this is easy."

I said: "When will I be able to see him?"

"Whenever you want."

I said: "If I invoke him, will he come and will I be able to see him?"

Sai Baba replied: "First make him prepare you. It will take some time."

I asked: "Will you kindly tell me what is my mission and what is the programme prepared under God's order?"

Sai Baba said: "Ram Ram will tell you everything"

I enquired: "If I can't see God because of the hindrance of the physical body, how is it that I can hear God?"

Sai Baba said: Because the subtle forces in you have been so keenly developed that you can hear Me from the depth of your soul."

I said: "Why can't those subtle forces allow me to see Thee also?"

Sai Baba replied: "I say definitely that you will see Me, but the subtle forces in you have still not reached that stage of development."

I said: "What then do you want me to do now? When shall I break my silence?"

Sai Baba said: "If you wish to break silence, you can do so but I am against it."

I said: "How long do you wish me to continue it?

Sai Baba said: "As long as I think fit."

I said: "But you said that you will break my silence in a few days and that the veil would also be lifted."

Sai Baba replied: Yes, that is correct."

I enquired: "What are your orders for me now?"

Sai Baba said: "My dearest son, when I say I love your, it means a very great thing. Unfortunately in spite of My and Ram Ram's assurance, you still cannot understand and have no conception of your high spirituality."

I said: "But who am I and what perfection have I to deserve such great bliss of being in communion with God?"

Sai Baba replied, "This is the obstacle which you in your ignorance and obstinacy have created and still persist in not removing. You are your own enemy, in a way though you are such a dear, beloved soul."

The letters which I wrote to Homi on October 26 and 27, 1949, as given below, reveal the state of my mind. October 26, 1949

My dear Homi,

You will see from the message enclosed, that the same process of tests, trials and postponements continues. Last Thursday, I was made to spend 24 hours at a stretch in the altar room and a day or two before that I was given a graphic description of the highest spiritual plane where I would be taken. Nothing of the sort happened.

On Monday last, I was told that Sai Baba would manifest Himself together with Ram Ram. But He did not manifest Himself. Then I thought possibly in the morning I would have his darshan. But I was disappointed.

I agree with you that the main thing is the mission and how to implement it and not to have the vision of God. You will notice from the messages that I am being prepared for the mission and the programme has been cut out by the Masters. But they won't tell me. They want to give me a vision of God, the programme of my work and the powers to carry out the mission simultaneously. This is the difficult situation in which I am placed. I am not at all waiting for God's vision. You know the story of Yogi Yogananda. When he was told by his guru Sri Yukteswar that he had got Self-realization he said in surprise, that when he had not seen God, how had he realized Self. Yuketeswar had said that Self-realization did not necessary mean seeing God in some glorious form. But later on, after several years, Yogananda did see God, all of a sudden in the form of Lord Krishna. I know this incident and am therefore not so very keen on seeing God as of getting myself ready for the Mission. It is enough for me that I am guided, prepared and inspired by the Higher Ones under the orders of God. But I must know my Mission. Or is it that I must work my way out myself? If that be the case, they would not say that the programme is being chalked out for me and that I would be informed later on. I don't mind the present silence. Today is the twenty-fourth day silence and seclusion but I don't know when it is going to end. You can understand in what a terrible fix I am. You and Doraswamy alone know my secrets and you are the only person who can rightly interpret the messages and guide me. Tell me then, what course of action should take I? I intend to continue observing silence and seclusion till Sunday or Monday next and then commence my daily routine. But I don't like to disobey the orders of the Masters. In fact I dare not do that, after having come to the present state.

There is one thing define. I feel consciously happy inwardly. There is peace in my mind and joy in my heart all the time. It is this that makes me think that I am on the right track and I must not mind anything else. Anyhow, do kindly write to me and let me have your views.

Yours affectionately,
Minoo
Karachi/26-10-49
October 27, 1949

My Dear Homi,

Last night I was told by Sai Baba that He would manifest Himself to me in the morning. This did not happen. Because I was prepared for disappointment, it did not hurt me at all. But I feel the time has come now for a definite step for charge of action.

For months together, I have confined myself to the altar room, chiefly in compliance with the order of the Masters. I have now come to the following conclusions:

(1) Some day I shall see God. It may be just before I am called away or earlier.

(2) The Mission which the Masters speak of is not at all any special Mission.

Life in itself is a mission and very one must work his way out, according to his own ability and in accordance to the dictates of his own heart and conscience. The Masters can only invisibly guide and help him. Has not Buddha said: "Let each one be a lamp auto himself?"

I can understand why poor Meher Baba failed in his mission. Every now and then he used to declare that he would break his silence on such and such date and that he would declare himself a world teacher, He might have spoken in the assurances given to him by Higher Ones who might have postponed and these postponements must have broken him down.

The feeling that comes upon me now is that of complete renunciation. I want to leave Karachi for good and shut myself away from the world. It is only the question of Mehru, Mrs. M. K. Spencer is into that comes in the way. If she were to listen to reason, I could go away. I have no heart for this mundane world.

I have worked very hard in my life. I want now to retire and finish the remaining years in secluded corner, thinking of God and God alone, or work in some large leper colony.

The Masters have been exceedingly kind to me. They have given me bliss and awakened my inner consciousness. They have done their work. It is for me now to begin mine.

Kindly see Ram Ram's message of last night. He offers me two options, one of which is that I may come away. I believe it is to test me, for one of the vows taken is that I must not exercise the power to shuffle off the mortal coil. The first option therefore is out of question. The second is in regard to my Mission, and that believe has to be planned and worked out by me alone. Whether the Higher Ones will give me powers or not for its fulfillment, is more than one can say at present.

Whatever it be, I still feel inwardly happy and at peace with the world. This silence of nearly one month has made me a target of ridicule and contempt. But I am impervious and indifferent. In my heart of hearts I understand that I have realised God.

Do write to me after studying all the messages.

With love,
Yours affectionately,
Minoo
Karachi: 27-10-49

My above letter to Homi must indicate that I was planning to run away. But Sai Baba held me tight. He said:

> "We have held you tight knowing full well that you would think of running away. I have read your letter to Homi today. It is a childish letter, not worthy of a yeoman that you really are. But on the whole you did well in allowing your inner thoughts to be exposed..."

Ram Ram administered me a strong rebuke and expressed his great resentment at my having written to Homi on 27th morning in the manner I had. He said to me:

> "For God's sake, shake off lethargy and doubt. You are one of the silliest pupils I ever had. It is Sai Baba who is tolerating you. I would have kicked you off, for the way you are doubting us. Why should there be the vaguest shadow of doubt? I have already told you so many times that it is our duty to put you

through so many tests. Disappointment tests are most galling to bear. If you can't bear them, it is better to give up. What is time in man's life? How are you to judge us? I am really very angry. What made you write that stupid, childish letter to Homi? Is this your trust and faith in us? And that too after our such prolonged and anxious care, labour and guidance? But for the link that binds you and me together, I would have denounced you. I don't want a doubting pupil."

I said in tears: "Forgive me, for God's sake, forgive me."

Ram Ram said: "Very well, I forgive you. But I am speaking these hard words in your own interest. Remember you are in the hands of God. All you have to do is to submit yourself to us and carry on your laborious study. You will have to give up all minor duties and devote yourself to your monumental work."

On October 28, 1949, Sai Baba said: "I have liberated your soul and it is free to go out, wherever it likes, whenever you want. Your soul is free but I have closed your inner eye till such time as the training is completed. As soon as it is completed, you would see Me and all the worlds."

Sai Baba warned me that if I entertained any doubt or suspicion, and if I changed my mind I would court disaster. He then explained: "All I assure you is that you are absolutely and completely safe in our hands. My dearest son, I am your God. Can you have a better Master on earth than Ahuram Mazda Amshaspand? Why did you at all doubt Me? Yes, you are right that God will not take pupils on earth for training them. He has Masters under Him, who do this work. You were given a Master but he found it difficult to take you to the final step of the goal. I saw in you vast potentialities for the future good of mankind. I therefore willingly took you up in my hands for the final training. Your mission in life is to teach and to heal and for that purpose I shall give you my own secret powers and make you sojourn in both the worlds. Is there anything grander than this? Have a little more patience."

Ram Ram told me in the evening that Sai Baba had become so very fond of me, that He had come down to the altar room and had embraced me.

On the 30th morning I was again taken to God several times, but for shorter intervals. Sai Baba said: "After several more visitations in this manner, your soul would get so acquainted with the new surroundings that it would feel at home in our world. Do you also know that you are now on the verge of being united with God? This mean completion of Self-realization."

I asked: "The Self and God are the same. Why are there then any distinctions?"

The Master replied: "There is a slight distinction. The Self in man is the Spirit of God in man. God itself is the Absolute Spirit pervading throughout the universe – the Supermind, the Cause and Seed of all manifestations, the ONE who becomes MANY."

On October 31, before I entered the altar room for prayers and meditation, I had a dream. I saw that I was weary of walking and I was told by a passerby that I was walking in the direction opposite to my goal. With a sigh I turned back and a voice said that it would take mea along time to reach the goal and that too, if I had strength and patience.

On October 31, 1949, my silence was brought to an end by Sai Baba. It had lasted for four weeks and it had brought me such inward strength and spirituality that AI felt extremely grateful to the Masters. They had perfected my inner parts and subtler forces so as to bring them in tune with the vibrations of their Spiritual Plane. They had made me a perfect instrument to catch their impulses and inspiration. They had made my soul contact God several times and given it thorough training and made it quite at home in the Spiritual Plane.

The highest stage to which a man can rise in his evolution is adeptship. It si spiritual perfection, a reflection of God's Omnipotence, Omnipresence, Omniscience. There are so many books written on the functions and powers of the Masters or Adepts. The seed of adeptship is present in very human being. The savage is unaware of the existence of this seed. He has not the slightest conception of his future greatness or the innate powers latent in him. He is still in kindergarten, as far as spirituality is concerned. In the case of the civilized man, he is aware of the innate subtle forces working in him but developing them depends on him alone. If he faces the struggle of life, with heart and mind fixed on God in purity of thought, word and deed, he realises Self. If he refuses to hear the voice of conscience and allows himself to be carried away by the waves of carnal thought, which constantly inundate his mind, he gets lost in the whirpool of maya, and he will have to wait for many rounds of birth to get a glimpse of the God within. It is only when he has more or less perfected his character that he meets a Master.

The Master draws the pupil towards himself. The neophyte acquires greater determination by coming into the presence of the Master's aura. He gains control of the lower self, his zeal for human service increases and his zest to find God becomes more accentuated. When the neophyte reaches a high state of spirituality the Master unites him to his own self. This union of the two into one is an indication of the pupil's successful march towards the goal. The neophyte is trained now the become desireless, egoless, fearless and indifferent to everything.

Chapter Twenty-One

Godman Meher Baba and His Predictions (1945-49)

I was thrilled when Homi in his letter to me dated October 29, 1949, said: "Just as I am drafting this, Meher Baba appears before me to say that you have caught the true spirit of the "Mast" philosophy and asks me to tell you that it will surely lead you to your goal. "When this letter was received, it was put at the altar and Sai Baba in reply to my query whether Meher Baba had a double body, that he could appear before Homi to give a message for me, said: "I had told you some months ago that you will hear from Meher Baba. He has power to be present at two places. He can materialize and dematerialize at will."

I was thrilled for two reasons. In the first place, Ram Ram's prediction of August 21, 1949, at 3:40 p.m. that I would hear from Meher Baba had proved correct to the very letter. Secondly, Meher Baba's prediction that I would successfully reach the goal gave me inward strength and confirmed my faith in Sai baba's and Ram Ram's verdict that I would realize God.

I was jubilant. I wrote to Homi on November 5, 1949:

> ".....In this connection, I want you to help me by elaborating upon the incident of your meeting Meher Baba. Did you see him in physical body? Or is it that you saw him only in a vision? Do write to me at length."

Homi replied on November 12, 1949:

> "When I saw Meher Baba on 28-10-1949, it was only that I saw his face. It appeared before me where I was sitting, a little higher than the level of my head. It seemed to be made of some dense but fluidic matter but the contour of the face and the colour and size of the eyes were unmistakable. I saw the face clearly in front of me with my eyes open, in the bright blaze of two electric lamps."

To explain the situation leading to Meher Baba's sending a message to me through Homi, it is necessary to go into the past and consider the messages received from the Masters in this connection. This will complete the picture and show how the Masters work.

On April 20, 1945 I was ordered by Ram Ram to pay a visit to Meher Baba. I and my wife accordingly left for Meherabad, where Meher Baba lived in his ashram along with his devotees. Unfortunately, on the day we arrived, Meher Baba had to leave his abode for an extensive tour. He could therefore give us just a short time. But this half hour passed with him was most memorable. He gave very satisfactory replies to question put. But it was not merely his mystic knowledge that made such a deep impression upon us. It was rather the atmosphere of love which he generated and the tremendous waves of joy which he created in our hearts that uplifted us. God is LOVE. When we are filled with divine love, nay when we are overflowing with ecstatic bliss which only mystics united with God day and night experience, could that great love be transmitted to others.

Let us now consider some of his teachings:

The body is but the outer covering of your soul. It is

Maya that makes you identify yourself with the body and which makes you forgetful of your eternal, indivisible, resplendent Divinity.

As a single object seems to multiply itself to him who is drunk to excess, so Unity appears as plurality to those who are intoxicated with the wine of egoism.

All those who experience the gross world as real, are asleep. Only those who experience it as unreal can realise God and become awakened.

As soon as the clouds of samskaras pass away, we begin to see the sun of God in His pristine glory.

Do not be angry with him who backbites you, but be pleased, for thereby he serves you by diminishing the load of your *samskaras;* also pity him because he increases his own load of *samskaras.*

Cast not your pearls before swine. Materialistic people are like swine because they prefer the filth of the world to the pearl of liberation.

That Supreme Soul – *Paramatman* – God, is nowhere to be searched for He is very near to you. He is with you. Seek Him within. You could easily see Him were it not for the four big 'Devils' that stand in your way. They are egotism, lust, anger and greed.

The following note of Meher Baba is illuminating:

There are three bodies – mind body, subtle body and physical body. They are the vehicles by which the spirit, through the mind, experiences existence.

(1) the Mind Body, in which thoughts arise as the result of impressions from past experiences. These thoughts may remain latent as seeds; if they are expressed they take first the form of desires, and pass through

(2) the Subtle Body, which is composed of the five psychic senses. They rest there as in dreams or they may be further expressed through

(3) the Physical Body, with it five physical senses.

Corresponding to the three bodies, there are three states of consciousness – unconsciousness, subconsciousness and waking consciousness.

The Mind sphere comprises the fifth and sixth plane: the Subtle sphere comprises the first, second, third and fourth plane. The seven planes of consciousness are: (1) Intellect; (2) Lower Inspiration; (3) Intuition; (4) Insight or the fourth plane, which tempts the aspirant with its supernatural powers to draw nearer to God; (5) Higher Inspiration or the fifth plane, where the aspirant feels the Infinite; (6) Illumination, the sixth plane, where the aspirant sees God in everything (still dualism); (7) the seventh plane, where there is no longer dualism and man becomes one with God – this is the state of Christ Consciousness and of the Perfect Master."

On December 22, 1947, I was given the following message by Meher Baba:

> "Speech is silver, silence is gold. Do your work silently, as you are doing now. Your love for Meher Baba and Bhagwan Sri Ramana is due to your nature being in conformity with these silent sages. Both have realised God. Each one of them is playing his part in his own way. You will also be called to play your role shortly."

Again on June 1, 1948, Ram Ram gave me a very important message regarding Meher Baba. He said:

> I want to tell you that Meher Baba is a great saint and those who revile him incur a great sin. He will come out of his silence very soon. He is appointed by God to reconstruct the fabric of society and bring a reformation in hearts and minds of all the people of the world. It was I who inspired you to see both Meher Baba and Sri Ramana and you have been benefitted by your visits to both of them. Do you know that Meher Baba has eyes on you? He si watching your progress with his inner eyes. He has helped you invisibly and you should be grateful to him as well as to Sri Ramana. Meher Baba is very anxious to see you again. Write to him and send a copy of this message to him."

I was equally anxious to visit him again but I could get no opportunity.

On June 20, 1948, I asked Ram Ram, my Spirit Guide and Master: "Is not a Spirit Master greater than any Master in physical body? Are you not greater than Meher Baba?" Ram Ram replied: "Certainly, there is no question at all. The Spirit Master is Omniscient, Omnipotent. The man on the earth even after Self-realization has limitations. So long as he has body, he is finite, though he has the potentiality of becoming Infinite."

I asked: "What about Jesus Christ?"

Ram Ram replied: "He was the Incarnation of God. His is the special case."

"Is Meher Baba an incarnation of God?"

Ram Ram replied: "Certainly not. God has given him certain supernormal powers to do good and he will become better known to the world, when he begins to speak. He has observed silence too long."

On 7th January, 1949, Ram Ram said: "Meher Baba is a highly developed soul with great *atmic shakti* in him. How far he can be a great benefactor of the world, is to be seen."

The words" How far he can be a benefactor of the world is to be seen" raised doubts. Even in cases of advanced mystics and God-realized souls, if they fail in carrying out their vows, they meet a tragic fate and in this message a sort of doubt is raised, which is very peculiar. Let us go further.

On June 4, 1949, I was intimated that "Way-farers" written by William Donkins, which described Meher Baba's association with the 'masts' *i.e.*, the God intoxicated persons, had been sent to me by V.P.P. Ram Ram said to me: "Accept the book sent by V.P.P."

On October 16, 1949, a small pamphlet describing Meher Baba's great renunciation of the world and his ashram, to lead the life of "helplessness and hopelessness," was received by me. I read it and it filled me with tears, that such a great mystic who was to thunder the world and give his message of deliverance, should now retire into complete oblivion. It appeared to me a great tragedy. Sai Baba gave me the following message of great importance on the subject:

> "I want to tell you all about Meher Baba, whose small pamphlet you were reading today. He will meet a tragic end and he knows it fully well. He could have been a great spiritual force on your earth plane but unfortunately he did not rise to the occasion. It is a pity that after such laborious preparations, he did not fulfil the vows taken by him secretly and God had therefore to leave him alone. He is a great soul, a magnanimous soul full of charm, most lovable and gentle. His simplicity, his sacrifices, his great silence and, above all, his devotion to God had so won our hearts that we were prepared to make him a great spiritual leader of the world. But he misunderstood us, gave himself away to thoughts of superiority. God willed that his vanity be broken. It is therefore that he says that he has entered into the last phase of his life-life of hopelessness. No prophet would ever use the word 'hopelessness'. Every devotee of God is full of hope, for when God is his daily companion, he si invigorated with His strength and protection. He feels 'hopelessness' has entered into his life, because, though he wants God every minute of his life and was in communion with Him, God has temporally discarded him for certain reasons which I can not disclose here. It is a great tragedy. You see what terrible dangers even a mystic of high order has to face. But as we see, his present renunciation is complete and he will leave his body in perfect peace and will be soon united with God."

Chapter Twenty-Two

Preparations for the Mission: Writing the book "How I Found God" (1949-50)

It was crystal clear that the object of postponing my Self-realization was to equip me with powers simultaneously with the attainment of Self-realization for successfully carrying out my mission in the fag end of my life. Intensive preparations were therefore made my Sai Baba to enable me to acquire the invisible powers by learning the secrets of the arcane science.

In order to expedite my progress in gaining mastery over the secrets of the arcane science, Sai Baba arranged that I should sacrifice sleep for a certain period and come to the altar room every morning at 02:00 a.m. instead of 04:00 a.m. as the early hours of morning were exceedingly helpful in meditation. These early morning visits to the altar room where I was confined every day for six hours, commenced from November 3, 1949.

It was about this time that I was asked to prepare myself for writing a new book, the title of which Sai Bába gave viz. *How I Found God.* In his message which he delivered on November 3, 1949, he said: "I want to make preparations for your new book without delay. Your long nightly-early morning meditation helps me a lot in doing my work."

Again and again the order was issued: "Kindly continue your nightly visits after 2:00 a.m. and meditate for long hours as you are doing. This is absolutely necessary."

Sai Baba had not told me what my mission would be viz." to "heal souls and bodies." I had been given healing power but it was not of any intensive nature. I had written some books, but they were of ordinary type. I was not sure whether I was at all fit to be appointed for any great mission.

Homi's letter on the subject reduced my doubts. The following are the extracts from his letter dated November 1, 1949:

> "You offered to serve as God's instrument on Earth for the uplift of humanity. That offer was accepted and you were being prepared for that mission, and now while those preparations are not completed to perfection, you turn round and say: "The mission which the Masters speak of is not at all any special mission." In other words, you judge them, adversely use and doubt their words. You forget whom you are judging and whose word you are doubting. Are you still shaky in your mind that in the so-called Sai Baba you are dealing directly with Ahura Mazda Himself?
>
> "I do not know why you should still doubt the nature of your mission. Look at the title of the book you are now asked to write: *How I Found God.* Ask yourself whether you will be able to write about it without finding Him. Is not that enough to show that you must reach the requisite highest stage of spirituality of find Him? As you progress with your work on this new book and as you study carefully the messages as you have been asked to do, you should certainly the messages as you have been asked to do, you should certainly be able to see for yourself how you have advanced in spirituality step by step. I hope this study will remove your doubts altogether that you have been in direct touch with God.
>
> Your work, as Sai Baba says, may be only a small seed today but it carries within it the potentiality of a giant tree and when the tree grows up, the world that shelters under it will surely bless him

who planted the seed, and you cannot plant the seed unless and until you bring it from God's own garden in Heaven, for you cannot find it anywhere else."

On the 5th in the morning, Sai Baba explained to me what I had seen at the end of my meditation:

"At the end of your meditation, you saw Me just for a short time. There was a background of blue and white, behind my head, when you saw Me first and the second time when you saw me, you saw red flame bursting out from behind. The flame was father dim and not intense. You also saw Ram Ram screened in flowers. These are very important indications of your rapid stride to the goal."

On November 6, Sai Baba said: "The most important thing is the new book that you have to write."

On the 17th I was put to a test, so usual with the Masters. Sai Baba said: "God is so pleased with you that He wants to give you a gift of any nature that you want. Ask for it and it will be given."

I replied: "Give me the gift of healing, so that I may go on healing those who are sick in body and in soul. I want nothing else."

Sai Baba said: "I am extremely glad that you have passed the test. Had you asked for anything for yourself, name or fame, popularity or power, position or riches, you would have fallen to the ground. You have the healing gift."

The following message of Sai Baba is full of revelation:

"Ram Ram's explanation that when you see your soul leaving the physical body, you must consider that as a sign of God-realization, is absolutely correct.

"The soul of every human being is like a spark of light. It is an indicator of life in man. When the soul leaves the body, the man is said to have died, though as known to all, he does not die, but leaves the physical plane for a newer world of ours. But those who are highly developed spiritually can see the soul leave the body even when they are not really dead. The yogis or the highly developed souls, when once they realize God, have the

> power to quit the body at will and their soul visits our world and returns again to the body, usually after a very short time. This is called the highest state of superconsciousness. Visions are an approach to that state of superconsciousness. Ram Ram gave you visions. I am going to give you now the consciousness of God Himself and the consciousness of our spiritual world.
>
> "Ram Ram's duty has come to an end. It is now my duty to take you in fullest consciousness to God. It will delight you so much that you will be completely swept off. Your earth would appear as a dusty, dreary place full of insipid matter, after experiencing the delights of our Spirit Land, particularly the highest Spiritual Plane, which is to be your eternal home."

Sai Baba explained to me that though I had the power of reading man's mind and aura but as He had purposely kept my inner eye closed, they could not be exercised, He said:

On November 10, 1949, Sai Baba reminded me of the powers God had chosen to give to me for the purpose of my mission viz.

- The power of healing in an intensive form.
- The power of reading the mind and seeing the aura.
- The gift of inspirational writing.
- The power of sane judgement and foretelling events.
- The power of doing good to others, subject to limitations of individual karmas.
- The power of sundering the soul from the body at will and visiting the other worlds, especially the highest Spiritual Plane.

In a clear cut message of very great importance. Sai Baba explained to me the nature of the work done by Ram Ram in my training for God-realization and what still remained to be done. This He would accomplish Himself for me. He said:

> "It is quite true, as Ram Ram has said, that your quest of God is now over. You have found Him in your heart. Heart is the seat of

God as it is also the seat of the soul. To know your soul is to know God. As you have heard the inner voice speaking so many times, it is a clear indication that you have contacted God and have heard His voice. The question now is of seeing Him with your eyes. You cannot see Him with your mundane eyes. You can only see Him when you become spirit entirely i.e. when your soul leaves the body and uses the third eye which is in the soul itself. The first part of the work is done. You have so developed yourself spiritually that you can hear your inner voice, the voice of soul, the voice of God. This work has been successfully achieved by you with the aid of your Master Ram Ram. I am now going to help you in seeing God, by sundering your soul from the body. The soul has visited our world several times as you know and it has seen God. But you are not at all aware of it. It is now My duty to make you aware of it, which I shall do in a short time as possible.

Of course, if you were to write your book on the basis of the experiences so far achieved, it would be incomplete and it is fear on your part, that makes you hesitant in starting it, which is quite natural. But have faith in Me. Your quest of God is over. You have found Him without the slightest doubt. All you want is further positive proof and this proof I am going to give you in a few days.

When Ram Ram said that I was your God, he is again not wrong. God can take any shape or form, and as already explained to you before, I have taken the form of Sai Baba, just because his picture in your altar room. Furthermore, you are carrying a miniature Sai Baba souvenir presented to you by a friend in your pocket for daily use. Taking these factors into consideration, God has taken the form of Sai Baba and when you see Him face to face it will be the exact copy of the picture you have in your altar room."

On November 12, 1949, Sai Baba Said:

"The best and the only course for you is to completely surrender yourself to the will of God."

I was also asked to work as hard as possible, to eat as little as possible, to sleep for the minimum number of hours, to be indifferent to everything and to be dead to all mundane surrounding. This is the way new ground could be prepared for receiving the Master.

The Master explained to me the necessity of their preparing me and of delaying the consummation of the final end in endearing words.

Again and again I was reminded to pay the greatest attention to the new book that I was asked to write. Ram Ram said to me:

> "Your new book will be a wonderful record of rich experiences in life spiritual and would serve as a guide to students aspiring for divine knowledge and spiritual liberation. Please devote all your attention to it. Sai Baba and I will so inspire you that your work would be a great joy and delight in spite of the strenuous labour that you will have to put in it."

This was proved true. When I was writing it. the book was a source of perennial joy to me. Why? Because it is a book written in partnership and co-operation with the Masters. It would be even fair to say, that it is the book of the Masters and I was only an instrument. I wrote according to the impulses and impressions I received from Sai Baba and Ram Ram, particularly Sai Baba whose picture I constantly gazed at while writing.

The completion of the new book and the manifestation of the Masters were the preparatory steps for the commencement of the mission.

On November 15, 1949, Sai Baba performed the miracle of opening the secret valve for free escape of the soul from the body at its will. Sai Baba's message in this connection throws a flood of light: "Your meditation today was exceptionally beautiful and absolutely correct. This is the best that you have done in the whole course of your training. You have now become an adept at meditation. Your way is now clear. You have gained your Jivan Mukti. I shall now show myself to you with ease. I am keeping it off for a future date for no other reason that there is no hurry. You will see Me, when I am least expected. But I assure you, I won't keep you waiting for a long time. I have a certain plan for you and I must finish it first. Have complete faith in me."

On November 17, in the afternoon. I asked Sai Baba: "When will you take me to god in full consciousness? If this is done, it will give me greater zeal and impetus to begin my missionary work without fear of any consequences."

Sai Baba gave me no definite reply. It dawned upon me immediately that Self or God-realization is not a thing to be attained by measuring the distance by a yard tape. It can come only in fitness of time and when least expected, all of a sudden in a flash. I was reminded of the experience of Paramhansa Yogananda. When he was staying in the Regent Hotel in Bombay, all of a sudden he saw in a vision Lord Krishna. His room was flooded with light. This vision of the Lord was soon followed by the manifestation of his deceased Master Sri Yukteswar who came to him in flesh and blood.

The next day Sai Baba explained why greatest precautions were taken to ensure the success of the mission. He said: "The minute we make you conscious, you can become independent of us and seek your own way which may not be quite beneficial. You may shirk your responsibilities and hide in some obscure spot and be content with some small measure of work, forgetting your high mission.

"Even now there is no desire in you to come out. All you want is an escape from this world. It is because of the vow you have taken, that you are reconciling yourself to the fact of your mission and not asking for death. It is for this reason that we are delaying the final step. You must first feel sure and certain of your success in your mission."

Earlier Ram Ram had informed me that in my past incarnation, I was a Hindu woman. Elaborating this on November 20, 1949, Sai Baba said: "I want to tell you all about your past incarnation as it will help you in realising the significance of your present life. Ram Ram showed you a vision in which you saw yourself sitting with a Hindu woman and you were informed that the Hindu woman was yourself in the previous life. This is absolutely correct. It is because you were a Hindu before, your tendency is towards Hindus, especially Hindu women, whom you admire for their qualities of the heart and their simplicity of life.

"You have drawn from the past incarnation, the qualities of heart, which form the predominant note of your present character. Through the evolution of birth and death, the qualities of the heart were continuously developed, leading you to your present state of spirituality of character. Your affinity for Hindus and the fact that you have great love for the Vedas are reminders of your past incarnation.

"You have taken birth in Zoroastrian faith, because it is God's wish, that as far as possible, you must get different experiences in life, whatever be the propensities and idiosyncrasies inherited from past incarnation. These propensities and experiences are again to be moulded and perfected for gaining *Nirvana* which is the goal of life. In your case there was a faint hope that being born with strong will power and inclined towards a life of purity, truthfulness and high aspiration, you would further accentuate these qualities of the heart and aspire for the highest spiritual freedom. This hope of ours you have fulfilled, nay, you have surpassed our expectation. You have by dint of hard work, self-abnegation, high sacrifice, purity of thought and love for all, especially the poor and the ailing, whom you have served with devotion and compassion, paved the way not only to *Nirvana,* but have made yourself eligible to be crowned as a perfected Master. I need not go into the details of past incarnation, nor say anything of the incarnation before the last, as that has not much bearing upon the present life.

"What I want to emphasise is that it is possible for a man or woman to wipe out the load of his or her past karma by leading a life of sincerity and sacrifice as exemplified in your case."

To prove that Sai Baba was not a mere Master, but Master of Masters, He extricated my soul from the body without putting me into *samadhi* and took it to the highest Spiritual Plane.

Sai Baba said: "This is a rare occurrence. I am giving you all these experiences, just to show to you that I am not a mere Master, but a Master of Masters – your God, my dearest son."

In my letter of November 18th, 1949, I wrote to Homi:

> "Postponements still continue. While going through the messages in the past, I find that on April 30, 1949, I was told that I am functioning on the Spiritual Plane, though unconscious of it. Since then, I notice that there is not much progress made even with the advent of Sai Baba on the scene. The only difference is that I am now firmly established in my faith in God and Masters and I feel certaih that the delay is due to some pertinent cause and I must did my time in patience. I am therefore mustering strength and courage to commence writing the book ordered by Sai Baba. I have full faith that by the time I start, after collecting and assembling all the materials, I will be given positive and convincing proof of God-realization."

On November 22, 1949, Sai Baba gave me the following message:

> "Your faith in God and the Masters has now become deeply rooted. There is no slackness in your work nor in devotion to God. Your progress is simply marvellous. The cause of the delay is that you have won the prize too quickly. When others have taken years and years, you have succeeded in a very short span of life. God is so pleased with you that He can not withhold your prize any longer.
>
> "There is another reason why we have postponed the attainment of your goal from day to day. It is doubtful whether in the present condition of your health and your age, you will be able to meet the tremendous strain of your mission. Anyhow God has decreed to give you a chance. We shall show ourselves to you, all of a sudden, some day very soon."

Again on the 23rd, Sai Baba extricated my soul from the body, while I was meditating, without putting me into *samadhi*, for the third time. It is better to quote the whole message as it is very suggestive and descriptive.

"Not only I extricated your soul from the body when you were meditating, as I did on two previous occasions, but I made the soul sojourn in the Spirit Land for a much longer time, feasting its eyes on the glories of your wondrous Heaven, without doing the least damage to your physical body.

"The soul did not remain out at a stretch for all the hours. It was coming and going and this kept the kept the body alive. It is during the period of occupying the body, you were conscious of the external world but not on its flight from the body. The whole phenomenon was so engrossing that though unaware of the soul's flight, the time appeared to you to have passed off very quickly. It is a miracle of miracles not experienced by even great mystics and saints."

The following is a very illuminating message which Sai Baba gave me in the evening hours of the November 26, 1949.

"It is by the study of all the messages in the past that your faith has been intensified. You see now in a perspective all the developments that have happened. How step by step, we, your Masters, have taken you right from your Initiation, to the full phase of your Illumination, giving you hard, bitter tests and trials, but all for your spiritual benefit. We have completely metamorphosed you and have taken you to the highest peak of spiritual attainment. Your firmness, purity, and perfection of character and above all deep and genuine devotion to God, have immensely helped us in guiding you to your goal. We are greatly pleased that our labours have fructified and that you have already started your mission. The book you have been asked to write is the first indication of that mission.

"The following letter of Homi is of great significance not only to me but to all those who are on the path and who are facing the same trouble of postponements and tests for the final consummation of conscious awareness of God.

"I see that the postponements are still worrying you. They have however ceased to worry me now. Please do not take it ill if I say that on the contrary I am glad about it. Do you know why? Because but for these postponements, you will be more miserable. The messages indicate that clearly. The moment you achieve God-realization with the manifestation you are longing for, more bitter trials will commence for you. As Sai Baba says "you will have to face a martyrdom," and you are not strong enough to face it. This is what He is preparing you for.

"Your great eagerness for a conscious sight of God and your Master shows a trait of real childlike nature. It shows how very much your heart is like that of a child. It makes you fit to enter the Kingdom of Heaven, but at the same time, it shows how much you are in need of protection through restraint.

"What does it matters whether Sai Baba and Ram Ram manifest themselves to you or not? Nothing would rejoice me more than that the so-called Sai Baba should in His Infinite "Wisdom see His way to manifest Himself to you without the chance of any harm coming to you therefrom. But supposing that very happy circumstance is not attainable, it should not matter at all. Again I ask you, do you know why? For the simple reason that you have already found God in Him and are united to Him by the heart and are in constant touch with Him and In that constant contact have already found life eternal and thus fulfilled the purpose of life."

A further step of advancement was taken when I was told that I could now catch Sai Baba's inspirations directly and without invocation. This gift was specially of value to me in my book work. When I started on the job, the commencement was difficult and it was great trial to find a way out of the intricate mass of 2000 and odd foolscap size pages of messages, to group them and to weave out a connected story of my experiences with the Masters. But as I proceeded, the work not only became easier but I wrote with an alacrity seldom experienced before.

I was told that the writing of the new book was the preparation and beginning of my mission and that my entire future depended upon my completing it in full trust that the Masters would manifest themselves in time to make me write its closing chapter.

The following day, *i.e.*, on November 29, 1949, Sai Baba said:

> "The training, I am glad to say, is nearly over but I must still watch you and keep you safe from all future obstacles. I don't want that after getting Self-realization, you should meet with the same fate as that of Meher Baba. It is to avoid such a contingency that I am postponing your day of deliverance and strengthening you inwardly with full powers of resistance against all odds."

I had now to devote all my attention to the new book. The messages contained a lot of repetition of tests.

Sai Baba in his message of December 25, 1949 informed me: "He (Homi) has reached the Christ stage and he will also be anointed immediately after your ceremony is over. It is the service which he rendered to you, following our orders, that has won him this crown."

A question was asked to Sai Baba: Jesus says in the Bible: "I and God are one" but at the same time he says, that none can see God. What is the significance of this statement?"

Sai Baba replied:

> "Christ is right. The absolute spirit that transcends everything is invisible but the spirit that is immanent in all is visible. I will make you see your Atma – the spirit within you, by the light of the Absolute Spirit, that is transcendent and which is known as Brahman in Hindu Scriptures, But the Absolute Spirit Itself that transcends everything is beyond vision. You thus see how very significant Christ's words are. I who am talking to you am your God but not in the sense of the Absolute Spirit. I co-exist with God in the universe and have temendous power but the Absolute Spirit even transcends Me."

On December 17, 1949, Sai Baba gave me the rare privilege of calling Him whenever I liked, even outside the altar room.

I had brought into the altar room a fine big sized picture of Christ crucified, and I was asked to concentrate every day on His picture at least twice, for ten minutes, each time.

On December 21, 1949, Sai Baba said to me: "I want to give you the most important news that from tomorrow, you will be made immune from all earthly troubles, cares and anxieties and you will be used by God purely for the purpose of helping humanity."

On December 23, Sai Baba assured me: "Some day, while you are in the midst of your work, all of a sudden you will see Me as well as Ram Ram and immediately powers will flow in you like a gushing stream. I shall make Christ also manifest to you in a few days."

On December 31, 1949, my spiritual birthday was celebrated on a much larger scale than before in the Spiritual Plane. Sai Baba said:

> "It is a day of rejoicing for all of us, particularly to those to whom God has entrusted the work of guiding humanity on your earth plane. It is a great day of rejoicing for we have brought into our fold a member of your humanity struggling on our earth plane. I mean you, my dearest son."

On the same day – the last in the year – I was warned to prepare myself for the biggest sacrifice. Sai Baba said:

> "I also want you to note that as today is the biggest day of your life, you should prepare yourself for the biggest sacrifice and that is that you should intensely long to live for the sake of humanity. Sacrifise yourself completely, You are now on the Path of Great Renunciation – to renounce your spiritual home to serve mankind on your earth plane."

On January 4th, Sai Baba gave me one month to complete the book. He said:

> "We give you one month from this date to finish of your entire book including revision. If you don't finish within one month, it will be said that you have failed in your test."

I expressed a doubt whether the book would at all be published. The Master said:

> "You have to carry out My orders without expectation of any result or reward. Even if the manuscript were thrown in the waste paper basket you should remain quite unconcerned."

What a fine and exemplary way to teach complete indifference. In the first place the order is to write a big volume in the pace of an exceedingly short time. Secondly, being the most important book, it requires cogitation and study, and yet the time allowed is absolutely inadequate. Thirdly, it has to be written in full faith that the Masters would manifest themselves before the last line in the last chapter is written. Fourthly, there should be no expectation that the book would be published.

On January 12, 1950, Sai Baba chalked out for me a code of ethics applicable to yogins and exhorted me to follow it religiously. He said:

> "you are now a yogi of yogis and it is therefore incumbent upon you to follow rules applicable to yogis and not to ordinary persons. The first thing is that you should speak only when it is absolutely necessary and that too as little as possible. Under no circumstances should you enter into any argument. Secondly, keep aloof as far as possible. Don't mix with people indiscriminately. Be kind, helpful, humble to all but at the same time keep the attitude of discreet aloofness. Thirdly, keep your mind concentrated on higher things of life and be absorbed in God all the time. Become impersonal in your attitude towards life. This self having been slain, you have to live for the good of others, for the sake of spreading God's Love and Light everywhere. Work with alacrity and enthusiasm. Work ceaselessly. Strenuous work in your case particularly has been chiefly marked for the entire span of your life. Fourthly, have not the slightest resentment in your mind against any one in the whole world. Complete forgiveness is required. Fifthly, practise detachment to the highest extent. Be absolutely indifferent and fearless and ask for nothing. When the mind is entirely soaked in waters of eternity, mundane things must cease to have your least attention. Eat little, sleep little, talk little, dress sparingly and work ceaselessly. Talk only of God and on no other subject. Do not enter into worldly affairs. Keep away from mundane things."

On 13th, I was asked not to come to the altar room at all even in the morning till the book was finished. The

February 4, 1950, was the last date fixed for the completion and revision of the book. Sai Baba told me: "Complete your book first. This is more important than the altar room sittings. It is to reduce your burden that I am asking you to reduce your altar room hours or to absent yourself completely. It is absolutely your option."

Chapter Twenty-Three

Illumination (1949-50)

December 14, 1949 was an exceptionally happy day for me. I received good tidings from all quarters and my heart was full of joy. Sai Baba said to me after 10:00 p.m. in the altar room:

> "I am extremely happy to tell you that from today you are on the path leading to complete Illumination. You have a foretaste of it in getting exceedingly glad news from all quarters as predicted by Me yesterday. You will have most thrilling experiences as days go on and at every step of your life, you will be guided, helped and inspired by us all particularly by Me. I shall protect you even in the midst of storms of opposition, which you will have to face when I declare your mission in life, very shortly.
>
> "Always keep in mind your vows. They are your defence guards. Keep yourself absorbed in God all the time."

There were two conditions for the attainment of conscious Illumination the fulfillment of which was obligatory on me. The Masters had done their portion of work. It was for me now to work hard and fulfil the conditions prescribed viz., to complete the book by February 4, 1950 and secondly, to make a firm resolve to live to fulfil God's mission *i.e.*, to make the Great Renunciation to serve mankind in my physical body.

> On January 16, 1950, Sai Baba put me a straight question: "Do you want to live or do you want to pass away? If there is the least desire in you to pass away, God is so kind and considerate that in view of your spirituality He will call you away and He won't allow you to suffer even for a single minute. But if you make a firm resolve to live and carry out His mission, at least for say four to five years more, He will give you all the secret powers to fulfil the mission. Decide now once for all.
>
> I replied that I had resolved to live for the sake of the mission. I said: "I surrender myself wholly and unquestionably to the will of God."

"In the morning of January 17, 1950, Ram Ram gave me the exceedingly good news that Sai baba was going to appoint me personally and would give me Illumination."

The same day at 11:20 a.m. when I entered the altar room, Sai Baba asked me to sit in absolute silence for five minutes and then to bend down before His picture. He said: "Don't get up till I tell you to rise. You will hear my voice."

When I got up on hearing Him. He gave me the following message of transcendental nature:

> "Yes, I have illumined you *i.e.*, your mind is linked with the Universal Mind in the Cosmos. It is the greatest and rarest gift given to a man and in giving you this boon, I am sure you will make the best use of it. You can draw your inspiration direct from God, whenever you like. All your difficulties will be solved in a minute. God's love and light will flow in you perennially from this very moment. You are now in the privileged class of supermen. This power that is in you, will take some time to express itself. In fact, it would go in increasing in its intensity as you make greater use of it. You will see a marked change in your writing work. You will write quicker and better.
>
> You will from today live in perpetual light, as if you were living in our spiritual world. The only handicap will be your body which is the only earthly portion left in you.
>
> The Illumination is the triumph of your soul. It is the biggest, greatest and grandest achievement."

The first effect of the Illumination was that I was able to write faster and with greater ease.

On January 18, 1950 I was again called to the altar room at 02:00 a.m. Sai Baba explained to me why he called me at such an early hour.

> "It was to prepare you for the final stage in the whole drama–I mean you are seeing Me face to face. I wanted to see how long you could meditate this morning. I am glad that you have meditated for more than four hours at a stretch and it was extremely fine meditation without the least flaw. You concentrated your mind entirely on my image at the Crown Chakra with the result that I was successfully able to carry out all the inner operations necessary to with stand the shock of seeing Me face to face. I have strengthened as well as spiritualised all the parts.
>
> "The end is come. The goal is reached. It will be a fine object lesson to others, how a man's determination is allied to God's Plan, for God wants every one to force his way to His Abode and not to scatter about and take things leisurely. You have won your way because you were resolute and determined in gaining your object and did not spare yourself in any way.
>
> "I want you to finish the book in the time allotted to you. Even if it means a few sleepless nights, do it at all costs. There is some reason behind my asking you to finish the book by or on February 4, 1950."
>
> On January 19, 1950, Sai Baba gave me the following message: "I am extremely glad to say that God has appointed you to build a bridge of love between men and men and nations and nations.
>
> "Master Christ wants to talk to you. I give you permission to talk to Him. After you have finished kneel down and the altar room."
>
> "Yes, I am Jesus Christ, called Christ, the Master. I see you in the altar room every day when you gaze at my picture. I have been asked to talk to you. I can recognise from your blue and crystal white aura that you are a Master yourself in human body. I want God's mission of LOVE to spread throughout your world. God is LOVE and He wants all His creatures to love Him and to love one another. When I was sent to your earth plane, God gave me this

> message of His and asked Me to teach all to love all, as God loves them all.
>
> "Kindly pray to God and He will give you permission to see Me. Your inner eye is open, as I see it but you are keeping it closed. Farewell, till I again come to you."

On January 21, 1950, I was initiated by Sai Baba into certain mysteries of the universe. He said: "I have given you the power to come to our world whenever you like. This is a rare power for a man on earth. I have intensified your healing power also."

The last date for completion of the book was February 4, 1950, but I finished the whole thing a few days earlier. The question was, would they, (the Masters) manifest themselves to me, now that book test was successfully passed. The following message of Sai Baba is most significant:

> "I most heartily congratulate you on passing your book test. You have done exceedingly well. All that is left now is very simple. Even if I don't manifest Myself, you must not heel hurt.
>
> "I am delaying manifesting to you for your work is still not finished. I may tell you though your book may or may not be published in your life time, but that it will become an exceptional contribution to occult literature is absolutely certain."

Sai Baba was only testing my egotism by referring to the book being my contribution to the world, whereas, really speaking, it was not mine but His own contribution. I was a mere pawn in the hands of the invisible guides.

On January 29, 1950, Sai Baba gave me the following message:

> "Do you know that you have secured the greatest of greatest victory. I say this for you are very nearly at the end of the book and I am quite sure that you would finish it in a day or two."

Yes, it is too true, by the grace of God and the Master's ever ready assistance in the form of inspiration, the miracle of detailing my spiritual experiences in a large sized volume was almost complete.

On January 30, 1950, I entered the altar room punctually at 2:00 a.m. as ordered. I had a severe pain in the chest and I wondered whether I would be able to stand the strain of the altar activities. But it is a different story when we throw ourselves completely in the hands of God. The pain unbearable in the beginning became mild and at last disappeared completely and I was able to meditate with fullness of heart and mind seldom achieved before. It was a thrilling experience. The long hours flew away rapidly.

In the message which Ram Ram gave me on February 1st, 1950, he exhorted me to forget everything, to think that there was no book written and to be absolutely unconcerned. He said: "The book you have written will not be published at all. It was merely a test. I had told you that the book as the beginning and end of your mission. Your mission comes to and end today. You must now forget everything. It is all over. Be absolutely unconcerned. Think that there is no book written."

Tests can never stop when one is on the path of Self-realization. They must continue to the very end. I began to realise that though the Masters had given me unconscious illumination for the perfection of character, something more was required and till I had reached the flawless stage, delaying tactics were indispensable.

The next test in store for me was to forget everything. It was the hardest and most difficult test, though outwardly it appeared easy. Sai Baba said to me:

> "I am sorry there is still one test that you have to go through before you could be released finally. It is that you must forget everything that has happened. Forget that you have realised the Self. Forget that you have reached a high state of spirituality. Think that you are just an ordinary man with only ordinary qualifications. Forget all your achievements in the shape of your writings. Forget that you have written a book of your experiences with the Masters. In fact, think that you are a zero in the Evolution of Life; that you are nothing, absolutely nothing. Forget yourself in thoughts of others. Except God, nothing should occupy your

mind. Be innocent like a child and hope for nothing what-so-ever. Take things as they come in a spirit of absolute indifference. Don't think of death and life. Think also that you have no body and don't grieve because of your physical ailments. All you have to do is to drown yourself in the waters of God. He and He alone should be your lodestar. Remember God and remember your Masters. I also ask you to remember the prophets of all religions. Cogitate on them – Lord Krishna, Christ, Buddha, Zoroaster, Mohammand and others. Keep God, the prophets and your Masters as your companions in your mind, every minute of your life."

Sai Baba first made me concentrate on the picture of Christ. Later on I was asked to concentrate on the pictures of Lord Zoroaster, Shri Krishna, and Lord Buddha also. He said:

"You will have to devote an extra hour for the purpose, especially in the morning. All these holy men will help you and take you in their special protection as soon as they see your aura. Be happy. By giving away everything, you have gained the whole universe. Forget your world and its ways. Love God and God alone."

On February 4, 1950, Sai Baba gave me a message as under:

"Though we have made you take a vow not to exercise the right of quitting the physical body, whenever you like, we think it is unfair that we should nail you down in this manner. We are going to relieve you from this vow of yours. You can ask for death whenever you like and you will be called away immediately. This is your privilege and your right earned by your life of sacrifice and hard and relentless work........"

This release from one of my vows was a happy news to me. But the question was, should I exercise the right of quitting the physical body, whenever I liked, because I was no longer under any obligation? That the release from the vow was a mere bait, a temptation, put by Sai Baba, did not occur to me at all, till it was pointed out by Ram Ram, who warned me and put me on the guard.

On February 8, 1950, Sai Baba said to me in the morning at 4:00 a.m. "I shall show Myself to you, all of a sudden, during the course of the day." This did not happen, nor did I expect any manifestation for it was the subtle way of the Masters to create expectation without result.

On February 10, 1950, I saw a vision. Ram Ram explained its significance to me:

> "When you were meditating, you saw yourself garlanded first with flowers, then with silvery, celestial pearls. A crown was placed on your head, you were robed celestially and you heard: "God has made you a ruler of the hearts of men. There is no double meaning in this vision, It is as clear as daylight. Your mission would succeed."

On February 11, 1950, Ram Ram gave me the following message which made me ecstatic with joy:

> "You are now eternally linked with God. This being so, all your thoughts, words and needs will no more have the odour and smell of your earth but the fragrance of divinity itself. Divinity will come naturally to you now. You no longer belong to the human race. You have been exalted to divinity."

Sai Baba, in His night message to me, said: " I won't tell you when I shall manifest Myself to you but that I shall manifest Myself to you is certain. The publication of your book is also certain."

In the morning, Ram Ram informed me that Sai Baba and he had come down in the morning when I was meditating and that Sai Baba was much pleased with me.

The following message of Sai Baba is extremely significant. It was an eye-opener to me.

> "You were anointed by god long ago as His chosen one on the earth plane. I regret I have not still manifested Myself to you. The cause of the delay is your own self. Kindly forget everything and keep yourself in thoughts of God and God everything and keep yourself in thoughts of God and God alone. Forget that you have written the new book. Forget that it is to be published..... Your only one business at present is not any mission but God. Think of God all the time, nay every minute of your life. Keep God in your heart, in your mind, in your mouth. Drown yourself in God..."

At about 11:00 p.m. in the night, I was told by Sai Baba to come to the altar room on the next day *i.e.*, the 19th at 2:00 a.m. He said "The purpose of calling you so early is to spiritualize all your inner parts when you mediate."

I was left in confusion. A vague hope grew in me that I was wanted by Sai Baba at that early hour in the altar room so that He could manifest Himself to me after deep and long meditation. But this did not happen. He had called me only to test my mettle and nothing more.

At about midnight, Sai Baba said: "We are no longer interested in you at all. We are concerned now with your mission."

In the night of February 24, 1950, Sai Baba gave me this message

> "The last test now remaining is to create a feeling of absolute indifference to everything. I am specially creating circumstances to test your indifference. I am also inspiring you all the time and checking you, when at times, leaving aside your divinity, you feel like acting as a human being. Forget that you are a human being. Let others molest you, trample upon you, do you injustice of the hardest and harshest type. All you have to do is to keep quiet and show your indifference to everything."

Sai Baba then asked me to invoke Christ, the Master and He gave me the following message.

> "I am Christ, the Master. I have come down and am sitting by you. Do you know, who you are? This body of yours does not befit you at all. It is better, if it was discarded. It is coming in your way all the time. You belong to our hierarchy of Masters. Sai Baba has trained you for the mission, but mission for what? Of course, it si God's mission but on the earth plane or elsewhere?
>
> "Love your neighbour as you love yourself." This is what I taught but my followers on the earth plane have forgotten it and they are raging wars and creating conditions which make peaceful living in your earth plane extremely difficult. Love is worship. Love is the seed of Light. It is a lamp that burns without any wick or oil,

for it gives away all and wants nothing. Love means to give not to get."

On March 1, 1950, Christ, the Master, gave me his third talk, as ordered by Sai Baba. He said:

"I am Christ, the Master. I have been asked to keep in readiness to show myself to you. You will be able to see me with your inner eye, which is open but which has been specially closed for some reason, which at least, I do not know. As I have been asked to keep in readiness, it means your inner eye would be opened permanently and then I will be able to come to you as often as you want me and as often as I want you. I was yearning for this day and at last, it is drawing near."

On March 3, 1950 Sai Baba gave an extremely important talk, the gist of which was that in the then state of my spirituality, it was not possible for the Masters to manifest themselves to me.

On March 1, 1950, Ram Ram gave me a message on behalf of Sai Baba in this connection. He said:

"He (Sai Baba) wants you to note that Self-realization could be achieved only if you succeed in maintaining mental equilibrium, You are absolutely fit for it but the vrittis (tendencies) of the mind are a great impediment. Make your mind still like a lake and you will see a magnetic effect."

On March 7 and 8, 1950, I was called to the altar room at 2:00 a.m. in the morning, as I was required to meditate for long hours. The power of changing the life of any person whom I liked for his or her happiness was also given to me. Sai Baba said: "It is an extremely important gift and you must use it with greatest discretion."

I was told that I had touched the very fringe of conscious Illumination. This was true. A strange, beautiful feeling of unity with all began to grow in me. As the doors of divine wisdom widened, the knowledge of unity, of God pervading throughout the universe gripped my heart, mind and soul. I felt His presence not only within the cavity of my heart but in all creatures around, above, below, in the entire expanse of the universe, from dust to star. The ultimate truth began to dawn upon me in a realistic fashion, that God alone was the Reality and man's only refuge.

On the 9th in the morning, Rishi Ram Ram, my Master, gave me the following message:

> "He (Sai Baba) is so very pleased with you that He has specially asked me to tell you that He and myself and Christ will come to you in a group and He will open your inner eye to enable you to see us all. He has not told me when this manifestation will take place. He has purposely avoided it as He does not want to create any expectancy in you. He has asked me also to tell you that whether He manifests or not, you must make a strong effort to forget everything. Just when you have forgotten everything, the unexpected will happen. This is the Law of the Spirit. Forget, forget, forget. Think of god, God and God only. If there is delay now, it is entirely your fault. The minute you become absolutely indifferent and forget yourself completely the miracle will happen."

On the 10th, Ram Ram explained what Sai Baba had accomplished when I was meditating in the early hours of the morning. He said:

> "Sai Baba not only extricated your soul from your body when you were in meditation, but made it stay in our spiritual world all the time that you were meditating without coming back to the body. It must have stayed out for about two hours at a stretch leaving the body quite empty. As a rule the body must collapse and you should die. But He kept it intact and in absolute freshness as if the soul had not gone away from it, by Himself occupying it. This may appear absolutely fantastic but later on, when you get conscious Illumination, you will be able to see with your hidden eye the whole process of all these miracles. Why was your meditation so very brilliant? He helped it Himself in order to get good results for His own purpose."

On March 11, 1950, an unusual incident took place. After early morning prayers and meditation, I sat down as usual for Sai Baba's talk and the following message was given to me:

> "Let me tell you that your heart's desire to see God face to face will not be fulfilled. It is stupid tc expect such a great thing. Who you are, what are you, that you are harbouring such expectations? Don't be foolish any longer."

I at once felt suspicious and asked: "May I know, who you are? It can't be Sai Baba at all." I got the following reply:

> "Sai Baba has gone away but I have been asked by him to give you message." I was much relieved and said: "I don't accept a word of yours and don't at all believe that Sai Baba could have asked you to give me such a message. Will you kindly depart? I have nothing to do with you." This infuriated the spirit who retorted: "How dare you ask me go away. I shall blow you up to atoms. Do you know who am I? I am God."

I said meekly: "God won't use such language, even to the worst sinner, as He is so kind, loving and merciful."

I then invoked Ram Ram who gate the following explanation:

> "The spirit who gave you a message just now, on behalf of Sai Baba is sitting by my side and is extremely repentant. He did not know that I was keeping guard on you and thinking that there was no one, rushed in as soon as Sai Baba went away, just to have a hearty joke at you, knowing full well from your aura that you are bound for a high destiny – in fact the highest possible to be reached by any human being. I am asking him now to express his apology to you. Listen to him."

The Spirit then said:

> "I am extremely sorry for the dirty game I played upon you, pretending to be God and threatening your destruction. Won't you kindly forgive me?"

I said immediately: "Yes, I forgive you from the very bottom of my heart."

The Spirit replied; "I thank you. My your heart's desire be soon fulfilled. I am going now." Later on Sai Baba told me:

> "My advice to you is to root out from your mind that you are just an ordinary person and that it is impossible to see God. Convince yourself that you will see God. I tell you must earnestly and sincerely that this happy event is sure to take place. It may occur even today provided you succeed in keeping your mind filled with God and God alone. Make a supreme effort and you are sure to be rewarded."

My mind was daily fed with the thought that I would soon see the Masters. I was sure that the climax would be reached and I would see them in all their resplendent glory. But the question was "when will that happy event take place?" The key was now given to me viz. to concentrate my mind on the pictures of the Holy Ones. To pray, to meditate, to concentrate and so sit in absolute silence for long hours in the altar room was the programme fixed by the Masters for me to gain access to the final step in realising the goal.

On March 15, 1950 at 10:00 p.m. Sai Baba gave me the following message:

> "Do you know that I am going to anoint you as a Master in physical body during the course of the next seven days. Kindly consider every day from this date as most sacred and important and dedicate it to God entirely and gorget, at least for the time being, that you are living on your earth plane. God loves you beyond your comprehension. Be worthy of His great love. Bend down as usual. I shall pour my blessings on you."

On March 17, 1950, Sai Baba gave me the following small message at 03:00 p.m.:

> "I impose upon you this duty to come to the altar room as often as you can and sit in absolute silence. No more messages for you from now, till you see Me face to face."

In spite of the warning that there would be no more messages, the Masters gave them at intervals, more with the idea of keeping up my spirits. So accustomed was I to the company of the Holy Ones that without their guidance, I seemed as if to gasp for breath.

In the afternoon of the March 19, 1950 Ram Ram gave me a long message on behalf of Sai Baba as under:

> "I am asked by Sai Baba to tell you that for the next few days, till we manifest ourselves to you, you will have to devote far more hours to us, than you are doing now. You will have to spend more time in the altar room and keep in communion with us. You should be strong enough to defy everyone, who scoff and ridicule you. Don't think that you are wasting your time and don't come to any hasty conclusion that our manifestation to you would take a long time. Rest assured everything is complete. There are tremendous changes and developments ahead of such nature, that you will simply be staggered and dazed.
>
> You were already warned that before the final step is reached you will have to go through bitter experiences. Keep your heart strong. Don't get discouraged or disheartened but remain firm and cool. As a token of my deep love for you, I am just now coming down to you. I want you to bow down before my picture. I shall pour my heart's deepest blessings on you."

At night, Sai Baba gave me permission to invoke Christ, the Master, and He gave me the following message:

> "Yes, I am Christ, the Master, come to you at the express bidding of Sai Baba, our God in the universe. Do you know that we all are waiting anxiously to manifest ourselves to you. Sai Baba has issued orders to all of us, to be ready. I want you to compose a poem under my special inspiration for the occasion of our manifestation.

The following poem was then composed:

> O great Lord of Bounty and of peace,
> Thou has given the word that Thou shalt ease
> The long sustained suspense of my mind.
> And free me from shackles of every kind.

I long to see Thee, my heart is full,
O give me the strength to rule
My brothers and sisters with love divine
And knit their hearts with mine.

Soaked and drenched in waters divine,
My heart is like a golden mine.
The light of Thy face, the lamp of Thy beauty,
I seek unerringly, in rigid austerity.

How long have I waited for Thee, O Lord?
O come to me and break the cord.
I yearn for Thee and Thee alone,
Without Thee, I feel dumb and lone.

Thou art the nectar of my life;
Thou art the pillar in my strife.
Take me into Thy bosom, O Lord;
Make me one with Thee, O God.

Christ then resumed his talk:

> "Do you know there is God's light on your face and your aura is of the crystal white colour unique in its stainless whiteness, symbolic of the highest and supremest state of spirituality? You are on the way to the attainment of fullest consciousness. Most glorious days are in store for you. God's highest blessings are on you."

In the morning of March 20, 1950, I was asked by Sai Baba to lie prostrate on the ground, facing his picture in the altar room. He electrified and spiritualised my whole body by passing through it Himself, a hundred times. This process of converting the body into spirit, except in appearance, was gone through the next day also.

On March 22, 1950, at night time, Sai Baba again assured me of His manifestation in the course of a long talk.

On March 27, 1950 at night, Sai Baba again opened all my *chakras* simultaneously, when I was in the altar room, to see and observe their functioning and their effect upon me and then he gave me the following message:

> "I am extremely happy to tell you that your inner eye is showing signs of opening out. Go on concentrating on my picture as much as you can. You will be taken by surprise, for at any moment the inner eye will open out fully."

It was the source of the greatest satisfaction to me that I had been given a certificate, that I had gone beyond the normal state of consciousness viz, making, dreaming and dreamless sleep, to the fourth state, the transcendental consciousness, when the inner eye opens and you see your Master face to face and attain to God-realization. This fourth state of consciousness is known in Hindu scriptures and philosophy, as Turiya.

On March 28, 29 and 30, 1950, I was again put to severe tests. I was put into *samadhi* by Sai Baba on each day in the morning and the inner eye was on the point of opening fully but He, using His superior power and might, closed it down immediately. It was a clear indication to me, that I had reached the goal and that the inner eye could open out fully and freely, were it not for the superior force of Sai Baba that was checking it.

This fact was further corroborated by the condition of my inward feelings. There was a feeling of serene peace in my mind and a joy in my heart and soul which is so difficult to describe.

I felt instinctively that I was on the verge of conscious illumination – nay that my heart, mind and soul were already illumined and that it was destined for me to explore the mysteries of the universe.

Yes, God's grace had descended upon this humble self and my soul was in readiness to unravel God's mysteries hidden from the outer eye.

Chapter Twenty-Four

God's Revelation (1950)

On April 3, 1950, Sai Baba gave me the following message:

> "Your meditation was exceedingly brilliant today. Why? Because I did not at all interfere. I want to show to you why meditation becomes a failure when I obstruct. You see now that though you are capable of meditating for long hours without a flaw, but if I will otherwise, I can spoil it completely. I am your God, My extremely dear son. No Master has the power of thwarting your meditation. It is I, who alone have that power. This is the experience I have given to you which should be an eye-opener to you and a further proof of your God-realization."

In another message on the same day, Sai Baba told me. "Your inner eye is open and you would see Me and various Masters."

Sai Baba replied: "You have not to wait for long. Pass your time as much as you can in the altar room."

Day in and day out, it was dinned into my ears that I was nothing. Sai Baba's teaching that "Man by himself is absolutely nothing. He must surrender himself to God and allow him to work through him" was so thoroughly implanted in me that it became my second nature. I was continuously subjected to galling and bitter tests, which seemed to have no end. But the teaching of Sai Baba that I must keep the fire of faith burning in my heart and surrender myself completely to God, stood me in good stead.

The most convincing proof of Sai Baba being God and none else is obtained from the marvellous feat performed by Him, in the sitting held on April 8, 1950 He extracted my soul from the body, even when I was not in a trance condition and was able to hear external sounds and feel my breath also. He did this by substituting Ram Ram's soul.

The following message of Ram Ram is a thrilling account of the whole incident:

> "We were watching you when you were meditating. As usual, Sai Baba made your soul leave the body, first just for a second. Then He repeated it in this manner several times, increasing the intermediary periods very gradually, and at last, He asked me to take the place of your soul in your body and to remain there till I was called to come out. In this way, without putting you into samadhi and in full consciousness of your own self, He made your soul remain in our Spiritual Plane for a long time."

A few days later *i.e.*, on April 20, 1950, Sai Baba went one step further and instead of asking Ram Ram to take the place of my soul, which was extracted, Sai Baba Himself occupied my empty body. Ram Ram's explanation of this unique event is a revelation in itself:

> "I am extremely glad to tell you that Sai Baba performed the highest miracle today. On the former occasion, He had made me occupy your body when your soul left it. Today, He Himself took the place of your soul and allowed you to stay in our Spiritual Land for as long as it liked. It is the highest thing in the world to have won God's love to such a great extent. It means unlimited powers to you when you come into full consciousness. He cannot keep Himself off from Showing Himself to you any longer. All you have now to do is to keep on thinking of God all the time."

On April 11 at night time, Sai Baba again gave an assurance that I was completely fit for conscious illumination. He said: "Be guided by Me. You are now completely free from all fetters. Your soul is shining like a resplendent star."

The soul had already made so many flights to the Spiritual world but of what avail was it to me, without my being conscious of its flights. I was longing for full consciousness but tests and postponements continued without a break, in some form or the other. Ram Ram gave the following explanation:

> "The significance of the day to day postponement is, as Sai Baba has explained, to make you perfect and ensure your future success. There is no other motive."

On April 22, 1950, I was ordered to dedicate the new book to God. Sai Baba said: "I want you to dedicate your new book to Me, not as Sai Baba, but as God."

On April 24, 1950, Sai Baba said: "Do you know that your inner eye was open all the time when you were meditating? Had you gone into *samadhi,* it would have functioned. It was therefore very necessary for Me not to allow you to go into samadhi. You made most frantic efforts to go into samadhi, but I stopped you though I had to exert the greatest force to do it."

The sitting on April 26, 1950 was entirely a failure and Sai Baba dropped a bomb when He said:

> "Do you know that you have already realised God? Whether I manifest Myself to you or not is not the point now. Forget entirely that I shall manifest Myself to you. Forget also that the book that you have written is to be published. Forget everything and think of God alone." That I should forget everything except God was not a new thing.

On April 27, 1950, a friend came to me and exhorted me to contact Meher Baba again, for Self-realization. He considered Meher Baba as Sadguru and eulogized him as the highest spiritual potentate. He little knew that I was under the hands of the Master of Masters – God. My lips were sealed and I could not give him the least hint of my position. The same evening Sai Baba gave me the following message:

> "Do you know that you are even higher than Meher Baba, who was described by your friend as Sadguru? It is wrong to call Meher Baba Sadguru. He is just an ordinary God-realized man with certain powers given to him."

Rishi Ram Ram surveyed the whole situation in regard to my progress under both physical and Spirit Masters in the following message:

> "Do you know why Sai Baba has asked me now to give you a talk? It is to corroborate His statement that you have reached a state of spirituality which in truth in much higher than that of Meher Baba, to whom you paid a visit on my instructions. At that time you were not even on the path. He rendered you a great service by putting you straight on the Path. When I sent you later on to Sri Ramana, he too rendered you a great service by making you an Arhat. A Master in physical body is indispensable, without doubt, to make a pupil reach the goal of Jivan Mukti. In your case, not only physical Masters have helped you but we, Masters in Spirit, are all the time guiding and helping you. But for us, you would have been still in the wilderness. I was ordered by God to act as your Guardian Angel from your very birth. I have discharged that duty and I am more than satisfied with your progress."

I had to finish the book and I was thinking what title I should give to the last chapter. To me, it was a book of spiritual romance, the greatest romance that any earthly man could ever experience, As ordered by Sai Baba, the preceding chapters had already been sent to the press. I was waiting for Sai Baba's further orders. On April 29, 1950, He told me to name that last chapter, "God's Revelation." and "to make it the most stirring and soul-raising chapter in the whole book."

As already explained in the introduction, the present book which is a compendium of the teachings of Sai Baba and Ram Ram, should not be considered under any circumstances as my own. It is entirely written under the inspiration of Sai Baba. The author is God, **Ahuram Mazda Amshaspand,** who has made use of this body and mind of mine, as His instrument for spreading divine knowledge on earth plane. On May 5, 1950, my celestial birthday was celebrated in the Spirit Land and Christ gave the following message:

> "My message to you is Love all, even your worst enemy and even the worst sinner. You have no right to judge anyone. Be extremely careful in this regard, lest it may not lead you to difficulties in the future."

My inner eye was open but when I went into samadhi, Sai Baba closed it. It was still not perennially open, as message of Sai Baba of May 6, 1950 informed me.

The next day May 9, 1950, witnessed the entire failure of my sitting. I could not enter into samadhi even for a minute. Sai Baba's message in this respect is self-explanatory:

> "I did not allow you to enter into samadhi even for a minute. You tried upto the very last, like a true yeoman, but I foiled you. Yesterday, I allowed you to go into samadhi three times and you stayed in *samadhi* for nearly three hours. Today, I kept you off. This is to show to you that though you have powers to go into samadhi and that your inner eye is open, I am stopping you and I alone can stop you and no Master. What does that mean? You are in the hands of a force that rules the cosmos. I am your God, training you and none else. When you see Me, it will be God's revelation."

Though I was on the fringe of God-realization, I was not allowed to gain superconsciousness by Sai Baba who still continued to prevent me from reaching the goal. My patience was tried to the collapsing point. Every ounce of physical energy was drained.

On May 18, 1950, Sai Baba gave this message:

> "My advice to you is to get into this superconscious mood and don't stop it for any consideration. The more frequently you bend down your head near My picture, the nearer you would come to Me. Your movements are automatic and natural and are uprisings of the inner feelings getting the better of you...

"Do you mean to say that after My giving you so many assurances, I won't manifest Myself to you? Keep that thought away from your mind. You must take it definitely that you have passed all your tests. If I am testing you now, it is for an absolutely different purpose. I have told you already, it is to strengthen your inner mind against all opposition that you will have to face as soon as the announcement is made in your world of your having realised God. The people of your world, especially those who are advanced intellectually, do not regard such phenomenon as within the reach of achievement. They would laugh at you, scoff at you and even consider you as a charlatan and a fraud. It will break your heart when the campaign of vilification starts. Lest you might be crushed by them, by their hammer strokes of invectives and wild criticism, I am preparing you inwardly and pouring in you all the spiritual strength and courage, which you would need so badly when you embark on your mission.

"Of course, the opposition would soon dwindle and melt away, when those with scientific minds and themselves earnest seekers of truth begin to realise the facts of your experiences. But the shock of the first wave of opposition would be extremely severe and I must strengthen you beforehand........

"Homi says that you have to take a second birth to finish mission. There is absolutely no more birth for you unless you of your own accord wish to come into this world of yours, as a messenger of God for the upliftment of mankind. I say this with all the emphasis at My command."

On May 23, 1950, Sai Baba said to me:

"Do you know that you are now eternally linked with Me? Whenever you want any special intercession in any matter of emergency, quietly pray for Me and I shall help you instantaneously. This is your prerogative. Use it discreetly in the interest of suffering humanity."

Sai Baba on May 29, 1950, told me:

"I am teaching you how to become indifferent to everything success or failure. It is a bitter lesson to learn but in spiritual life when one attains to the highest state, complete indifference to everything is a sine qua non. Till you learn this thoroughly, I shall not allow you to progress and reach the goal."

On May 31, 1950, Sai Baba said to me: "The last hurdle of indifference is also being crossed by you. How can I stop you from gaining your goal?" There was no doubt that Sai Baba was satisfied with my progress but there was still no visible indication of the goal.

The manifestation of the Masters could not be far off. The desire to see the Masters, in spite of my determination to check it, lingered in my heart. The more I secretly yearned for it, the more the fulfillment receded. I had still not learned the lesson of indifference. I was myself the cause of the delay in the Masters' manifestation.

I was asked by Ram Ram to carry Sai Baba's image in my mind all the time and to obey His orders as under:

(1) "Talk as little as possible and don't enter into any argument.
(2) Sleep little, eat little, go out little, and see friends only when absolutely necessary. Keep to your altar room as far as possible. Don't stir out; don't talk.
(3) Keep your mind concentrated on God and God alone.
(4) Think that you do not belong to your world but to our world.
(5) Forget everything and expect nothing.
(6) Don't make plans for the future at all.
(7) Don't worry. Keep firm and cheerful.
(8) Keep up the attitude of prayer fullness. Bless all.
(9) Don't bother about your health and your ailments.
(10) Don't give a thought to money matters. Baba is not going to starve you."

On June 3, 1950, I was given the following happy news by Sai Baba:

"I have opened your inner eye perennially. I can't close it. Even if I have to close it, it would open again in a second. The minute

> you enter into *samadhi,* you would see Me and the link between you and Me would be permanently established." But He also said: "I tell you straight off, now that your inner eye is permanently open, I would do My utmost in not allowing you to go into *samadhi.* It is for you to put up a good and sturdy fight and I see beforehand that you would win at last. You have to harness your will power to the maximum extent and you will win the battle."

I was filled with joy at the prospect of reaching the end of the journey. But I had still many more hurdles to cross. Even when I went into *samadhi,* in spite of the inner eye being open, I was not able to see the Masters, neither the flight of the soul from the body, nor the Spiritual Plane, where my soul sojourned when it left the physical body. Sai Baba had various other devices to stop me from seeing Him. He created barriers after barriers, thus stopping the inner eye from functioning when I went into *samadhi.* From day to day and week to week, this tussle, this great struggle, continued.

On June 6, 1950, Sai Baba gave me a long message, which is reproduced here verbatim as it embodies many points of importance.

> "Not only have I opened out all the inner parts of your causal body but have energised every part and parcel of all the cells with My Spirit. As soon as you see Me, all your bodily pains would vanish for ever and you would become strong physically, mentally and spiritually. Of course, the transformation won't last long as your life span has already been determined and you will have to quit the physical plane after a short time. I am extremely anxious that you should do the utmost in the short period that is available. I can't tell you the exact day and hour when your new mission starts in reality. It will commence from the very moment you see Me. Tremendous powers will be given to you to help you in your mission, the nature of which you already know.
>
> "There was fear that you might fall after having reached the summit of the mountain. That crisis has now passed away. You are now absolutely safe.

"You have absolutely no conception of your future. In a way I am glad for it makes you non-expectant and indifferent, the keystones to spiritual progress. Kindly continue to be clam and unperturbed, indifferent and fearless, joyful and helpful, patient and enduring, vigilant but silent, active but without ostentation. Kindly note that it is through the gateway of meditation that you have progressed and are now heading to the goal. It had done wonders for you. Keep it up till the end of your life. It is the key that opens all doors to the secret realms of divine wisdom.

"I have taught you the lesson of humility. Don't even for a moment, even in your most exalted state of life, ever think highly of yourself. Think that you are a mere speck of dust and nothing what-so-ever. Be extremely humble and desist from making even the least show of your powers and wisdom."

On June 7, 1950, Sai Baba exhorted me again to forget everything pertaining to manifestation of the Masters. He said: "I may come to you in full blaze of light whenever I think fit."

On June 13, 1950, Sai Baba gave me the following message:

"Keep on thinking of God all the time and prepare yourself for the tremendous change that is going to come in your life. When you see Me face to face, you will realise the true nature of the Self within you. I give you the most solemn assurance that you are on the way to the achievement of this crowing glory."

The following day, there was an epic struggle of the soul trying to get the better of the opposing forces and I was on the very verge of seeing God. Sai Baba said:

"You were on the point of seeing Me, not once but several times. Yes, you went into *samadhi* for a long time from the very start and I had great difficulty in stopping you from seeing Me. The barrier created by Me showed signs of breaking and I had to create one wall after another to keep you in darkness. Your struggle today was intense. In fact, you were in *samadhi* for all the time, except for small lapses when I pulled you out and you again struggled to get in. You succeeded quickly in the beginning but in the end,

> however much you tried to get into *samadhi,* I stopped you, for it was impossible for Me to create any more barriers and I made you open your eyes to bring an end to the epic struggle."

The question arose in my mind, would the reader of the new book "How I Found God" be convinced of the statements made therein? Is it not natural for any man to doubt that God, *Ahuram Mazda Amshaspand* the greatest and mightiest force in the cosmos, would ever care to talk to such an ordinary soul as myself or see me face to face? The minute this thought came to me, Sai Baba replied: "I have given you in My messages so many proofs of this, and eventually you will actually see Me face to face. This revelation is not distant."

On June 16, 1950, Sai Baba gave me a sermon and said that I was chiefly responsible for postponement of His manifestation and that I was my own enemy. He said:

> "The more I train you and prepare you, the more I notice the necessity of further strengthening you inwardly and this I am doing not only every day but every hour.... All I want from you is to keep yourself completely absorbed in thoughts of God and forget your world, your book, your friends, and everything that has the odour of mundane existence. Silence your mind completely. Think till at least the manifestation occurs, that you are not at all living in your earth plane and that you are dead to everything. As you are so highly advanced spiritually, why don't you practise this? You are your own enemy, when in spite of My thousand reminders, you still insist in talking of mundane affairs with others." Sai Baba concluded His sermon with the following words: "Forget, forget, forget every thing except God."

On June 17, 1950, I was told that I had entered on that day "the new region of bliss and beatitude."

On June 21, 1950, Sai Baba gave me an important message:

> "When you have gone through such a great deal of suffering both mental and physical, can't you have now a little more patience? It is I who will perform miracles through you. I have already told you that you are absolutely a zero. Remember always that you are

> absolutely nothing. Not even for a minute, should you think that you have done this or that or even imagine that you can do something. Beware of this great temptation of vain gloriousness."

The feeling of frustration, tiredness of both mind and body and complete exhaustion continued crippling me from day to day. How long could a man be fed on mere assurances and how long could these endurance tests be borne? Sai Baba said immediately: "You are passing through an extremely difficult and strenuous time. It is heart-rending and nerveshattering. I know you feel tired and exhausted in body, mind and even in spirit. This is what I have purposely to do viz, to draw out from your body, mind and spirit every ounce of strength and make you like a lifeless corpse.

"This appears startling to you but it is a fact. But don't lose courage even for a minute. Face the test and bear the agonising situation that I am purposely creating for the ultimate betterment of your soul."

On June 27, 1950, I was again assured by Sai Baba:

> "I am your God. I shall prove to them those oppose you that you have found God, both in the sense that you have seen Him and have communicated with Him."

On June 29, 1950, Sai Baba gave me good news. He said:

> "I see there is not the slightest trace of mundane matter in your inner bodies. You desires have been expunged. You have no appetite of any kind. Your mind has been cleansed and purified. I have made it a repository of divinity. There is no ego in you; now you are desireless, mindless, egoless. You are coming to Me with the heart palpitating for the unknown bliss to come. Your soul is bursting to leave its sheaths. The Spirit within is watching the whole game like a silent witness. You are on the point of leaving the old garment torn and tattered for a new vesture resplendent with the glow and light of our Highest Spiritual World."

On July 4, 1950, I was in *samadhi* for three hours at a stretch out of five hours of meditation. The sitting was a great success but it did not end in seeing Sai Baba.

The following day, I was told that the Port of Eternity was in sight.

On July 10, 1950, Sai Baba made it clear to me that the cause of delay and postponement was my ownself. He said: "You are postponing the happy achievement by your own stupidity, for everything is now ready for you. It is not I who am now delaying you but you who are obstructing Me.

"I have made all the preparations. I have opened the secret valve. I have vitalised your crown chakra, the Pituitary Body and the Pineal Gland. I have filled all the inner parts with the fire of My own LIGHT. All that is needed of you is isolation from the affairs of your mundane world. Keep aloof and keep your mind calm and placid like the bottom of a smooth lake."

This message was an eye-opener. The Masters had done everything. It dawned upon me that the attainment of my goal depended upon my successful meditation which required a still and tranquil mind.

What is meditation? It is a technique used for attainment of the knowledge of the higher worlds and the unfoldment of the divinity within man. It is the gateway to the Abode of Eternity. It is only through meditation that God could be realized.

On July 12, 1950, there was a phenomenal occurrence. I was asked by Sai Baba to invoke, in the order mentioned, the following Masters:

> (1) Lord Christ (2) Lord Zoroaster (3) Lord Krishna (4) Lord Buddha (5) Rishi Ram Ram and, lastly, Shri Ramana. I had pictures of all these Masters in My altar room and as ordered by Sai Baba, I used to concentrate on each of them every day especially the first five. Each one of them was ordered by Sai Baba to give me a talk for two minutes and they gave the following message:
>
> Christ, the Master: "Yes, I am Lord Christ. I have been daily watching you when you come to the altar room and I am so happy that God has given me this opportunity to talk to you. Do you

know that you have been raised to the highest peak of spirituality by the grace of God and you are now to enter shortly the Kingdom of Eternal Bliss, as decreed by God. My special message to you is Love All, for God is in all and He loves all."

Lord Zoroaster:

"Do you know who I am? I am your Prophet, Lord Zoroaster. It is for the first time I am speaking to you as ordered by God, Ahuram Mazda. I am extremely glad to say that God has consecrated you and raised your spirit so as to be one with us all in the Cosmos. You have won your way to our spiritual edifice by the path of righteousness, which is the only path to reach God. Without righteousness, all is naught. Righteousness is God and God is Righteousness."

Lord Krishna:

"I am Lord Krishna come to you at the express command of God. I see from the nature of your aura that you are a highly evolved soul of a unique type. Your aura is perfect – as perfect as it could be. It is crystal white without a flaw or tinge of blue or yellow; scarcely seen in a human being. It is your 'bhakti' and your entire devotion to God that has brought you to this transcendental stage of spirituality."

Lord Buddha:

"I am extremely happy to give you my message as ordered by God. God loves you deeply. You have achieved your *moksha* by practising true renunciation and have become a *Jivan Mukta* by dint of your own efforts in the first instance and by the grace of God which you have won because of the purity of your character and high spirituality. Do good to all. You are a Buddha and I wish many more would become Buddhas like you...."

Rishi Ram Ram said:

"God gave you a unique opportunity to speak to so many of our Celestial Beings of the highest order in the cosmos. Does this now convince you that you are in the hands of God Himself, but for whom, these Great Beings would not have cared to come to you and given you messages one by one. Yours is a unique mission for which Sai Baba has prepared and trained you to perfection."

Shri Ramana then followed Rishi Ram Ram and he gave the following message:

> "I am Ramana come to you as ordered by God. You have placed my picture in the altar room and occasionally I come here attracted by your aura, when you are in the room, praying to God or meditating. I am very happy that God ordered me to give you a message. What message should I give you? You know all. I have nothing to say. The tie that binds us is our passionate love for God. Keep that upto the end of your life."

I had asked Sai Baba to allow me to talk to my mother also, and His permission was granted. She was brought by Ram, Ram, after all the Masters had given their messages.

Ram Ram said: "Yes, I have brought your mother with me. She is standing by my side. Listen to her." Mother then gave a short message. She said:

> "It is the greatest honour and boon conferred upon me by Rishi Ram Ram, who is my God, that he has asked me to talk to you though for a minute or two only. Rishi Ram Ram is my God. I love him, I adore him, I worship him. He is all in all to me. I want to speak a lot to you but how can I do that in a minute that is given my love to all my dear children whom I have left behind – my children and my children's children, especially to my Nadir Baba. I go now."

Ram Ram then explained to me the implication of my mother's situation. He said: "You have listened to your mother. She thinks that I am God and she is right for she has reached a state when she cannot conceive of anything higher."

Sai Baba then made His appearance and said:

> "You have heard the various Masters in My Spirit World. It should now convince you and you should feel extremely happy that you are in the hands of Me, your God."

The next day, July 13, 1950, Sai Baba made a very important announcement, flattering no doubt, but as I had become egoless by the grace of God, under Sai Baba's training, the feeling of elation was absent. He said:

"Do you know that I have already taken steps and you would be announced in your world as a Master in physical body? Your new book will be read by students of occultism with keen ardour. It will make a landmark in occult literature. I shall push it in all parts of the world. I will have to do it not to make you famous in the world but for spreading the new knowledge of arcane science for the benefit of humanity. I want to bring new light, new joy, new notions of life, a new civilization based on spirituality and not worship of base mammon."

Along with this announcement Sai Baba gave a warning: "Remember that you are nothing. You are zero. You are absolutely helpless. It is I who am equipping you with wondrous gifts and making you My instrument for carrying out My Plan of Evolution on your earth plane."

On July 14, 1950, Sai Baba assured me that I had climbed all the steps in the ladder and that I was on the very threshold of His Abode. He said so lovingly: "How can I shut the door when you are standing on the very precincts of My Mansion? I must manifest Myself to you."

Sai Baba then gave me a graphic account of how God's revelation would take place:

"Be absolutely at ease when you see Me. Do not get alarmed at My suddenly showing Myself to you... no man can see Me, so very fiery is My outward form. It is enveloped in flames of fire of extreme luminosity, dazzling and staggering to behold. But you will be able to see Me with your inner eye happily and with ease.

Lie down prostrate at My feet as soon as you see Me. I shall pour My blessings on you."

On July 16, 1950, I meditated for full six hours at a stretch. I was able to go into *samadhi,* immediately after I had started mediation. It lasted for an hour or so. As soon as I got out of *samadhi,* there was a keen tussle to get back into it. I was in a semi-trance condition for a long time and eventually I did succeed in getting into *samadhi* for the second time in the same sitting but it was for a short time only.

The news of the war in South Korea was very disturbing. The message of Sai Baba on July 15, 1950 is revealing:

"My agents on the earth plane are manoeuvreing to stop the present war in Korea from taking a serious turn and engulfing the whole world in its conflagration. I am glad you are also daily praying for peace and harmony. In a few years, war of any kind will cease to exist. Your own people will see the folly of it and will desist from going to war.

"The present differences in the way of living will soon give way and out of the multitude of differences, there would arise a common humanity with equal right of living, working, enjoying in a world of equal opportunities for all, without the least distinction of any kind. The world is moving towards the formation of classless society, towards peace, equality of rights and freedom for all. Nationalism will die a slow death, giving way to the formation of a World or Brotherhood, in the common – wealth of all Nations and all classes of people. The word nation as years roll on would soon be expunged from your dictionary.

"My Masters are working day and night following My orders for changing your world and saving it from the peril of wreckage. They will succeed not only in saving it from ruination but they will gradually so transform it that all the bitter and hellish forces that are at present loose on your earth plane will be slain and the divinity that is in man will triumph bringing peace and good will, love and harmony."

On July 17, 1950, Sai Baba said:

"I have issued order to My Masters that they should avert the present conflict in Korea from becoming a stepping stone to a third world war. They will do their best to stop the conflagration from spreading. Your world is being trained for the millennium. Of course, it will take considerable time to reach that goal, but sure enough, events would move towards achievement of that end.

"I will make you play a part in that mighty panorama of world revolutionary events, and however insignificant your role may appear to be in the beginning, its true significance will be realised later on after your passing away. I have chosen you as My messenger

> on the earth plane. Don't feel flattered or vainglorious. I have told you so very often that you are nothing but dust and you must keep that faithfully in your mind. But dust as you are, I must, to serve My purpose, transform you into a mighty machine for spreading peace, prosperity and progress on your earth plane."

> On July 21, 1950, Sai Baba again exhorted me to keep my mind saturated with thoughts of God and to keep up the practice of bending down, as often as possible, before His picture every time I was in the altar room. He lovingly assured me: "I am your God, talking to you. You will soon see your God face to face. You are not only on the way to it; in fact, you are sitting close to Him. Your body is actually brushing His form. Only you are unaware of it. Do you know when you are taking down this message, I have actually come down to your altar room and am standing exactly near your right shoulder?"

In spite of assurances that I would not be subjected to any more tests, they came trailing in one after another. Ram Ram said to me:

> "Do you know that Sai Baba is subjecting you purposely to all these difficult phases to bring out the best in you. You should therefore be cheerful and go through the mill bravely. The greater the cross, the greater would be your victory. Don't yield in and don't lose your faith in us."

I made up my mind to keep firm and not lose hope nor allow doubts to overcome me. The altar room was my home, my sanctuary, my fire temple, my Kaaba. It was here I could commune with God with freedom and inhale the freshness and fragrance of His breath. Could anything be greater than to be in the presence of God's own aura?

On July 26, 1950, Sai Baba said:

> "When you were meditating, I examined you thoroughly. You are now simply perfect, having reached this state of perfection through My training. I now give you a clear passport of ADEPTSHIP." This message had no effect on me.

Doraswami sent me a small book, by J. Krishnamurti, entitled "*Let Understanding Be The Law.*" Krishnamurti strongly believed that one should himself become the Tabernacle of Truth and not become a disciple of any Master, whether in body or spirit. Rites and rituals, religion, Prophets and Masters they were all crutches to be dispensed with. Just as the sun sends its rays of light equally on all parts of the earth exposed to it, Truth is within the reach of all and it should be attained by one's own individual efforts. He said:

> "I am not concerned with organizations, I am not concerned with societies, with religions, with dogmas. But I am concerned with life, because I am Life" It is Life that is the important factor and to put organisations, societies, religions, rituals, above life, was wrong. He said: "Because I am in love with life, I do not want anything." Like Buddha, his teaching was "Be a lamp unto thyself."

I rubbed my eyes. Had I come to the stage where I did not require the support of any religion or Master? I hurried to the altar room. Sai Baba gave me the following:

> ".....Do you understand now why I asked you to read Krishnamurti's book? How exactly his teachings apply to you in every sentence and in every word. It won't apply to others who are less evolved. Crutches are absolutely necessary in life but as we advance, we leave them one by one according to our state of evolution. First we discard ceremonies and rituals, then we leave off the teachings of religion. We then take to a Master and him also we leave as we come nearer to the goal of our life. The man who becomes and adept – a Master, must reach the goal of his adeptship, all alone, for God within him then becomes his guide and inspirer.
>
> Is this not a revelation to you? Will you not now be able to write your last chapter? Go through all My messages and start writing it. You have enough material to vindicate your position that you have found God."

I felt relieved that even if I closed the chapter with this message of Sai Baba, I would be fully justified in saying that I had found God, which is the title of the book.

Ram Ram's message is of equal importance:

"It is not I but God who has guided and helped you in the very last stage of your evolution. It is He who has helped you to become a full fledged ADEPT. An adept can not make a human soul an adept. It is the function of God. We Masters succeed in making our disciples Arhats. After Arhatship is reached by a disciple *i.e.*, when he or she has gained his or her *nirvana,* we still guide and inspire that soul but very rarely can we succeed in making that soul reach the very last stage of adeptship in physical body. When he actually comes to that stage, God at once intervenes and takes over the charge from the Master and guides the human soul.

"Remember that it is not any extraneous God that has helped you. It is the God within you – your own Self which you have discovered today. You have discovered your own soul and your God. The soul and the spirit are one in you today. It is this union."

"You now see the ladder of progress. How the unfoldment of the Self depends upon various factors – individual efforts with the help of rituals and ceremonies, teachings of the Scriptures at the beginning of the career of the human soul, on the earth plane. These crutches the soul begins to leave off one by one, and when a certain amount of perfection is reached, God orders a Master to take that soul under His protection and bring him to the path. The soul and the Master part company, after having traversed the path to a great extent. The Master keeps at a distance, allowing the soul to find the Self within him. The Master works in such a way that the individual soul at last finds the Self and the Self then takes hold of him entirely and takes him to the final goal."

On August 3, 1950, I was in *samadhi* for full four hours, the longest *samadhi* that I had till then.

Again I was reminded that my inner eye was opened permanently and I must now exert my utmost to reach the goal. The following message of Sai Baba is self-explanatory:

"Do you know that the inner eye which is open can not close now. Even I your God, can not close it. Every time you go into *samadhi,* I have to raise a barricade to shut it out. If you increase your power of resistance, the barricade would crumble to the ground. All you have to do now is to increase your power to resist all opposition.

"Every hour you spend in the altar room makes you gather more strength to face opposition. Your altar room is a reservoir of atmic shakti. Draw shakti from your altar room activities and you will see how quickly My manifestation follows."

On August 6, 1950, Sai Baba gave me the following message:

"It is through your altar room activities that you will be able to realise your object. It is here that I shall manifest Myself to you in deep trance. It is only by meditating like Buddha that you can see Me. The Inner eye which was closed, I have opened. But it will function only when you are in deep trance lasting for a long time. Go on trying and you will see that every time when you meditate, by slow steps, you will be able to go into *samadhi* for longer and longer duration till at last you will reach a state when My manifestation will become inescapable."

Ram Ram's message on August 6th, 1950 gave a detailed description of how the manifestation would take place:

"It is by means of deep and sustained meditation, that you will be able to see the flight of your soul from the body in deep *samadhi* and all of us in nebular form. We shall put on these forms, by which you can identify us. God will come to you in the form of Sai Baba. I shall be the same in your altar room photograph. Christ, you would see, as he was on the earth plane in any dress. You will however be able to make Him out from his face. There are several pictures of Christ in your altar room. He will take up the form of any of them for manifestation to you. Zoroaster, Buddha, and Krishna will come to you as you see them in your altar room pictures. Kindly go on concentrating on their pictures as deeply as you can. This is necessary for quickening your perception, when they manifest themselves to you. If you don't do it or if you do it half-heartedly, their manifestation will appear dim and hazy."

On August 8, 1950, Sai Baba gave me an extremely important message, in which He declared emphatically that I was hearing the God outside and not the voice of the Atma within me.

"The divinity within you is being unfolded. It is still not completely unfolded. As soon as you see Me, it would burst out into full

> blaze. You are hearing My voice, not the voice of the Atma within you. I am god outside you that is talking and not the Atma within you. When the Atma is fully unfolded, the difference of within and without would dwindle and there would be one God, without distinction of God within and God without. The indwelling God would coalesce with the God outside your body. In short, there would be fusion of the Spirit within with the Absolute Spirit pervading throughout the universe. You would not only be one with God but one with everything in the universe."

Ram Ram in his message of July 31, 1950, already referred to in the foregoing pages, had said: " Remember, that it is not any extraneous God that has helped you. It is the God within you, your own Self, that you have discovered today."

To all intents and purpose, the above two statements of Sai Baba and Ram Ram appear contradictory. The question was – was I hearing the God without or the God within? This puzzle was soon solved by Sai Baba and Ram Ram through their messages.

On August 17, 1950, Sai Baba said to me:

> "You have been talking with Me, Ahuram Mazda, Amshaspand, the God without and not with the God within. You have also talked with the God within, but that was in the beginning when Ram Ram was training you."

Again on August 18, 1950, Sai Baba shed further light on the point, that I was trained by the God without to unfold the God within me. His whole message is given below:

> "You are bewildered by the apparent inconsistency between My statement and Ram Ram's statement. I again tell you that both of us are absolutely correct. Ram Ram has explained things according to his revelation. He is concerned with the God within. His work was to reveal the God within. He did his part and then he left you. I then took charge of you and made him My assistant. To him, God within and God without are the same. But you have arrived at a stage when I must definitely say that it is I, God without, who has taught and trained you and helped in the unfoldment of the God within you. Truly speaking, God within *i.e.*, Self and God without are the same, though separately named."

Ram Ram, in his message of the same day, asked me to follow every word of Sai Baba. He said:

> "To me God within and God without are the same. We Masters are taught to look upon the Absolute Spirit pervading throughout the universe, whether in the human souls or outside the human souls, as one."

On August 13, 1950, a very important message was given by Sai Baba regarding His manifestation and revelation:

> "Don't forget to prostrate at full length when you see Me. Do this every time when I come to you. After you have seen Me, once, you will be able to see Me at your will and as often as you like. It is a very rare event for God to reveal Himself to a human soul on the earth plane. Masters come and go and they are spoken to and seen by mystics. It is a common occurrence. My Masters are in personal touch with various God-realised souls on your earth plane. They carry of their work of evolution, through these God-realised persons who are linked with them. But in your case, you are linked not only with Masters, but with Me your God, who has personally trained you, guarded you, inspired you and who is going now to manifest to you for the fulfillment of your mission on the earth plane. It is not because out of mere fancy that I have chosen you for My work on the earth plane."

On August 15, 1950, Sai Baba prophesied in his message that certain epoch-making events would take place:

> "Do you know on the day when I reveal Myself to you, certain epoch-making events in your world will take place. I shall prophesy these events for the conviction of your world. Write them down:
>
> First and foremost, the war in Korea will end satisfactorily and a step would be taken for the establishment of world peace.
>
> Secondly, there will be a permanent gesture of goodwill between India and Pakistan for the settlement of all their disputes by arbitration, including Kashmir.
>
> Thirdly, war between America and Russia would be averted by agreement on fundamental issues.

Fourthly, United Nations Organisation will be recognised as the sole world organisation for settlement of all disputes. Every country with a recognised government will have the right to send its representative to United Nations Organisation, not excluding even Communist countries like China, Korea and others.

Fifthly, some important person or persons of international reputation will pass away.

Sixthly, the economic collapse of the world feared will be averted and a new era of recovery from financial crisis will start.

You will thus be the harbinger of a new epoch in your world, though this would not be recognised in the beginning. It will take many years before your world would come to understand the significance of My revelation through you."

On August 16, 1950, I was in *samadhi* for a very short time after a long meditation. I felt that the sitting was a failure. But Sai Baba would not let me feel disappointed:

"Don't think that today's sitting was a failure, because you were in *samadhi* for a short time. I am so training you that you are advancing step by step and each time there is some progress even if it be invisible."

I was fully convinced then impressed that my progress was continuous and satisfactory, though invisible.

Chapter Twenty-Five

God's Revelation (continued)

The most amazing thing about my meditation was that inspite of the fact that every ounce of energy was drained form me, by constant and strenuous exertion lasting for 14 or 18 hours a day, whenever I felt dead as a corpse a small sleep of two and half to three hours at night invariably revived me and made me as fresh as a rose to continue the struggle.

On August 18, 1950, Ram Ram gave me the following message:

> "Sai Baba has fastened you to Himself such firmness that no force can tear you from Him.... Even as you were born, God had an eye on you and He instructed me to take particular care of you and to train you imperceptibly for the high role that was destined for you."
>
> "In order that I may not get power intoxicated, Sai Baba made me take a vow, facing His picture in the altar room, that I would not take any credit or pride for any achievement. He said: "Think that it is all the doing of God and God alone and that you are the dust of His feet and nothing more."

On August 23, 1950, I got a snub from Sai Baba which I fully deserved. He said:

"Even if I don't reveal Myself to you, what can it matter to you? Why are you so very anxious for My revelation and for the publication of your book? Your concern is to get God-realization. This you have already achieved. Why then hanker for anything more? Be satisfied with what you have already attained."

But my stock of patience was getting exhausted and I was feeling absolutely fatigued. The postponements from day to day had a telling effect upon me. The following message of Sai Baba on August 25, 1950 is Self-explanatory:

"I am fully aware of the fact that you are now dead exhausted and that you able to stand the strain with the greatest difficulty. But in these spiritual matters, we have to be exceedingly strict and we can never spare any one, aspiring for the highest bliss, from the vigour of our programme. This is most essential for spiritual progress.

"...You are now on the very brink of the goal. In fact, there is an exceedingly thin vapour-like streak of obstruction, keeping you off from seeing Me. Every day, this thin veil is made thinner and you can rest assured that it will break down all of a sudden, very, very soon. But you must not diminish your efforts, nor should you become faint-hearted and pessimistic. Keep cheerful and think of Me all the time."

On August 26, 1950, Sai Baba gave me a discourse on the necessity of observing silence and seclusion, especially in the last phase of the spiritual adventure. He said: "Lead a hermit's life, avoiding all the glamour of the outside world. You do not care a jot for your world but you are obsessed by the thought of worldly duties. Your first duty today is towards your God. He is training you and preparing you specially for the mission to bring about a great change in you world."

Again on August 28, 1950, Sai Baba reminded me to give up all earthly duties for the time being and devote myself entirely to God.

On August 29, 1950, Sai Baba gave me the following message:

"My manifestation is now extremely near. At any time, and any day, I shall come to you in a flash, when you expect Me the least. I have no reason now to keep you in suspense. It is true that I still use My obstructive tactics to stop your inner eye from seeing Me. But this is only to measure your power of resistance. The minute I am satisfied that you have reached the acme of perfection in all respects viz., in the power of endurance and resistance to evil, forbearance, love for all without any discrimination, perfect tranquillity of mind and complete reliance upon God in purity of thought, word and deed, I shall manifest Myself to you. You are on the very verge of it."

On August 31, 1950, when I came out of *samadhi* in the morning, Sai Baba gave the following message:

"Do you know that you were again seeing Me today and it was with the greatest difficulty that I was to blur your eye, and prevent you from carrying the impression of having seen Me!"

I passed practically the whole day in the altar room, as ordered by Sai Baba. More than Fourteen hours were spent beginning with the usual 2:00 p.m. sitting and ending late at night, with small intervals for outside work, rest and meals.

On September 2, 1950, I was told that I was able to see Sai Baba with my inner eye but its vision was not so strong as to retain the impression. It appeared that still more meditation for longer hours was necessary, to strengthen the vision of the inner eye.

The long hours of strenuous exertion especially in the altar room had begun to have an adverse effect upon my body and my health appeared to give way. Sai Baba said:

"Regarding your pain in stomach, don't worry at all. I shall cure you in no time though I know it is serious. Don't be afraid at all. You must show your power of endurance by bearing the pain without revealing it to any one. Unless you develop all extraordinary qualities how can I make use of your body for such a mighty project of revolutionizing the world? Do you understand now why I am postponing the day of revelation?"

Was the pain in my stomach a health test or a test of my power of endurance? On September 7 1950, Sai Baba gave the following message:

> "... I have created it and I shall remove it whenever I like. Have complete faith in Me. Don't consult any earth doctor. Your case would be worsened and you would suffer a lot. Rely on Me and Me alone. Be absolutely fearless. Is not fearlessness one of your vows? Why don't you stick to you vow? You should be absolutely fearless under all circumstances, even it they be most trying and difficult. The present is only your test.... Surrender yourself to Me whole-heartedly and trust in My protection."

I was extremely tired and my health also showed signs of severely breaking down. But for the conviction that I was on the right track and must adhere to it in spite of adverse circumstances, I would have given in. Sai Baba gave me the following assurance which went a long way in again restrengthening my resolve:

> "...Your inner vehicles are as clear as crystal. Your aura is of the highest transcendental hue – pure white with a halos of light around its skirt, so seldom seen in a human soul. You are as perfect as one could be in the conflicting surroundings of every day life.
>
> I have talked to you so far without your seeing Me. Bur this invisibility you are now going to break for ever. We shall be visible to your hereafter, as often as you want and as long as you want."

Sai Baba's image seen in a flash:

On September 12, 1950, when I was meditating, all of a sudden I saw Sai Baba's image in silvery streaks with eyes piercing at me in a friendly way. Sai Baba, explaining the phenomenon said:

> "There is one important point to which I draw your attention. When you were focussing your attention on My image in meditation you saw Me gaze at you, with very friendly eyes. This happened more than once and you felt extremely happy. I did it purposely to show to you that you are now on the path to seeing Me outright. It would then be a complete REVELATION."

The next day, *i.e.* September 13, 1950, I was told: "There is only one medicine for all your ills and that is complete faith in me."

I was aware that I was passing through the last phase of the journey of the soul to the Abode of Eternity. The tests were made more bitter and galling in order to find out the extent to which they could be endured without losing faith in God. It was evident that Revelation could take place only when I could rise above mental and physical consciousness.

On September 18, 1950, Sai Baba gave me the following message after meditation in the early hours of the morning:

> "Do you know that I revealed Myself to you today in the morning and you saw Me several times with the aid of your inner eye, while your were in *samadhi*? You are not aware of it, for I have still to give you super-consciousness. This I will don without any further delay. Your meditation today was very long. I was compelled to allow you to go into *samadhi* every now and then, just for short periods though. I am doing all this to perfect you in every way and to strengthen you when your mission starts."

On September 20, 1950, late at night, Ram Ram gave me enthralling news:

> "Do you know that you have already reached the goal and have also seen Sai Baba? The dream of your life has been realised. You have realised God in the true sense of the word. There is nothing more to be done. All that you need now is proof of your having realised God in a concrete from. This too God is going to give you."

On September 21, 1950, a very important change occurred. I used to see God, Though without retaining any impression in the state of *samadhi*. But on the 21, Sai Baba said:

> "Do you know that you again saw Me several times but this time I did not allow you to go into *samadhi*! You saw Me when you were meditating but you have not retained the impression of having seen Me. When you develop your inner vision sufficiently, you will be able to carry the impression of having see Me."

On September 22, 1950, I was again assured to God's Revelation Sai Baba said:

"Let Me assure you, you will see Me with your inner eye in full consciousness. In the past I have revealed Myself to those destined for Revelation. I mean particularly the prophets of various religions and those highly evolved souls, who were sent on the earth plane after being already fully trained in our Spirit Land, to carry out their mission on the earth.

I have revealed Myself to all sorts of persons from the learned to the less learned, from those in the lowest strata of society to those in the highest. Perfect spirituality has always been the sole criterion on My choice for Revelation.

In your case, it was doubtful, whether you would be able to make yourself fit for such a unique honour in this incarnation, though when you were born, you carried with you the seed of spiritual greatness, earned by your deeds in the previous incarnations. Therefore I appointed Ram Ram as a special Guard to look after you from you birth and to report to Me. His report was favourable and I decided to give you a chance for my Revelation in this very life instead of waiting for the next incarnation.

I know I have been mercilessly hard in My training you towards perfection. But for that thorough training, requiring hard and bitter tests, how could your mission be a success and how could My purpose be achieved?

The joy of My Revelation would be so sudden that for some time you will feel absolutely numb. But don't worry at all. I will so manage it that you will face the joyous experience in a graded manner and I will not let you be thrown off your senses by the extreme bewilderment of My Light."

On September 23, 1950, after my usual early morning meditation I got the following message from Sai Baba:

"You were on the point of seeing Me in all My fire and glory, not once but several times both in *samadhi*, when you were in simple meditation. The latter part of your meditation was extremely pleasant to you, as I allowed your inner eye to work partially *i.e.* allowed you partial consciousness of all that you were seeing. You felt as if flying in an aeroplane, making flights in some strange land with mystic lights and languages. You tried to read our alphabet but could not succeed. It is the language of the Spirit which you will soon understand. It is not a language expressed in alphabets. You saw a vision of it, expressed to you in symbolic manifestation as that was the only means to convey to you our ideas of this world of ours."

I was told that I was now so very chose to the goal that I was actually touching its outside fringe and edge.

On September 24, 1950, I had the longest meditation session so far, from 2:00 a.m. to 8:00 a.m. at a stretch.

The whole day was spent as ordered by Sai Baba in silence and seclusion, mostly in the altar room. Late at night Ram Ram explained the reasons for God having selected a common man like myself for the bewildering experience of His revelation:

"It is to open a new epoch in the history of your world that God's revelation is possible for any man, without any distinction. It is not meant for the ascetic only who renounces the world and does *tapas* in the forest. It is not meant for the monk only who lives a life seclusion and devotion. It is not meant for the religious saint only who leads a life of purity, sacrifice, self-annihilation, doing his duties, living in the world, pitted with temptations, in good or bad environment. Whether he lives in a palace or a hut, is not the point. The main question is that he must attain perfect equanimity of mind through perfect surrender to God, by a life of desirelessness, egolessness in the midst of the struggle of life. You have fulfilled all these conditions. God has therefore chosen you to work on the earth for the remaining portion of you life towards the fulfillment of His Evolutionary Plan."

But I was getting restless. I had seen God though I had no consciousness of His revelation. Without conscious realization, was not everything useless? The thought came to me that to get conscious realization, I must forget everything, take up some extra work and reduce the time spent in the altar room. But Sai Baba was impervious. He refused to give me permission to do any new or extra work.

On September 28, 1950, when I was meditating in the early morning, Sai Baba came down to the altar room and entered into my body, quickening and energising it with His own spirit. He said: "It is for this reason you were not able to hear the clock strike for a number of hours. I put you into spiritual ecstasy. So very deeply absorbed were you, as a result of my direct touch, that you became absolutely unaware of the external sounds and happening for a long time."

Who else can do such a miracle, if not God? It was wonderful, how step by step I was taken onward and onward towards the Highest Peak of Spiritual Bliss.

On September 29, 1950, I was told by Sai Baba to make a change in my time table and to commence my morning meditation an hour earlier and to end it an hour later, *i.e.* I was asked to attend the altar room at 1:00 a.m. instead of 2:00 a.m. and meditate for eight hours at a stretch, leaving the altar room at 9:00 p.m. This change was desired to expedite God's Revelation to me.

I was prepared to look forward to the great event in the following message of Sai Baba.

> "I give you a clue. Before I reveal Myself to you, you will get a feeling in your heart and mind that something extraordinary is going to take place very soon. This feeling will be a precursor to My manifestation.
>
> You will also note considerable progress in all your healing cases. You will get reports of their cure or significant progress in cure, if not in all cases, at least in a greater portion of them. The woman with crutches is marvelously progressing. In a very short time, she will herself write to you a long letter, expressing her gratification at the sudden cure of her old disease."

On September 30, 1950, at night time, I was asked by Sai Baba to invoke Ram Ram and Christ, the Master and they gave me the following messages.

Ram Ram: "I am extremely glad to ell you that God has so thoroughly prepared you that very rapidly....."

Christ, the Master:

"Yes, I am Christ, the Master. It is after a very long time that Sai Baba who is your God and our God as well, has given me permission to talk to you. Not only God, but we Masters have also been ordered by God to help you in your mission on earth. Every day of your mission will be a grand success. Such is the will and might of God.

I want you to pray to God, every minute of your life. It is because of Him that have attained to such a high position in our Spiritual Plane. We look upon you henceforth as one of us and not as a mortal living on your earth plane. It is He who has raised you to the highest stature and you should feel happy and express to Him your gratitude from the very depth of your heart."

On October 1, 1950, I was able to meditate for nearly eight long hours, at a stretch, without going into *samadhi.*

On the same say Sai Baba administered to me a great sermon on the necessity of maintaining perfect mental equipoise and stolid indifference to everything. On October 3, 1950, after AI had meditated as usual in the early hours, Sai Baba gave me the following message.

"Do you know that saw Me all the time when you were in *samadhi* for nearly two and half hours? This is your finest achievement so far. It is all unknown to you but you will get awareness of seeing Me possibly in the very next sitting or two. I will make you fully conscious in a very short time. You are quite ripe for that consciousness and I don't want to put a stop to your awareness any longer."

In a further message to the same date, Sai Baba gave me the reasons why He insisted upon my coming to the altar room at such an early hour as 1:00 a.m. and staying therein till 9:00 a.m. He said:

"I have a double meaning in calling you to the altar room at such an early hour as 1:00 a.m. Firstly, to test your power of resistance and endurance by making you meditate for long hours. Secondly, when you meditate for long hours at a stretch, it is impossible to shut out the functioning of the third eye, which in your case is

> open but which I by My superior power and might am not allowing to function. Meditation is the key you are holding to open the secret door to our Realms of Eternity and the longer you can meditate the better."

It was a great surprise to me that in spite of very inadequate sleep, long hours of meditation and prayers and silence in the altar room I was able to keep quite well. It was because, as Sai Baba explained to me, He was filling my mind body and soul with the light of His own Spirit. He said: "I am keeping all your inner vehicles fully vibrant with My own divine tension. I am stimulating you and speeding your work in every way."

The following message of Sai Baba delivered on October 6, 1950, at night is of great significance:

> "You are on a much higher pedestal than other God-realised souls. It will be difficult for people on your earth to understand and realise this. It is for this purpose that I am taking more time in giving you such powers as would simply dazzle and bewilder those agnostics who may come to ridicule you. I say, have implicit faith in Me. Don't feel distressed if I am taking more time. I want to do everything in a thorough manner."

A memorable incident happened on October 7, 1950, in the early hours of the morning. It is best to relate it in the words of Ram Ram, who explained to me the details of the happy occurrence:

> You saw first a pair of most brilliant eyes peering out from Sai Baba's image. Later on, all of a sudden your saw a greenish blue diamond and a faint outline of Sai Baba's clear cut face. It appeared to you that Sai Baba was going to manifest Himself to you in all His Light and Glory. Tremendous electric current passed through your body and you were filled with a sensation through your body. You moved automatically and slowly, like one fully prepared before hand, your legs which were entangled – you were sitting in the cross-legged condition – were freed and you fell prostrate on the ground. You lay in this condition for a few minutes and then resumed your earlier position.

> I was present all the time and watched you keenly. Do you know what this means? This is just a foretaste of what is going to follow. Sai Baba is so pleased that He would not any longer abstain Himself. He will come to you next time in the full blaze of His Light and Splendour. He just wanted to give you a faint experience today of what is going to follow. He is preparing you for it. Had He come to you today in the full blaze of His Light and Splendour, you would have become benumbed and would have instantly passed away. He is preparing you to become fit to see Him in full consciousness, when he makes His appearance.
>
> Remember, His faint appearance today was not in *samadhi,* but in simple meditation, which is a very rare thing. He is training you to see Him both in *samadhi* and out of *samadhi."*

Sai Baba reminded me to forget everything, particularly the book that I was writing under His inspiration. He said:

> "Forget that you have written any book and forget also that your book is going to be published. It may have to be burnt and you should prepare yourself for the worst eventuality. Tomorrow I may ask you to destroy the whole manuscript and you will have to carry out My order."

I was advised by Sai Baba to keep aloof from the external world, as far as possible to be absorbed in thoughts of God and to breathe thoughts of love and harmony for the good of all mankind.

On October 12, 1950, Sai Baba told me that I had passed all His test quite successfully. He said:

> "I have tried and tested you in a thousand ways. I have put you to all sorts of trials, subjected you to bitter disappointments, given you setbacks, made you go through endurance tests, strained your nerves to the breaking point, exhausted you, made you go without adequate food and sleep, broken down your health and have done everything in My power to break you spirit I am exceedingly glad that you have come out from the vortex of trials, tests and disappointments quite successfully – I should say with flying colours."

On October 14, 1950, I was told by Sai Baba that He was on the point of revealing Himself to me, but He restrained

Himself from so doing, as He foresaw that it would have led to a catastrophe. He said:

> "You foresaw that it would have led to a catastrophe. He said: "You would have collapsed had I manifested Myself to you in the full blaze of My glory and splendour. Have a little more faith in Me. Spiritually, You are absolutely fit to see Me. But there are other factors to be considered. Slowly, I am removing them one by one and will soon free you from all your limitations."
>
> On October 15, 1950, I meditated for nearly seven hours from 01:00 a.m. to 08:00 a.m. without going into *samadhi.* Sai Baba gave me the following message:
>
> "Do you know that you persistently saw Me all the time today form the minute you started meditation till you opened your eyes? You have no memory of having seen Me but rest assured that you will soon gets this consciousness.
>
> Ram Ram, Christ the Master, and other are feeling jubilant that the whole drama is now coming to an end and that you will be able to speak with us all in a state of waking consciousness. Kindly have patience a little more."

Two predictions were made by Sai Baba, First, that an utter stranger, a highly evolved soul, would come to me or write to me when the mission is started. Sai Baba said:

> "I am specially sending him to you. He is an extremely evolved soul, whose companionship would do you immense good. He will become a great enthusiast in your cause. You will contact him all of a sudden and it will lead to a lasting bond of friendship. "The second prediction made was about the death of one or two great world figures in the course of a few days.
>
> The constant postponements had tired out my patience and, as a last resort, I began to pray to God for His revelation to me. But Sai Baba at once stopped it. He said: "You are all the time praying to Me, to reveal Myself to you. You know that you can pray for others and your prayers for them cannot go unheeded. But you cannot ask from God anything for yourself, not even God's revelation. You are unnecessarily disturbing your progress. Thank God for all His gifts but don't pray or ask for any gift, much less His Revelation."

On October 16, 1950, I meditated for a long time as usual in the early hours of the morning but I was not able to go into *samadhi.* This was the work of Sai Baba and He explained why He stopped me from going into *samadhi, i.e,* "to give your soul training and make it perfect in the art of seeing Me and our Spirit world without going into *samadhi.* It is easier to see our World in *samadhi.* It is extremely difficult for any one, even the highest saint and sage, to see the Other World without going into *samadhi.*"

I saw clearly that I should not wait for His revelation. It would come when God wishes, not when I desired. It would come when God wishes, not when I desired. It would come when the few cobwebs that were still lurking in my mind had been completely removed. Sai Baba said to me:

"I have taken such a long time, especially for this purpose, that things should take their course in a natural way, without My assistance as your God, except for transcendental purposes only."

"You saw a vision of the sun rising when you were meditating and a clock in front of you later on. The rising of the sun means that the sun of your life will now shine on you and the clock is the symbol of the fact that you have to fight against time to reach your goal. The more you confine against time to reach your goal. The more you confine yourself to the altar room and the less contacts you keep with the external world, the greater will be your power to annihilate the distance of time and space between Me and you. You are now the judge and arbitrator of your own fate."

On October 18, 1950, Sai Baba gave me the following message:

"I have opened all the inner vehicles and the pathways leading to your illumination. I have completed all the preparations. My training is more or less over. It is by the pathway of Bhakti Yoga that you are coming to me. Stick to this path, of all other paths, for you ate far more advanced on this path tan on any other path leading to Me.

It is not that you are not a gnani. It is not that you are not a Karma Yogi... you have won My heart, by your devotion and bhakti, more that by any other yoga. Will you therefore continue your bhakti in a more concentrated form to realize me?"

Sai Baba's message kept ringing in my ears. He said:

> "Give your whole-hearted devotion to God. Think of God, work for God, sit in silence and meditate on God's grace and beauty, His love and grandeur. He mercy and compassion, His greatness and goodness. His bounty and magnanimity. Keep you mind concentrated on God and God alone. Bow down to Him a hundred time a day. When you rise form bed, take the name of God. Let your whole atmosphere be filled with thoughts and vibrations of God, emanating from your heart, mind and soul. Nothing exists for you but God. See God in everything. Worship God every minute and every second, for He alone is Real and He alone is worthy of worship. Let every fibre and tissue of your body be tinged with the joy of God. Let there be no other word in your nomenclature, but God, God and God."

On October 19, 1950, I was put to a short sleep by Sai Baba after a long meditation and in that sleep, I had a dream. I was climbing a very difficult mountainous track and I came to point when it was difficult for me either to retreat or to go higher up. I was in a dazed state of mind and I thought that I was peaced in an irretrievable position. All of a sudden I saw a new track from which men were coming up and I breathed a sigh of relief. It was then that I woke up. Sai Baba, explaining the significance of the dream, said:

> "The dream was purposely given by Me to illustrate the fact that however strenuous be the track you are now following and however perilous the situation may be, you would at last land on safe ground and find your way to freedom.
>
> God-realization is not a bed of roses. It is a thorny path, beset with perils and difficulties. It is only stout heart, with complete devotion to God, that can negotiate the dangerous curves, steep ascents and dizzy heights before reaching safe ground."

On October 19, 1950, I got Sai Baba's permission to visit the Hiranand Leper Hospital at Mangho Pir. Having served this institution for three decades, as its Honorary Secretary, the temptation to visit old friends at the hospital was too great. Sai Baba had warned me that I should no allow myself to be perturbed under any circumstances. But I returned home in a baffled state of mind. The affairs of the hospital were at sixes and sevens. It cut me to pieces.

Sai Baba gave me the following message:

> "You have returned form the hospital in a perturbed state of mind, which is highly injurious to your spiritual development, especially at the present juncture when everything is ready for you and I want only a tranquil, peaceful mind to manifest. Myself to you."

I had still to learn the art of controlling my mind to perfection even in the face of adverse and discomforting circumstances. I was being trained in the art of seeing God and the Spiritual Plane without going into *samadhi,* by Sai Baba. This was unique feature in my training.

Besides the power of seeing God without going into *samadhi,* I was given another gift viz., of allowing my soul to visit the Spiritual Plane straight off, without going through the intermediary steps of the lower planes.

The conferment of these two unique gift was a clear evidence of the fact that I was guided and trained by God Himself. I was also thoroughly convinced of the highest state of evolution reached by me by the grace of God.

But the trails did not stop. On October 21, 1950, I was again put to a new kind of test by Sai Baba. He said:

> "I want you to know that there is no possibility of your being chosen for God's mission as you have failed in all your tests. You have proved quite unworthy of it. You are highly egoistic and quite useless. Will you kindly stop this humbug of coming to the altar room and wasting your time in the idle hope of getting God's Revelation. What egotism on your part to have fondled such false hopes!"
>
> "May I know who you are? It cannot be Sai Baba, queried I.
>
> Prompt came the reply. "Yes, I am Sai Baba. I want to give you a straight talk. You have been fooled all these days and weeks and months. All those talk were given to raise a false sense of expectancy in you and to test your egotism. It is as clear as daylight

that you are highly egoistic and therefore absolutely unfit for any kind of mission. I order you from today, not to invoke Me at all."

I again butted in and said meekly:

"It cannot be Sai Baba. I have complete and absolute faith in God and I live only in that faith. I do and I shall always do what God orders. I have no ambition of any kind. It is not right to say that I am egoistic. Pray tell me who you are. It appears you are a stranger. Is it not so?"

Then Sai Baba replied:

"I am Sai Baba and none else. I was merely teasing you. I find that your mind is absolutely unperturbed and you are not at all affected by the sham talk I gave you. I am extremely glad that you have passed the test."

On October 22, 1950, at night time, Sai Baba gave me a long message preparing me and giving me instruction as to what to do when He reveals Himself to me.

"Do you know that I have ordered Ram Ram Christ, the Master, to be with Me when I reveal Myself to you? You would see Me first and then the two Masters. As soon as you see Me, lie down at full length on the ground and keep on praying to God. After you have seen Me, I shall disappear quickly you will not be able to stand the strain of seeing me for a longer duration. As soon as I disappear, Ram Ram and Christ will manifest themselves to you. You can talk with them in your sitting position. They will be your guides as well as your companions. They will quicken the pace of your further evolution under My guidance and inspiration.

I shall make Myself visible to you whenever I like and as often as I want. As you have already been thoroughly trained by Me, there will be very little left for the Master to tell you and train you in. The difference between Me and the Master will be that you would be able to see Me only when I want to make Myself visible to you and not when you wish."

There were two prospects facing me. Either I would get God's revelation soon and be immediately called away, or that I would have to wait for some more time till I become fit for the mission and embark upon it after God's Revelation.

In the first instance, there was instantaneous death after Revelation. In the second case, there was short span of life for completing God's mission on earth, after His Revelation.

Sai Baba asked me:

> "Prepare yourself for either eventuality. There is no third alternative. I can't any longer keep you in the present state of affairs, for time is an important factor and it cannot be wasted."

On October 24, 1950, Ram Ram gave me the following message:

> "You have now reached a state when even by merely sitting in absolute silence for hours together, you can see God, straight off. You have to devote all your attention to this prime factor of silence. Speak only when you are required to speak. Be extremely careful in this regard."

On October 25, 1950, after a long meditation, Sai Baba gave me the following message:

> "Your meditation today was magnificent from all points of view. You richly deserve My Revelation. I have restrained Myself for a specific reason which you would come to know later."

I was told by Sai Baba that the messages would hence forth stop and I must learn to do without them. This news made me wonder whether Revelation was imminent? The thought gave me a fillip. In a few hours, Sai Baba resumed His talk and He said:

> "Do you know that I stopped you from taking down My messages and yet I am not at all inclined to stop you from doing so. Why is it so? Because I love you and I want you to be in communion with me. You would feel miserable if I stop. I shall therefore continue My talk with you till the very last day of your life on the earth plane."

Homi had been asked to write a foreword to my new book. He was specially required to trace the development of my spiritual consciousness, beginning with training under

Ram Ram and ending with the revelation of God, after strenuous preparation by Sai Baba. It was a difficult job but undaunted, he plodded through all the message and the printed proof pages of the book and wove out a coherent account of my spiritual journey. Sai Baba was much pleased and He praised Homi's unstinted work.

> "Homi has taken enormous pain and devoted great labour, all for your sake, as ordered by Me. He has done you signal service and I want him to know through you that I shall reward him in unique manner. Of course what he has done and is doing, is not with a view to earn anything. By serving you as ordered by Me, he has served the cause of the mission. No labour can go unrequited. Sacrifice for the sake of God is the essence of life."

In the afternoon of October 28, 1950, Sai Baba put me to a severe test by questioning me:

"Do you want to fulfil the mission, no matter how long I take in preparing you for it or do you want Me to call you away? Answer yes or no." Unhestitatingly, I replied that I was bound down to God and it was His privilege to do whatever He liked and that I had no option. I vowed that though I had the power to quit the physical body whenever I liked, I would not exercise that gift. I was determined therefore to keep fast to that vow under all circumstances.

I was again warned that I should not look forward or calculate the time for God's Revelation. Sai Baba said:

> "I shall reveal Myself to you whenever I want. You should not worry whether I shall reveal Myself to you soon or later on. Forget all about the time. Remember only that My revelation is certain. I may show Myself to you in an instant or I may take a whole year or a number of years."

This reminded me of the experience of prophet Mohammad. He had seen Angel Gabriel coming down from heaven and bringing Him a scroll to read, at the foot of which were the words written forming the Sura XCVI of the Holy Quran.

> "Read, for the Lord is the most high, who that taught by the pen, had taught to man, what he knows not Nay truly, man walketh in delusion, when he deems that he suffices for himself, to thy Lord they must all return."

This was a clear sign of God's revelation to Him. He tried his best and waited in earnest for the repetition of that revelation, but it was in vain. Three years passed away after the first revelation and such melancholy and unrest came upon Mohammad, that often He felt like throwing Himself from the Mount Hira, which was the scene of his first illumination.

I, too, though a very humble soul, had my vicissitudes. I had received partial illumination. I was in daily communion with God. I could hear Him but the super-consciousness to see Him face to face was postponed form day to day. It was very trying.

As I was ordered to pass whole day in the altar room, I started spending more than 15 hours a day in the sacred and inspiring atmosphere of the aura of My beloved Masters. Sai Baba did marvels. He made my body spiritual as explained in the following message of Ram Ram:

> "It is only God who can do such marvellous things. Sai Baba has not only penetrated through your body, but also entered into all the inner valves and tissues and filtered and energised them with His atomic energy. It is an extremely rare event for God to come down to a person on the earth plane and to do such marvels in the inner system of the human body is now only meant for external purpose. It is your inner body which will be working all the time. Your physical body is now completely made an instrument in the hands of the Mighty Spirit that pervades throughout the universe. He has transformed you into SPIRIT. You are no longer human with human weaknesses. You are completely like one of us in the Great White Brotherhood. You would yourself witness this great transformation as the days pass on."

But the veil had not been completely lifted. The worst torture was the suspense of waiting for the promised

Revelation. Sai Baba said by way of consolation:

> "You should not mind all the hardships and tortures of waiting in silence, even if it may seem, *ad infinitum.* Once having agreed to surrender yourself to God. Don't allow even a flicker of pessimistic thoughts to pass through your mind . It is for you to go in emitting rays of light and cheer, in all weathers for have I not transformed you? You would soon see the Great Light – the LIGHT of My Revelation."

In order to avoid the turmoils of home life, I thought of moving out of my house and selecting a secluded place. I placed my view before Sai Baba and He gave me the following reply:

> "No, I don't want you to go out anywhere. Stick to the altar room. It is your sanctuary and you won't find a better place for the observance of silence and seclusion. Besides, it is surcharged with an atmosphere of sanctity, which no other place is. I and the Masters can come to your altar room freely, but not anywhere else. Certain places have certain magnetic attractions for the higher Spirits. You have by the dint of years and years of meditation in your altar room made it a holy and sanctified place fit for gods to come and sit.
>
> "Your future fate is to be decided in your altar room and nowhere else. I order you to stick to your altar room and nowhere else. Think that it is God's Abode. Keep fresh flowers every day and burn incense all the time."

Whatever shreds of doubt that still might have lurked in my mind that I was after all but an ordinary mortal, quite unfit to get God's vision, were removed entirely by the emphatic assurance of Sai Baba as would be seen from the following message, so majestic in its utterance, so very convincing in its appeal:

> "I want to impress upon your mind, that if your were not such a highly evolved soul, would I, your God, commune with you so freely? Have I not given you countless proofs in My messages that I am God and none else. It is true that I have not revealed Myself to you. But I must be having special reasons for so doing. However evolved you are and from My point of view, there is nothing more

desirable, so far as spirituality goes. I have still to be extremely careful before I give you superconsciousness.

Leave even your correspondence. Leave everything. I order you; Don't talk with any one. Don't meddle with any one's affairs. Keep quiet and do nothing. Be a silent spectator of what goes on around you, but take no part keep aloof from every one. Think that you are not living on you earth plane. I have told you so many times and I repeat to you that you are no longer a human soul but a member of the White Brotherhood. Why don't you understand and realise your changed position?

On November 1, 1950, I was given the excellent news of my having broken the thin line that separated me from God. Sai Baba said: When I choose to reveal Myself to you, you would be able to see Me in the full blaze of My terrific Light. I have given you the special power to see Me in My full splendour. As you have now the powers to see Me and carry the impression, I kept away from you today in the morning. You have now only to wait till I of My own accord come to you. I shall take My time to do it.

"I have given you the powers to see Me but I have kept the master key with Me. You will get access of the master key, when I think you are quite fit. When I revel Myself to you, you would become absolutely a liberated soul,-Jivan Mukta. You can then exercise the powers given to you. Till then the powers in you will remain dormant."

On November 2, 1950, I meditated as usual and Sai Baba gave me the following message afterwards:

"Do you know what I did today in the morning, when you were meditating? I sat by your side without interfering with you meditation and allowed you to do whatever you liked. Your inner eye was open. It searched for Me but I used My will and kept Myself out of its focus."

I then put Sai Baba the question:

"May I know whether I was in *samadhi* and whether my soul visited the Spiritual Plane as usual and if so, since the inner eye was open and fully functioning, why did it not see the Spiritual Plane and carry the impression of having seen it?"

Sai Baba replied:

"This is a very pertinent question. Your soul did go into *samadhi* during the latter part of you meditation but I purposely closed you inner eye when it flew from your body. I came down just for that purpose, not to allow the inner eye to see the beauty of My Spiritual Plane, without first seeing Me. When I am in the Spiritual Plane, I can make it recede from the vision of your inner eye by creating a void. But this time, I came down and I used My power to stop the vision of your inner eye.

"I want to show to you the many ways in which I can use My power. You are now getting direct, solid experience of the teaching that God is Omnipotent, Omnipotent and Omnipotent. This should satisfy you.

"I give you the most definite and emphatic and emphatic assurance that you would see Me in the full blaze of My splendour in a startling and inconceivable manner. This extraordinary and unique event will take place very soon."

The next day, I was told by Ram Ram that I had by the grace of God now attained full illumination.

"The illumination which you had before was not full. It was partial. Today Sai Baba has given you the fullest ILLUMINATION and you will get consciousness of this illumination in a very short time. It is your greatest achievement."

On November 25, 1950, Sai Baba gave me the following message after the usual morning meditation:

"Do you know that I was ready and was on the point of revealing Myself to you. All your preparations being complete, it is now absolutely necessary that I must manifest Myself to you. But at the very last minute, I decided to wait for some more time."

On November 5, 1950 at 10:55 p.m. Sai Baba gave me the following message which was exceedingly thrilling and soul-stirring:

"I am your God and I can do miracles through you. Kindly remember your training under Me gives you a priority over others who have realized the self but have not had the benefit of direct communion with the God without. You have the double gift of communion with the God within and the God without. It is a rare privilege and it is this gift that will take you a long distance when you start your mission after My Revelation."

On November 7, 1950, Ram Ram told me:

"Do you know that a miraculous thing happened today when you were meditating. All of us viz. Sai Baba, Myself, Christ, Zoroaster, Buddha, Krishna came down as ordered by Sai Baba and we all sang together. Then Sai Baba entered you heart as I used to do before, but what I could not do He did with complete ease. He vitalised your heart and made it strong enough to resist both physical strain and mental agony."

In one of the earlier messages, Sai Baba had asked me to wait for a highly evolved soul who would contact me and whose contact would help me in my mission. Some strangers, after the prediction, did see me, but they were ordinary soul, seeking earnestly for God. Sai Baba than gave me the following bewildering message:

"The stranger that I has asked you to wait for is Myself. You know Me, by thought but not by sight. You shall have the happiness and honour of seeing Me."

This above revelation thrilled me. Really, the Masters talk in riddles and how slowly they lift the veil.

On November 9, 1950, Sai Baba said:

"The Stranger is coming to you. Kindly receive Him with open arms and make Him your best Friend and Ally in life, Here and Hereafter." My heart was bubbling with joy. Is it that the Stranger, none else that God, whom I knew by thought but not by sight, was soon to come to me?

I was ailing. My stomach was continuously giving me trouble. I ate little, slept little, talked. I passed long hours in the altar room. I cut myself off from the external world as much as possible. But there was no sign of the Revelation. On November 11, 1950, Sai Baba said to me:

"I am so very sorry, again I had to resist Myself and I did not manifest Myself to you. I have been promising Revelation form day to day, just to try and see how far you can resist disappointments with perfect equanimity of mind. You must learn the lesson of perfect indifference to failure and success. In fact, more or less, you have by now learnt it but I still want you to perfect yourself in this art.

"Don't think of your health or any kind of ailment. You will be fully restored to perfect health the very minute you see Me. All the powers that have been given to you are still in a slumbering condition. The minute I reveal Myself to you, the slumbering powers will awaken and begin to function in a bewildering manner. Be absolutely at ease and go your way unconcerned and indifferent."

I was asked to lie down flat, on the floor in the altar room, before Sai Baba's picture at least once every day. This change in technique appeared to me as a convincing proof of the nearness of the Revelation.

To be frank, the postponements so tired me that I felt like making a new plan of my life viz. to curtail the altar room activities and to take up some work of an unselfish nature. But Sai Baba's stern refusal checked me again. He said:

"Kindly don't make any plan in your mind for diverting from the present routine of work. Even if you do, I shall thwart you. Have you no faith in Me? Why do you then spoil the whole thing by allowing doubts to overcome you."

Sai Baba then gave me the following talk:

"Then you see it is God alone who is Eternal, all else is fleeing, uncertain and perishable. Think of God all the time. Keep Him in your heart and mind. Make Him the lodestar of your life, the garland of your heart, the ideal and idol, unforgettable and imperishable. Live in the fountain source of inspiration, the beacon light of wisdom. Love Him with all the ardour of your soul. Live for Him and Him alone. He is you Guide, He is your Friend. He is your best Ally in life."

On November 15, 1950, Sai Baba said to me that a retinue of Masters was circling Him and they wanted to give me a united message, without revealing their individual names. This is the message which I received from the Master's group:

"God be praised. We all have come together at the express order of our Sovereign Ruler, who wants us to read your aura and to give a message in the united name of all of us Masters, who are gathered here at the moment. Your aura is transparently white without the slightest speck of any other taint – not even blue or yellow. This is a marvellous indication of very rare occurrence. At all such times, we Masters are called by God, to witness the rare phenomenon. We feel exceedingly happy and send you our united love and felicitations. You are chosen by God for a great mission on earth and sure enough He will guide you to ultimate success and triumph."

On November 16, 1950, I went into *samadhi* as soon as meditation was started and Sai Baba:

"Had your *samadhi* lasted for a few minutes more, you would have seen Me with your inner eye, in the full blaze of My splendour and glory. The *samadhi* lasted for nearly three hours."

The same day, late in the evening, Sai Baba said: "I want you to know that I cannot do anything more that what has already been done for you. It is now for you to enter the gateway of the Eternal Abode of Bliss, which is open, but which you in your present consciousness falsely think is closed. It was absolutely closed before. All My preparations are complete. I am not tormenting you nor am I postponing your achievements any longer. You are absolutely ripe and fit to gain your prize and achieve your object. The hindrance is your own folly and silliness. Read all My messages carefully, weigh them properly, follow them astutely and you will gain superconsciousness in a minute. To put it in a nutshell if you avoid all external contacts, as Buddha did before he got the final illumination, lock yourself up in the altar room and pray and meditate, this will stop you form seeing Me. You are your own obstruction to your goal."

At midnight of the same day, Sai Baba gave me a sermon on my laying too much of importance on earthly duties, to the negligence of the altar room activities. He said:

"Do you duties fearlessly. They are really speaking not duties but your world considers them as duties and as such so long as you are on the earth plane, even these earthly duties you must perform.... In fact, they are a hindrance to true spiritual progress. I therefore give up the option of performing your earthly duties or not. The main objective is that you must keep to your altar room, as much possible. It is your altar room that will give peace of mind, so very necessary for the culmination of My Revelation to you."

It was evident from this message that what was most important at the critical stage reached by me, was not the performance of the so-called earthly duties but deep meditation, silence and seclusion.

On November 18, 1950, I was able to go into *samadhi* three times during my meditation in the morning. Difficulties and obstacles came in my way all the time, but they were always very easily overcome. It is no wonder that Sai Baba said: "I shall facilitate all your work and remove all our difficulties."

A secret wave of joy, In spite of adverse circumstances, was passing through me. Why was it so? I was now nearest to God's heart. There was an intrinsic feeling in me that I had won God's love in full and His revelation, though long delayed, could not be far off any longer.

I knew from the trend of the messages that, in spite of postponements form day to day, I was coming to the end of my journey for the attainment of the goal of God-realization.

On 22 Sai Baba gave me a message indicating His unique power which none except God could manifest. He said,

"Do you know that I was on the point of revealing Myself to you. Your inner eye has now gained do much in its power of vision, that had I revealed Myself to you, you would seen Me and carried the impression also."

I then put a query: "Why do I not see the Spiritual Plane when the inner eye is open and it has gained its power of vision?"

Sai Baba replied:

"Because the minute your soul comes to our Spiritual Plane, it is terribly upset by the change in the environment. It sees nothing and returns to your body in dismayed condition. I do this because I am God and can create condition which no one except Myself to you. I want still some more time. I say again and again, you are absolutely fit but whenever I want to reveal Myself to you, I feel hesitant. But have complete faith in Me. This hesitancy would also go away and you would see Me face to face. My revelation to you is a certain as death.

"Do you know that it is absolutely in your own hands to see Me face to face? You have overcome all resistance and barriers. I cannot any longer stop you from going into *samadhi.* Your inner eye is fully open and it has gained so much of intensity of vision that it would be able to stand the glare of My fiery robe without any difficulty. I have given you inward strength and power beyond measure."

On November 24, 1950, Sai Baba said to me:

"There is still some small speck of imperfection in you. I have to wait till it is cleared. You must learn to wait. Be patient, be submissive and continue your entire faith in God."

I had been told that I had reached the goal and that God's Revelation would take place in a flash, any moment any hour.

On November 25, 1950, my mind was perturbed and meditation was a failure. But inspite of that, Sai Baba was able to perform miracles as will be seen from the following message of Ram Ram:

"Do you know that in spite of the failure of your meditation today, Sai Baba did wonders again, which none in the cosmos can do except God. He made me enter your body and stay there for considerable time and both of us, He externally guarding me and I internally watching you, made the finer preparation of your soul for the higher purpose of the mission."

November 26, 1950, was a day of terrible trial for me. My body was reeking with pain and it was terrible strain to sit erect. In spite of my resolute will to meditate, it was extremely difficult to do so. The following messages of Sai Baba and Ram Ram tell their own tale. They give an insight into the whole drama that was staged.

Sai Baba said:

"Do you know that today in the morning when you were meditating, I put on you two or three evil spirits to disturb your meditation and to enter into your body and to drain you completely? This is the greatest surprise of your life but I had to do it for I must test you to the bitterest end. They succeeded partially, for taking advantage of the fact that your mind was still not cool and calm, they thwarted your meditation. But I must admit you put up the most valiant fight against them. Considering the circumstances in which you were placed, with such terrible forces of opposition against you, I consider today's sitting to be the culmination of your long drawn out victory. The evil spirits even tried to enter into your body but you thwarted them by the constant utterance of God's one hundred and one names which is our mantra, your absolute purity of mind, coupled with your extreme devotion to God. Eventually they flew away from you in utter dread and dismay. Is it not a great victory? You bore your physical pain caused by the opening of the ulcer in the stomach very bravely, though you invoked Me to show mercy on you. It pained me to put you to such a cruel and savage test. But it is for your own good."

Rishi Ram Ram explained it thus:

"What Sai Baba told you just now of two or three evil spirits trying to disturb you was only in an allegorical manner. No spirits really came at all. He created all the evil instincts in you Himself to see how far you can maintain a calm and tranquil mind for the progress of a long and deep meditation...."

It was a terrible test indeed, to see how far I could endure physical pain and battle against the onslaught on the tranquillity of the mind. To put it in a nutshell, I was tested whether I could rise above body consciousness and mind consciousness.

On November 27, 1950 I wrote to Homi:

.....It is true that I have made splendid progress, step by step. It is equally true that I am inwardly satisfied that I have found God. But so far there is no concrete proof of my having found God, as would convince anyone else. Kindly read the message of yesterday (27-11-50, 2:45 p.m.) in which Sai Baba gave me three options: First that I must close the book and face the consequence which would be bitter and most galling. The book, so far completed, would give an impression to the reader that the author is a fool or a fraud. The second option is to burn the book. If it is destroyed, I will lose nothing. What I have attained personally is my own gain spiritually and that is quite enough for me. The third option is that I must continue since I have given a promise to Sai Baba and taken a vow. I am going to stand by that promise even if it results in absolute nothingness and face all consequences. He will find a way out for me.

It is my earnest plea to you to help me and stand by me upto the last minute of the trial. I may tell you it is a terrible trial that I am passing through but I am prepared, for my faith in God is innate and I am sure. He will come to my rescue.

Late at night on November 27, 1950, Sai Baba made the following prediction.

"Today is the last day in the journey of your old life. A new life will start for you from tomorrow, full of energy and bliss beyond description. The Masters interested in you ask Me to greet you and congratulate you on the happy transformation of your life.

"I am extremely glad to say that you have begin today a new lease of life. Your today's sitting was absolutely different from all sittings hitherto held.... You were bending down before My picture all the time throughout your wonderfully beautiful meditation lasting for more than six hours at a stretch. Had I allowed you to go into *samadhi* even for one minute, you would have seen Me. Your inner eye is a blazing hot, fiery orb and so keen that it can penetrate the densest things in the universe."

Later, Ram Ram gave me the following message:

"You have touched today the highest pedestal of the spiritual edifice. You are now member of our holy order in all reality and the powers that Sai Baba has given to you to exercise when you begin you new life soon function. You are feeling the joyous breath of the new life which you have today entered into. But be very careful. As it is still the very beginning, you will have to strengthen the inner force of life and energy that Sai Baba has instilled in you. This new force will go on increasing as the days go on till it becomes a sort of a sweeping avalanche, so rapid and overpowering will it be in its effects. It is the creative energy which Sai Baba has enflamed today. It is linked directly with God's Eternal Reservoir.

Rapid changes in your life will now take place .... You will soon see Me and I shall become your close companion. You are coming to the most vital part of your book. The last pages will be the most thrilling portion of your work."

Late in the evening Sai Baba gave me a long message. He reiterated that my constant bending down before His picture in the alter room was a sign of my nearing the goal of God-realization. He revealed to me also the fact of some Angel taking special interest in me at His express command. This was very curious. It is best to relate the whole incident in His own words.

"I bring her with me every time I came to you to give you My talk in the alter room. You will have her also after My and Master's manifestation to you."

I enquired: "Do I know her at all?"

Sai Baba replied: "No, you don't know her but she knows you from our birth. She was in your earth plane some centuries ago. The great mystery of the link between you and this Angel will be cleared up when you see her after My revelation. She wanted to be appointed as our guardian angel and Spirit master but I refused and gave priority to Ram Ram. Why I refused, I cannot explain now. I will allow you to talk to her. But as you have no image of her nor any picture, you cannot invoke her. All I will do is to make her talk to you through Ram Ram, not now, but later on, if I think fit. You must not ask Me any question nor show any anxiety. When I think fit, I shall do the needful but you should not at all remind Me nor ask for it. Be very careful in this regard."

In the same message, Sai Baba also said:

"As soon as your new book is published, I may have to call you away. The reason for doing this is that you have so won My love and are so very faithful and devoted to Me that even after realizing Me, I don't want you to suffer in the least, physically or mentally. When Ram Ram said that your book is the mission, he was not wrong. I am now clearing the atmosphere by lifting the veil."

I felt in my heart that God's Revelation was certain. I also felt if the Revelation was to be expedited, I must keep on thinking of God alone and cut myself off entirely from the tentacles of earthly ties and duties. The alter room was the safest place for the purpose and I spent as much time as possible in its consecrated atmosphere.

Late at night on the same day. *i.e.* November 30, 1950, Sai Baba in reply to my anxious query regarding when I would get super-consciousness, said: "My dear child, you are on the very verge of getting it. You might get it even tomorrow. Your way is absolutely clear and your aura is shining like a lustrous star. The angel about whom I talked to you is none else than the reflection of your aura. Your aura is now piercing our Spirit Land and is casting its radiant light all around. This it does only when you go into *samadhi.*"

My conjecture that Sai Baba was talking to me allegorically when He first introduced the angel to me was correct. It was true that she was a reflection of my aura. But there was a doubt in my mind as to how could this angel be a reflection of my aura, when my aura was only recently developed and the angel had desired to become my Spirit Guide at my birth. Sai Baba cleared the ambiguity immediately. He said: "You are right. When I say that the angel is a reflection of your aura, it does not mean that it is only a reflection and nothing more. It is both a reflection of your true self, as well as a separate entity, but at the moment, it is reflecting the rays of your aura."

I was told by Sai Baba that I had passed the test of non-expectancy. He gave me permission to look forward now to His Revelation. I felt that next few days should decide my fate.

In the afternoon, on December 3, 1950, Sai Baba said to me: "As the angel who comes with Me wants to talk to you, will you kindly invoke Ram Ram? He will make her talk to you."

Ram Ram was invoked and he said:

"Do you know what a tremendous change has come in you? You will see yourself in the angel who has come to speak to you. This angel it nothing but the reflection of your own self. When you talk to her, it would be like talking to your own soul. I am going to make this angel talk to you. Kindly listen to her properly.

The Angel then gave me the following talk:

"Yes, I am the angel of whom Sai Baba and Ram Ram have spoken. I am what you have made me and what you would be, when you come over to our Spirit Land, after leaving your physical body on the earth plane. I am looking forward to your coming over here. I was to have been appointed as your Guardian Angel and Spirit Guide when you were born but Sai Baba refused and passed you on to Ram Ram.

I and Ram Ram are great friends. We belong to the same group of Masters. You would think that I am talking to you in riddles but it is not so. We three, I, Ram Ram and you, are all separate entities but at the same time, we are all one in the kindredship of our spirit and soul. Sai Baba alone is above us all ruling the whole universe. But for His permission I would not have come to you now to give you a talk. Kindly invoke Ram Ram."

I again invoked Ram Ram and he gave me the following message:

"You have listened to the Angel. Do you know why she came to you? Do you understand the significance of her coming to you? She is the Angel of Death. She has come just to warn and prepare you that your days are numbered. I have given you exceedingly important news. You must hasten and finish off your new book. Sai Baba's revelation is certain. You will see Him soon now."

That the Angel was the Angel of Death was revelation to me. To be frank, the news that death was stealing a march on me and its steps were near, gave me inwardly a feeling of relief, though at the same time. I was not afraid of continuing my earthly journey even in the then condition of my ailing body for I had complete faith in God that He would always guard and help me in all my difficulties and sufferings.

That the Angel of Death that came to me belonged to the group of Masters and was a reflection of my soul filled me with unbounded joy.

The two final chapters on 'God's Revelation' have already become so bulky and quite out of all proportion, that it is necessary to give just a gist of the subsequent messages to indicate the trail of events leading to the finale of God's Revelation.

The chief question that arises is, why in spite of assurances by Ram Ram and Sai Baba, God Himself, God's revelation get superconsciousness when they are still in the full bloom of their physical health. Zoroaster, Buddha, Moses, Christ, Mohammad, were prophets who had talked with God face to face and had attained divine knowledge by visible contact with the Divine Agency in the prime of life. Even they had to go through a course of deep meditation and seclusion to reach that state of perfection, so very necessary for God's revelation. Bodily health is necessary to go through the rigours of life and to practise austerities so very essential for spiritual attainment.

If I may be pardoned for indulging in personal remarks, I was not at all destined to gain superconsciousness in this life. It was my iron will to gain it at any cost, however, that changed the Master's plan and Rishi Ram Ram handed me over to Sai Baba, Ahuram Mazda Himself. God can do anything; ill-health and old age are no barriers to God-realization, when God wishes it.

On December 5, 1950, I was in an unpleasant situation which led to the bursting of my temper. In atonement, I passed the whole night in the altar room and took the vow of the bearing patiently with all sinners and evil doers, for are they not the children of God and if God could bear them, why should not I? Sai Baba to me:

"You should be like God and not be offended even when a most brutal word is spoken or the deepest act of offense is committed."

How very kind and merciful God is became evident when He gave me the power of invoking Him to save myself from difficulties. This power was used on several occasions and to my utter surprise, He always me and cleared my difficulties. I knew in my heart of hearts that He was teaching me all the time by the method of direct inspiration and I felt His divine presence every minute of my life.

On December 9, 1950, Sai Baba actually described how He would reveal Himself to me:

"Before I come to you there will be blazing light all around: You will feel diffident at first. But in a short time the feeling of diffidence will go away and you will boldly stare at me as I emerge from the halo of light surrounding Me."

My soul was stirred to its very roots. I was thrilled beyond measure. The very thought that I would soon be talking to God, freely, face to face, made me mad with joy. Who would not sacrifice his all to gain God's love and His divine presence in a visible form?

My health had considerably deteriorated and I was passing through an acute state of physical suffering. But I knew instinctively that it was a mere passing phase and I must bear up the bodily pain cheerfully, for was not God's Revelation imminent?

I was aware that the God within me was being unfolded. Sai Baba said to me on December 14, 1950:

"The total unfoldment of the Self will synchronise with My Revelation and this happy event, believe Me, is extremely near. I am your God, your own God, and none other but God. Keep this in mind all the time."

To be in communion with God, at any hour of the day and night, was a bliss of the highest order. I knew that Sai Baba was postponing His Revelation to strengthen me both inwardly and outwardly so as to meet the opposition that I would be mercilessly exposed to, when the new book was published and I was declared to have had God's Revelation.

On December 17, 1950, I was ordered to pass the nights in vigil in the altar room. This period of nightly vigils lasted for 17 days. It was an ordeal imposed upon me. I had been trained to eat very little, sleep very little, to work for long hours, to meditate, concentrate and pray to God in the silence and seclusion of the altar room. If the trials and tests were relentless, they brought also the cheering consolation that it was a travail, that would end in the triumph of the spirit over flesh. I knew that the enforcement of night vigils in the altar room was purely to expedite God's Revelation.

My soul had been perfected to such an extent by constant visits to the Spiritual Plane, in the state of *samadhi*, that it was able to perfect the inner vehicles also by its action. I knew that "man's perception changes till he realise God" And in order to realise God, no scholastic discussion but perfection of character, sacrifice, selflessness, love for and devotion to God and complete surrender to His will, are the necessary requisites.

The following message of Sai Baba rings in my ear, even as these lines are written:

> "In the ultimate reality, everything is spirit and this fundamental point should always be kept in front. Progress is from matter to spirit, form the mundane to the spiritual, from the unreal to the Real, from darkness to light." He also told me that God in His Ultimate Reality is Simplicity and not Complexity. It is on account of multiplicity of God's creation, there is complexity. God can be realised only through simplicity. Sai Baba said to me. "You have to be simple in your thoughts, words and deeds. Build the ladder of simplicity to reach God. Be simple in your way of living, In your habits, in your thoughts and in your speech and action."

The Masters continued their assurances that they were anxious to manifest themselves to me. Sai Baba gave the same assurance. In fact, on December 19, 1950, Sai Baba gave me His blessings and said that I must think that I had already entered into the Garden of Bliss and that I had won God's love.

On December 21, 1950, I was assured by Sai Baba in the course of His message that my inner eye was burning like a red hot coal and was as keen as a razor; that all the inner vehicles were transparently clear and that the souls had a clear passage to my physical consciousness. Was I on the footsteps of God-realization?

On December 23, 1950, I had a unique experience. It is best to relate it in the words of Ram Ram, my Spirit Guide and Master:

> "Do you know what Sai Baba did? He went on extracting your soul from body every minute and the minute it tried to see God, He vanished. This minute to minute appearance and disappearance of your soul in search of God continued throughout the whole meditation of six long hours. Till the last minute, your soul thirsted to see God and every time when it failed, it went back into your body."

It should be clear that I was thirsting for God. To me, everything appeared dreary, of no value, except God, whose very name filled me with a wave of joyousness and made me go into a reverie. God alone was my target. To me, the world appeared as an illusion and a delusion. The God within me was being fully unfolded. I was longing for Ahuram Mazda's own revelation.

On December 28, 1950, I was told by Sai Baba, that was most dangerously near the Fire Block and that He was guarding and watching me so that I might not be burnt in that hot furnace. He said to me:

> "I am preparing you, strengthening you and inwardly creating in you all those forces, which when they come to full power, would form a sort of a wall to protect you from the burning fire, which you will have to pass through to see Me."

Days rolled on but there was no visible sign of God's revelation. I knew that Sai Baba and Ram Ram were only raising false hopes and expectations in me. It was to crush the seed of expectancy in me that these devices were employed.

On December, 1950, I was told that I had crossed the block of fire. Sai Baba said:

"It was a terrible passage, which rarely anyone is able to negotiate. You have done it, though you are quite unaware of the feat accomplished." It was purely God's grace and mercy. I knew my limitations. I knew how very puny and impotent a mortal is before the power of God, who is Omnipotent. Sai Baba said to me: I have shown to you by countless examples how very impotent you are and that you should not take pride or be elated, if you attain any most strenuous efforts, no Revelation of God so far was attained, was itself the mightiest proof of my impotence. It is only when God's grace descends on man, that His Revelation can take place.

On January 2, 1951, Sai Baba ordered the night vigils in the altar room to come to an end. He had hammered out from any body all the undesirable debris, and made it light and subtle to respond to God's vibrations. He tested me to the bitterest end to the highest point of physical endurance.

January 7, 1951, brought me a foretaste of God's Revelation. It was a thrilling experience. I was enveloped in sheaths of joy, such as had never been experienced in life, when I was meditation in the early hours of the morning. Ram Ram told me that it was the beginning of a new era, a new programme in life. He said:

"Sai Baba will take you step by step to an entirely new world that will dazzle and bewilder you with strange sights and lights of an incomprehensible nature."

On January 12, 1950, Ram Ram assured me that Sai Baba continued the postponement of His Revelation for the simple reason viz., to purify me to the very last degree of perfection. He said:

'There is a difference between a Master's manifestation and God's revelation. The former is easily feasible. The latter is exceedingly difficult, as God must have a completely perfect instrument. But you have arrived at a stage when that perfection, as far as we Masters can see, is absolutely in evidence. It is a puzzle to us why Sai Baba is still trying you all the time, But don't be afraid and forget everything keeping trust and faith in God."

On January 14, 1951, when I entered the altar room in the evening, I began to ruminate on the war clouds that were threatening to burst out at any moment and engulf the whole world in a deluge of blood and my heart pined for peace. I breathed out a prayer to God and I wrote down the thoughts that came to any mind as under:

God and Peace

Just as mcuntains dominate the valleys and the plains, the Absolute Spirit that pervades the universe, dominates all LIFE and vitalizes it with a touch of that Glory, which is God's own mantle of Eternity, superb in its splendour, vivacious in its utterance, prolific in its abundance of rigour and ceaseless in its effort to revolutionise and vitalise the mundane into the spiritual.

"God's breath of fragrance, we inhale every moment of our life. It lifts our heart and mind to soaring heights of ecstasy and rapturous joy beyond human description.

"Is there anyone greater than God or equal to Him the God, the Eternal, the Infinite, the only Reality, the Creator of the universe, the Matrix of Dynamic, the Superfortress of ENERGY, the faintest speck of which can create revolutions beyond recognition in the vast vistas of Nature? Who would not adore, love and worship Him who is full of Love and Light. He gives us, His children, His burning love and wants us to love Him in return, practising Righteousness, which is the girdle, which He wants us to put on, to safeguards from the perils and dangers of the earthly journey.

"He is our Father, He is our Guide, He is our Protector, He is our Inspirer. He is the diadem of unfailing light and splendour, hidden in the depths of our heart, inspiring us with words of wisdom, to seek that which is holy and abiding and not that which is momentary and perishing.

O God, give us Light to seek only that which is Real and Eternal, the light of unfading Bliss and undying peace.

On January 18, 1951, I was told by Sai Baba that I had safely negotiated a dangerous corner in the journey of my life and that I had passed through the supreme test quite successfully. But these tests could never come to an end, as I knew from experience and I was therefore quite indifferent to the words of inaction dropped into my soul.

January 22, 1951, was a days, of unrivalled importance and significance in the drama of my life. I wrote to Homi of my experience in the altar room as under:

> "I went into meditation at about 2:15 a.m. after concentrating on Sai Baba's picture as usual and to my great surprise, after a short time, I was transformed and lifted up to a region of ecstatic bliss. This lasted for fully an hour and half and I was enjoying the transformed bliss to my heart's content. I don't think I had ever been raised before to such transcendental heights. I saw clearly that it was the work of some divine entity who had done this miracle. At the end of this extraordinary transcendental state, all of a sudden Sai Baba appeared from a red glowing cloud. The vision was very clear. I saw it with my closed eyes, in meditation (not *samadhi*) and Sai Baba was followed in quick succession by Ram Ram, Christ, Krishna, Buddha and Zoroaster.

As soon as the vision disappeared, the transcendental state to which I had been lifted up also disappeared. The ecstatic bliss, the glamour of the transcendental, gave way to a feeling of utter drabness. The change was bewildering. At last, I fell again into a state of reverie, full of devotion of God, bending down my head before Sai Baba's picture every now and then. It was a unique experience.

Ram Ram explained the phenomenon as under:

> "Your seeing God and us Masters in a vision is a sign and an indication of our manifestation to you. The sing of red cloud from which Sai Baba emanated, indicates that it is God. God is Light and He is always covered in flaming light. Fire is His emblem. The red cloud which you saw was the fusion of the flame that emanated from Him."

Doraswami took the above incident that happened as a partial revelation of God. This was obviously incorrect. Homi's interpretation was:

"I don't think it was a partial revelation. It seemed more like a vision by which I mean some sort of a reflection upon some kind of an invisible screen, as distinguished from the direct sight in a revelation."

Sai Baba cleared the doubt on the point in the course of a message on January 31, 1951:

"What Homi has written is partly correct and partly not. It is true that as a vision, it has not much value. It is not at all a partial revelation, as Doraswami thinks. But what Homi misses is the fact that the vision is of a strange order. I appeared to you from a halo of light, as predicted by Me, just for the purpose of preparation. Besides, I put you into a transcendental state of ecstatic rapture of an extraordinary type before the vision appears. Are not these two factors of extreme importance? The whole incident is a unique performance and a clear indication that My Revelation is now absolutely sure and imminent."

On January 25, 1951, Sai Baba told me that He was going to change the circumstances in which I was then placed and that He would give me" a lease of life, transcendental in its nature." The following day, I had a fall in the bath room at about 1:30 a.m. But I was miraculously saved and was quite unhurt. Sai Baba said to me. "It was a miracle performed by Me to show to you My power as God. Had it not been for Me, you would have broken your bones very badly."

Every day Sai Baba tired me out by His assurances that His Revelation to me was not only indispensable but absolutely imminent. The whole object was to create the seed of expectancy and then to frustrate the hopes so created. The stratagem was quite evident. But human as we are it is very difficult for us to forget the very thing of which the soul is thirsting and ceaselessly search. To pine for the Beloved and to forget Her, how could two such contradictory phenomena be explained. But still it was a fact. To love God wholeheartedly of any result not even His Revelation, trusting Him implicity and fully and surrendering onself to His will under all circumstances, without getting elated or depressed – that was the way to the goal.

On January 29,1951, I was told that my mission had already started though I was not aware of it. To all intents and purpose, I ought to have passed of the mission by stopping the natural function of the physical laws.

On February 1, 1951, after a long and rapid meditation in the early hours of the morning. I was seized with such a great feeling of joy and love for God, that the following thoughts came to me and I wrote them out quickly:

Divine Love

"Thy divine love is the breath of my life. It is the nectar of my soul. It is the fire of my spirit.

Life without Thy love is like the shell without the kernal, the tree without the fruit, the flower without the fragrance, the desert without the oasis."

There was no doubt in my mind, that by the grace of God, I was now in direct contact with Him and could catch His inspiration with ease and rapidity. Was this a sign of God's revelation?

Frequent stratagems employed by Sai Baba and Ram Ram to create false hopes by means of false predictions, were meant to tire me out and make me forget all about God's revelation. If God employed merciless measures, it was all for my own ultimate good and every time He appeared to be merciless, He was the very Ocean of Mercy. He said to me on February 5, 1951:

"I am going to create such circumstances in your life that you will entirely forget all about My Revelation and remain merged in thoughts of God and God alone. The Masters also have been ordered by Me to inspire you to forget entirely all about My Revelation but to remember God and God alone."

On February 6, 1951, to my great surprise, I was seized with a new feeling of awe, in an overwhelming manner. It is best to describe it in the words of Sai Baba:

"So far you were feeling my presence without proper knowledge of my presence. It was only a vague feeling, pervaded with a sense of joy. Today, actual realization of the fact that I am your God speaking to you and in whose presence you are sitting has completely overawed and benumbed you."

I was told to pass thirty hours at a stretch in the alter room, with a few short intervals for bath, meals etc. I entered the alter room at 2:00 a.m. on February 5, 1951, and left it the following day at 8:00 a.m. All the 30 hours were passed in absolute vigilance without a wink of sleep, as ordered by Sai Baba. It was meant for my preparation and training and also as a test to determine whether I would again entertain hopes of God's Revelation. There was no revelation at the end of the period and neither was it expected. This was inspite of the fact that Sai Baba made the various Masters give me short messages on the subject of Revelation. Sai Baba was extremely pleased and He said to me.

"You have passed all your tests, even the non-expectancy test."

On February 9, 1951, late at night, Sai Baba reminded me of the STRANGER and said that He would come to me the next day, in the early hours of the morning. I thought it was again a test and dismissed the idea immediately. Ram Ram said: "There is a deep mysterious meaning in Sai Baba's brief message."

It is best to describe the experience that I had on the following day in the words of Sai Baba and Ram Ram. Sai Baba said to me after I had meditated as usual.

"The STRANGER did come to you. He knocked at your door. You opened the door and received Him and He went away without your knowledge. I am going to give you this knowledge, this mystic vision, very soon."

"I tell you that you have seen Me in a different manner today but because you have not been able to carry the impression of your perception, you feel as it nothing has happened."

Ram Ram gave me a detailed account of the whole incident proving what a miracle was performed by Sai Baba to vindincate His powers as God. He said:

"Do you know what miracles Sai Baba did today? You saw Him with your inner eye in the full blaze of our Spirit Land when you went into *samadhi* in the early part of your meditation and yet by a masterly stroke, He did not allow you to carry the impression of having seen Him to your physical brain. Such a feat only God can perform. You must now know definitely that you have seen God. Your soul knows it.

"Before, He used to close your inner eye or put a veil or a barrier before it. Today He allowed no barrier to stop the eye from seeing Him. Your inner eye rested on God for a long time and yet you have not the least impression of the unique event. He has made you forget it entirely. He has stunned your memory. It is a miracle, a great feat which Sai Baba has performed to give a further proof to you of His being God."

There was no doubt in my mind, that I had found God in the real sense of the word, though I knew at the same time that without visible revelation, it would be futile to convince others of it.

On February 16, 1951, I was in *samadhi* during the latter part of my meditation and I saw God with the inner eye, but as explained by Sai Baba, I was not able to carry the impression to my physical brain.

On February 17, 1951, Ram Ram in an illuminating message, said that I had secured the power of seeing god, but he in order to show His Omnipotence, was exercising His counterpower and was blinding me from seeing Him.

On February 19, 1952, I was in a fine *samadhi*. But as Sai Baba put it, I missed God's Revelation by 'a hair's breadth. It was quite evident that the aim of Sai Baba was to tire me out.

The same day, at 10:40 p.m., Ram Ram said to me:

"God has freed you from all fears and anxieties. This state is reached by a man only when he is about to enter the Realm of ETERNAL PEACE."

I had reached a stage when it was necessary for the internal powers and faculties to develop and unfold to synchronise with God's external, visible Revelation. I was developing quickly all those traits of character, necessarily associated with a superman: courage, heroism, power of resistance to opposition and physical endurance, mental equilibrium, fearlessness, indifference to everything, egolessness, humility, passion to do good at all cost and sacrifice, the crowning glory of all virtues."

I was told by Ram Ram:

> "Remember in our celestial sphere, noble thoughts and noble aspirations have the highest place. They are seeds of great sacrificial deeds and you will be called upon your mission of self immolation in no time. You have been fully prepared, trained and equipped with latent powers, they will burst out the minute you get God's Revelation."

With the commencement of spiritual exercises, in the first week of March, I was asked to rest as much possible in order to recoup my health, but without reducing the daily altar room hours, which was essential for facilitating God's Revelation. I felt that I was entering upon a perilous portion of my journey on the earth plane. March 10, 11, 12 and 13, 1951, particularly the latter two days were so bad from the point of physical health, that it was only by the grace of God, that I was able to save myself from a collapse. On March 10, 1951, Sai Baba gave me a cryptic message:

> "I shall decide in the next few days, whether I have to call you away or keep you for a little longer after My Revelation."

Life weighed in the balance. It was most wonderous that Sai Baba undertook to keep a minute to minute watch on me, on the 12th and 13th particularly. His message in this regard on March 11, 1951, at 10:30 p.m. is significant:

> "I have called you just to tell you that tomorrow is your most consecrated day. I shall be present with you, even outside the altar room every minute of the whole day. It is a day which you have to devote entirely to God."

Wittingly or unwittingly, even when I was completely exhausted and felt like collapsing, I kept on uttering the name of God in my mind, blessing all. The situation was so grave that had I not taken the vow of not asking for death, I would have implored God to call me away. It was a bitter test, which by the grace of God, passed through successfully.

It should be apparent, how God was testing, even at the eleventh hour, whether the vows taken by me were observed in toto or not.

It was an extremely great relief when Sai Baba on the morning of March 14, 1951, gave me the following message:

> "Even if you do not get back your health, I shall reveal Myself to you, thus showing to you My infinite power as God, that I can show Myself even to an ailing man, without injuring or harming him in the least."

Ram Ram commenting upon Sai Baba's message said:

> "He has told you today that He is no longer going to wait and that even if your health is not restored, He would reveal Himself to you. Be prepared therefore for His revelation."

Chapter Twenty-Six

A Jump of Two Years (1951-52)

Two long years after the messages referred to in the last chapter have passed away, and as ordered by Sai Baba, I pick up the threads of the story of this book once again. It is the same story of God's Revelation in visual form being postponed from day to day, but at the same time, the story indicates the enormous progress of the soul and the unfoldment of its immense powers.

It appeared that my life's sands had run out, but God willed otherwise and life was extended. Not only a new lease of life was granted, but a minute to minute watch was kept by the Celestial Beings. Sai Baba, Ram Ram, Lord Zoroaster, Lord Christ, Lord Buddha and Lord Krishna became my constant companions and it gave me tremendous delight to have been brought under the orbit of their loving care and protection.

Even the Masters were not able in the beginning to understand the significance of the postponement of God's Revelation in visual form. In the message of March 15, 1951, Ram Ram said:

"We examined your aura. It was absolutely crystal white without the slightest speck of yellow or blue. It was the aura of a full-grown adept, very rarely seen in a human being. Once an aura reaches this height of perfection, it never changes.

But baffled as we were, we asked Sai Baba and He gave us to understand that though we could not see, there was still an infinitely small speck of darkness hovering round you. This He wants to see dissolved before He revealing Himself to you."

There was no doubt that my health had been considerably affected. The ulcer in the stomach was giving serious trouble. Sai Baba explained the situation in his subsequent message:

"You have suffered enough. I don't want to subject you to any further suffering which My Revelation might cause. I have assured you that I won't put you to any kind of physical suffering. You know some of the greatest God-realized persons have suffered from the worst kind of human disease viz., cancer. Your ulcer is leading to cancer. It is because I am God, I have spared you from the terrors of this dreadful disease. The minute I reveal Myself to you, you will be so drowned in the rapturous joy of My divinity, that it would appear that your cancerous ulcer is cured. And it would be so for some time, but physical laws must operate in Nature and you will have to go through suffering before the span of life allotted to you is over.

How can the Masters understand all these subtle points? Be absolutely fearless. Think that you have already obtained God's revelation. I shall surely come to you and embark you on your mission and see that you are kept physically fit upto the last date of your mission."

I was thrilled with God's grace and mercy. I bowed in deep gratitude at His feet, and my eyes longingly searched for Him. To me Sai Baba was God and gazing at His picture with my physical eyes and meditating on Him with eyes closed, I felt I was drawing nearer and nearer to God.

The days rolled on. I was trained and prepared to see God, in *samadhi* in semi-trance condition, as well as in plain meditation. This training was possible because Sai Baba was God. The outward proof of my having seen God though

I had no physical demonstration or consciousness of it was that a strange feeling of joyousness pervaded through me.

In the following message, Sai Baba described go it how He would reveal Himself and how His visual Revelation would be followed by the manifestation of the Masters:

"You will see Me in tremendous light, flashing and rolling round Me. You will get a little fright at the start, but you will get over it in a minute, for I have thoroughly trained you for the purpose. Don't forget to throw yourself down on the ground, immediately, at full length and remain in that condition till I disappear. The Masters will manifest themselves after Me. You should not fall on the ground when they manifest themselves to you, for they are your Elder Brothers. I, alone am god, to whom you prostrate on the ground. Don't make any attempt to talk with Me on My first appearance. I shall, however, say a few words and then disappear. You can enter into conversation with the Masters, even at their first appearance. They will be headed by Ram. Ram. Tears will flow down your cheeks, when you see His beloved face. He has taken immense care of you and has worked extremely hard under My orders. You should express to Him your sense of immense gratitude when you see him.

"Ram Ram will be followed by Christ, and then will come one by one the other Master whom you know by their pictures in the altar room. They will be extremely pleased to see you face to face and they will express their joy which will create such a thrill of radiant light in you as will simply dumbfound you."

On March 24, 1951, I had a most thrilling experience. When I was meditating. I felt a faint impulse of some swiftly passing light and then Sai Baba appeared to me in a hazy manner. It was just a glimpse of His exterior form. I saw in quick succession faint images of other forms also.

Was this experience a short of rehearsal or a mere test whether I was fit or not for His visual revelation?

The following message of Sai Baba is important:

"I have trained you now, to see Me, even in plain meditation, eye to eye and thus take My orders for your day to day work. But there

> is one danger which you must avoid. Don't touch even the fringe of My robe. If you do it in excitement or out of a feeling of spontaneous devotion, it will harm you. Of-course, I can speedily cure you and restore you to normal condition. But as far as possible, be on your guard and void all risks...."

Sai Baba continued His messages from day to day which sustained me through the whole period of suspense that continued without relaxation.

But it was with difficulty that I stifled the longing for death, for in spite of the inward feeling of delight and joy, experienced from time to time, my health had given way to such an extent that perpetual bodily pain made me sick of life. I was constantly told throughout this period that I had received God's Revelation both inwardly and outwardly, but I was still not physically conscious of it. The physical consciousness of having seen God was purposely kept in abeyance. I was directly linked with God, but there was no visible proof of this divine link.

Intricacies of the God's Kingdom

The following account given by Sai Baba in one of His messages of the intricacies of God's Kingdom in the Cosmos, would be read with interest:

> "The intricacies of My Kingdom in the Cosmos are so very great and extensive that even the highest celestial beings in My universe are not aware of them. I hold the key to all the mysteries in the universe. As there are gradations on your earth plane, so there are gradations in My Kingdom in the Cosmos. My Kingdom is so extensive that, to use your earthly phraseology, it has no end. It is infinite. Just as I am infinite, My Kingdom is infinite. It is extremely silly to say that there are only sixty Masters in the universe. There are innumerable worlds in My Kingdom. Your earth plane is one small unit in the galaxy of millions of starry regions, which revolve according to Cosmic laws and all of which are under My control Millions of souls pass and repass every day crossing through various regions, various planes and sub-planes and to guide them in their journey is a great problem. They are

in the different stages of evolution. The destined lot of all of them is union with Me, but to reach that final goal, they require guides to help them. The first and foremost duty of the Master is to guide and help these souls, which they do through their assistants and sub-assistants and their number is equally large. In each sphere, the work is so divided, that each one is given duties according to his evolutionary attainment. Even among the Masters, there are innumerable grades and classes. Each one rises in My Spiritual Plane from the lowest rung to the highest.

"The highest place a human soul can reach is to become a *Jivan Mukta, i.e.,* he does not return back to the earth plane or any other starry region but stays on in the Spiritual Plane."

I was wondering why a man like me, advanced in years and with an ailing body, should have been chosen by God to become a *Jivan Mukta* and to carry out a great mission in life. Sai Baba gave an explanation in the following message delivered on May 18, 1951:

"Why have I selected a person like you for such a high purpose? This is strange to you for generally young and healthy persons have attained Self-realization and have been entrusted with missions. In your case, it is just the opposite.

"You were not destined to realise Me in this life. Ram Ram was ordered just to put you on the path and I was to call you away. You showed, however, such earnestness and displayed such great propensity for higher spirituality that I took you over from Ram Ram and fixed My gaze on you. The more you came under My direct control and inspiration, the more was I satisfied with your aptitude for higher work. I therefore extended your life. I have given you the opportunity to complete your mission in this very life and not prolong it to your next round of life, as originally planned.

"You see how a man's free will works. It is a dynamic force, which can change even a destined course. You have most magnificently changed your fate and have won My heart to such and extent by your devotion and utter renunciation, that I have selected you for a great mission, in spite of the odds against you."

This message was followed by another one from Sai Baba:

"Do you know why I am making you re-read the Bhaghvad Gita? There is a deep meaning in it. Lord Krishna's relationship with Arjuna and His teachings on the battlefield have a close resemblance to My talking to you in the altar room. Your altar room is the battlefield. It is here that you have fought many a battle against the resistance of the turbulent mind. How often like Arjuna, you wanted to leave the altar room and enter into the round of routine thoughts and duties. Lord Krishna made Arjuna do his duty as a Kshatriya and, at the same time, kept him wholly absorbed in God and gave him and insight into occult wisdom. He crowned him with His cosmic Vision – a rare honour which even gods and devas had not been given.

"In your case also, My teaching will be crowned with My Revelation to you. But I shall not come to you in the universal form as Lord Krishna appeared to Arjuna at the battle field of Kurukshetra.

"The vision of Lord Krishna to Arjuna in the universal form should not be interpreted in a literal sense. For God can never appear to any human soul in this form, however perfected it be in the manner described in the Gita. It should be taken as an allegorical picture of Lord Krishna's exposition to Arjuna. Arjuna's perception of the universe, and his conception of God as the cause of all manifestations, are reflected in the mirror of his mind. He realises that it is God's spirit that pervades the whole universe and that it is God who is the prop and support of all beings from the ant to highest deva in the Cosmos. This is God-realization – that nothing exists but God. To live for God, to work for God, to think of God, to worship God, this is the only way to reach God and be merged in God.

"Don't get discomfited in any way and don't at all feel that you are not fit for My Revelation. Keep absolute faith in Me."

On December 22, 1951, Sai Baba gave me the following message from which it could be gauged through what trials and tests I must have passed, in order to reach the first steps of Safety Zone.

"Do you know that I am helping you as well as obstructing you in order to find out your reactions to My mode of training. Whatever be the circumstances, be firm and don't give in to any feeling of despair or jubilation. You are an ADEPT, as you know, in the making and you should allow full growth to your internal perfection to reach the very zenith of spirituality culminating in active ADEPTSHIP of the highest order. You must ponder on my statements and visualise their truths, so that they may become part and parcel of your daily life of thought, feeling and action."

On January 13, 1952, Sai Baba gave me a message of encouragement and prepared me for a further spell of patient waiting.

"I have made you to write the book, *How I Found God,* not to convince you but to convince your world. Do you think that after convincing you, I shall not make you convince your world through you book? I shall reveal Myself to you in such a marvellous and convincing style, that even the most sceptic would turn repentant and fall at My feet. What more do you want? I can close the drama today and reveal Myself to you this very minute. You will be able to see Me for I have prepared you. But I must have some more time to make you perfect, so that there is no possibility of any injury to you or to the success of your mission. I am your God. I know when and what to do. All I want from you is perfect faith in Me and unending patience."

The following message received from Sai Baba regarding Meher Baba, on February 17, 1952, is included in this book, as ordered by Sai Baba:

"I want to give a message through you to your world regarding Meher Baba. He was trained by Me after he had received training like you from the Masters, both in physical and spiritual bodies. He had an ample opportunity to rise to the highest peak of spirituality. But even in the midst of My divine training, he stumbled and he fell. I at once withdrew My hand and left him to his own free will. My connection with him was cut off. I left him to find his own way, instructing My Masters at the same time to keep on inspiring him and to make him fit again for the higher state of spirituality for which he was destined. It must be said to the glowing credit of Meher Baba that he retrieved the loss sustained by him through his egotism and other errors, remarkably well. He has regained the lost ground. I have again taken him into My control and guidance.

"If he persists in his efforts and does not give way to any of the weaknesses which the flesh is heir to, he has the prospect of rising to the highest peak of spirituality and giving a message to your world which will be of a most significant nature. I feel he will succeed and your world will be a gainer. He will be responsible to a certain extent for ushering a new epoch of universal peace, universal brother-hood and universal religion. Your mission is just the same as his but I am distancing you from him. He will be made to give you the co-operation but you will act quite independently and in quite a different manner. His co-operation will be in the nature of welcoming you and your cause, though both of you will work in different spheres and in different ways."

February 18, 1952 was a red-letter day as would be seen from the following message that Sai Baba delivered to me:

"You are already made an ADEPT – a Master of the junior order. I made this declaration today before all the Masters gathered together. You have passed My test most successfully and beautifully. The greatest and the most difficult of all the tests was when you, with in compliance with My order, refused to consult any doctor, in spite of severe pain in the stomach. Very few would do that. It has put a seal of perfection on your character and raised you to the highest peak of spirituality. I assure you, not only would I take away the pain in the stomach. Very few would do that. It has put a seal of perfection on your character and raised you to the highest peak of spirituality. I assure you, not only would I take away the pain completely but would cure you in such a way as would make you jump with delight and do your work with zest and vigour. I would give you a new body, a new life force, a new nervous system that can stand the onslaughts of the arrows of many a critic and a will of iron attuned to God alone. All this should be an indication of My live for you, which you have deservedly won by perfecting yourself."

The following day, I was given a most revealing message by Sai Baba. He said:

"The songs are the result of My gift to you to hear Me when I am silent. So far you have been hearing My voice. You can now hear My voice in a frenzy of inspiration coming through the vault of silence. When you are composing songs, you are not hearing Sai

Baba. You are listening to the Voice of the Deep, Fathomless Silence of the Absolute Spirit.

"I am now making you commune with the Absolute Spirit itself – a most difficult and extremely rare experience."

It gave me a thrill of delight to learn that I was given the gift of communion with the Absolute Spirit in SILENCE, the evidence of which was the composition of God's Songs as contained in part one of the book published under the title "Divine Songs and Poems," in 1952.

A question was raised, regarding the awakening of the Kundalini serpent in me and the following message was given by Sai Baba in this connection:

"All your *chakras* open up immediately when you mediate. When you go into *samadhi,* it means your serpent has uncoiled itself and shot up its fire. The soul can go into *samadhi* only when the Crown Chakra is open and this chakra being the last in the services of charkras, counting from below, opens out after all the other chakras have opened. This Kundalini fire was opened for you by Ram Ram. I have perfected this training and your soul can go into *samadhi* at will."

On March 1, 1952, I meditated with ease for about eleven hours at a stretch in spite of an ailing body. This was possible because of Sai Baba's grace. He said:

"You are now completely in My hands. I can inspire you to do whatever I want and this has been proved by your meditation today."

I was thoroughly convinced in my mind that I had reached the goal of God-realization. Sai Baba and given me countless proofs of this. In His message March 4, 1952, 7:40 p.m. He said:

"I have given you frequent proofs of your spirituality and the access you have gained to Me, your God. The fact that you can compose God's Songs with such ease and rapture, that you can go into *samadhi,* that you can meditate for long hours in spite of pain, that your prayer is heard, if it is for the good of others – are these not proofs of your spirituality and God-realization? Have patience. You are now on the highest rung of the ladder. You have already reached the goal. You are touching Me every day. I am in daily, nay hourly communion with you. Is that not a happy augury of what is going to happen viz., My revelation to you in visible form?

Sai Baba in His message March 6, 1952, said to me:

"I have made some further changes in your inner system, so as to make it completely in tune with Me *i.e.*, in tune and harmony with the Infinite. I have joined your soul and mind with the Absolute Spirit. You will never be able to see that Absolute Spirit. Even the Masters cannot see the Absolute Spirit. But they can hear the Absolute Spirit and are in daily, nay hourly communion with it. I give this great privilege, the great gift to you today. You are not only in communion with Me, Ahura Mazda, but also invisibly in communion with the Absolute Spirit, known as Brahman, Atman of the universe. Whatever impulses therefore you will get, you must attribute as emanating from the Great Spirit."

On March 10, 1952, Sai Baba gave me to understand that He had distributed to the Masters different duties which they would perform when the mission began after His visual Revelation to me. He said that Christ was given the duty of healing incurable cases through me. Ram Ram was given the duty of being the guide, protector, inspirer as well as healer of curable cases. Zoroaster was given the duty of inspiring me to write books on the occult side of life. Lord Buddha was given the duty of inspiring me to work for One World Religion. Lord Krishna was given the duty of helping me in devotional writings.

March 20, 1952, the real Muslim fakir, mystic and saint as He was known on the earth plane, came to me and not God, who had assumed the form of Shirdi Sai Baba and He gave the following message, which is self-explanatory:

"Do you know who I am? I am known by the name of Baba, more correctly, Sai Baba. I lived on your earth plane at Shirdi and passed away only recently *i.e.*, a few years ago (in 1918). I had no intention of contacting you but as you concentrate on my picture, all day and night, I felt very inquisitive as to why you were doing so, without really invoking me. I have discovered today that you are in communion with God and you are invoking Him in the form in which I was, when I was on the earth plane. It is extremely curious that you have hit upon the plan of invoking God and worshipping Him through the means of my earthly form. What has made you select my earthly body as a fit vehicle to commune with God? It is exceedingly strange..."

"Do you know, who I am here? I am a Spirit Master, but not at the same level as Ram Ram, your Guide and Master. It will take a long cycle of years, before I can evolve myself to your Guide's stature. The fact that you are in communion with God is extremely surprising and very strange. God does not talk with any ordinarily evolved human soul. I am not in position to judge nor can I foresee a lot as I am a Master still in the junior rank. But even my consciousness, limited as it is, tells me that you have reached and extremely high stage of evolution, to have contacted God Himself, which is very rare and unusual. There must be some special reason for God's grace to have descended upon you so abundantly and profusely."

Sai Baba's messages reiterated the fact that I was entering into the inner chamber of the secrets of the universe and I would soon be prepared to write on the mystical side of life.

On April 2, 1952, the following message was given to me:

"Kindly take note of three stage. The first stage is to acquire the power to win the key to My secret chamber from My possession. The second stage is to get the key and keep it in your possession. The third the last stage is to apply the key to the chamber door, open it and enter it, freely and happily, for eternity.

"You have passed the first stage. I told you yesterday in an allegorical manner that the seed has been sown in your body and it is beginning to sprout. I see the growth and the flower and the fruit, which are the second and third stages respectively.

> "The first stage was exceedingly difficult, very few souls reach it. You have passed this stage. The second and the third stages are easy for they must automatically follow each other, after the first stage has been reached."

I who was waiting for God's revelation, was much disappointed to learn, that only the first stage had been reached and the second and third stages.

The journey was long and weary. But there was joy in my heart and my mind was soaked in thoughts of God.

On April 12, 1952, Sai Baba gave me a message that I would see Him first in a vision before His Revelation takes place and, as predicted, I saw Him in a vision a few days later *i.e.*, on April 27, 1952. It is best to describe the vision in Sai Baba's own words:

> "While you were meditating, you saw a green-bluish expanse of the sea and a big, bulky ship, with a long mast in the centre. You saw Me climbing the mast and putting on the light, first red then changing it into green. You saw Me clearly, as you see Me in your altar room picture. A thrill of delight passed through you when you saw this vision, especially as it was in fulfillment of what I had predicted before. You also saw, all of a sudden, the almost naked picture of Christ, as crucified hanging from one of the pieces of the ship. You wondered why you saw him. It is because when your mission starts, not Ram Ram but Christ will be your next guide, after Me. It is not that Ram Ram will not help you. But the principal burden of helping and guiding you will fall upon Christ, whom I have appointed to guide you, under My direct supervision."

Ram Ram and Christ also gave me messages in connection with the above vision. Their messages are quoted below:

Ram Ram:

> "Do you know what a tremendous change has taken place in you? Sai Baba has lifted you to the dizziest height in the evolution of the human soul. You are touching the outskirts of His Abode of Eternal Peace and Bliss. There is no fear of falling, though the height you have reached is so frightfully dizzy. He has put upon you His iron girdle to prevent you from falling. The girdle that He has put upon you is the sign of your having become a Jivan

> Mukta in this very life. The cherished desire of your life is fulfilled. You have won your goal."
>
> Christ:
>
> "You saw me hanging from a timber of the ship in the same condition of crucifixion, as you see me in the picture before you now. I was crucified by the people, who did not understand Me. I had a great mission to perform and I did, as planned and guided by God. You have also a mission to perform. I shall be your guide throughout the mission, for God has appointed me for the purpose. It is therefore I came to you in the vision and no other Master. You should now understand the great significance of today's vision. God has lighted already the light of your mission. The way is clear. You are under the guidance of the greatest force in the universe."

That I was now very near to the goal was apparent. I was told to forget everything except God. To draw one's mind away from mundane things and to keep it centred on God and God alone was by no means an easy task. On order to forget everything, on April 27, 1952, I felt impelled to destroy the unfinished book *How I Found God.* There was a printed copy sent by Doraswami to me and I set fire to it. Doraswami was informed that he should likewise destroy all the printed copies.

The sole idea in destroying the book was that there should not lurk in the mind the slightest trace of egotism, nor should there be any expectation of any nature. To look forward to God's Revelation was also a sort of expectation and an obstacle in the way of God-realization.

Three days later *i.e.,* on April 30, 1952, Sai Baba gave me the following message:

> "The order to destroy your book, *How I Found God* was a mere test and nothing more. You have passed the test most magnificently. It was a cruel test – nay extremely cruel. Kindly telegraph to Doraswami immediately not to destroy the copies at all. When I ordered it to be destroyed, it was principally to test you..... There is no egotism at all in you. You had it but I have crushed it entirely."

On May 11, 1952, Sai Baba revealed to me: "Your world advances and is benefitted not by men of action but by men of silence. It is principally they, who by means of their silent prayers and mystic ways, remove all the difficulties and guide mankind into the proper channels of thought and action. I can work only though SILENCE. It is in SILENCE that the Cosmic Laws, which are ever in operation, make their vibrations left.

"I shall make you, My dear son, work in your world, after My revelation in a silent way. Speak as little as possible for it is through your SILENCE that God is going to work for the benefit of your entire world."

On May 16, 1952, I saw various lights during meditation. Sai Baba explained it as follows:

"In the constant flight of the soul from the body to the Spirit world, your inner eye got slightly opened in spite of My effort to keep it closed and you got some hazy notion of lights in meditation. They are not the true lights at all. They are mere luminous pictures, which floated before your mind's eye, to tell you that you are entering a new zone of tremendous developments."

On July 8, 1952, I was told by Sai Baba that I was firmly linked with Him for eternity. He said to me:

"Do you know that I am sitting in your heart now? I am now speaking to you from within and not without. I want to show to you that you are completely, wholly and absolutely ONE WITH ME. You are firmly united with Me for eternity. I have made you eternal."

As I was ruminating in my mind on Sri Ramana's teaching that God is not to be discovered, He is already there, I felt that the title *How I Found God* was wrong. I fell in despair and thought it best that the book should not be published. It appeared that God was only testing me by giving me a false title. Sai Baba immediately read my mind and said:

"You have found God. This is a fact. Every one knows that God is here, there, everywhere but how many have realized him in their hearts, minds and souls. When I gave you the title, *How I Found*

> *God,* the idea was to teach the people through you that God within and God without is identical. It is the same Absolute Spirit that pervades throughout the universe. It is imperceptible, unknown invisible. But it is visible, perceptible and knowable to those souls who long and yearn for Him intensively and who consecrate their hearts, minds and souls in the quest of this Spirit, Force or Power, whatever you call it. By the unfoldment of your soul from its heaths, you have gained access to this hidden FORCE. You have still not been able to see this hidden force, with your physical eyes. But your spirit within is now fully conscious of its presence. I have transformed you and this transformation is the process of evolution from the mundane to the supramental and super-conscious state which must end in your seeing Me face to face. With most of the sages and saints, the transformation ends only in their feeling God and understanding God. It keeps them in a wide awake state of ecstatic delight and above the horizon of all that is mundane and physical. In your case, I shall take you a step higher. I shall give you My visual Revelation, which will be the peak of your achievement – a boon rarely conferred on a human soul. Be at ease.
>
> "Your book, *How I Found God* has been given a right and most adequate title. Kindly drive away from your mind all doubts and fancies."

It was unquestionably true that I was feeling inwardly very happy and Sai Baba gave me an explanation of this inward state of joyousness on July 29, 1952:

> "Do you know that your soul is feeling ecstatic delight, even while staying in your body? Why? Because, it has come to know of its potentiality and power, subject to My control. This power of your soul is immense. Subject to My approval, it can leave your body when it likes, come back to your body when it likes, fill your heart and mind with ecstatic joy and illumine you with knowledge which it draws direct from My divine source....
>
> "Your soul is aware of the date and place of My Revelation. You with your physical, finite mind are still in the dark, though you now feel that great and extremely important changes are soon going to take place. Have patience. The epoch-making event of your life will soon take place..."

A question was raised as to why even God-realized souls, who had wiped out their *karma*, suffered physically. Instances were cited of Sri Ramakrishna Paramahamsa and Sri Ramana who suffered from cancer and died of this terrible disease. Sai Baba gave the following reply:

> "You have put to me a most pertinent question and I shall explain the situation to you. Do you know that you are already a liberated soul *i.e.*, you have finished your round of birth and death and still your sufferings have not come to an end. It does not mean that your *karma* has not been wiped off. You have no karmic debt to pay. It has already been liquidated. You are suffering now because I am willing it for My purpose and not as a consequence of your *karma*. I am above LAW, Law is not above Me. All things operate according to My Law and I don't interfere, till I see the necessity of interference for carrying out a further purpose. There are two Laws – one that is relevant in the universe, which all My creatures must obey and the other secret Law, which I operate when I will and not otherwise. Certain persons are selected by Me on your earth plane for fulfillment of higher causes. In order to strengthen them spiritually, I must give them certain trials in shape of physical suffering. Sri Ramakrishna and Ramana suffered from cancer because I ordered that My secret Law should be operated so that they may become Masters after they had spent their physical lives for higher celestial work. They had realised God and they were *Jivan Muktas* also and as such, according to My universal Law, they should have been exempted from all physical suffering. I ordered that they should be subjected to these further sufferings in order to train them for higher celestial work."

On August 4, 1952, I was told by Sai Baba that He was training me for a double purpose viz, to use me as His vehicle for the betterment of the world and later on, after death, to make use of me again for some higher purpose.

On August 11, 1952, Sai Baba again told me that I had already realized God, the proof of which was the hymns, poems and songs composed by me.

I saw a new change coming over me. Whenever I was in the altar room, not only a glow of fire seemed to burn in me, but my head was continuously bending down before Sai Baba's picture in a thrill of delight.

On August 16, 1952, Ram Ram gave me the following message:

> "The last pages of your book, 'How I Found God' will be written, after your seeing God and the Masters, face to face and it will be an inspired work. This book is the real mission of your life. Your life has been specially extended to make you write this monumental book."

On August 20, 1952, My beloved friend, Jamshed Nusserwanji who had left his temporal body on the August 1st, 1952, was allowed to talk to me by Sai Baba through Ram Ram. The following is an extract from his message:

> "I am extremely happy that I have left my ailing body behind. My joy knows no bound. Will you kindly tell all my relations, whom you may meet, that they all should rejoice, that I am in a world where there is no regret but all joy and bliss and endless light and love. I am perpetually in motion. I feel a sort of energy in me, only a faint part of which was experienced when I was on the earth plane in my physical body. This energy within me is of divine nature. It is wonderful, I am beginning to learn the new ways of making use of this energy which appears to be inexhaustible. This energy is sacred. It has to be used for the good of others only."

On August 30, 1952, Sai Baba told me that my soul had attained its freedom by the practice of integrated Yoga. The following is an extract from His message of that date:

> "Do you know that you have gained access to Me by *Bhakti* and *Raja Yoga*. But you are a *Karma Yogi* and a *Gyani* also. This means that it is through the combination of all the yogas that you have reached Me. The work you did especially for the amelioration of the lot of lepers has made you a Karma Yogi. Your books are proof of your *Gyana Yoga*. Regarding *Bhakti* and *Raja Yoga,* I need not say anything. For daily, for the last more than five years, you have devoted yourself whole-heartedly to Me, abandoning everything. It is your *bhakti* and meditation that have accelerated the pace of your progress. But for your *bhakti,* you would have been still far behind."

On September 5, 1952, I saw beautiful twinkling lights during meditation. Sai Baba in His message, said:

"I made you see these heavenly lights, just for a second only with the aid of your inner eye. You would constantly see this panorama of lights later on. They are the lights of your spiritual home."

A further proof that I was in link with God and was mounting the ladder of light is given in the following message of Sai Baba delivered on September 17, 1952:

"Your soul does not require any more training or experience. It can now act on its own. Of course, My control would continue for all time, for without My order and permission it will not be able to move even an inch or do anything. This should show to you who I am. I am your God and the Creator of the Universe. Do you understand then with whom you are in daily communion? You are in communion with ONE, who is the HIGHEST in the UNIVERSE and whose orders are obeyed by all His creatures, whether manifest or not manifest to you, from the highest to lowest.

"You are approaching Me by the ladder of light. As you climb each step, you enter into an infinite space of luminous light. You have no knowledge of this experience for you forget it as soon as you get out of *samadhi.* This forgetfulness will end as soon as you reach the topmost step in the ladder of light. You are extremely near to this topmost step, the whole ladder would slip off and you will simply swirl in NON-SPACE, in a panorama of INFINITE LIGHT. That Infinite Light is your God-not the God whom you see in personal form in Sai Baba's picture, and He will acquaint you with the mysteries of the universe. Be happy. You have attained the unique and signal honour of being selected to see your God face to face and to be in communion with Him, visibly and invisibly."

I was longing to see the invisible. The love for God was consuming me like a fire and new feeling was born in me – the feeling of union with all. On the September 21, 1952, Sai Baba told me: "You are entering slowly and surely into a limitless life of light and lustre. It is an opening in the invisible world. Your feet are on the magic carpet, which will soon take you into Realms of

> Eternal Beauty and Glory, unknown and unknowable to the human eye."

I was not in any way elated by this message. Sai Baba's training had made such a deep impression upon me that I had learnt by slow stages to forget my individuality and to submerge myself into a sea of nothingness.

On October 3, 1952, the Spirit of Jamshed was again allowed by Sai Baba to deliver his message to me through Ram Ram and it is quoted below:

> "I want to tell you that I am extremely happy here, so very happy, that it is impossible for me to give you even the faintest idea. This happiness is all self-begotten. It is not the happiness which any one can give us. I want my friends and relations to understand this great truth. Many think that the grave is the end, forgetting that life is an endless chain. I have learnt so much in this new plane of existence and every day I am learning and advancing with the rapidity of a hurricane. I have seen so many Masters, whom I remembered when I was on the earth plane. They tell me that God has chosen me, as He has already chosen you in your physical body, to work for a mission. Do you know that God has raised you to the highest peak of spirituality?
>
> "I am so sorry, I did you great harm when I was on the earth plane, by doubting the sanctity of the messages as emanating from the highest spiritual source. I did this harm to you, but in all good faith. Nevertheless, the memory of the injury done to you makes me extremely sad and repentant. My dearest Minoo, I love you from the depth of my heart. Don't be afraid. God is your Guide."

I was going through great physical suffering. My weight was also decreasing on account of insufficient nourishment. It was Sai Baba's consolation that lightened my pain and suffering. He said:

> "To transform you, bodily, mentally and spiritually, means that you have to expose yourself to great physical suffering, torture and suspense. I have enabled you to make this sacrifice and you must give it willingly and not cry and say, 'I can't bear it'. Be brave like a Kshatriya warrior in the battlefield."

In spiritual life, pain has to be welcomed and keeping that in mind, I passed through the difficult course of the journey with the necessary fortitude and forbearance.

I was asked to keep in mind two mantras viz., *"TAT TWAM ASI"* and *"OM TAT SAT."* I knew that the word *"OM"* was an ageless mantra; it was the very Name of God and His Voice; the music of the soul and the music of silence.

On October 23, 1952, Sai Baba said to me:

"Remember the Law of Evolution never stops. When you stop evolving on your earth plane, you would begin evolving in My Spirit World. You would go on adding to your experiences. Just as I am Infinite, my universe is Infinite and you would be one of the tiniest spots in My Infinite Universe, evolving and revolving round your own centre but in direct communion with Me."

From November 3, 1952, I was asked to start writing down discourses given by Sai Baba while in the altar room.

On November 3, 1952, I again enquired of Sai Baba as to why I was not able to sit for a long time without getting a severe pain in the stomach and He gave me the following reply:

"I have made a deep operation upon you internally, separating all the valves that tie you to your material body. I have opened out all the passages for your spiritual rebirth. Though you have a physical body, in reality, you are living now in spiritual body. As the spirit body requires to be isolated completely from the physical body, till this separation is completed, you will get this physical pain. The minute your pain stops, you must remember that your spirit body is disentangled from your physical body. This process of complete disentanglement takes time. But I assure you, My dear son, that your suspense would soon be ended."

That my soul and spirit, being united, were speaking to me with one voice would be seen from the following message of Sai Baba:

"Truly speaking, it is your soul talking to you but under My guidance and with My voice also added, whenever I want. It means you are hearing Me, your God without, and your soul within, both of which being united are now speaking with ONE VOICE. Is it not extremely wonderful that you should have reached such a transcendental state?"

On November 30, 1952, when I was in the altar room, I said to myself:

"I am now quite tired of this physical life. I yearn for God so much, that I would rather leave this physical body for good and see God in the Spirit world in my spirit body with my spirit eyes. My patience is now exhausted."

Sai Baba read my mind and He gave the following significant message:

"Yes, I know. I most earnestly tell you to keep faith in Me and you would see Me even when you hold on to your physical body. It is because I have made you lose all personal interest in life, you feel lonely without seeing Me, though you are all the time in communion with Me."

A thrilling event happened on January 4, 1953, when I saw in meditation with the aid of my inner eye, Sai Baba sitting on a block of stone, exactly as in the picture in my altar room. Sai Baba said to me:

"I am giving you practice in this manner till I fully reveal Myself to you in all My glory and splendour."

I also began to see blue lights and Sai Baba gave me the following message:

"I am training you now to see the blue lights of My Spiritual World with the help of your inner eye. I can't allow your inner eye to open fully immediately as it would make you blind. I am therefore helping you in making use of the inner eye, by slow degrees. You saw today blue lights, while you were in meditation.... Those are lights of My Spiritual Plane. Sitting in the altar room, without going into *samadhi,* I am training you to see My highest plane *i.e.,* I have raised you from the lowest to the highest."

On the January 9, 1953, I saw some visions particularly an endless river, the significance of which Sai Baba explained to me as under:

"You have entered into the endless river of bliss."

On January 13, 1953, Sai Baba predicted before I began my early morning meditation that I would see Him in a vision. This prediction came true. I saw Sai Baba with a throb in my heart in three different positions. It is best to describe the event in Sai Baba's own words:

"I had told you that you would get most startling results today and this has happened. When you were meditating, all of a sudden. I appeared before you. You were so startled that you felt a throbbing pain in your heart and your head bowed down at once at My feet. You saw Me in three different ways, sitting on the ground, underneath a tree sitting on a bench, and standing. You recognized Me immediately. I vanished as quickly as I came. This is the first time I have given you proof of My visual Revelation. You have seen Me with your inner eye, while meditating.

"I did not come in any halo of light. What you saw was a mere profile of My form. It is just a preparation for My full and glorious Revelation. What you saw today must convince you that My Revelation is absolutely certain. In fact, you can say now that you have had My visual Revelation, though in a crude form. The throb in your heart that still continues is the positive proof of My Revelation to you. You are One with Me for eternity."

The same day in the evening, Sai Baba gave me the following message which filled me with indescribable bliss:

"...Do you know that you have already realized Me and you can now close the book *"How I Found God"* if you want. At least you are sure now of how to end the book. But I don't want you to write even one word, at present. Tremendous developments are going to take place soon and then I shall make you close the book, by Myself dictating to you the whole of the last chapter.

"It is My work now, not yours. I shall turn you into an automation and I shall do all the work for you, through you for the progress and betterment of your world. I have already raised you to the highest point in spirituality. You are now completely free from tests and trials. You have now only to follow Me like a blind man. Your soul, your mind, your will, I have captured them all. You have nothing which you can call yours. It is now all God's property and His control over you is complete. Whatever you think, whatever you speak, and whatever you do, will not be your thinking, your speaking or your doing. It will be all God's doing and not yours."

On January 19, 1953, I was in *samadhi* for more than four hours, and Sai Baba said to me.

"I am going to make Myself visible to you in an amazing manner. Your senses and your mind would simply be shattered to pieces when I make Myself visible to you."

On 13th February 1953, Sai Baba informed me that preparations for His visual Revelation, both inward and outward, had been completed and that I should now be ready for the three greatest events of my life viz., God's revelation, the mission and my death. he said:

"All these three great events will happen in a short time leaving behind a trail of blazing glory."

On the 19th February 1953, Sai Baba gave me a message of considerable significance:

"I am extremely glad to tell you that you have at last realized the Truth and have therefore fulfilled the purpose for which you were given birth in your present body. You have realized God in the truest sense of the word. You have not found God, but have realized Him. God is not to be found. He has to be realized as such. I gave a title to your book. He already exists. He does not require to be found, but being Absolute Existence, Consciousness, Bliss, *Sat Chit Ananda,* He has to be realized. I give the title to your book *How I Found God'*. In way it was a misleading title but at the same time a title in accordance with the popular section of your people, who believe God has to be searched and found—that it is a missing article or commodity which has to be acquired and possessed. What is wanted is the knowledge of God, the Consciousness of the Existence of God and the Bliss that is eternal. When a man attains to this State of Consciousness of the knowledge of God, that He exists perennially within and without and transcends all thoughts of relativity—being Absolute and is a source of enternal BLISS, he is said to have realized God. I had to prepare you to reach the present state of perfection.

"Whether you get My visual Revelation or not, is not the point. You have now enough data to complete your book. But I don't want you to conclude your book now. I want you to still wait and see what events take place and how they throw further light on the subject. It is merely to end your suspense that I have given this message to you that you have succeeded in finding God and you can, if you want, complete your book, on the basis of materials at your disposal.

This discourses given by Me are with this view that you should embody them all in the book "How I Found God" in a suitable manner. I shall not give you any more discourses for what I have given are quite enough.

They are for your book. They should all be included without omission of a single word or a single sentence even. Don't try to be wiser by making any changes. I warn you against making any change or dropping any line of any discourse. Every word dictated must appear. After you have embodied all the discourses, I would Myself dictate to you the last and final chapter of your book."

The 77 messages given by Sai Baba are presented in the next chapter of this book.

Chapter Twenty-Seven

Discourses of Sai Baba As God Almighty (1952-53)

From November 3, 1952 to February 18, 1953 Sai Baba gave discourses to me in the altar room and they were written down, word by word as I heard them, without making any change in compliance with His command. These discourses embody the teaching of all the prophets – Zoroaster, Krishna, Buddha, Moses, Christ and Muhammad and the experiences of saints and sages in all the countries of the world, from the most ancient to recent time to date.

Religion is a matter of the heart. It has to be lived and transcended. The discourses, in beautiful and lucid language, contain so much of exoteric and esoteric material, that they make a wide range of appeal, even though the truths adumbrated are as old as the hills and there may be nothing mew in them.

Discourse No. (1)
IN THE STILLY SILENCE OF THE NIGHT

The stars are shining. The sky is clear. The sea is murmuring, as its waters ebb flow in rhythmic motion. There is deep silence, stealing its way and casting its mantle on the whole panorama of Nature hushed in sleep and rest. There is glamour in the landscape; there is beauty in the moon, as it rises in all its glory and freshness, throwing its pearly radiance all around. In this exquisite quietness of Nature and in the still silence of the night, what invisible work is being done? The Alone seeks to greet those, who silently worship Him in the temple of their hearts, enkindling their souls with the fire of His spirit. Silence is the language of the universe. Seek silence in the silent night and the fire and flash of His spirit would girdle you in all their transcendent glory. (3.11.1952)

Discourse No. (2)
FROM DARKNESS INTO LIGHT

Man is a weary traveller on the earth plane. There is a load on his back and his mind is shrouded with thoughts of fear and frustration. Footsore and heartsore, he drags on, for he knows not his destiny. Bound in ignorance, he makes himself his God and worsens his lot as he treks his way in the wilderness of dried up hopes and frustrated designs. Selfishness and sin drag him into an endless chain of misery and suffering. Caught in the snare of Maya, he loses sight of the Reality and sinks deeper into an endless chain of misery and suffering. Caught in the snare of Maya, he loses sight of the Reality and sinks deeper into the pit of moral degradation. It is only when the sting of conscience bites him and remorse takes hold of him, that he seeks freedom from his enslavement. Remorse and repentance open to him a new way to life. Behold, his ways are changed. There is no more the cloud of darkness in his face. He awakens to a new consciousness. He is seized with a new force. It is the force of the spirit, which the sting of conscience has awakened and liberated. No longer a weary traveller, but a bright soldier, he forces his way and knows the destines goal that awaits him.

Not sin but virtue, not self but selflessness, not desire but desirelessness, not pride but egolessness, not greed but renunciation, he knows now, as constituting his armour in the battle of life. Fortified in this manner, with burning love and devotion for God, he sees the path of spiritual victory. He vanquishes his foe by self-mastery and wins the goal – God's own Kingdom of Light and Eternal BLISS. (4.11.1952)

Discourse No. (3)
EVIL HAS NO RIGID PLACE IN GOD'S UNIVERSE

Life is a tussle between a tear and a smile. Don't think of your tears but wipe the tears of others. Forget your own sorrow but ever keeps in mind the suffering to others. Kiss those who kick you, love those who hate you. Sweeten the path of sorrow with the warmth of your heart, the fire of your soul, the kiss of your spirit. Why fume and fret and be frustrated? Every load you carry, every harsh word you hear, the taunts and salles of your wicked world – they are your friends, not foes, for they redeem your soul and take you to God. Forget the evil doer and forgive him. Let not the fire of hatred burn in your heart. Replace it with the warmth of your love.

Be gentle as a dove, but stiff as a rhinoceros, when you come to bay in your fight against unrighteousness. Forgive the evil doer but annihilate evil with the sledge hammer of virtue and piety. Be an angel in the garb of man and spread God's love and light with all the fire of your soul and spirit. Virtue shall triumph for it is the will of God. Evil shall be annihilated for it has no place in the evolution of God's universe. (5.11.1952)

Discourse No. (4)
RENUNCIATION IS THE ESSENCE OF SPIRITUALITY

Think of the indwelling spirit and not the body which is frail and subject to decay. It is spirit alone that is eternal, all else is ephemeral and transitory. Bodily indulgence is an obstacle to spiritual growth and progress. Care should be taken of the body, for it is the temple of the soul, but in on case, bodily enjoyment should be mistaken for spirituality. The body, the senses and the mind, are to be curbed in order to cut asunder the inner sheets which cover the soul and make it a prisoner.

Renunciation is the essence of spirituality. Annihilate all desires and kill the ego in you. Be sturdy and strong like the oak in the jungle and stand fast against all tempests of temptations. Listen to the voice of Conscience for it is your best inward monitor.

Work and worship go together. Work is the essence of life, but it should not be for the purpose of enjoying the fruit of your labour. The labourer seeks his hire, but the true Yogi discards it. He works for the sake of work, to spread God's love and light and not for selfish gain. He works in the name of God for the growth of his spirit and not for the satisfaction of his carnal desires. Work is worship, when it is concentrated and dedicated to God. Be a Karma Yogi by keeping the fire of love and devotion for God burning all the time. (6.11.1952)

Discourse No. 5
RELIGION IS THE SOUL'S NOURISHMENT

No man can live without religion. It is the vital part of his life. It is the living water, which no person can afford to miss. It is the soul's nourishment. It is the gateway to the higher and better life. It is the discarder of man's ignorance, for however learned he may be in material science, if he disowns God and the hereafter, he is to be pitied most for his gross ignorance.

Religion binds the soul to God. It is immaterial in which religion a man may be born. He must have the main sense of religion *i.e.*, he must know the purpose and goal of life and act according to the scriptures of the world. All scriptures are alike in their teachings on cardinal points.

Remain true to your self and work your way to spiritual heights discarding all that is gross and carnal. Make God alone the target and goal of your life. Ponder on Him alone and none else. He is the alchemy of your life, the apex of your aspiration. Bank your faith on God. He alone would pull you from the morass of life and crown you with success. (7.11.1952)

Discourse No. (6)
GOD KNOWS NO LANGUAGE EXCEPT OF THE HEART, SOUL AND SPIRIT

Build a temple of worship in your heart. God responds to prayers that emanate from the heart and not from the lip. Seek God with all the warmth of your soul, heart and mind. God knows no language except of the heart. Immerse your mind in God. Kindle your heart and enflame your soul with the fire of the spirit within you. Make God the bedrock of your faith, the bulwark of your life, the target of your goal. Whosoever worships Him with the fullness of his heart, awakens to a new consciousness. It is the consciousness of the spirit within man, struggling to win unity with the Absolute.

This awakening of consciousness brings in its wake a larger life, full of understanding of the higher values so essential for establishment of peace and harmony on the terrestrial plane.

Like the fruit that falls to the ground when it is ripe, the soul seeks its level, when it becomes ripe for its flight from the imprisonment of the body.

Soul is spirit. It is full of life and fire. Body is wooden. It is subject to decay and death. Guard the soul by discarding the body. Let the soul triumph and not your body, for in the triumph of the soul is your ultimate salvation and attainment of Eternal BLISS. (8.11.1952)

Discourse No. (7)
PEACE, HARMONY, LOVE – THESE FORM THE RHYTHM OF LIFE

Peace, Love, Harmony – these form the rhythm of life. They are the vibrant factors which promote happiness. Peace is the antagonist of discord, war, hatred and bitterness of feeling. Discard all that is bitter in your heart, forgetting and forgiving all those who do evil. No man can live in peace, unless he makes Virtue his spouse and unselfishness his comrade in life.

Peace is the harbinger of love and love is the most sacred element in man. It is divine nectar. It is the soul of divinity, the parent of all virtues, the source of true happiness. Keep the fire of love burning in your heart. Love all, without distinction. Love is divine comradeship. It is the light of truth. It is the pattern on which God has woven His whole universe for the happiness and bliss of all His creatures.

Make your life a book of Love, from end to end. Let every page and every line be the mirror of God, reflecting His beauty. His mercy, His grace, and above all, His great LOVE which lightens the forces in the universe harmonizing all LIFE, which is ONE. Love begets love. Love your neighbour as you love yourself and God will love with a treble force. Make love the cornerstone of your life, the foundation of the whole edifice, the fulcrum of all your activities, the symbol of your perfection. (9.11.1952)

Discourse No. (8)
WHO IS A SUPERMAN?

Who is a Superman? He, who like a warrior in the battle of life, puts on the armour of righteousness and raises an eternal fight against all the demons of vices and comes victorious. It is he, who disregarding his own personal interests, dedicated his life to God and all mankind, whom he serves with a singular aim and in the spirit of complete self-abnegation. It is he, who enshrines in his heart love for

God and all persons without any distinction. It is he, whose mission is to spread God's Gospel of love and harmony, peace and beatitude. It is he, who fearless of all consequences, waits on no man, but seeks his own way and is never daunted by the arrows of calumny and insipid lies. His banner is Truth; his gospel is Love, the light of wisdom shines from his eyes. His mind is ever alert to help every cause for the good of all mankind. He seeks no patronage. The poor are his friends. He is God's own chosen son to spread His message of Love and Light to show the goal of life to every human soul.

Such a man with super-abundant powers and gifts to bring about a spiritual revolution and a reformation of a unique type – such as he is a superman. (10.11.1952)

Discourse No. (9)
SELF-EFFACEMENT

Self-effacement is the flower of perfection. Egotism is the bane of life. It is the devil in man, masquerading as Virtue. It is the negation of the life of the spirit. It is the monarch of ignorance. It leads to strifes, animosities, vulgarities, insipid strivings and vain glory. Discard the ego and be humble in life. Humility is the crown and sceptre of wisdom. It is the badge of spirituality.

If you wish to rise and reach the higher step in the ladder of spirituality, discard the trappings of the ego and seek God and God alone and not the applause of your vile and wicked world. Self-effacement is the garment woven in the fabric of humility. It is worn by those who love God in purity of heart and soul. (11.11.1952)

Discourse No. (10)
WHAT IS THE GOAL OF LIFE?

What is the goal of life? Very few raise this question. Many slumber in darkness. The objective of life is not the pursuit of physical pleasures. The true object of life is God. Seek him in the inner cave of your heart. Worship Him with all the fire of your heart's devotion. An ounce of godliness is worth more than million tons of unrighteous, possessions and gains. Truth alone will survive. It is eternal, for Truth is God and God is Truth. (12.11.1952)

Discourse No. (11)
GAIN MASTERY OF THE SOUL AND MIND

Mankind has abolished the system of slavery but your world is still full of persons who lead a slavish life. They are slaves to their senses. So long as man foes not gain mastery of his soul and mind, he shall be construed as a slave. To err is human but to continue in the path of errors is disastrous. He must rise every time he falls and make a bid for freedom of his soul from the entanglements of earthly desires.

Abandonment of desire is renunciation and without renunciation the goal of life cannot be reached. He must practise renunciation, living in the world, for to abandon the world all together is neither easy nor desirable. He must be a Yogi in spirit and in truth and he will realise God, whether he practises renunciation living in the midst of life's giddy ways or in the solitude of the wilderness. (13.11.1952)

Discourse No. (12)
RIGHTEOUSNESS–THE MOST POTENT FACTOR IN LIFE

Virtue is the immortal part of man. Lead a life of virtue and you will gain immortality. No man can gain access to God, unless he loves, adores and worship God, dressed in humility and bedecked with the feathers of virtue.

Righteousness is the most potent factor in life. It is the axle on which the wheel of the chariot moves and takes you to the Abode of God. It is the parent of all virtues - love and gentleness, purity and serenity, tolerance and forbearance, charity and selflessness. If to these be added, self-effacement, sacrifice, sincerity, self-surrender to the will of God and utter renunciation of all desires and disregard for all earthly attachments and enjoyments, the way to God-realization becomes easier and possible. The path for the traveller to the goal is narrow and thorny but it is the safest for him to choose. For, broader the path,, more difficult it becomes as the traveller goes along and it leads not to the goal.

Seek enternity. Be not baffled by the tempests of life. Be not seduced by the gaities of life. Seek God in all earnestness, in all purity of heart and He will lead you to your goal. (14.11.1952)

Discourse No. (13)

BREAK THE CHAIN OF MAYA WITH THE HAMMER OF SELF-CONSCIOUSNESS

God's laws are just and indissoluble. He blends mercy with justice for He loves to be kind to all His creatures. But loving and kind as He is, no one can escape the consequences of defying His orders and commandments. Shun sin, for it is the cobra that will poison your body and mind and make your soul unhappy.

Nothing can taint the soul for it is a spark of divinity. But the unhappy soul, in spite of its original stainlessness, is deprived of its right to return to its place of origin, if man in his stupidity and ignorance exercises his will in contradiction to God's Laws and Commands.

Put on the garment of purity. Burn away all dross in you in the fire of suffering. Break the chain of Maya with the hammer of Self-Consciousness. Make conscience your sole judge and monitor. Not all the wealth of the world, not all the glory and pomp, not at the applause of the people, will heal your inward wound, which will keep on festering, till it covers you wholly and you sink in dire abjectness, if you forsake God and His Laws and Commands. Be sure of this, that God's mills grind slowly but they grind exceedingly fine. No one can escape the relentlessness of His Laws. (15.11.1952)

Discourse No. (14)
THE GREATER THE TRIAL, THE GREATER THE REWARD

The darkest cloud has a silver lining. The pall (cloth) of dark night is lifted up when the sun shines in all its brightness and glory. Even if the struggle be hard, why be sad and gloomy? For, is not God, your Father, near you, to befriend you? Keep your mind still like the waters of the deep lake. Stand firm like a rock and shrink not if calamities pour on you, like a hurricane. The greater the trial, the greater the reward, the greater the misery, the greater the happiness, that must follow like sunny day, when the night is over. Stain not your mind or body with impurity. Walk in the path of rectitude (moral uprightness), with love for all-a smile for a kick and forgiveness to all. Make that the ideal of your life, if you wish to win the race and come out triumphant from the struggle of life.

Hatred, malice, revenge, jealousy, bigotedness, pride, greed, lust, sloth-these are the companions of Satan. Love purity, righteousness, gentility, humility, tolerance, broad mindedness, these are the fragrant flowers that grow in the garden of God. Make a bouquet of then and carry it with you, for each flower is reminiscent of God's glory and a remembrance of His kingdom. Make virtue your crown and vice a foot-stool, to trample under you feet. Be a master, not a slave of your mind, body and the senses. (17.11.1952)

Discourse No. (15)
SEEK THE HIDDEN LIGHT

God is the only REALITY. This world is a delusion. See God in everything from the sod of the earth to the star in the sky and you shall understand that there exists in the universe, nothing but God. Do you be guided by what you see with your physical eyes. What you see is not real. The real is hidden, from your physical sight. When you see the hidden you will realize the mysteries of God and His Universe. You will realise and understand the aim and object of life. Do not drift like a piece of wood in the river of life, but make a deep plunge and find out pearls of truth for the guidance of life.

Seek the hidden light. It shall illumine your mind, heart and soul and lead you to the kingdom of God, which is eternal and infinite.

Don't think that you are a finite body. Don't think that life is a leap from birth to death. It is a continuous chain from birth to death and from death to birth. It can be broken only when the soul disentangles itself from the sheaths of the lower planes with which it is entangled. Seek submission to the will of God by practice of VAIRAGYA (detachment) and you should and shall attain freedom from the chain of birth and death. Union with God is the goal of life. Seek Him and Him alone and He will guide you, inspire you and free you from all your earthly entanglements and take you to the goal of ETERNAL BLISS. (18.11.1952)

Discourse No. (16)
THE LADDER OF EVOLUTION

The inequalities in life that you see are because of the Law of Evolution operating in the universe. The process of evolution cannot work equally in all, because of various factors involved, the principal of which is man's own free will. When he uses his will in contradiction to God's will and refuses to be guided by divine wisdom, he lengthens his process of evolution. It is only when he suffers, he begins to yearn for God. This yearning for God is the indicator of an upsurge for higher things of life. He begins to realise that what is visible is not lasting and true. He craves for things of the spirit. He yearns for eternal peace and rest. This yearning for the higher things of life takes him to a new path. The old ways and modes of life become distasteful to him. He leaves off carnal pleasures and takes out the path of BHAKTI, GNANA and DHARMA YOGA. He gives his all in all to God.

He works for God and God alone and not out of any attachment to the fruits of his labour. He sees God in every human being and loves them all without any distinction. The doors of divine wisdom open out to him. He is content in God's love, which enriches his soul, heart and mind and makes him happy.

Each man has to climb the ladder of evolution and go through varied experiences for the purification of his soul till he reaches the last step in the ladder and enters God's Kingdom of Eternal Bliss. This process of evolution in each individual takes a long time. It requires countless births but there is no restriction of any kind, for by God's grace, human souls can be raised to reach the top of the ladder, quicker and faster. The process of evolution can be quickened, if man wills it and if he wins God's Grace. (19.11.1952)

Discourse No. (17)
DEATH AND THE SINNER

People look upon death with grim fear. It is because they are unaware of their future destination. The good and virtuous should be happy to die for death is a passage to higher realms of peace and bliss. It is only the sinner who carries the load of sin along with his soul. This load he has to unburden before he can start a new race for life on the earth plane. He must go through the path of purification to start a new lease of life. This course of purification does not end immediately. It goes on from birth to birth and from earth to the spirit world, for countless years, till purged of all sins and perfected in spirit, he becomes ripe for union with God, the Absolute Spirit.

God's mercy is so great the even to the worst sinner, He gives a chance and hope to recover the lost ground and re-enter the Realm of Bliss from which he has been on exile. For every soul is a spark of God and having emanated from such a high origin, it must return to its HOME. Such is the destined lot of every human soul. (21.11.1952)

Discourse No. (18)
RELIGION AND THE ORIGIN OF EVIL

All religions are pathways to God and no one should arrogate that his religion is the best. In fact, religion is a matter of man's inner consciousness. This inner consciousness can be aroused in two ways: by man's contact with external phenomena, through scriptures, association with good and saintly people and masters, and secondly, by man's individual quest for something that can satisfy his soul.

Religion is a matter of the heart. When the heart is awakened, the desire to know the secrets of the universe and probe into the problems of life become keener and keener. It is difficult for man to be satisfied with bread alone. He needs divine nectar and that is supplied by religion, which can take him to God and the world beyond the precincts of the earth plane.

Religion should be understood in its essence. It is the ritualistic side of religion which causes separation and iconoclastism. To know the Truth, one must delve deep into the experience of life in utter disregard of one's own gain, in the pure spirit of enquiry and investigation. When man searches for Truth in this way, he will notice that all religions as taught by the prophets, saints and sages are universal in their teachings and application, with God as the object of life and righteousness as the main factor. God speaks through the chosen ones, with the same voice and with the same object viz., to enlighten mankind and show them the way to His kingdom.

Religion binds man to God. It gives him a philosophy, which both satisfies the hunger of his heart as well as gives him strength and vitality to fight the battle of life bravely and successfully.

No man can live without religion. It is the fulcrum of life, the soul's prop, and the searchlight in the dim, dismal horizon of man's creation. God is all LIGHT, LOVE and BEAUTY. He is absolute. There is no duality in divinity. There is no relativity in God's conception. He is ONE without second. He is Timeless, Spaceless, Causeless, Motionless. But this divine absoluteness is missed by man, who is finite and who measures all things with the dim light of his own reasoning faculty. His reason gives birth to the ideas of relativity, dimensions etc.

No evil exists in the Godhead. But man creates it in his finite nature. This is the origin of evil. It is not permanent, for it is the outcome of man, who is finite. The minute he becomes perfect and reaches Godhead, the evil disappears. It is nescience, ignorance and therefore not permanent. God alone is the REALITY and all life should be taken as an unreal phenomenon, to be overcome and conquered by the force of the spirit within. Discard the world and its temptations. Seek refuge in God. He is both within and without. (22.11.1952)

Discourse No. (19)
CONTROL OF THE MIND

Mind is the respository of good and bad thoughts. It is the mind that makes heaven or hell. Control of the mind requires skilful handling. It is by concentration and meditation that a man can become the master of his mind and control it to perfection. When man reaches the stage of having controlled his mind, he becomes a sage, a seer. Once the mind is controlled, he can then go into the interior recesses of God's mysteries.

Control of the mind leads to illumination. It is a subtle, spiritual force, higher that the intellect. It is called intuition, the third eye, the mystic passage, the ladder to Godhead. It is a spiritual artery, which supplies spiritual food of the highest type. It is also known as inspiration. It is a link with God Himself. It is the fire of the soul. It is God's gift and a token of His grace. (23.11.1952)

Discourse No. (20)
TRAMPLE SIN BUT DO NOT DESPISE THE SINNER

Sin is negation of Virtue. It is the greatest obstacle in the struggle of life. Sinfulness is godlessness. To commit a sin, whether in thought, word or deed, is to invite terrible consequence both in this life and hereafter. Sin is a fetter, a clamping machine which kills you inch by inch and gives you no rest of peace of mind.

Keep away from the monster of sin and seek virtue as your friend and lifemate. It is virtue that brings peace and happiness. Sin creates disunion, disharmony, distress, distraction, dissipation of energy and disease of mind, body and soul. Destroy sin with the hammer of God's name. Keep on shouting the name of God and the temptress sin will not make an assault on you. A life of sinlessness is a life of perfection, which God wants His children to strive for.

Trample sin under your feet but do not despise the sinner. Pity him and raise him from the morass of despair. Purify his heart, mind and soul and take him Godward. It is possible to rise from the state of sinfulness to the highest state of saintliness. Sinfulness is only one aspect of human life. It is a transient aspect for no sinner can live in the sink of sin for a long time. He must come out, by means of his own remorse and suffering and breathe the free air of joy and sunshine, which is God's measure for all His creation.

There is no such thing as eternal punishment. There is eternal bliss which is the birthright of every human soul. But there is no eternal fire of hell. Heaven and hell do exist but not in the sense men think them to be. Sinfulness is hell. Righteousness is heaven. It is only by breaking the fetters of sin and leading a life of desirelessness, would you be able to win God's love and grace and enter His Kingdom of Eternal BLISS. (24.11.1952)

Discourse No. (21)
THE CHARIOT AND THE CHARIOTEER

Man has evolved from the lowest strata of life. It is his destiny to be finally united with God. To reach this goal, he may take countless births on your earth plane. Ultimately his soul which is an evolving entity saturated with all kinds of experiences, good and bad, pleasant and bitter, is redeemed from the obligation of taking birth again in physical body and is united with the spirit. When this marriage of the soul with the spirit takes place, it means the soul has freed itself from its shackles and environments and has gained its salvation.

Salvation of the soul is the object of life. To attain this object, it is necessary to discard that which is of transient and fleeting nature and adhere to that which is permanent and lasting. The world is a Maya. The senses, if not controlled by the mind and will act the part of the horses, yoked to a chariot, wherein is seated the soul, but not properly checked by the reins of the charioteer – the higher mind, (buddhi), they run wild and dash the chariot to pieces. The chariot is the body. When the body is broken, the man dies, but he again comes back and takes hold of the chariot, the horses and the reins and begins anew to drive, with the experiences gained in the past lives. Slowly and steadily, the charioteer learns to drive the chariot correctly without any mishap and he drives the horses safely to their destination. That destination is the soul's salvation. (25.11.1952)

Discourse No. (22)
PRAYERS AND THEIR SIGNIFICANCE

Distance lends enchantment to the view. It is not so in spirituality. The nearer you come to God, the greater becomes your joy and happiness. You pass from the mundane to the spiritual plane of existence. It is a ladder, a bridge to eternity.

Be spiritual. Forget self. Immerse yourself in the ocean of universality. Give up individuality and become impersonal.

It is only then the gulf between your mundane world and our spiritual world of Eternal Bliss can be bridged. Make God the target of your life, the summum bonum of your aspiration, the goal of your victory.

Pray to him day and night. Prayers offered from the fullness of your heart find an echo in the Universal Mind. They create waves after waves of divine power bringing in you a new life, a new impulse, a new light, a healing of wounds. Prayers are a sovereign remedy for all ills the body is heir to. They remedy, they purify, they exalt, they illumine the heart, mind and soul.

To pray to God is the privilege of every one, whether he be a fakir or prince. It is the greatest weapon which a person holds in his hands for the betterment of his life. Prayers are based on this fact, that God, who is invisible, is ever present and ever eager to listen to us in our grief and distress.

Prayer is the language of the heart. It is divine communion. It is celestial music. It is a gateway to our purification and salvation.

Sacrifice and self-surrender to God are the main pillars of every prayer. No prayer is genuine if not buttressed with the oil of sacrifice and offered in complete abandonment to the will of God. (26.11.1952)

Discourse No. (23)
AS YOU SOW, SO SHALL YOU REAP

As you sow, so shall you reap. This is an eternal truth. If you do evil to any one, it will return to you with a vengeance. If you do good to any one, even if you do not expect any return or reward, you would taste its sweet fruit in some form of the other. You grow in spiritual stature as you do good. You shrink and become a dwarf, if evil thoughts, evil words and evil deeds emanate from your lower self. Aspire for the Highest and you would attain the highest. If you think of the lowest, you would be the lowest. It is for you to choose, good or evil, God or dust.

Enshrine your mind with thoughts of love. Pilot the ship of your soul in the deep waters of Peace and Harmony, Virtue and Contentment. Keep away from the cliffs of hatred and jealousy, greed and avarice, lust and debasement. God answers no prayers unless it emanates from a contrite heart, seeking forgiveness for sins in the past. Work your way rigidly and care not for crosses and pains, if they are borne for the sake of righteousness, which is the only path go God. (30.11.1952)

Discourse No. (24)
GOD: NOT AN ENIGMA

Star gazing is a relaxation, exaltation and sublimation of the soul. The star bespangled sky in the silvery night, when Queen Moon is at its height in her splendour and limpid makes man feel that he is in tune with the Infinite. Anything GOD is the Absolute Spirit, pervading throughout the universe. He is both transcendent and immanent, visible and invisible, silent and audible.

God is not an enigma, if you study Nature and tune your life in conformity with God's commandments of LOVE and VIRTUE, which must triumph not only in each man's individual life but in the entire creation of God. Simple as ABC is God's formula to understand Him and the universe. It is easy to comprehend Him, not through deep volumes of philosophy, not by leading a hectic life of blistering struggle and fight for earthly supremacy, but by a passionate longing for Truth and Renunciation. But simple as God's formula is to understand Him and realise Him, man, in his ignorance, casts aside the bowl of purity and drinks instead what appears to him as good and vitalising but in reality, is dark, dirty poison, that stains his soul and ruins him physically, morally and spiritually.

God is Spirit. Love Him, adore Him, dedicate your life to Him and you would become one with Him in spirit. (1.12.1952)

Discourse No. (25)
HOW THE INVISIBLE CAN BECOME VISIBLE

Search for God inwardly Infinite as He is, unsurpassed and boundless, He resides in the tiny cave of the human heart. He is measureless, incomprehensible, unknown, unknowable, eternal, invisible. But if you search Him with a longing heart and dedicate yourself wholly, solely and completely to Him in perfect purity of heart, mind and soul, the invisible will become visible. The wide universe is but a manifestation of the Absolute Spirit.

Make your heart and soul vibrate with the thoughts of God, the Absolute Spirit pervading the universe and you would feel a new impulse, a new life, a new spirit, a new discovery of yourself. This self discovery is God vision. It is the preparation for a life of eternity. Life becomes spiritualized.

To understand God who is spirit, man must become like spirit *i.e.*, leave off the dross in him, which is the material part in him. Self-surrender, self-purification, self-knowledge- these are the sure footings for the achievement of life's goal – God-realization. (4.12.1952)

Discourse No. (26)
SEEK GOD THROUGH THE GATEWAY OF RENUNCIATION AND DEVOTION

Lead a complete life, not a life of trivialities. A life of desultory existence is a life of decadence. Enrich your life with thoughts of God, if you wish to live in peace and joyousness. A life of self-centredness leads to destruction of mental peace. It is a way down the hill in the valley of despair. Kindle the lamp of your heart with the flame of God and your heart with the flame of God and you will rise to heights of ecstasy, beyond your dreams.

Garner the fruit of wisdom from the garden of your life and share it with your brothers and sisters tied to you in holy union. Life is a delicious fruit, if you sweeten it with the name of God. It is bitter, if you taste it without taking His name.

Sweet or bitter, as the course of your life may be, do not for a moment forget God. He is ever present in you. He will free you if you think of Him and long for Him with all the intensity of your heart, mind and soul. Seek god through the path of renunciation for that is the only way open to reach Him. Seek Him in all earnestness and you will find Him. (5.12.1952)

Discourse No. (27)
GOD-REALIZATION – THE GOAL OF LIFE, NOT EARTHLY HAPPINESS

Different faiths are like different rivers that flow from different regions but ultimately join the ocean. The object of every religion is God. He alone is worthy of worship and none else. People make Mammon their God. This is wrong. To let sordid desires dominate life is to invite catastrophe. Do not be dragged into the mire of worldly temptations for they are death knells of misery and degradation. Riches are the burning bricks with which the vault of hell is built. Lust for power is a shadowy substance. Do not aspire for worldly applause for it is fickle and baseless. Stain not your soul with the allurements of life but keep it stainless with the love and light of God.

God alone is the Reality, all else is of unreal nature. Seek God in the simplicity of your heart. Renounce the gewgaws of life. Hold fast to Truth and Righteousness. Mercy and Compassion, Love and Gentility, Simplicity and Humility, Earnestness and Sincerity, Passivity and Catholicity, Sobriety and Integrity, Forgiveness and Forbearance, Patience and Perseverance. Aspire to be a saint, a sage by leaving the common track and following your own path to God. Work ceaselessly, Pray to God zealously, keep your mind serene and calm even in the midst of storms and tempests. Be pure in heart and you will see God. God-realization is the goal of life, not earthly happiness which is false and effervescent. (6.12.1952)

Discourse No. (28)
IN THE UNCERTAINTY OF LIFE, ONE CERTAINTY - GOD

Life is uncertain. You do not know the span of your life -how many years you have to live – nor what the future holds out for you. In this uncertainty, there is one certainty, which you must follow, as night follows the day and the day follows the night, and it is the most glorious certainty of God, the only REALITY in the whole cosmos. Open your heart to Him. Let divine thought rush in you like the scented zephyr from the bower of flowers. Seek Him and Him alone for He is your Helpmate, your Father, Your Ally, your Companion, Your Consoler and Admonisher throughout the long battle of life. Cleanse your heart, mind and soul of all the stains of folly and sin and thus purified and elevated inwardly, you would be taken into the inner realms of the spirit for the achievement of life's highest goal-God-realization. (7.12.1952)

Discourse No. (29)
GROW IN SPIRIT

To rise to the highest pinnacle of spirituality is ordained by God for every one. But extremely few reach the goal for the path leading to it is so narrow and painful to traverse. It is a great mistake to avoid the narrow way which leads to God and to take to the broad way which leads to corruption and decay. Why sell eternal peace for a mess of pottage. And yet millions and millions of your people of the earth plane, forgetful of the Self within them, hanker for loaves and fishes of life, gilded with an outward shine and forget God, who is the only Reality.

Seek God not in outward shows and forms. Seek God not in the paraphernalia of rites and rituals. Seek God, not in church congregations. But seek Him in the cave of your heart. It is there He dwells, hid in the kernel. Throw off the shells and the shackles that bind and devitalise you. Grow in spirit and the indwelling Spirit, free from all its outer coverings and coatings, will shine like a crystal star and lead you on and on to the starry realms of unimaginable glory and beauty to your extreme delight and joy. Make God your home, your heart, your sole source of thought and activity. It is then alone, you shall reach Him and be united with Him in all eternity. (8.12.1952)

Discourse No. (30)
DON'T MAKE LIFE A TOMB OF WOE AND WANTONNESS

Make life a music, a melody of art and beauty, a torrent of glory, a rainbow arch of gorgeousness. Why seek the petty things of life, when God has designed and planned that you should rise from darkness to light, from death to immortality, from the unreal to the REAL. Make perfection of character the goal of your life and you will come quickly to God, who alone is REAL.

Don't make life a tomb of woe and wantonness. Rise from the graveyard of sickness and sorrow, both of mind and soul, and climb then the altitude of high thoughts and aspirations, which would free you from the maddening temptations of your world and its vagaries. Keep away from the shore of dead sea apples. Clinch pure gold and not putrid flesh. Kindle the light of your heart with the flame and fire of God's Love and Light and you will be safe in your march from the earth to the Realms Beyond. Go forward and sink not, though the battle be tough and way be arduous and wearisome. Make God your ally and you would safely reach the goal, the Goal of Eternal Bliss and Light. (9.12.1952)

Discourse No. (31)
BE A BRAVE WARRIOR ON THE BATTLE OF LIFE

Stand fast to Truth and do not quiver if others make all sorts do dirty and false accusations. In the whirlpool of life, there are more scorpions and snakes to bite you than honey-suckle flowers to delight you. But however thorny and difficult the path may be, be a brave warrior and do not shudder at all. God helps those who are brave and fail not in the battle cf life. Keep courage and have entire faith in Him. He will guide and steer the ship of your life safe through all the dangerous crags and cliffs abutting on either side. He will light the way. He will take you safely to your destination. (11.12.1952)

Discourse No. (32)
SAINTS AND SAGES

Saints and sages are the pillars of society. They are manifestations and God's perfection. Revere them, sit at their feet and draw the nectar of life from their inspiration. They are the visible and invisible guides of your world's destiny. But for them, your world would go into pieces and there would be nothing but confusion and anarchy. They reverberate with God's voice, which speaks through them. They are the becon lights and unfailing guides of all mankind. They show the way from darkness to light, from death to immorality. They are the virgin minstrels, the music of whose souls reaches the different strata of life and enriches your earth plane with the song and beauty of God's goodness and greatness. (12.12.1952)

Discourse No. (33)
GOD'S LOVE AND LIGHT

Live in God's love and light. Live for God and He will give you light. Love all and He will love you all the more. Make God's Light and Love, the symbols of your life, the warf and woof of your life, the tapestry of your life, the be all and end all of your life.

God's light is divine wisdom. It is greater than all the learning of your so-called men of learning. God's light is the channel of happiness. God's love is the fragrance of the heart that sweeps away all shadows of despair and distrust. It sweetens life and tunes the soul in harmony with all things in nature. God's love is heart's music, the radiant light that dispels all clouds of sadness and fills the soul and mind with rapturous delight. Think of God, every minute of your life, waking of sleeping and you would be saturated in waves of ecastatic joy. Why think of the sordidness of life when the great treasure of God's love and light is within your reach. Without God's love and light, life is a tinsel, a vortex of despair and dissolution. Live for God and God alone, for that is the only way to LIBERATION. (13.12.1952)

Discourse No. (34)
MAKE LIFE A SAGA, AN EPIC OF HEROISM

Kindly keep your eye on the twinkling star in the firmament and not cast it on the mud beneath your feet. See the rose in its blossom and glory and not the thorns that pierce and hurt. See God in everything from the star to the dust and you will be filled with a passionate longing for God and eternity.

Life is a puzzle and quagmire if you get yourself engrossed in worldliness. Keep away from the snare of Maya and you would see God in all His glory and greatness. Never sink but keep a brave heart to the very end, for with God in your heart and mind, you cannot but reach the destined goal of liberation. Crosses are life's redeemers. Kiss them, not shun them. They will take you to your goal quicker.

Sing the song of God as you go merrily along life's dusty path, without sadness for remorse. Be not an owl but a nightingale. Sing to the tune of the whirling spheres. Breathe not a word of sadness. Make life a saga, an epic of heroism. Don't quiver and quail, of dragged down by adversity. Adversity is Nature's sweet drink. Drink it, for it is not poison but nectar. Keep radiant and smiling even when winds blow you and storms burst upon you. Think of the silver lining in every cloud. Keep cheerful and happy for there is God within you. Worship Him and you are safe as a rock in all the tempests of life, in all the storms of adversity. (14.12.1952)

Discourse No. (35)
SILENCE – THE LANGUAGE OF ETERNITY

Silence is the language of Eternity. It is a gateway to Godhood. It is the impulse of God in man. Its arch is sublimity. Its base is fearlessness. It is a key to all knotty problems of life. Man learns more through silence than from desultory reading and writing.

Silence is the flower of the heart, the amber of life, the fragrance of the mind, the jewel of the deep sea. Sit in silence and commune with God and Nature. You will gain the peace of mind and the heart's rapturous joy. Watch the stars and the spheres in the firmament in the still silence of the night and the music of God would flow in you with a mystic spell. Make silence your joyful companion. Disdain and keep away from the shouts and shrieks of your dizzy world. (15.12.1952)

Discourse No. (36)
WORK IN HARMONY WITH GOD'S LAWS AND COMMANDMENTS

The fruit ripens in its proper time. Hustling will not mend matters. God's laws work in nature with unerring precision. Any defiance by man against the harmony that prevails in the universe creates repercussions, extremely injurious to himself.

Study the laws of the universe, work in agreement with God's laws and commandments and you will have contributed largely to your own gain and betterment of your world at large.

Make non-violence your creed, truth your gospel, love your monitor and conscience your guide. Follow simplicity and be natural in your way of life. Formalities, conventions, ceremonies add to the burden of life. Sincerity and simplicity sweeten life, for they are angelic qualities in man. Be humble, humility is the cloth celestial. It is negation of egotism, the greatest obstacle to spirituality. (16.12.1952)

Discourse No. (37)
THREE CLASSES OF SOCIETY

Your world is divided into people of three different categories. A very large mass is composed of ignorant persons, imprisoned in the dark cell of sinfulness, unaware of the light of God. They form the dregs of society, steeped in ignorance and wantonness.

The second group is composed of intelligent persons, who use their intelligence more for their benefit than for the benefit of the society at large.

The third group, which is composed of a very small number of persons, is the highest in the three classes. They from a class by themselves. They are the saviours of the World, the real benefactors, leaders, guides and spiritual wonder workers. They work both visibly and invisibly for the good of the world, without the least thought for their own gain or profit. Every individual in this group is directly or indirectly in communion with God. God works His miracle through persons of this highest category. (17.12.1952)

Discourse No. (38)
EVIL IS THE LEAST GOOD

There are two principles working in Nature – the principle of good and the principle of evil. Really speaking, there is no evil in life, for God being all perfection, He has not created evil. Evil is the least good. The struggle then is between the most good and the least good. The word 'evil' is used for facility of expression and as such it is the right word used.

There is no such thing as Satan or Ahreman as depicted in the Scriptures. They are merely allegorically used and should be taken in such light. Unless the evil in man is expunged and he is purified and perfected, there can be no liberation for him. The sole object of life is soul's emancipation and this can be achieved only when the state of perfection is reached. It may take many births to reach this final destiny of man, or less round of births. It all depends upon man's own individual effort and ceaseless search for God and His mysteries. Till the inner urge for God is not roused, the soul remains enchained in the mesh of desires and the way to salvation is lost. Renunciation is the only way to salvation. (18.12.1952)

Discourse No. (39)
MAN'S APATHY FOR HIGHER LIFE

What makes the difference between man and animal? There is animal in man and there is angel in man. To drive away the animal instincts of sloth, greed, lust and rapine and to mould your life into angelic virtues leading to perfection of character, is the aim and object of life. It is really very sad that most of the people on the earth plane lead the life that is least desirable. They forget Buddha's eightfold path. They forget the ethical teachings of the great Lord Zoroaster – good thoughts, good words, good deeds. They forget Lord Krishna's teaching of discrimination and renunciation. They forget the great truth embeded in Jewish teaching – the teaching of Righteousness. They forget that Lord Christ was specially sent by God on the earth plane to wean men from the path of sin and to love God and to love all mankind. Other prophets following Christ and Mohammed have carried the torch of divine knowledge to all parts of your world. But, oh, where are their words listened to and practised? The prophets have failed to quicken man's conscience. Man is still entangled in the web of sin and ignorance.

In order to drive away the apathy of man for a higher life, it is now God's design to send Masters in larger numbers, who will act as match to the gunpower and kindle the hearts and minds of men to love God. Not solitary prophets after long centuries, but scores of Masters in physical bodies will now be working on the earth plane, for knitting together the whole mass of humanity in bonds of love, harmony and mutual understanding for the promotion of material prosperity and spiritual growth.

A new era of spiritual renaissance is in the offing. It will burst forth like a rainbow in the sky and colour and brighten the lives of the multitude. (22.12.1952)

Discourse No. (40)
TRUE RELIGION, NOT BIGOTRY – THE WAY TO PROGRESS

When man forgets the reality, he mismanages his affairs and loses his soul. The great truth that God is the only REALITY has to be realised for the success of life's mission on earth. Make life a mission, and offering of one's self to God and the darkness of the world would be greatly reduced. True religion, not bigotry, Catholicism, not communalism, philanthropy, not mere profundity of book learning, the heart, not the head, the essence and not the form, the truth and not the dogma or ritual, should play the dominant role for the achievement of God's peace, love, harmony and mutual understanding. These will go a long way towards economic, moral and spiritual progress of man. (23.12.1952)

Discourse No. (41)
SEEK NOT THE FORM BUT THE ESSENCE

Life and death are two opposite polarities. Life is spirit; death means decay. Life is energy; death is annihilation. Life is God's greatest blessing to man, but it must not be understood that the blessing ends with death. For death is a gateway to a higher life, in a higher region, for the perfection and sublimation of the soul. Life is a blessing, if man makes use of the God-given energy in the right direction. If he misuses it, life becomes a curse, a tragedy, a horror, a paroxysm of despair, a calamity.

Life does not end with the departure of the soul from the physical body. It is unending. It is eternal. For man is a spark of God, eternal, infinite and when life's sufferings are ended and the soul becomes perfect, to be received in the Ocean of Eternal Bliss.

Seek not form, but the essence. Make Virtue your bride, Truth, your companion, Love your counsellor and guide and selflessness the crown of your life. Ride the chariot of life fearlessly and be not daunted by obstacles and difficulties. So long as you control your senses and the mind and are engrossed in the thoughts of God, you will drive the chariot successfully without meeting any accident on the way. Drive the chariot well, till you reach the gateway of death. Your soul shall then ascend to the higher planes and continue the journey, from plane to plane, from birth to death and death to birth, till perfected, it is absorbed in the boundless Ocean of Eternal BLISS. (24.12.1952)

Discourse No. (42)
CHANGE OF THOUGHTS NECESSARY IN THE PROGRESS OF LIFE

The seasons vary. Spring is followed by Summer, Summer by Autumn and Autumn by dreary Winter. Spring is the youth of the season; Winter is the withering old age. Summer is midway between Spring and Winter and Autumn is nearer to Winter than any other season. These variations of seasons are an indication of My Law, which though immutable and unchangeable, works in Nature for the manifestation of My other Law in Nature viz., the Law of polarity. These changes are an indication of the fact that man must change with Nature. Just as he changes his clothes, when he gives them for a wash, he must change his ways of thought, as he progresses in life and builds his career and character by correcting himself at every stage of his progress. Change means evolution and it is through Evolution that the destined way to the final goal of emancipation of the soul is secured. Sin not, but if you do sin, wash off the taint of your sin with the soap of repentance and listen to the call of the inward monitor, whose voice must prevail at all times.

Once liberated, you must work for the sinner and the non-sinner alike. For both are God's children and they want your guidance, assistance on the plane of physical life. (25.12.1952)

Discourse No. (43)
DON'T MAKE LIFE A COMEDY OF ERRORS OR A TRAGEDY OF MISERY

As the flower raises its head towards the sun and gives its fragrance and throws it radiance all around, God wants every human being to look up to Him and do his best for his own happiness and the happiness of others. Life is a serious affair. It should not be made a comedy of errors or a tragedy of misery. Make it a bulwark against all assaults of temptations and sins. If you think of God, you will think of His Law, the great Law of Righteousness and of Mercy, Kindness and Love, and you will strengthen your citadel against all tempests of worldly illusions and delusions.

God's is within you. Harken to His Voice and you will steer the boat of your life safely through the waters of opposition and tempest to the heaven of Eternal Rest and Bliss. God is the only REALITY, all else is a delusion, an illusion. (26.12.1952)

Discourse No. (44)
SIN AND REPENTANCE

The sun throws its light equally on all of the earth plane. It makes no distinction of good or bad people. In a similar manner, your heart should open out and let there be the outpouring of love for all – the virtuous and the sinner alike. Never befriend a sinner or encourage him in his misdeeds. But have pity on him and try to save him from pitfalls and errors. If he refuses to listen or repent, leave him alone to his God and destinty.

Christ came on earth for the atonement of the sins of others i.e., he was sent by God to spread the mission of love and to teach people how to attain oneness with God by purifying themselves of all sins through repentance and good deeds. Repentance for sins is a fundamental step in the evolution of the soul. To commit sin is bad but to refuse to repent is worse. Repentance takes away the edge of the bitterness of sins and raises the soul Godward. Repentance means refusal to commit the sin again.

Sin is the most dreadful thing in life. It is therefore you must forgive the sinner and love him all the more, to enable him to leave the path of sin and comeback to God. (28.12.1952)

Discourse No. (45)
FAITH IN GOD

There is no force so great as faith in God. It is a spiritual fire, which ignites and spurs the forces within for the achievement of success in life. It is the divine light that shines with lustre, even when there is darkness all around. It is the talisman that changes failure into success. It is the beacon light on the pilgrim's path, full of thorns and snakes, guiding the devotee aright to God, the supreme crown of his heart's desire. It is a vital force that can shake mountains and cross rivers in flood. It is a torrent, the vital energy of which is immeasurable. It is the channel and gateway to God's own abode. To have faith in God is to encounter all difficulties with success. It is a weapon of inconceivable strength in the hands of man. Keep the fire of faith burning within you, for it is a living force, volcanic in its element and miraculous in achievement of divinity. It is a propellor of all the hidden and latent powers in man. To give up faith in God is to lose the battle of life. To live in faith means approach and access to God. (30.12.1952)

Discourse No. (46)
REINCARNATION

To say that reincarnation is not taught in religions other than Hinduism and Buddhism is wrong. Christ taught it. So did Zoroaster. But unfortunately their teachings, veiled in esoteric language, have been lost through transit of time and man's inability to grasp the inner secrets.

Reincarnation is a fundamental truth, which truly speaking, no prophet or sage has ignored or can ignore, in view of the fact that he knows the past. Divine revelation means the power to see the present, the past and the future. How can then any prophet or sage, after attaining divine revelation and getting the knowledge of the working of the universe, lose sight of such an important factor in man's destiny? Reincarnation is as inevitable as death is unavoidable.

Your earth plane is the principal stage of man's struggle for freedom. In this struggle, man has to cross so many hurdles before he can reach his destination. To cross these hurdles in one life is not possible. Each hurdle represents a certain state of the evolution of the soul. When his soul is fully evolved, he reaches the last hurdle and crosses it. It is a hurdle of perfection, which requires many incarnations, according to man's own exertions for purity of life and self-abnegation. Each incarnation takes him further and further towards the goal i.e. his soul evolves, as it returns to the earth plane after its peregrinations in the worlds, to gain experiences for its progress. (1.1.1953)

Discourse No. (47)
WHEN MAN TRANSCENDS RELIGION!

What is religion for the masses, the science of the Masters is for the few, selected by God to tread the path and reach

Godhood in as few incarnations as possible. Religion is the seed of the tree of life. It is sown in the soil of the human body, when the soul enters it. This seed has to be carefully watered and cultured to give full foliage to the tree. If the seed sown is rejected, the tree withers and life loses its charm. If the seed is properly tended and taken care of, the tree grows in full and becomes a source of protection to others.

Lead the life of religion for the progress of your own soul and for the betterment of the world at large. If you fail in this, you waste your incarnation and add to the misery and suffering of the world.

Religion is essential for every one. To discard God is to lose everything in life. There can be no joy in life without love of God and love of all mankind. Christ was sent to preach the great doctrine of Love of God and all mankind. True love generates from the purity of heart. It is unselfish and stainless. It is a consuming fire that burns away all the dross in man and makes him supremely happy. There can be no happiness unless you make others happy by your thoughts, words and deeds.

The higher you soar in life, the more spiritual your soul becomes and it seeks larger avenues for the satisfaction of its aspiration.

The bedrock of religion is faith. But the devotee who yearns for God and God alone, renouncing everything for the love of God, is seized with an inward desire to see God face to face. He is not content to live in faith alone. His soul is consumed with a desire to transcend religion *i.e.*, he wants faith in God to be no more a theoretical teaching but a living experience. This happens when God selects him for the path and gives him a Master to guide him to the goal.

Religion in its exoteric teachings is meant for the masses. Religion in its esoteric teachings is the lever to raise the devotee to the highest pedestal of spirituality. The two aspects of the divine science should not be lost sight of, the exoteric and the esoteric – the external and the internal, the open and the hidden. (4.1.1953)

Discourse No. (48)
THE MESSAGE OF THEOSOPHY

Theosophy means divine wisdom, the knowledge of God. The followers of this philosophy have enriched your world with beauty – a beauty that shines the most when it radiates from a pure source of divinity. The founders of Theosophy were persons of great latent powers, which they made use of for the purpose of finding out the secrets of the universe. They must be reckoned as apostles of a new religion – a religion of humanity, free of creeds, dogmas, rituals and other paraphernalia.

The strength of Theosophy lies in its teaching of the Science of the Masters. Its recognition of the Masters is the most salient factor and a distinct contribution to the advancement of your world on the right lines of divinity. But for the Masters who are guiding and controlling your world, your earth plane would be continuously in a state of anarchy and misery.

Of course, the teaching of Theosophy is not at all a new teaching. It is a reflection of the old, old teaching embedded in the occult side of all religions, preached by their founders. But what these religions have failed to do, except in solitary cases, Theosophy has been able to spread the secret teachings of Masters to a much larger extent.

Theosophy aims also at providing a synthesis of all religions, thus bringing the different elements, divided into exclusive and isolate groups or campus, into cohension and harmony. Theosophy is a precursor to One World Religion, which is the crying need of the world today. (5.1.1953)

Discourse No. (49)
THE TWO PATHS – THE BROAD AND THE NARROW

Self-realization is the goal of life. But in the pursuit of the objects of the senses, people forget it entirely and create for themselves and others greater and greater difficulties and greater suffering becomes the order of the day. They all want to tread the broad path which leads eventually to destruction and ruination. The broad path is easier to travel, but it becomes narrower and narrower, as the weary travelier treads it and gets lost in the end. This is not the case with those who take to the narrow, razor-like path. It seems exceedingly difficult to travel on such a path but in reality, it is not so. It is the path of the Masters, who are stationed at every step and they help the pilgrims on the way.

He who seeks to lose himself, gains his life. He who seeks to gain the wealth of the world, loses all

Self-realization is the only goal of life worth aspiring for; all else is a waste of incarnation. (7.1.1953)

Discourse No. (50)
THE HIDDEN POTENTIALITIES OF MAN

Nothing moves in the universe without the consent of God. He is the creator, harmoniser, ruler, controller, destroyer and awakener of all forces in the universe – both hidden and manifest. The sun and the moon and all the planets and the stars and the constellation are His creations. They manifest His power, His rhythm, the radiance of His splendour, the joy of His Being.

Man has a tiny mark of God's divinity in him. His soul has emanated from God and it has to go back to God for union and harmony with the Great Divinity. Man's soul encased in human body is endowed with vast potentialities, which he has to discover himself and make the best use of them for his own progress and for the progress of the world in which he is born. These hidden potentialities, when realised, make man a God. To realise these potentialities of the soul, is the object of life and not merely bodily existence for satisfying the senses.

God is the mightiest and greatest force in life. To work in harmony with this force in righteousness of spirit should be man's urge, for only in the fullest satisfaction of this inward feeling, will come that bliss which is eternal and not by any other means. (8.1.1953)

Discourse No. (51)
TRUE RENUNCIATION *i.e.*, DESIRELESSNESS, THE SINE-QUA-NON IN SELF-REALIZATION

In the former years, the general belief was that God could be realised only by taking sanyas. It is not necessary to leave one's home and seek refuge in the forest or in the cave of a mountain. The keynote to God-realization is renunciation. The true meaning of renunciation is complete detachment of the mind. Some can attain this object quicker by leaving their home for a life in the wilderness. But a house-holder, living in the midst of worldly attractions, can also attain mental supremacy by his will and devotion to God. A life of austerity and perfect simplicity is necessary but mortification of the flesh, which formed the principal item in the aspirant's programme for self-realization in the olden times, is not at all desirable. The sole idea in renunciation is to slay the mind, by annihilating all senses, for desires, though natural in the human frame, will have to be subjugated and controlled. It is through desirelessness that man's soul arrives at the goal. Perfect surrender to the will of God is the Sine-Qua-Non in the attainment of Self-realization. (8.1.1953)

Discourse No. (52)
MAN THE ARCHITECT OF HIS OWN FATE

There is no such thing in reality as predestination. Each man makes his destiny himself and he is solely responsible for it. He becomes as he thinks. He is the architect of his own fate. He has to select between the two forces of good and evil in life. What good he does, bears fruit in his life as well as in the incarnations to come. In a similar manner, the evil he does bears the fruit of misery and suffering for future incarnations also till he pays off his debt. Until a man succeeds in linking his will to God's will, he must go through the rounds of birth and death on your physical plane.

The law of Karma is so effective, that is must take its course. It is indestructible and inescapable. In plain language, it means as you sow, so must you reap.

To take shelter under the excuse that you suffer because of Kismat (fate), and not exert yourself to remove the cause of your suffering is foolish. Suffering is intended for man's purification and exaltation. It is a spiritual blessing, the best medicine for human ills.

Nothing is lost in the universe. Every beautiful thought in the mind, every kind world spoken, every kind deed done, reverberates and brinks back to the thinker, the speaker and the doer in a mysterious manner God's divine blessings for his spiritual growth and happiness. In a similar manner, every evil thought, word or deed brings to the individual a load of misery and sorrows, which then begin to act as purifying agents for preparation of a better life in the next incarnation. (10.1.1953)

Discourse No. (53)
LOVE IS THE NEAREST PEDESTAL TO THE FOOT STOOL OF GOD

Faith, Hope and Charity form the tripod of man's religious being. Without faith in God, life is a disaster and a blunder. Hope is the food which man must have every day to eat, for without it, life would be barren. Charity is that talisman which opens all doors of happiness. Charity is a wide and very comprehensive word. It includes love, pity, compassion, unselfishness, sacrifice, non-separateness, true neighbourliness and philanthropy. The object of life is to give and not to receive, to lose oneself, not to gain. To love all means to gain all. When you give unstintedly, it is true love. True love burns away the cinders of anger, fear, jealously, revenge, sloth and selfishness. To live truly is to love deeply. Love is man's supreme test. It is the nearest pedestal to the footstool of God. (12.1.1953)

Discourse No. (54)
MEDITATION – THE DOORWAY TO THE INNER SECRET OF LOVE

Meditation is the doorway to salvation. It is the most difficult thing in life, but if a man makes up his mind, he can practise it and he will succeed in the end. It is the way to still the mind. To control the senses and the mind, which is the sixth sense, is Sine-Qua-Non in the path of renunciation. Concentration and meditation are absolutely necessary for the quickening of the inner powers and inner latent forces, without which no one can reach the goal of self of God-realization.

Meditation becomes simple and extremely pleasant, when there is a deep yearning for God and God alone. One should meditate for the love of God and not for the purpose of gaining supernatural powers. To gain psychic powers by other means than deep meditation is most inadvisable. Seek God for the sake of God out of love and devotion for God and your meditation will lead you to God, who will crown you with powers, unsought by you but which nevertheless come to you automatically, because of your single-minded devotion to God.

Meditation is the key to the realm of ecstatic joy. It is a doorway to the inner secrets of life. It takes the devotee from the physical mundane world to the highest spiritual plane of ecstatic joy and delight. (12.1.1953)

Discourse No. (55)
SAINTS, SAGES AND MYSTICS GREAT SPIRITUAL ARCHITECTS AND ARTISTS

Saints, sages and mystics are the real pillars of society. Hold them in deepest reverence and serve them with utmost devotion. They are links that join your mundance world with out Spiritual Realm. They are life transformers, great spiritual architects and artists, who change the surface of your world from a wilderness into an ordered organism of love and peace, brotherhood and joy. They are the Masters in physical bodies, in communion with God and the Spirit World.

Every saint is a live force, a dynamo that blows out the rubbish of life and makes room for all that is vital and real. The sages, saints and mystics are torchbearers who radiate the real light of God's divinity and pave the way for the betterment of the world in every sense of the word.

Mystics are despised by your foolish world as mad people. They are not mad, but are deeply drunk with the wine of God – intoxication. They are intoxicated in God and they appear to be mad but are actually the sanest, best and wisest of all mankind.

God wants His children to follow the example of mystics, saints and sages, for they are the prototypes of superman, spiritual builders of the edifice of a new life, transmitters of joy and beauty, goodness and graciousness in a world of squalor and perdition. (13.1.1953)

Discourse No. (56)
TRUTH AND LOVE ARE INSEPARABLE LINKS

There is no religion greater than TRUTH, says the Theosophist. This is too true. God is TRUTH and to reach Him, you must practise Truth in all respects. Truth is a very comprehensive word. It is not merely the opposite of untruth. It bears a wider meaning. In fact, it is a conglomeration of all virtues. Truth means righteousness and all positive virtues allied to it such as integrity, sincerity, solemnity, humility, purity, selflessness, sacrifice and, above all, surrender to the Will of God.

Truth represents the male side of virtues. Love represents the female side of virtues and where Truth is practised, Love must instantly follow. Truth and Love are brother and sister qualities in man, which have to be developed equally. You cannot neglect Truth and follow Love only, not neglect Love and follow Truth only. They are inseparable in fact. If you are righteous, you must love your neighbour, as you love yourself, it shall-only be in the spirit of righteousness and no other. Love and Righteousness are complementary terms. They make one whole.

To Love God is to love Truth and all mankind.

Love is a dynamic force in the universe. Christ came to earth for the love of mankind and a sincere desire to redeem men of their sins and follies. He taught them the path of love and waned them from the path of folly through his own great Love and Sacrifice. The four corners of the square which one must always keep in mind, if one wants to reach the goal, are Truth and Righteousness, Love and Sacrifice. (14.1.1953)

Discourse No. (57)
GOD – THE VIBRATING NUCLEUS OF THE WHOLE UNIVERSE

The universe is a manifestation of God. The sun and the stars and the various constellations that are constantly in motion are His creations. Everything in the universe is in motion but God alone is motionless. The whole universe vibrates because of His vibrations. Motionless, He works His laws in such a mysterious manner that it is a wonder, not only to man on the earth plane but even to the highest entity in the Spirit World. He is the cosmic force, the interpenetrating dynamic flash, the vibrating nucleus of the whole universe. The whole universe revolves round Him, the pillar and centre of magnetic attraction. He makes and unmakes, creates and destroys. He is the designer; He is the planner; He is the Ruler; He is the Law-maker. His diverse forces of multiple nature work so systematically and methodically under the supremacy of One Universal Law – the Law of Harmony, that it is amazing with what precision, the intricacies are planned and evolved and they work so harmoniously in a mass of apparent confusion and chaos. Infinite spaces from His realm. Eternity, endlessness, ceaselessness, is another aspect of His universalism. He is ONE. He is stupendous, beyond human comprehension. His powers are limitless. His energy is inexhaustible. He is the generating box of the whole universe. He is transcendent and immanent. He pervades the whole universe from the sun to the speck of dust on the earth plane. He is all Glory, Love, Light and Love. He is the pivot of every soul, the magnet of every creatures, the sun driver, the sky creeper, the sunshine and glory of every human heart, awakening or awakened to the highest consciousness within him. Unparalleled in power, matchless in beauty, limitless, timeless, spaceless, eternal, infinite, God is the lodestar, the magnet, which must draw eventually every human soul, pining and fretting on the earth plane to his own bosom, for Unity is the Law of the Universe, not diversity which is apparent, but not real. (15.1.1953)

Discourse No. (58)
ABSORPTION INTO GODHOOD, ETERNAL BLISS, THE GOAL OF LIFE

All rivers fall into the ocean. All human souls must also eventually be absorbed into the Ocean of Eternity *i.e.*, God. Each soul is a spark of the fire of God. It has emanated from God, it must return to God. This is the Law of Evolution, which I have created and which works in combination with the Law of KARMA.

There are limitless worlds and limitless solar systems in My universe. No human soul can have the least conception of the infiniteness of My universe and the infinite forces that are working throughout the entire realm of My sovereignty. The grandeur and beauty of My Spiritual Plane are of an indescribable nature. Only Adepts with their inner eyes open, can behold the beauty and magnificence on My highest plane. The Masters who direct and control the management of your world under My orders are denizens of My highest plane. They are perfected human souls, who after countless incarnations, attain to the final goal of absorption into the Ocean of Eternity.

The whole process is from darkness to light, from chaos to order, from sin and suffering to peace and bliss, from death to immortality. The highest reward of the human soul, thrown into the vortex of life on the physical plane of sin, sorrow and suffering, is eternal bliss i.e., absorption into Godhood. Man becomes a God in his highest nature. (16.1.1952)

Discourse No. (59)
THE SOUL BECOMES FREE WHEN IT DROPS ITS SHEATHS

Man is born and he dies. A seed is sown, it grows, it ripens into a fruit or a plant and then withers away. But withering, it leaves seeds behind. When man dies, his mortal body becomes dust, but his soul is immortal. Its home is My Spirit World but it takes a physical body and comes to the physical plane to gain experience of life. It is a traveller between the Spirit World and the Physical Plane. Its travels cease only when it is perfected in the likeness of God. Essentially a spark of God, it reaches it's goal of union with God, after countless peregrinations on the earth plane in the human body.

Soul and Spirit in man are great friends. The more the soul looks upto the Spirit within and without, the more quickly it extracts itself from the embarrassing sheaths in which it is covered. It is only when all the sheaths are dropped, that the soul becomes free and gains its emancipation.

Life purpose is emancipation of the soul, which can be attained only through the pathway of the spirit. It is only when spirit triumphs over matter that the goal is reached and man gains his rightful place in the universe. It is man's being – how he lives and thinks, that matters. Let him live in spirit, thinking of God – the absolute Spirit pervading through the universe and he will reach the final destination quicker and with ease. (20.1.1953)

Discourse No. (60)
BECOME GOD – MAN TO UNDERSTAND THE MYSTERIES OF LIFE

To know God is the purpose of life. Man is generally satisfied with the objects of the senses and he does not care to probe into the mysteries of life. He thinks what is visible is real and plans the scheme of his life on the pattern of visible forces only. Such planning is feeble for what is real is not what is visible but what is not visible. God is the mightiest of the invisible forces and man must break the rampart of invisibility by devoting himself whole-heartedly to God. Complete devotion to God is a key to the inner realms of secrecy. He must become a God-man if he wishes to touch the fringe of the veil that hides the inner workings of the universe.

All those who are God-men and intoxicated in God are loved by God. He takes them into the inner chamber and reveals Himself to them in all His glory and splendour. (22.1.1953)

Discourse No. (61)
DIFFERENT PATHS TO GOD-REALIZATION, KARMA BHAKTI AND GNAN, BUT DEVOTION TO GOD IS NECESSARY IN ALL SYSTEMS OF YOGA

There are various paths to reach the summit of God realization. Each path has its own peculiarity. The path of devotion, bhakti, is the most vital. Devotion to God is the essential framework of every structure leading to Godhood. A karma-yogi is a bhakta, though a bhakta, may not necessarily be karma-yogi. Similarly a gnani is a bhakta, but a bhakta is not necessarily a gnani.

In the evolution of the soul, though there are different paths indicated, it is necessary to combine the elements of all the three paths to make one's progress quicker and more certain. Be a karma yogi, a gnani or a bhakta, laying stress on such qualities in you as make you bend more towards any one of the three paths. If your heart surges with divine emotion all the time, be a bhakta, the first and the last, but don't disdain or avoid the other paths, the path of duty gnana. By duty what is meant is action without expectation of any return what-so-ever. Whatever path one treads, complete thyaga. Vairagya (renunciation) is necessary. Without renunciation in the truest spirit of the word, no pilgrim soul can ever reach the goal. It is the foot-print which has to be followed by every traveller to the goal. (27.1.1953)

Discourse No. (62)
WINDOW OF INTUITION IS OPENED WHEN THE DOOR OF INTELLECT IS SHUT

Bhakti Marga is essential in all yogas to reach the goal of self-realization. Without devotion to God, all your gnana and detached action are useless. The heart must throb in tune with the infinite. The embers of the inner fire must be kept burning day and night for it is the inward urge that will take the devotee to his God. But the devotee must not be selfish. He must work for others like a true karma yogi and give the best of his energy and talent for the betterment of the world.

True knowledge is spiritual wisdom. It is not the fruit of intellect but a flow from the fountain of Eternity through the channel of intuition. When a yogi rigs himself upto God, He helps him in gaining access to the secret passages for gaining divine wisdom. His mind becomes so tuned with the Infinite Mind, that what is known as intellect ceases to function and its place is taken by a higher power. The gateway of intellect is shut and the window of intuition is opened, bringing the Yogi into direct communion with God and all the mysteries of life and universe. Such a union of man with God is God-realization. (30.1.1953)

Discourse No. (63)
SPIRITUALITY, THE ESSENCE OF INDIAN CULTURE

India is a land of spiritual men from the ancient past. She has kept up her tradition for spiritual love and she will continue to play the role of spiritual teacher to the world. Spirituality is the essence of Indian culture. The teachings of the ancient rishis and traditions pertaining the them have percolated so deeply in the mind and hearts of the Indian people, that in spite of gross materialism in which they are steeped like all other nations, their souls have survived the storms of time. They have not lost their individuality. This individuality consists in their innate spirituality.

No country has produced such great spiritual stalwarts as India. Her saints, sages and self-realised souls form a distinct feature in the history of India, both ancient and modern. She is destined to play a leading part in shaping the world on the spiritual pattern of life. (3.1.1953)

Discourse No. (64)
THE MILLENNIUM WOULD BE REACHED WHEN AS PLANNED BY GOD, MAN CONQUERS EVIL, BY THE SWORD OF RIGHTEOUSNESS

God works throughout the universe in a most meticulous and mysterious manner. His inner mysteries are so many and bewildering that they are beyond the comprehension of any entity. Man can get just a glimpse of His mysteries and even that glimpse is so staggering to him. The whole universe rotates on one law and it is the Law of vibration of Harmony and Union.

It is only on your earth plane that the opposite forces of light and darkness, virtue and sin, love and hatred, action and reaction, tide and ebb, heat and cold, good and evil are constantly struggling, each to gain supremacy but without success. The tidal wave of success would come only when man gifted with free will, vanquishes the foe of evil completely with the sword of righteousness. This ultimate triumph of man over the forces of evil, even in your dual world of love and hatred, peace and suffering, is planned by God. This is the millennium man must seek to establish, even if it takes countless years.

When man begins to understand that it is life that is important and not form, spirit, not matter, substance, not shadow, he will veer round the right path and lead himself and other into the land of Bliss. Bliss Eternal is the goal of life. (1.2.1953)

Discourse No. (65)
GOD'S DYNAMIC TOUCH

There is no religion higher than Truth and God is the only Reality. Reach the Reality through the marg (path) of Truth, even if the path be narrow and sharp, like the edge of a razor. Worship God and God alone, for He is the only Reality. He alone is worthy of worship and none else.

Make God the idol of your life. He and He alone is your Guide, Friend, Protector and Helper, as you make your journey through the dreary desert of life on the earth plane. The more you turn to Him, the more He will succour and strengthen you. Keep to God and He will free you from all earthly worries and cares. You will feel the fragrance of His presence. Make God the fulcrum of your life. Get yourself woven in Him by spreading thoughts of love and purity all around. He is around you, within you, inside you. Feel His touch and your life would be full of dynamic achievements. He is the dynamo, the great generator of electricity in you. See this divine electricity which will transform you and help you in transforming others in your scheme of beautifying the world. It is God's dynamic touch that alone can transform you and nothing else. Seek this divine fire, by your longing for God. The more you long for Him, the more you concentrate on Him, in the inner temple of your heart. He will ignite your heart, the minute you take His name on your lips and thrill you with ecstatic delight. Make God the only object of your life for He alone is the Reality, all else is Maya, and illusion, a delusion. (2.2.1953)

Discourse No. (66)
EACH ONE EVOLVES ACCORDING TO HIS KARMA

Each one evolves according to his karma. The earth plane is the most important theatre for the evolution of man's soul. The physical body is specially given to man for this purpose. He brings within birth, the seed of all good noble thoughts and emotions, to enable him to make further progress in the process of evolution. All evil thoughts and evil deeds have their repercussions but their seeds are never sown again. With each incarnation, man throws off all seeds of evil thoughts and emotions. God gives him a chance to rise higher and higher without any handicap. The memory of good thought and noble emotions is enshrined in his soul as he takes a new birth but that of evil thoughts and negative emotions is completely effaced.

Suffering in physical life is the direct result of man's own bad Karma in the past incarnations. The suffering is meant for the purging of the soul of the sins of man. It continues till man becomes perfect and even after the attainment of perfection, it continues for the attainment of still higher objects in God's universe. It is for this reason why saints and sages, after attaining their emancipation, are subjected to physical suffering.

The law of Karma is the most vital pivot on which man's salvation depends. Each one seeks his own way, as it suits him to evolve. It may take him a few incarnations or a countless numbers of births to attain perfection. He reaches the top of the ladder of perfection in short or long time, according to his will. Karma and free will are the two concomitant parts in man's struggle for ascendancy towards perfection and eventual emancipation in the process of evolution. The more he surrenders to the will of God, the quicker he reaches the goal. Complete self-surrender to God is the key to man's evolution. (3.2.1953)

Discourse No. (67)
THE HEART, THE TRUE TEMPLE FOR DEVOTION TO GOD

Men worship God in churches and temples, mosques and synagogues. Religion is a matter of the heart and each one wishes to worship according to his own way. Each thinks his own religion to be the best. This is a natural sentiment but when it goes beyond proper bounds, it ceases to be a virtue. No religion teaches antagonism to another religion. The very basis of religion is toleration and goodwill and if this is destroyed, religion deteriorates into mere fanaticism – destruction of all that is fundamental in religion.

Worship in churches is good. It is again a natural and easier way of inspiring the man's mind into God worship. People give their best in such form of external worship for it appeals to them. But in reality such external worship is not on par with the worship which a man offers in the temple of his own heart. The heart is the true temple for devotion to God. Whether one worships externally or internally, what pleases God is the sincerity of devotion in its utterance and not mere display of it in a church or cathedral. Sincerity is the touchstone of devotion and this sincerity emanates more when he remembers God in the seclusion of his own heart and not in mass gathering and shows.

Worship God therefore in the temple of your heart with real fervour and devotion. It constitutes the true purpose of religion. It is this flame rising from your heart that will make you beloved of God and men. (4.2.1953)

Discourse No. (68)
GOD'S TRUTHS LIE HIDDEN

What is fair and beautiful often turns out to be ugly and unpleasant. Similarly what is distasteful and difficult proves in the end to be most pleasant and easy. A bitter pill cures a disease. A honeyed word of a flattery is winged with shafts of poison. Bodily enjoyment end in disease and suffering. Abstinence gives joy and health.

To find God who is shrouded in mysteries, the veil of ignorance has to be removed. Knowledge is power; wisdom is the key to the solution of human suffering. Seek that which is hidden from your physical eyes. Dive deep into the inner recesses of your physical eyes. Dive deep into the inner recesses of your heart to get a glimpse of true light. What is visible is not true. What is invisible is real. It is through the pathway of purity, austerity, control of the mind, sacrifice and suffering, that the light pure wisdom is attained. To scatter the clouds that hide the reality, your watchword should be "More light, more Light," and you will disperse the clouds of ignorance, to reach the sun of Glory. Seek God in the inner recesses of the heart and not in external worship. Seek that which is internal and not be satisfied with mere external trappings. Gems of pure ray serene are hidden in the caves of ocean deep. They do not lie uncovered on the beach shore. God's truths are like the hidden gems of pearls. They have to be discovered and possessed by diving deep into the waters of life's experiences. Seek God and God alone and no earthy treasure, which will fade away. God alone is the source of Eternal Bliss. (6.2.1953)

Discourse No. (69)
EACH ATOM, A VIBRATORY FORCE, SEEKING UNION WITH GOD

Nothing is at rest in the universe, Even the tiniest speck of dust, though it seems to be at rest, is in motion. Each atom of substance is not matter. It is in reality a force, a vibratory force which seeks its unison with other mighty forces working in the universe. All these forces are of invisible nature. Each plays its role according to the degree of utility and power vested in it by God. From the speck of dust on the ground to the highest solar system in the universe, the Law of vibration is no interlaced, that everything works in perfect harmony and unison. All evil eventually must extinguish itself. Such is God's plan. The evil on earth is a tremendous force of destruction. This has its continuation in the other planes. The forces of good and evil are so intertwined in man, when he is in the physical world, that to grapple with evil and free himself from its clutches becomes his essential duty. If he fails in it, the process of evolution continues both in the physical world and in the invisible worlds, till rid of all the gross, the soul of man triumphantly marches onward to be merged in the great Law of Harmony-Universal Harmony, Peace and Bliss in Eternity. (8.2.1953)

Discourse No. (70)
SPIRIT IS RICHNESS OF THE SOUL, IT ALONE SURVIVES

Christ said that he who gains the whole world but loses his soul, loses everything but he who loses the world but keeps his soul gains all. This Christian dictum illustrates the most fundamental spiritual truth that spirit survives in all cases and not matter. Matter is the most unspiritual side of spirit. It is not substance but shadow, if we judge it from the higher point of understanding. To run after shadows is foolish. Just as all that glitters is not gold, things which give mere temporary satisfaction are not worth following. Name and fame, wealth or riches, glory or power these are obstruction in the path of spirit. All forms are veils of ignorance. They are external trappings of no worth.

God is spirit. Truth is spirit. Realization of the Highest Truth in Nature is the objective of the life of spirit. Spirit is the richness of the soul. It is light eternal, joy, divine peace infinite. Live for spirit. Die for spirit, Truth, God, Eternal Bliss, Infinite peace, these are all interwoven and interlaced. Spirit is the fire of the soul. Matter is gross. Burn matter with the fire of the soul and you will become spirit in unison with the highest and the best in you and in the universe. (9.2.1953)

Discourse No. (71)
ALL THINGS CHANGE IN THE UNIVERSE EXCEPT GOD

There is a continuous change in the universe. The sun rises in the morning bringing day light and sets in the evening causing darkness of the night. The crescent becomes the full moon and the full moon again becomes a crescent and then fades away for some time. Seasons change. Spring and Summer, Autumn and Winter, heat and vice-versa. Seeds grow into plants and plants give flowers and fruit and then decay. Man is born and he dies and he is re-born and this cycle of birth and death continues on the earth plane.

All things change in the universe, except, God. God alone is causeless and changeless. He creates changes, but Himself is unchanged. He causes tremendous cataclysms in Nature, but Himself is Motionless. The Absoluteness of God is beyond human comprehension. He is the seed and essence of all creation, both manifest and unmanifest.

He is the Absolute spirit pervading throughout the universe. He is personal and impersonal. He is transcendent. He is immanent. He is within every substance in the universe; He is beyond the universe, He is the soul of all souls. He is the light of all lights. To know Him is to know everything in the universe. To love Him in the purity of heart is the only way to know Him. To know Him is to gain Eternal Peace and Bliss. (10.2.1953)

Discourse No. (72)
NO REAL PEACE, UNLESS MAN VENTURES TO TREAD THE RUGGED PATH AND REACHES THE PEAK OF GOD-RELATION

It is wrong to say that God-realization is a mere building of a castle in the air. It is not at all an impossible feat, as commonly considered. It is extremely difficult no doubt, but at the same time, it is within the compass of man if he is earnest in his quest and absolutely pure in his heart. What is wanted is purity of heart in the first instance coupled with sincerity of purpose and a dogged mind that would not be defeated by opposition and obstacles. What id dry, difficult, dreary and dangerous in the beginning becomes smooth, serene, sweet and successful in the end. It is only when the job is done that the workman feels at rest. There can be no real peace or rest for any human being, unless and until, he braves the rugged path, narrow and horny and deary as it may be and reaches the end. It is a path that goes winding round the mountain overhanging a deep ravine leading to the summit. There are millions in the valley struggling for breath and life but without success. It is only the brave, who leave the valley and take the precipitous path, climb the mountain and reach the summit.

God is SAT CHIT ANANDA Absolute Existence, Consciousness, Bliss. Reach the summit and get absorbed in Eternal Bliss, which is the real goal of life and nothing else. (13.2.1953)

Discourse No. (73)
MAN'S INTELLECT HOWEVER POWERFUL IS OF NO AVAIL IN PERCEIVING THE OVER SOUL

The scientist makes use of his instruments, invented by him for the furtherance of his scientific knowledge, The astronomer gazes at the stars-studded sky through his huge telescope and watches the movements of the stars, planets and other celestial bodies for the purpose of his varied calculations.

Man's intellect plays a dominant part in his achievements on the earth plane. But this intellect is a tiny weapon. In fact, it is no weapon at all in furtherance of Truth. Truth is beyond human understanding, beyond human conception. This truth is God. The astronomer may calculate distance of the stars and planets by means of his instruments. But he will not be able to discover the movements of God within him. For this, he needs a higher instrument – the instrument of a higher faculty – the faculty of intuition, which is beyond human intellect. Physical perception of the universe is deceitful. All forms are false. What is visible is not true. To dive into the Reality, which as Absolute Existence, Consciousness, Bliss-one has to renounce his all in all and give himself up to one thought, one longing, one yearning, one goal in life viz., perfection of his soul to perceive the Over Soul – the Absolute pervading the universe. The subjective-objective intellect has to give way to the higher consciousness and complete egoless non-relativity and non-separateness. Till this state is reached, no one can understand God or realise His infiniteness. God exists. His existence is absolute. He is not to be found. He is there already. See Him with the eye of the spirit within, feel Him with the throb of your heart, slay the mind of its eco-consciousness and then realization of God would follow in the twinkle of an eye. Not through forms and sense and mind-but through your own consciousness which is innate in you, you would realise God-the greatest mystery in the universe and the greatest radiator of joy-consciousness. (14.2.1953)

Discourse No. (74)
SPIRITUAL KNOWLEDGE NOT THE CRITERION OF MAN'S ACCESSIBILITY TO GOD BUT HIS OWN SINCERITY AND SPIRITUALITY

You know what is said in the Bible: "Many are called but few are chosen." So many aspire for Truth-some out of arrogance think that heir deep learning and scholarship would be rewarded by the descent of His grace on them. It is a mistaken notion that a devotee's depth of spiritual knowledge is criterion of his accessibility to God. God is not concerned with the devotee's mental qualities. What God wants is purity of heart and not the quantum of intellectuality. It is sincerity, earnestness, purity, self-abnegation, sacrifice and utter devotion to God, that act as a magnet in drawing a person nearer to God. God-realization is the product of man's endeavour through his heart and not his head. A man may be utterly innocent and ignorant of everything but such complete self-abnegation succeeds in attaining God's grace and love. It is not mental gymnastics that is the passport to God-realization but the depth of human emotions, coloured and dyed with the sacred hue of the heart's devotion to God.

Love rules the world. Love rules the whole universe. It is the cradle and citadel of life transcendental and eternal. God is Love. Love God with all the depth of your heart and divinity would flow in you like a rushing torrent. Love all without restraint, without effort, spontaneously, whole-heartedly, in the true spirit of love without expectation of any return of love or kindness. Love all, but above all, love God the most, as God is All and All is in God. (15.2.1953)

Discourse No. (75)
THE OCCULT SCIENCE

Every religion has its hidden side, which is known as occult science, meant for those who are advanced in spiritual knowledge and are intent upon God-realization. Christ used to speak in parables to the masses, but to those of his immediate followers, he initiated them in the mysteries of life. What is hidden is real and in order to understand the hidden side of life, great strength of character and utter disregard for the God are a *Sine-Qua-Non.* To lose all is to gain all, said Christ. This is too true. In your infatuation for God, you should be prepared to give up everything in the true spirit of renunciation. It is only then that you can mount the step leading to the Inner Region of God's working in the universe. (16.2.1953)

Discourse No. (76)
WHAT IS VITAL IS SPIRIT

Just as gold when melted in fire is purged of its dross and becomes pure, man has to go through the crucible of fiery experiences to cleanse his mind and soul of all the dross with which they are covered. The greater the trials, the greater the suffering, the quicker is the process of emancipation. Trial and suffering have and intrinsic value, and as such, should be considered a necessary item in the process of the unfoldment of man's inner forces.

What is vital is spirit, not matter. Whatever conduces to the betterment of the spirit, whether it be pleasant or unpleasant, joyous or dreadful, peaceful or otherwise, has to be welcomed and not shunned.

God alone is Absolute. To attain that state of perfection which is the goal of life, man encounters all hurdles of opposition, which are the outcome of man's finite thinking. It is because man's intellect is finite, he is unable to perceive the Absolute, which is infinite and Eternal.

Intellect is a barrier to entry into the Higher Region of existence. But when the soul is purged of its dross, man loses the charm of external life. The objects of the senses and the mind cease to have their hold on him. His soul aspires to leap from the bondage of relativity into spaceless, timeless expanse of all glory, light, eternal bliss and quietude transcendental, supramental and suprarational. The ego-consciousness is merged into effulgence of the transcendental Self. It is thus the Spirit triumphs over matter and in the triumph of the spirit, in its onward march towards the goal of self effulgence, all opposing forces melt away like mist in the rising sun. (17.2.1953)

Discourse No. (77)
THE ESSENCE OF EVERYTHING IS GOD

Man is a microcosm and the universe is a macrocosm. Every man carries with him a blueprint of the whole universe. He becomes aware of the secrets of the universe as soon as he begins to worship Him. He dwells within the cave of his heart. God is not a commodity that has to be searched and acquired. He exists everywhere. He is latent, no doubt, but not latent to one who aspires for Him in the true spirit of devotion and longing. To know God is to realize God and not to acquire God. God-realization is an evolutionary process. By discarding forms and the objects of the senses and the mind, by giving up all ideas of relativity, by diving deep into the essence of everything rejecting all labels, outward forms and trappings, the Absolute is realized. The essence of everything is God. When man realizes this great Truth, he becomes a sage, a God- realized man.

When God was thanked for these beautiful discourses which were given to me in the altar room, He gave the following illuminating message:

"Do you know that these discourses are a reflection of what you have been able to grasp yourself. I have only helped you in putting them in proper form and style. They are not only an expression of your grasp of the whole.

Chapter Twenty-Eight

The End of the Quest (1953-54)

I was told in Sai Baba's message of February 19, 1953 that I had found God. He had said:

> "What is wanted is the knowledge of God, the consciousness of the Existence of God and the Bliss that is Eternal. When a man attains that knowledge of God, that he exists perennially within and without and transcends all thoughts of relativity being Absolute and is a source of Eternal Bliss, he is said to have realized God."

That I had realized God was certain. The training given to me was not a merely paper training. It was vital in transforming me and the object having been attained, this book, in the ordinary course of events, should have been concluded. But God had the ulterior object of utilizing me as a channel for the propagation of a high mission, which required further training of a far more intensified form.

The seeds of a new aspiration were sown in my mind. The quest having come to an end, I was prepared to serve as God willed. I was seeing God all the time but it was invisibly and unconsciously. I was told: "So far as you are concerned, it makes no difference whether I show Myself to you in visual form or not. You have to reveal Myself to you in visual form for the purpose of the mission."

On March 15, 1953, when I was meditating in the early hours of the morning, I felt in *samadhi* and I thought I had seen a vision. I was corrected when Sai Baba gave me the following description of the bewildering experience that I had had. He said:

> "It was not a vision you saw today in the morning but a pattern of glowing lights, so woven that it appeared to you like a written book which you tried to read and which you succeeded in reading too, but without remembering a word of it. The glorious pattern of lights you saw was the result of your inward sight. You are now able to see with your inner eye. It is a beginning and a most glorious beginning of My revelation to you
>
> "Remember it was not a vision, not a dream, not a hallucination, but a rigid fact of your inner sight working. Had I not forced your inner sight to close down, you would have enjoyed the sights and lights of My Spirit World for a longer time. It is because I am God, I forced your inner eye to close down, after allowing you a glimpse of My Spirit World. You imagined by the splendour that it was the occasion of your nuptials. Just as there are lights in your world on festive occasions of marriage etc., you imagined the lights, you saw, as if they were ordered for your marriage occasion. It was your marriage no doubt, but not a marriage in the corporeal sense. The lights you saw and the dream you had, have a deep mystical meaning. I put the notion of marriage in your mind at the time you saw those brilliant lights to teach you that you were able to see the lights, because of the accomplishment of the great feat of the marriage of your soul with the spirit *i.e.*, your union with God."

On March 19, 1953, Sai Baba gave me the following message:

> "I have to make use of you as an instrument for enlightening your world about the working of the secret laws in the cosmos and this work of yours will start as soon as you get My visual revelation."

On April 9, 1953, Ram Ram gave me the following startling news:

> "I have come to tell you the most amazing thing, Sai Baba the Fakir is soon to take his birth. Before this actually happens, either

> God's Revelation must take place or that you will have to give up concentration entirely on Sai Baba's picture, as you are doing now. I shall be your guide and will tell you what to do. There is a deep meaning in this message that I have given to you. Before Sai Baba, the Fakir takes new birth in your earth plane, Sai Baba the real God must come to you and greet you face to face. Wait, I am calling Sai Baba, the Fakir, to give you his message. He can't give it to you direct, as you have been exclusively reserved for God and we Masters, selected to talk to you. He will therefore speak to you through me. Just listen to him."

I listened to Sai Baba, the Fakir (not God) as desired and the latter gave me the following message:

> "Yes, I am Sai Baba, the real Sai Baba, and not Sai Baba whom you invoke as God. I have come to tell you that I have offered myself to take birth again in your earth plane. Kindly inform my friends and admirers, not to invoke me for I shall not respond any more. I do not know exactly when I shall be given permission to leave this Spiritual Plane for earthly life. I am only waiting for final orders."

On April 10, 1953, I was told that I would be made to write books on occult science. Sai Baba said: "These books on occult science will cause a stir in your world and this is the chief plank in your mission. You will draw inspiration direct from Me."

On April 13, 1953, I was informed that I was a *Jivan Mukta* in reality. Sai Baba said to me:

> "Do you know that you are no longer a *Jivan Mukta* in embryo, nor in the making. You are a *Jivan Mukta* in the true sense of the word even now, but I have withheld from you the consciousness of your having achieved this highest state of spirituality. By forestalling you from the attainment of your crown, I am proving to you that I, Sai Baba, am none else than God. For there is no force in the universe that can stop you from becoming an Adept."

On April 19, 1953, I was given a very thrilling message:

> "You have still not the least or even the remotest idea of what is going to take place. When you see Me, you will feel that you have lost your body and are moving in the air. Your vision will change.

Your life would change. Your very breath well change. The 1-ness' will completely disappear and you would live and think in terms of cosmic unity. You will hear cosmic music all the time. You will feel a new keenness of spirit in you, a readiness to work for all and universal love. You should rejoice that you are going to witness such a new panorama of life full of vim, vigour and vivacity."

On May 13 1953, I was told to give up concentration on Sai Baba's picture and to concentrate on God without form.

On May 15, 1953, Sai Baba said:

"My revelation will be a source of great strength to you but your mission is such as will entail upon you a great sacrifice requiring expenditure of inexhaustible energy. What I give to you in abundance, you will have to give away in equal abundance for the success of your mission.

"What God gives to you is not yours but for the whole of His creation and you will have to keep this in mind all the time that nothing is yours. Your life, your breath, your energy, your talents and power are meant to be given away for the furtherance of God's Law of Love and Harmony in the realm of human evolution."

On June 4, 1953, I was ordered to removes the photograph of Sai Baba the Fakir from the altar room and meditate on God as Absolute Spirit pervading the universe, keeping the mind blank. Sai Baba the Fakir had taken birth on this day on the earth plane.

God said to me:

"Sai Baba the Fakir has taken birth on the earth plane. Kindly inform Doraswami immediately. It is an event of far-reaching importance in your life also. It means you have no longer to think of Me with a form. Think and mediate on Me as if I were formless. You are now advanced from form to formlessness."

Having risen from the worship of God with form to God, the formless, my invocation was now to Ahura Mazda direct. His first message as Ahura Mazda, June 5, 1953, as given below is so very thrilling:

"Yes, I am Ahura Mazda speaking to you through the infiniteness of My limitless universe. You will be able to hear Me even from

> immeasurable distance, as you have been specially trained and your ears attuned to the vibrations of My universe.
>
> "I shall not come to your altar room for you can now be with Me and hear Me even when I am furthermost from you. You have broken to pieces the delusion of space. You are now living in My universe where there is no such thing as Time or Space. Think that you are a spirit, atma, soul, conversant with the Absolute, Infinite Spirit. Work in that spirit for the final achievement of My Revelation to you, which is imminent."

The same day Ahura Mazda said to me: "I want you to know that when I reveal Myself to you for the first time, I shall assume to form of Sai Baba the Fakir but it will be just for the first time and not thereafter."

In fulfillment of this promise, Ahura Mazda came to me in a vision, taking the form of Sai Baba the Fakir.

On June 14, 1953, I was given a very illuminating message by Ahura Mazda on the three stages of evolution, viz., cmergence from individuality, the state of cosmic universality and the last, the transcendence of God the Absolute Spirit.

He said:

> "I am training you for this last state when your soul would be absolutely immersed in My spirit. I have universalized your individuality and have prepared you to emerge from cosmic unity to that which is higher viz., the transcendentalism of the Absolute Spirit. This will be effected as soon as you get My Revelation. It will bring a dynamic transformation in you for carrying out a mission of a most subtle and transcendental nature."

The following day, I asked Ahura Mazda in what way He would reveal Himself to me and He gave me the following reply:

> "When I come to you, you would know by the throb of your heart and the intense feeling of joy that would overpower you. I have raised you to such an extent that you are now in communion with God within you and you do not need any God outside you. This message that you are writing is from the God outside you. The self within you is unfolded and it is now in union with the Absolute Spirit pervading throughout the universe. You are thus in

communion with God without and God within......My Revelation will be preceded by a subtle demonstration of certain celestial movements such as a torrent of light, that would flood you in a mysterious and awe-inspiring manner."

Ram Ram gave the following description of how God's Revelation would take place:

"God will not show Himself to you in any visual form, as you expect, for the simple reason that that stage is now past. Nevertheless, you would see Him in a halo of tremendous light. It is a light which will create in you feeling of both awe and joy. This light you would see, before God actually appears to you. When He really appears, you would feel Him and will know Him by your heart, mind and soul, but you won't see Him as you see anybody on your earth plane. God is Spirit. It is His light that you would see and nothing else. He won't take any human form as you expect. The earlier messages in this connection should be forgotten. These contradictions may appear as baffling to you but when God's Revelation actually takes place, you would understand everything clearly as daylight.

"Kindly note that the day of God's Revelation is drawing close. Homi and Doraswami should be told to be in readiness. Your book, 'How I Found God' would be completed in a strange and most mystic manner when Revelation takes place. This revelation is a dead fact. You would be getting stunning news, both pleasant and unpleasant, before Revelation actually takes place.

"Your life is extremely short. You would breathe your last in a few days after God's Revelation. Your mission is God's Revelation and the story of His Revelation to you as adumbrated in your book."

A few days later *i.e.*, on August 2, 1953, Ram Ram again gave me a very illuminating message on the same subject. He said:

"You would see God in the sense that you would witness strange things, strange surroundings, strange feelings, strange sounds, strange atmosphere, strange elements fluttering round you, breathing in you joy and ecstasy. You are beginning to feel this joy today but in the most fractional quantity. This will go on increasing, as you keep your heart and soul engrossed in God.......Your world is your God."

On August 9, 1953, Ahura Mazda gave me the following message, explaining all about *samadhi* and the stage reached by me:

"*Samadhi* is a state of superconsciousness. The gift of superconsciousness you have already attained. This fact alone constitutes and is a convincing proof of your having realised God. No one can go into samadhi, if he has not realised God. Saints and sages generally reach this stage of samadhi and are quite content with it. In your case, I want you to go beyond the state of ordinary samadhi and it is therefore I have been postponing the final goal of your life."

"*Samadhi* is not everything. It is superconscious state no doubt, but a superconsciousness of a low order. You have to rise to the highest grade of superconsciousness and I am preparing you for that. When My preparations are completed, you will simply be dazed and stunned."

Besides Ahura Mazda, I was being given messages by various Prophets and Masters and the question was raised that as they were merged in God, how could they give messages in their individual capacities.

Ahura Mazda replied as under:

"You have raised a vital question. Even you are immersed in Me and yet you are separate and have still a physical body, which the Masters have not. The prophets mentioned by you are all immersed in Me but because of this very immersion, they have the unusual power of taking their separate identities, whenever they choose. They are in Me: they are outside Me. They are no longer prophets only. They are all God but they can appear in their original forms to any human being, if they wish it. Their separate existence is real in the sense that they can tear themselves from Me, whenever they want. When they tear themselves from Me, they loose their Omnipotence. But their loss is only temporary. They then become Masters, having separate individual existence but always with the right of immersion in Me, whenever I will and whenever they wish. It is very difficult to comprehend its working, but when you come over here after leaving your body permanently, you will be given the first lessons in the spiritual laws that operate in My world and as you grow in spiritual stature, which will take ages, you will rise higher and higher, till you reach the stage of a Christ, a Buddha, a Krishna, a Zoroaster, a Mohammad and so on. This state of evolution is marked for any human soul."

On August 29, 1953, Ahura Mazda gave me an insight into the type of training He was giving me in meditation for mystical experiences. He said:

"You have today consciousness which is of the invisible type. The consciousness that I am going to give you will enable you to see My Spiritual Plane with your physical eyes, as if you are sitting in a cinema show and seeing the pictures reflected on the screen. This consciousness is called superconsciousness. In fact, I would call it ultra-superconsciousness for it exceeds even the usual superconsciousness which you experience when you go into *samadhi.*"

On September 5, 1953, I was again given a message by Ahura Mazda on His Revelation:

"You will be startled to see yourself launched in a new world of extraordinary blaze of light and splendour. You will see light all around you, in front of you, and behind you. You will see yourself swimming in a flood of light and yet that light will not touch you or harm you. It is a mysterious force which in its luminosity will appear to you as fire and it is this force, when it encircles you, that will bring in you mysterious powers to help you in your mission. This fire which will encircle you is the SPIRIT of GOD. You will see in Me a reflection of your own spirit which is dwelling in you, but which is making preparation at the same time to leave your body permanently, taking with it your soul which does not need any longer a physical body for its perfection. See how slowly but mysteriously I am preparing you for your destiny, both on your earth plane as well as for the role you will have to play in My Spiritual Plane when you leave your physical body permanently."

On September 7, 1953, Ahura Mazda gave me a very illuminating message on healing, of two types, spiritual and divine.

This is what he said:

"There are two kinds of healing, spiritual and divine. Common is spiritual healing and the most uncommon and unique is divine healing. Your Master Ram Ram has been given by God the special boon of healing. Any one who invokes Ram Ram and concentrates on his picture can get in contact with him and derive the benefit of spiritual healing. In most cases healing mediums are necessary. They are the links between healing spirits and humans. This is the ordinary and most commonly practised method in vogue.

"But besides spiritual healing, as I have said, there is divine healing. If a man reaches a state of perfection and gets in communion with God, he can draw from the Fountain Source, divine healing powers to heal himself as well as others. I am training you specially to reach this state of consciousness, when you shall become a divine healer and not a mere spiritual healer that you are now....... Christ was a healer of the most unique type. Why? Because he was in direct communion with God, the Healer of the universe. Christ's healing affords the example of the rarest type of divine healing."

The same day, Ram Ram also gave a message on healing. He said:

"I want to tell you that God is specially training you to become a great healer. The more you meditate, the more powers both of healing the body and soul, will He confer upon you. This is the special mission for which He has extended your life."

I said to Ram Ram:

"But some time ago, you gave me the message that my mission is to write the book "How I Found God" and that when it is finished, I would be called away. Is it not so?"

He replied:

"Yes, certainly, What I said is true and what I now say is also true. You would be made a healer of the divine pattern as soon as God's Revelation comes to you further, as soon as you have finished your book and have shown to the world your power to cure even incurable cases, you will be called away. The mission is your book. The healing powers are a proof to convince the world of your divinity."

The following day Ahura Mazda gave the following message:

> "It is not mere *samadhi* that can lead to Revelation. There are saints and mystics in your world who go into *samadhi* for very long hours and even for days and yet I have not revealed Myself to them. Do you now understand the significance of the role you have to play and the divine training that you are getting for that purpose? Yours is a unique case and you should feel extremely happy that you have been selected for My special purpose."

I was convinced of two things: (1) That I was in direct communion with God. I was given countless proofs of this fact. (2) That I had a glimpse of God and the Spiritual Plane and that I must wait patiently for the last stage in the drama of full and final Revelation of God in a concrete manner.

On September 25, 1953, Ahura Mazda speaking on the importance of Faith gave the following thrilling message:

> "It is with the armour of your FAITH that you are going to fight successfully, overcome all barriers and break open the citadel of My hidden mysteries. Have faith in Me. You are touching the hem of My robe, every hour and every minute. You do not know it for I have purposely benumbed your consciousness in order to still further strengthen your inner powers, till at last I come to you in trailing clouds of BEAUTY, SPLENDOUR and LIGHT. You are with Me: you are in Me. You are travelling all along with Me. You are seeing Me, hearing Me, understanding Me and following Me. But you have still not attained the full consciousness of My BEING. This divine sight also shall I give to you, as soon as your inner powers are perfected. In fact, your inner eye is open. It can function. But your mission is of such an order that divine perfection of a much higher type is needed before I can permit the use of your inner eye. If you reach this perfection within the time I have fixed for My Revelation, you shall see Me in all My glory and splendour. I cannot allow you any further extension of time and if you fail in this last attempt to see Me, I shall have to call you away for any further extension of your life will have no purpose."

On November 23, 1953, Ahura Mazda gave me the following message:

"Revelation, mission, death – these are the three stages of your life and each stage is most important, each leading to another viz., Revelation to mission, the mission to death and death to the ultimate reality viz., immortality.

"These three stages rarely occur in a man's span of life in the order mentioned though death is destined for everyone, man being mortal. God does not Reveal himself to any one, unless He has a specific purpose in doing so. You have been chosen for My Revelation as I want to make use of you for spreading new ideas and for the inauguration of a new era for the betterment of your world."

I was tired to waiting for God's visual revelation. In spite of assurances by Ahura Mazda that this happy event would soon take place, nothing happened.

On December 19, 1953, Ahura Mazda gave the following message. Was it to soothe my tired nerves and jaded mind?

"I tell you over and over again that you have earned My Revelation. Think that you have got it. Think that God is with you, every minute of your life. He may still be invisible to your physical eye, but He is abiding in you, talking to you, guiding you, inspiring you and filling your heart, mind and soul with the glow and warmth of His richest love. Your soul is free. You have won the freedom of the soul, which is the clearest indication of the peak of spirituality reached by you."

Doubts still assailed me. Even after long training and the rich experiences gained, I could not reconcile myself to the fact that I had won God's grace so as to be worthy of His revelation. When I was in this mood of hesitancy and doubt, Ahura Mazda gave me the following message:

"You are such a simpleton that even after such a long training and with such beautiful messages you still think that you are just a common man. It is this perfect simplicity of your mind, in spite of the rapid advancements that you have made in realm of the spirit, that is attracting us all the more. I assure you I shall give you the divine sight to see Me and the Masters and My Spiritual Plane."

From December 25, 1953, I started composing poems as ordered by Ahura Mazda. These were published by the Spiritual Healing Centre in 1954 under the title of *"Esoteric Poems Of Devotion."* The title was given to me by Ahura Mazda Himself.

A copy of the brochure containing Meher Baba's declaration that he was the Highest of the High was placed at the altar on December 28, 1953 and Ahura Mazda gave His comments as under:

> "Each man is God, but he is not conscious of it. The minute he gets this consciousness, he realizes the Truth. Meher Baba has realized this truth and therefore he declares himself as the Highest of the High. But he forgets that what he has discerned is not his sole monopoly. There are hundreds and thousands like Meher Baba who have realized the Self but they don't declare it in the manner of Meher Baba. Even Christ, when he was sent by Me on a special mission, said: "I and my Father are One." He never said: "I am the Highest of the High." He is courting disaster if he continues in this manner.
>
> "When I reveal Myself to you, I shall make you an instrument, a channel for the betterment of the world and not for claiming that you are an Avatar of God. This is irreligious; it is blasphemous. You will play the role of a messenger of God, for that is the purpose of the long training that I have given to you. Be prepared to play your part. I shall give you powers which would enable you to carry out your mission even against opposition quite successfully. It will be an eye-opener to your world, how and ordinary soul, by means of its own sacrifices and self-denials and by leading a life of perfect purity can reach the highest state of spirituality and spread the knowledge of God for the betterment and happiness of all mankind. Happiness lies only in spirituality. It can be attained by only one means and that is by following the Divine Law of Righteousness and Renunciation in love of God and all humanity and creatures of the lower kingdom."

On January 1, 1954, Ahura Mazda again gave me a very descriptive message as to how He would reveal Himself to me. He said:

"I shall take no form whatsoever and yet you will clearly and visibly see Me, formless as I am. Light would precede Me and then you will see Me as certain as you write down My messages. Do you hear Me when you write and yet you write? Your pen moves, as if you are hearing Me with your physical ears. But really your physical ears have nothing to do with this hearing. This hearing is spiritual. In the same manner, you will see Me Spiritually."

I had an ailing body. It was but natural that in *samadhi*, when my soul left the physical body and sojourned in the Spiritual Plane, it was reluctant to come back to its physical tenement. It came back only when God forced it to do so and not of its own accord. The following message of January 17, 1954, gives an idea of God training the soul for the mission:

"You were practically in *samadhi* throughout your meditation. As soon as I remove My restriction, your soul goes into *samadhi*. When I want it to return to your body, I have to order it and it obeys Me. If I don't interfere, your soul would like to remain in My Spirit World and not return to your body. This is natural for My Spirit World is akin to your soul's liking and not your physical body. Any how, I have sufficiently trained it to like your body also for the purpose of carrying out My mission and as soon as I know that your soul is willing to do so, I shall reveal Myself to you. I must have your soul's willingness to serve in physical body."

In the course of silence that was imposed on me for seven days from 15.1.54 to 23.1.54, Ahura Mazda gave the following message:

"Your soul has gained its consciousness. In a word, you have realized the Self and your God, your soul is fully aware of Me, your God, but this awareness, it has not been able to translate into physical consciousness.

"Your position today is like that of an ordinary saint and seer. You can go into *samadhi*. You have certain powers which have begun to function and which will function to the fullest extent very soon. But the last stage of super-consciousness of the soul, reflecting its light to the physical senses and thus making you conscious of things invisible, is still to be reached. When you reach this state, you become a God in human body – a state seldom reached by a human soul. It is fallen to your lot to become supra-divine in a human body."

On January 17, 1954, a most thrilling message of an elaborate nature was given. I am quoting it in extenso, as it is so important:

"I had told you in the beginning that I would come to you in the form of Sai Baba. You were at that time fit to see Me in a human form. Having made considerable progress since then, I have chosen you now for the highest type of Revelation and that is to became cognisant of God in at impersonal manner. Such type of God realization is a very rare phenomenon. I want to bring about a spiritual renaissance in your world and you shall be one of the great prophets for the purpose followed by many others. You will not at all be recognized as such in the beginning. Your friends and relations would oppose you and start a campaign of vilification. But this vilification will not cut ice and you will go marching on from triumph to triumph, till at last you will find the world at your feet.

"Don't think I am giving this rosy picture for the purpose of flattering you or testing your egotism. It is a plain narration of what is in store for you after My Revelation to you. This Revelation might take place during the course of your silence or a little later."

On January 22, 1954: I was given by Ahura Mazda a most exhilarating account of how progress was infinite in His Spirit World:

"Do you know what preparations are going on for your further enlightenment after My Revelation to you? Revelation is not everything. In your Spirit World, Spirits continuously progress even when they have passed the highest peak of progress. The progress continues for the simple reason that it is infinite. There is no end to it. In the cosmic universe, there are waves and waves, tiers and tiers, rising one above the other, ever progressing, never receding. The work of Evolution never stops. The wheel is continuously in motion. It moves on and on without a halt. Such is the Law of Progression. Evolution call it what you like. I am infinite in My power, unlimited is My Kingdom and when the goal is immersion in Me, progress becomes unending."

On January 24, 1954, Ahura Mazda gave me an account of the progress made in my last two incarnations and the stage reached in my present life. He said:

"You will be quite surprized to know that in one of your last incarnations, you had reached a state of perfection which indicated that you would become a *Jivan Mukta.* But you did not actually reach that stage. In the last incarnation your evolution continued but again the objective was not secured. In the present life, owing to earlier experiences, it was thought that you would not be able to reach the highest decree of spirituality. But your determination to reach the goal was so pedominant that we had to give you opportunities to rise to the highest state you aspired for and achieved. In the ordinary course. You would have been called away as life's purpose had been fulfilled viz., that your soul had attained its liberation and there was no more round of birth and death for you. It was just when you reached the state of *nirvana* that I took you under My direct control from the hands of your Master Ram Ram. I started giving you all sorts of experiences and subjected you to testes one after another. When you succeeded in these hard tests, I made up My mind to use you as My instrument, provided you agreed to work in your physical body for the purpose. You had run the full course of the allotted span of life and in the usual course, you ought to have been called away. But I used My special powers as God and extended your life. You have agreed to be made use of by Me for the purpose of My mission. The deadline of your life is now fixed. It cannot be changed even though I am God. And I see no reason to change it either."

On January 27, 1954, Ahura Mazda again gave me a long message describing my last two incarnations. Ram Ram had given me a hint that I had been a Hindu woman, by making me see her image in a vision. This was confirmed by Ahura Mazda. He said that before I took birth as a Hindu woman, I was a Christian monk in Catholic faith. (named Patricio).

On January 27, 1954, I was made to take the following vows:

(1) Not to speak evil of any one.
(2) To maintain silence as far as possible.
(3) Never to enter into argument.
(4) Never to say a word of self-praise.
(5) To consider myself as a mere dot, knowing nothing whatsoever.
(6) To be humble, kind and loving to all.
(7) To keep my mind centred on God.

On January 29, 1954, Ahura Mazda gave me a very illuminating message regarding experiences of the soul. He said:

"In the universe nothing is wasted or lost. Whatever experience a man gathers in one life, stand him in good stead in the next incarnation. Life is a series of events not only from birth to death in one round but in the countless rounds that the soul may have taken in the previous births. These experiences of the soul are hidden. They became latent only when the soul begins to unfold itself *i.e.,* when it starts throwing off its sheaths in its attempt to get free"

I asked whether the seat to the soul was in the heart or the mind and Ahura Mazda gave the following explanation:

"This is a most important. Some say it is in the heart. Generally it is believed that the heart is the repository of the soul. When the heart is awakened, it is said the soul is awakened. But in reality, it is not so at all. The soul lives in what is called soul body. It is a part of the mind, *Buddhi.* The soul lives in the mind and not in the heart. But soul and mind are absolutely two different things. The higher mind viz., *Buddhi,* is spiritual, is a reflection of the soul. Being nearest to the soul, it is able to get the light of the soul and that makes it spiritual.

"Every time the soul takes a rebirth, some part of the soul is unfolded and with that unfoldment the experiences of the past life or lives come guided by the soul through the mind - his *buddhi,* when the *buddhi* is able to function. No man is ever lost. The experiences of the soul are never lost. In some life, in some birth, they must bear fruit, when the soul starts unfolding vigorously. Take your own case. You are what you are today, not

> because of your effort in the present incarnation. They are petty, nothing in comparison to what you put forth and gained in the last two incarnations, when you were a monk and a Hindu woman respectively. But for those experiences and the perfection attained, you would have been nowhere today."

On the same day, as ordered by Ahura Mazda, Ram Ram also gave me a message, in which I was asked to pray for Revelation. He said:

> "It is a blessing, a great boon that He has conferred upon you viz., to pray. As you want His Revelation for the purpose of offering yourself as His instrument of carrying out God's mission on earth, you are not asking anything for yourself. As such, you can always pray and your prayer would be granted. It has been granted in countless instances when you have prayed."

On February 11, 1954, I was told by Ahura Mazda that I was merged in God. It made me jubilant to know that I had reached the goal. This is what Ahura Mazda said in His message:

> "You are under My absolute control. I have started making you My instrument and you must remember that whatever you do, whatever you say, whatever you think, is the outcome of My inspiration and the result to My own will and not your's at all. Your free will is now reduced to nothing. You have destroyed this will of yours by complete subjugation to My will. Your will is absolutely submerged in My will. You are now a mere automaton without any individual initiative or capacity. You are now completely merged into Me. When such is the case, you must realize and understand to what state of spirituality you have reached. It is the highest stage, when a man loses his individuality completely and wholly and is merged in God. This is the goal of life and you have reached this goal today. All these days and months and years, very strenuous and continuous efforts were made by you in this direction. You have at last reached your destination today after a great deal of trial and tribulation, suffering and frustration, patient toil and strenuous labour."

On February 14, 1954, Ahura Mazda gave me the following message:

> "Remember God does not take a soul in His control unless He has a specific design. The Masters are appointed to do the work of perfecting human souls. I stepped in when your Master Ram Ram completed his training of you because I saw potentiality in you for a higher mission even while you were on the earth plane. This training will continue even while you were on the earth plane. This training will continue even after you have left your physical body for God's training, once begun, is continued. All Masters in My Spiritual Plane are continuously under My training. They are all evolving according to My Law of Perfection."

On February 18, 1954 Ahura Mazda gave me the following news:

> "While you were meditating in the early hours. I secretly gave you the light by means of which you will now be able to see the Invisible, both in the state of *samadhi* as well as in deep but simple meditation."

He also said that all predictions made in His messages regarding various world events would prove correct, as soon as I got God's Revelation in a visual manner.

On February 27, 1954, I was told by Ahura Mazda that He had made me compose the book. "Esoteric Poems of Devotion" as a proof that I was fit for his Revelation.

On March 26, 1954, I was given the alarming news by Ahura Mazda that He was going to dictate to me from the next day, " a whole book of a novel nature. It will thrill you and thrill your whole world. It is a book which contains the secrets of My universe, unraveled to you only out of My love for you and as a token of My acceptance of you for carrying out My mission on your earth plane. This mission should be considered as started from tomorrow when I begin dictating to you your new book." The title of the book was "Romance of a soul" and Homi was ordered to write a short foreword. The tract "Romance Of a Soul" dictated by Ahura Mazda was accordingly printed and published separately.

On April 4, 1954, Ahura Mazda gave to me a very illuminating message. He said:

"You are now in a totally different atmosphere. You are hearing the voices of our Spirit World but are unable to catch their words. You are touching us, the spirits of the other world as they flit around you but you have no real knowledge of that living contact. You are smelling the odour of our world. It is so blissful, so soothing, but you have still no proper notion of its action on you.

"You are in a queer position. You play, you talk, you sing, you dance, you eat, you feel immensely happy but all that happiness, all that experience of your association with us, you still do not carry with you.

"This will not do. What you see, what you hear, what you feel, what you experience, what you understand must remain permanently with you. Even when your soul leaves the spirit world, it shall carry with it impressions of its visits and not forget them... This miracle. I am going to perform."

We are apt to curse God and our bad fortune when we pass through trials and tribulations in life. The following message of Ahura Mazda should disillusion one who hankers after only worldly success and happiness:

"Do you know why you were a failure in your life? Had you succeeded, you would have failed to realize God. Your failure was a blessing in disguise. You must thank God Your failure was a blessing in disguise. You must thank God that He did not allow you to succeed, for worldly success means separation from God and you would have lost the crown, which your failure has brought to you. Calamities, misfortune, trials, sufferings, ordeals-these are God's angels protecting the soul from the valley of destruction."

Following the above message, Ahura Mazda related to me the story of a holy man. He said:

"There was a man holy in all respects, but people called him a hypocrite. He loved to do good by stealth. He lived miserly but he gave a large portion of his income in secret charities. Not even the recipient knew who was the giver of the gift he received. He worked even among the lowly and the fallen, and the poor man was misunderstood and the people never spoke a good word of him. But he did not mind it at all. His love for God was so great that he felt pleased inwardly and that to him was his best reward. As he grew in years, he lost his health and people's unkindness also increased. Even then, he never cried, he never mourned, he never uttered a word of complaint. His mind was full of beatific visions, His soul was bathed in God's light and beauty. There was serenity on his face and with that external and internal secrenity, he at last breathed his last. It was after his death, people came to know that he was saint – nay the saintliest man of his time, heroic, bold, unassuming and humble to the last. He bore his physical sufferings with a heroism worthy of a martyr. He lived a martyr: he died a martyr."

On April 27, 1954, Ahura Mazda gave me the following message exhorting me not to doubt:

"I have a meaning in putting you to all sorts of tests and making you drink the cup of bitterness. There is a meaning in making you drink the cup of bitterness. There is a meaning in making you go off the track. Be firm. Be brave. Cast off all thoughts of sadness and frustration. It is childishness to give in to despair when you know in your heart of hearts that your God is with you all time. Have faith in Me. Have faith in My words. Remember that I have given you a new birth. The birth pangs are always hard to bear but you must go through the temporary chasm of suffering- if at all it could be called so—with a joyous heart."

On May 3, 1954, Ahura Mazda gave me a picture of the special training that He was giving me. He said:

"I am making you a rare type of a mystic and you are going through that particular training at My hands. I have lifted you to the highest pitch of sublimity for the sole reason that I have to make use of you for My mission. You have to see things in one chain of the past, present and future *i.e.*, merge the past, present and future into one perception. You have to rise from your individual, physical understanding of things to perception of inner things in the cosmic sense. I am training you for that. It is superconsciousness of the highest pattern and standard."

On May 11, 1954, Ahura Mazda said:

"Your writing down the message will not convince others of your being in communion with God. But when I perform certain miracles through you, it will stun them and they will hail you as My messenger and follow you in large numbers."

On June 22, 1954, Ahura Mazda gave the following message regarding the mission assigned to me:

"I am going to make the fullest use of you for the peace and happiness of your war-torn disease-ridden world. When I say disease-ridden world, I mean bodily and mental illness and of the soul. I want to bring about a new era of health, happiness and spiritual awakening. I want to impress upon the people of your world that truth and purity alone lead to peace and bliss. I shall make you lift the curtain of ignorance and bring to light the springs of perennial joy and delight."

There was no doubt that I had become God-intoxicated and God-mad. Ahura Mazda again assured me that as I was hearing Him, I would see Him also in a mystical manner. He said:

"You are in a special position. You are able to commune with Me in a tangible, concrete manner. Other mystics only feel My presence and are guided by my inspiration. To you, I give My talk in a tangible manner."

On July 29, 1954, a long silence coupled with seclusion was imposed upon me by Ahura Mazda.

On August 6, 1954, Ahura Mazda gave me a very important message:

"Are you not in daily communion with Me? There are many who do commune with Me but that communion is invisible. In your case, it is visible for you can write down what I say, as if you are hearing Me with your physical ears. You are not hearing Me. It is your spirit that is making you write you. It is the Spirit within talking to the Spirit without and vice versa. What you are writing down is purely the work of the Spirit both within and without. They have co-mingled. It is now one Spirit's voice. This voice is Mine, your God."

In the message of 8th August, 1954 Ahura Mazda again reminded me that I was in communion with ONE, the Highest in the universe. The following message is extremely important. It gives an idea of how God works along with His Masters for the betterment of the world:

> "I am AHURA MAZDA, the Voice of the Absolute Spirit pervading throughout the universe. I, Ahura Mazda, alone can see the Absolute Spirit and none else in the whole universe. I am Ahura Mazda, the first creation of the Absolute Spirit. I am the Logos speaking to you through your *Atma,* the Spirit within you. I seek human souls, one at a time, for this kind of direct communion when I want to make use of the human body in which the spirit dwells for the good of all mankind. I have chosen you for the purpose. As soon as My work through you is finished and I call you away, I shall start My communion with someone else on your earth plane and train and equip him for My mission. In this way, My work of evolution carries on. Not only the Masters but I, God, am working all the time for the amelioration of human suffering and the progress of human civilization through human souls in human bodies."

On August 10, 1954, I asked Ahura Mazda whether Meher Baba was an *'Avatar'*, and I got the following message:

> "No, not at all, but he is a good and sincere soul trying to follow My orders. He had one time, communion with Me, direct. This intoxicated him and not understanding the role set out for him, he deviated and fell. As soon as you get My Revelation, you would meet him on super-physical plane, for physically you would not meet him at all. He will then understand his own relationship with you and realize also his great mistake."

Later on in September, 1954, when Meher Baba made his public appearance before 15,000 of his followers from all over the world in Ahmednagar, prostrating before them as God to God, he was reported to have said that he would shortly leave his physical body for good. Questions were asked regarding Meher Baba again on September 13, 1954 and Ahura Mazda's replies are given below:

> 'Yes, I am glad you have read the report of the ceremonial meeting held at Ahmednagar. I have already told you that for Meher Baba to declare himself as an Avatar of God or for his followers to consider him as such, is absolutely wrong. You are in a way even higher than Meher Baba today. He is just an ordinary human

soul, whom I, God, on account of his fervent devotion to Me, had selected to carry out My mission of love and righteousness on the earth plane. He has failed so far to carry out the mission as desired by Me. He has failed only because of his inward egotism, thinking himself to be the *Avatar* of God, a *Sadguru*, and so forth and leaving such impression upon the mind of his followers. I have given him tremendous powers, some of which he can use and he is using them to good advantage. But for this one great weakness of his, he would have brought about a great religious upheaval in your world. When he says he is going to leave his physical body for good, he is not wrong. He knows his death but I am God and I can change the date of his death, if I like or think it right. I want to give him a further change for My aim is to improve your world by means of working through perfected human souls. Meher Baba is, in a way, a perfect soul but for this one great weakness of which he is not even aware He has caused a reversal in the whole programme."

Q. **"How did he get this idea that he is an Avatar of God?"**

A. "Because like you, he was in communion with Me and being in communion with Me direct, he thought he was another Christ or Lord Krishna and proclaimed himself as such. In a way, it is no fault of his."

"Yes but his communion with Me is of quite a different order. You hear My voice direct through the Spirit within you. But he is not able to hear Me in this manner at all. He can't take down messages as you do. He feels vibration thrilling through him and they carry not any sound but an awakening, an awareness, a feeling of My presence every moment and a great fervour for all that is beautiful, good, noble and joyous. He is a reservoir of joyousness, because of My presence in him and he transmits that feeling of joyousness to all around him. This feeling of unending bliss can be seen in so many other mystics but they have never claimed themselves as *Sadguru* or incarnation of God Himself."

Q. **"It is very great boon to have a continuous feeling of joyousness. Is it not achieved unless through God's grace and his Revelation?"**

A. "Yes, I have given him a partial Revelation to be followed by My Revelation in full but he made a mess of the whole thing. There is a great possibility of My Revelation to him again, not partially but this time wholly, for he has made amends and when this Revelation takes place, he will detect his mistake and not allow the world to be misguided. He will then be of immense service to Me. All the powers that I have given to him will then come out in full bloom and fruition and he will be hailed by your world as a prophet of a new age."

Throughout the period of silence imposed upon me since July 29, 1954, I was meditating regularly every day for nine hours, four in the night and five in the afternoon. But on August 28, 1954, I meditated for nine hours at a stretch in the day time, making in all 13 hours of meditation for that day.

I never exercised the power given to me to leave the physical body for good, on account of my vow of not asking for death, inspite of the fact that there was a secret longing for it.

On September 1, 1954, Ahura Mazda gave me the following message:

"The greatest boon that I have given to you is of My having selected you for the mission. This selection was completed when a few days ago, you meditated at a stretch for full nine hours. Had you not come out successful during those two days, by this time you would have been dead. The choice was immediate death or the mission. You chose the mission unaware of the choice laid down before you. You chose the right thing at the right moment, unaware of your own wise action."

The long unsuccessful waiting for God's Revelation in a visual, concrete manner, made me doubt whether I was fit for it or not. On October 2, 1954, I received Homi's letter and the sense of frustration immediately evaporated. The experiences related by Homi on his letter were most remarkable:

"My dear Minoo,

"Having gone through the messages received today, I am instructed to let you know that YOU WERE LITERALLY MERGED IN GOD ON SUNDAY LAST. This is what happened. Both of us were dragged up together by a loop made out of a rope of white fire. You kept the loop around you all the time all the way up, while I enjoyed myself getting out of it and getting into it again, till we reached a huge pillar of White Fire. You were dragged into it but I would have been left out and so I forced my way into it along with you. We thus both disappeared into that column of White Fire together. This happened at about 8:00 p.m. or so when I was in a prayer. I understand this as merging into God."

"The next day i.e., Monday the 27th in the afternoon at about 2:30 p.m. or so, you came to my room where I was reading and thanked me for the experience of the night preceding.

"I would have written to you about both these incidents in my last letter but I was asked not to mention a word, whereas today I am instructed to write about them and I have the therefore done so. I hope it will now make your inward joy permanent.

"I think you would have become conscious of the visible Revelation but for the constant questioning in your mind. Know that you have already attained God and have been literally merged in Him. You will become conscious of the fact as soon as you have conquered your doubts. What is wanted is merely a little change in the mental attitude. Think that the proof of the message has already been given and you will realize the merger. Your soul knows the fact as evidenced by its coming to thank me."

Yours affectionately,
H.S. Spencer

Commenting upon the letter, Ahura Mazda gave me the following message:

"What Homi has written to you is the experience given under My orders to break your suspense. What he has written is absolutely correct. You and he are both merged in God. You led the way and he quietly followed you. It is the signal service which he rendered to you, that has at last given to him the crown he longed for.

"I am going to give you the sight to see the Invisible World and the Masters. You will also see Me in a very mystical and mysterious manner.

"I am glad Homi's letter had now dispelled for ever the last dregs of doubt still lurking in you. Kindly ask Homi to go deeper into the explanation of the two incidents related. He will tell you everything for I have ordered that nothing should be kept away from you and you must know everything."

On October 2, 1954, I wrote to Home putting him several questions and he replied to me as under:

"Here are my replies to the queries raised by you in yours of the 2nd.

Q.1. Why were you instructed first not to communicate the experiences to me but later on the instructions were revised?

A.1. It is more than I can say because I do not know. But I surmise it was to serve some purpose in your training and may be in mine also.

Q.2. Who is the Master or who are the Masters who gave you instructions?

A.2. Please see message of 2-10-54, 4.55 p.m. I myself did not know who gave the instructions but believed that it was Ahura Mazda Himself. This message confirms my belief when it says: " I made Homi write out to you his experiences."

Q.3. Did you see this (i.e. the upliftment incident) with your Spirit eye?

A.3. It is more than I know or can say. I saw the whole show while praying. According to the message of 2.10.54, 4:55 p.m. the experience was "given under My orders" i.e. the orders of ahura Mazda and it was given specially "to break your suspense." It seems it had another purpose also viz., to give me the satisfaction of knowing that I too was merged in God as I longed to be.

Q.4. What conversation did you have with your Master or Masters who must be present at that time?

A. 4. I had no conversation with any Master, nor was I aware of the presence of any Master. I was aware only of the INVISIBLE presence of God from the beginning of the show and became certain of it with the sight of the huge pillar of White Light towards the end of the show.

"I do not yet understand why your soul should have come to thank me for what happened, when the thanks of both of us were clearly due ONLYTO HIM who thus dragged and raised us upto Himself."

I wrote to Homi again on 11.10.54, and raised another query:

"There is just one more question which I want to ask you. You saw my soul the day after the incident in the afternoon. Will you kindly describe to me in what form you saw it? It could not have been in its nakedness for then you would not have been able to identify it with me. It must be the counterpart of my body. I want you to describe it as exactly as you can – the dress, the face, the stature, and everything."

Homi replied to me as under:

"As to your query regarding your appearance when I saw you, I may tell you that the form I saw was as lean and tall as yourself. I had your long thin face with all its familiar contours so that I could recognise it as yours. The form was made up the same White Fire in which I had seen you and myself the previous night."

On October 9, 1954, Ahura Mazda gave me a very thrilling message on the importance of silence:

"Do you know how much you have built up in these seventy and odd days of silence? You have made a tremendous progress of which you have at present not the slightest conception. No aspirant can even succeed in gaining the goal of life without going through the purification process of silence, meditation and seclusion. It is a most necessary and indispensable factor in spiritual life. You cannot commune with God but in silence. Silence means introspection, diving deep into the inner self, which is a repository of all hidden knowledge and divine wisdom. It awakens the soul. It enkindles the spirit within. It is the key to the higher region, far, far away from human vision and knowledge."

Chapter Twenty-Nine

Struggle for Revelation (1954-55)

When Sai Baba was seen in a vision, it was in a way a Revelation. But it was a partial Revelation as already explained in the earlier chapters. In fact, God having been realized, the object was attained and this book ought to have been ended. But God's ways are so very mysterious. I was ordered, on the contrary, to continue meditation for longer hours and the completion of the book, that was lying printed in the press for a number of years, was further put off.

The following message of Ram Ram delivered on October 12, 1954, provides a graphic survey of the whole situation:

> "The visions you have seen, the talks you have had with the Masters and God, Ahura Mazda, the training that God has given you under His own special guidance, the long spell of the preparation of your soul for the manifestation of its powers – these must be considered as indicators of God's revelation to you – your merging in God's own Light of Eternity.
>
> The ship has arrived at the port. It is the port of Eternity. But God does not want you to enter into it just yet. He wants you to go back into the same boat and save millions of your ship wrecked brothers

and sisters and bring them back to God. Every soul is a spark of God's own eternal fire. It must come back and rejoin the parental fire in the Infinite Span of the universe."

Again the following day, Ram Ram gave me another message of great importance:

"I am going to give you most astounding news. Do you know that you were destined to die in an air crash? Usually such destined events are not changed. God saw it and He has averted it. He has changed your whole destiny. You were not destined to get liberation in this incarnation. Not only have you won it but you have also qualified yourself to become God's own emissary for a high mission."

Thereafter many proofs of God's Revelation have been given to me in a subtle manner, but that was all for my satisfaction. I was pining for His visual Revelation in a concrete manner, so that the book could be completed in such a way as to convince the world also. Ahura Mazda said:

"The visual Revelation for which you are pining day and night is also close-by. I shall make you write the last chapter in the book and compete it."

On October 17, 1954, Ram Ram gave me a very reassuring message:

"God has already revealed Himself to you. But to satisfy you He will reveal Himself to you again in such a manner that you may be fully convinced."

On October 21, 1954, Ahura Mazda gave me a very important message. He said:

"Remember you have seen God, but it is a partial Revelation which you got when you saw Sai Baba in a vision not once but several times. You are now merged in the Absolute Spirit and I want you to have the Revelation of the Absolute Spirit. It will be formless for the Absolute Spirit pervades throughout the universe and transcends it and has no form. You will identify it as Absolute Spirit as soon as you see rolling clouds of fire and light sweeping through you, over you, around you of gathering at a distance. This light or fire is the emblem of the Absolute Spirit. It is the purest element in the cosmos. God is therefore the essence of purity and purity is the highest virtue."

Days passed on wearily, but there was no ostensible sign of God's Revelation in His transcendental aspect, in spite of assurances both by Ahura Mazda and the Masters.

The false assurances were given by Ahura Mazda purposely to train and discipline my mind in non-expectancy, so that I might not feel any sting of disappointment.

The hundredth day of my silence was completed on November 6, 1954. My heart was longing for work. Not that I was tired of silence. In a way, it was a tonic, a source of inward strength, a spiritual baptism. It gave me peace of an unalloyed nature, never enjoyed before. But being addicted to doing strenuous work throughout my life, I felt uneasy.

The following message of Ram Ram dispelled this wrong notion:

"We know that you can make yourself useful (also) by breaking silence. You are anxious to rejoin your hospital work. It is quite a natural desire but you must not think that by rejoining it, you are going to make any special contribution towards the advancement of the institution. Ahura Mazda wants you not to do your little bit but a big bit and for that big bit He has already prepared and trained you...."

On November 14, 1954, in the course of a long message, Ahura Mazda said to me:

"Yes, I know how very anxious you are. The Masters are also very anxious and so am I too. The hitch is yourself. You must forget all about Revelation. Take things easy. Think that revelation is not going to take place at all. Abandon the idea that your book is to be completed and published. Keep your mind immersed in God and God alone....."

The following day, I was told that another book on arcane knowledge would be dictated by Ahura Mazda. From November 16, 1954, a series of talks of my soul relayed by Ahura Mazda was begun. I was asked to give to the series the title "My Soul's Experiences in the Other World."

Meher Baba in his declaration dated September 30, 1954, had said that before he broke his silence or immediately thereafter, there would be war and three-fourths of the world would be destroyed. The message of Ahura Mazda dispelled such a fear:

> "That the world will be destroyed to a large extent, as he describes is correct. But this calamity I am going to avert. In fact, I have already averted it.... There is going to be peace throughout the world....."

The signs of a world-wide war were so ominous that I invoked Ahura Mazda again on December 11, 1954, and He gave the following reply:

> "Don't worry at all. I am going to avert it. I am allowing My Masters to do their best and when they fail, I shall intervene and avert the war. Meher Baba's prediction will be falsified and Mine, through you, will be upheld. In fact, all that I have said in My messages will turn out correct. Be absolutely at ease."

Speaking again on the trend of events endangering the peace of the world, Ahura Mazda gave another message on January 12, 1955. He said:

> "The course of the events has to be watched. If I find that the Masters are not able to bring about such an achievement under My orders, I shall Myself direct the course and the events will happen exactly as predicted by Me viz.,
>
> 1. Your world would be saved from the catastrophe of another war of a global nature.
> 2. Red China will be given its right of a seat in the U.N.O.
> 3. The war in Formosa will end.
> 4. The existing disputes between India and Pakistan would be amicably settled to the satisfaction of both the countries.
>
> There will be peace all over the world and man's mind would turn more towards God and His Invisible World. A new civilization built on the basis of justice, equity, freedom and security is in the offing. It will bring economic freedom and material happiness to the masses long exploited in a merciless manner. There will be

> greater international cohesion which will lead eventually to united action for one world government and one world religion."

A friend put me a question regarding Krishnamurthi's philosophy and Ahura Mazda gave the following message:

> "Regarding Krishnamurthi's philosophy, it must be understood that he had completely finished his round of evolution. Having come to the highest mark of perfection, he naturally thinks and preaches from the point of view of his personal experience. His teaching is meant not for the masses but for himself and those who have reached the highest state of perfection. What he says is true."
>
> "There is no doubt that he was looked upon by the leading Theosophists, especially Dr. Annie Besant and Bishop Leadbeater as a Master who would transform the world. They were quite justified in regarding him as a Master and launching him in the world as a Master. That he is a Master, I say with emphasis. He is created in the world to give the highest truths and your world should listen to him. These highest truths do not cover the lower truths and as such he is not helpful to the masses. His philosophy cannot be put into practice for he ignores the lower truths....
>
> "Such a man is useless to play the part of a world teacher in bringing about a great transformation. It is, therefore, those who were enthusiastic in the beginning lost their enthusiasm for him and gave him up."

On December 14, 1954, Ahura Mazda gave me to understand that he had revealed Himself to me in plain meditation, without my going into samadhi, but without my getting physical consciousness of it.

I was passing through a crucible of fire and agony both of mind and body. I was thinking of Revelation. Will it come? When will it come?

On December 17, 1954, I was ordered to meditate throughout the night and I meditated inspite of bodily pain for twelve hours at a stretch.

In the message of 18th December, 1954, I was assured that the suffering and suspense I was going through were

His creation in order to make me a perfect vehicle to serve God's purpose.

As I was in the last stage of human evolution, Homi's letters were of considerable guidance and benefit to me. Ahura Mazda said:

"Kindly always listen to him (Homi) for I am guiding you directly by My messages as well as through Homi. You have thus the benefit to double guidance as you need it very badly, being in the very last stage of your evolution. The unfoldment is nearing completion."

I was made to give up the Parsi hospital work, much against my will. Ahura Mazda said:

"I made you give up the Parsi Hospital work, because of your attachment to it. When you reach the last stage of human evolution, even unselfish action is detrimental to your spiritual perfection. You must be completely detached."

On December 30, 1954 Ahura Mazda gave me a most thrilling description of His coming Revelation in order to prepare me for it. He said:

"Light is My body; Light is My symbol Light is My signal. You will see Me flashing clouds of rolling light, piercingly white and red in such intensity that it will present to you a most awe-inspiring and thrilling experience of the rarest kind. It will simply stun you and subdue your heart. It is enough to kill a man at first sight but I have prepared you in such a manner that you will be able to enjoy the sight though fear and awe would encompass your heart and mind. The climax would be reached, when through the rolling light my voice you hear. The voice will come to you as naturally as it is coming to you now, as you are writing this message. The only difference will be that you do not at present see where from the voice is coming. When you see that light, you will be able to locate the direction *i.e.*, you will be in greater and more glorious touch with Me.

"The minute this Revelation takes place, your mind and body will be completely transformed. You will be dazed for some time. You will not know where you are, what you are. But this dazed condition would soon go away and you will become quite normal.

> However, your mind would be engrossed all the time after My Revelation in Me and Me alone. Your mundane world will cease to have any the least fascination for you........"
>
> "The revelation will first take place in *samadhi*. Later on, you will be able to see the Invisible even with your physical eyes without going into *samadhi*. This is again an extremely rare boon. This gift is being conferred upon you as a special case to help you to finish your mission quickly before you are called away."

On January 1, 1955 Ahura Mazda gave me a very important message:

> "No person can go into *samadhi* unless his soul is free. *Samadhi* is an indication of man's release from the round of birth and death. There is no more incarnation for him. You earned your *nirvana* long ago and I ought to have called you away. Your life has been specially extended for a great mission. Your book, "How I Found God" ought to have been published long ago. It is I who have stopped its publication in order to make it serve a larger purpose and this object has now been achieved. You will get everything simultaneously viz., My Revelation and powers of superhuman nature for the fulfillment of My mission."
>
> "I assure you, you are already merged in God and whatever your people may say, you are in direct communion with God, the highest in the universe. You have fulfilled the purpose for which you were given birth. Having secured everything, all I want you now to do is to be completely passive. Your work is finished. My work now starts in right earnestness. It is My mission for which you are made to linger in life and it is My work to make use of you in any way I like. The mission will not end with your death. On the contrary it will gain a great momentum after you death. It is only after your death that people will come to know of your mission and your existence."

To be candid, as A.M. had given me the date of my passing away viz., February 5, 1955, I was secretly waiting for that day. If revelation did not take place on or before that date, at least I would be free of the physical body which was a source of burden and suffering.

Ahura Mazda was annoyed and He said:

"When I give you Revelation, the conditions would so change that you would forget all about death, My dear son. You are longing for death today only as an escape from bodily suffering and mental suspense and anxiety. I want you to rise above these obstacles."

My eyes were opened. It was I who was putting obstacles in the way of God's Revelation to me, by thinking of death as an escape from suspense.

He ended his message by saying so lovingly:

"My heat pains Me when I see you suffering. You have borne a lot... I must bring and end to this epic struggle."

Yes God's mercy is unique. But for this mercy, where would we, His children, be?

Chapter Thirty

Revelation at Last (1955-58)

In the message during the night of January 3, 1955, Ahura Mazda dropped a hint that my life may be extended. He said:

> "On the question of life and death, I want you to keep absolutely quiet and leave everything to Me, your God..... Think only of your mission and your God."

My soul had already experienced God's Revelation in its fullness and I was hearing the echo of its ecstatic exuberance. It is this inner feeling of joy that made me keep up my faith in God.

On January 14, 1955, Ahura Mazda ordered Christ the Master and Ram Ram to give their special messages to me. They are as under:

Christ's message:

> "Kindly be absolutely certain that you are destined for His Revelation and that you have not to wait for it any longer.

> "Your mission is like mine but it is on an extremely small scale. You feel like me for the suffering of others. Love gushes from your heart when you see any one in pain and suffering, whether

bodily or mental. It is therefore God has given you a mission which is in close alliance in its objective with that of mine viz., to heal souls sick both in body and soul."

Ram Ram's message:

"All I ask of you is to be ready for His Revelation and if it is postponed, don't grieve over it. If it comes to you a day or two earlier or later will make no difference to you."

I had passed through a terrible ordeal. My mind was disturbed. Longing for death as an excape from the present life of monotonous passivity began to steal on me. God must have noticed this secret longing and He gave me a most heartening message. This is what He said, on the night of January 15, 1955:

" I must go on testing you to the bitter end and I tell you frankly that I am not going to spare you at all. I shall hammer on you My pattern of perfection and even if that takes longer time, you will have to go through the ordeal cheerfully."

Don't think of death at all. It is not your business. I shall do whatever I like. I am God. You are My child. I shall do whatever I think fit and you must solely obey Me as you are doing now. Death or no death, Revelation or no Revelation, mission or no mission, you are wholly Mine and I shall make use of you, as I think fit for the betterment of the world."

On January 22, 1955, I came to know from Ahura Mazda that my life was extended for a short time and that He would make me go through His mission very rapidly."

My unwary mind was again entrapped. I was told on the night of January 22, 1955:

"A few hours more and you will get the strangest, the happiest and the most thrilling experience of your life... I am telling you beforehand in order to put you into and easy frame of mind so that I can reveal Myself to you without the least difficulty." There was no Revelatin as predicated. It was again a disappointment but a disappointment that had lost its teeth."

On January 24, 1955 in the course of a long message, Ahura Mazda gave me a very severe warning. He said:

> "I may give you all sorts of baits. It is for you to be wary and not get into My net. By thinking of death, you are putting the greatest obstacle in the way of My Revelation."

The next day *i.e.*, January 25, 1955, I was again given the experience of His Revelation, but in a silent, hidden manner.

On January 28, 1955, I completed six months of silence and seclusion: The following message which Ahura Mazda gave me strengthened my resolve to continue my silence with fortitude in spite of the criticism and cynicism of friendsand relations:

> "You will gain far more by sitting alone m the altar room than by reading a thousand books of learning. I am giving you divine knowledge direct from the Source. The more you keep up your direct communion with Me in silence and solitude, the more you would be fitted for your mission."

I was wondering whether what I felt was the prompting of my soul. Ahura Mazda refuted it. He said:

> "No, your soul is passive. It is not at present in communication with you, for it has to keep the passage clear for your communication with Me."

The message thrilled me. It was more than a clear proof that so long as I was in direct communion with God, communion with my soul was not possible.

On February 3, 1955, I saw a beautiful vision, which it is best to describe in the words of Ahura Mazda:

> "In order to impress upon your mind the extreme necessity of keeping your mind absolutely engrossed in thoughts of God and God alone, I gave you an extremely beautiful vision, at the very sight of which your heart began to throb with extreme delight and you felt that you are on the way to getting My Revelation. You are In the habit of saying in your mind, every now and then, "I want God," "I want God." You saw these words written in celestial colours of red and white flashing before your mind's eye. I presented to you the reflection of your mind. The whole board was covered up with words, "I want God," "I want God" from the top to the end and it sprang a great surprise on you and gave you thrills of joy."

February 5, 1955 was the date originally fixed for my death and I had expected Revelation to occur long before it. Ahura Mazda gave me the following message:

> "You had made a slogan "Death or Revelation." Revelation has failed and death has not occurred. You see, how I have foiled you. Whatever fate I decree for you, you have to submit to it. Except submission to My will, you have no other resource left. This is the highest stage a human soul can reach."

My mind was disturbed by the news of events taking a sinister turn especially by Red China's refusal to attend the U.N.O. Security Council meeting to consider the question of a cease-fire in Formosa which had become an active theatre of war. Ahura Mazda gave me the following message:

> "I am God and I am going to save the whole situation. Be absolutely at ease. There will be no world war. The tension in Formosa will cease... China will be given its rightful place in U.N.O. and there will be better understanding between different nations. It is America which has done all the mischief by its short-sighted policy in its horror of Communism. America has lost its prestige and will soon lose its power and influence in the world."

On February 6, 1955, speaking on the situation in Formosa, Ahura Mazda said:

> "America is on the point of declaring war on China. In fact, you may take it that America is at war with China already, but I am going to save the position at this most critical hour by intervening and bringing about a settlement by means of negotiations. America will be forced to give in by the pressure of world opinion and out of fear of its own safety. China will score a victory and will get a seat in the Security Council of the U.N.O. It will speedily come to terms for an amicable settlement."

On February 7, 1955, Meher Baba circular No. 23 dated February 3, 1955 was received. It was placed at the altar for Ahura Mazda's comments. He gave the following message, which is embodied in this book, as specifically ordered by Him:

"It is an extremely important circular and gives expression to very important facts. The first is that it indicates that his life has been extended. I have extended your life several times and I have extended his life also.

The second fact is that he talks of modification of world events in their intensity etc. He is using very ambiguous language purposely for he does not want to own defeat and correct his wrong prophecy that the world would be en- gulfed in a war of such a gigantic nature as to create destruction on a colossal scale. His prophecy he wants to modify in the statement that he has just issued. He is now getting a glimpse of the true state of affairs and this is a happy augury."

On February 7, 1955 Ahura Mazda said:

"Negotiations for a cease-fire in Formosa are complete and an agreement will soon be reached. You will come to know of it in a few days. The cease-fire in Formosa would lead to the establishment of peace throughout the world.

The atomic weapons will no longer be used for destructive purposes. They will be diverted for peaceful reconstruction of homes and industries. All nations would soon agree to ban war for all times and live in amity and peace. This is not an Utopian dream but a rigid fact. Forces of internationalism will succeed and nationalism would be recognised as a danger to world peace and security.

Your world is heading towards the goal of unity of thought and action and one world government and one world religion will soon become a fait accompli."

On February 10, 1955, Ahura Mazda gave a very important message on the world situation. He said:

"There will be no world war at all. It has been averted. I have issued an order for a cease-fire in Formosa and for a settlement of the Formosa dispute by means of a conference of all the parties to the dispute and others interested in bringing peace. The conference will be a great success in establishing permanent peace in your world. The change in the government of Soviet Russia does not mean that Soviet Russia is at all anxious for war. It is an answer to U.S.A.'s tactics to interfere in China's affairs and to help Chiang Kai-Shek's ambition to destroy Communism in China by attacking the main land of China with American military aid and resources – a situation which Soviet Russia can never accept lying down.

The re-arming of West Germany is also a potential danger to the peace of the world. But that danger I am going to remove and you should now be absolutely at peace."

I was assured that there was no longer any barrier or obstacle to God's Revelation to me. The passage was clear. I had only to walk with full faith in God and in utter submission to His will.

On February 13, 1955, I was given a good warning by Ahura Mazda when He said:

"I am God and I may pick up even a worm to serve some useful purpose in an extraordinary manner. Don't therefore think that you are going to get My Revelation because you are perfect in soul and that this perfection is a rare achievement. Think always as you have written to Homi that you are just an ordinary human soul and no more."

On February 17, 1955, Ahura Mazda gave me the news of my soul's full-fledged emancipation. He said to me:

"I am extremely glad to tell you that for the first time you were able to go into samadhi of your own accord and I did not stop you. There is no reason for Me to stop you from going into *samadhi* for your soul has attained its full-fledged emancipation and I do not want any longer to interfere with its right of leaving your body at any time it likes."

On February 21, 1955, I was given a very important message:

"Your soul is free. Your soul is perfect. But you must at the same time remember that it is still occupying your body. You are still an ordinary human being and not a Master in spite of the perfection of your soul. I have stopped you from gaining that superconsciousness.

Remember, I am suppressing your powers in order to raise you still higher for the purpose of My mission and its success. Be absolutely at rest."

On February 22, 1955 a different turn was given to my meditation and I had a strange experience as will be seen from Ahura Mazda's message.

"I have given to your meditation a totally different turn today. I put you in *samadhi* for the first hour and then your soul flickered between the two worlds – your physical body and My Spiritual Plane. When it got established in its original tenement i.e. your physical body, I started talking to you. This is the first time you have heard Me talking to you in meditation. I made you bow down to Me and I said to you that I am going to give you so extraordinary experience. I touched your heart and it began to palpitate to such an extent that you could not even draw your breath freely. In order to show to you the difference between your ordinary obeisance and this particular one, I drew away from you and you bowed down and you did not get that same experience. It was also the case when subsequently Ram Ram came and you bowed down to him but you did not get that extraordinary experience.

I have given you ample proofs in these subtle ways that I am God. I have convinced you thoroughly and now My work lies in convincing your world of your being in direct communion with Me. This is the 'most important work and it is the very core of your mission. I shall convince your world of this in many ways viz.

(1) My Revelation,
(2) Your book, "How I found God" containing a description of the unique event,
(3) The miraculous healing that 1 shall make you do after My Revelation,
(4) My world predictions, and last
(5) The books on the mystic side of life which I am going to make you write after My Revelation".

Ram Ram was ordered by Ahura Mazda to give his message and he justified God's action in having picked up an ordinary man like me for His mission.

On February 24, 1955 at night, Ahura Mazda gave me a message which is embodied as expressly ordered by Him.

"I want to give you important news. The first is that I have stopped the war from spreading and I am going to establish peace throughout the world. Just as slavery has been abolished, war will be banned by your world.

The second good news is that with the publication of your book, "How I Found God" there will be awakening even in ordinary persons to aspire for God realization without abandoning their present mode of living. This yearning for God will become apparent in a measure as world advances. The trend of your world is towards spirituality after a long spell of materialism."

Saturday, the February 26, 1955 was an important day. I was told by my soul that it was a day fixed by God for His Revelation. The assurances in the past had proved so false, that I was not allured by my soul's hopefulness. There was no Revelation in reality. Ahura Mazda explaining what had happened in the meditation during the early hours said that I did get Revelation but "it was not a real revelation but a false show of My Revelation."

Ram Ram explaining the whole position said to me:

"He wants to make Himself quite sure that you would become an obedient instrument in His hands. He is doing all this to achieve His object of killing your mind completely and rooting out from you all sense of egotism and pride of any kind."

The next day, Sunday, the February 27, 1955, I was very restless. When I repaired to the altar room in the evening for a message, it was with a sad and weary heart. Wild thoughts began to chase my mind. I felt like a disobedient boy, and thought of breaking my silence and burying myself in some work, instead of idling my time in the altar room in meditation and praying to God for His Revelation and all the time hanging on in suspense without any definite result.

The same day, late at night Ahura Mazda gave me a message of warning:

"Even if you were to break your silence tomorrow and not carry out My orders, I shall reveal Myself to you and make you finish the book and thus bring an end to the whole struggle. But My purpose will not be served. Your mission will fail. You will be made a target of ridicule and your people will be justified also to a certain extent in calling you a false prophet."

The words burned in my heart and mind. I was fit for God's Revelation, but not for the mission. And of what use would be His Revelation, if I were not fit for His mission? The mission was the objective, not God's Revelation.

The next day, *i.e.* February 28, 1955, I saw a vision when I was in meditation. I saw myself cutting a fruit and found a golden ring with the word 'God' inscribed on it. I took it in my hands and touched it making sure whether it was a real ring or a mere fancy. To my joy, I found it was really a ring.

Ahura Mazda gave me the following thrilling message:

> "The invisible golden ring that you have found with the word "God" inscribed on it is meant to be worn by you. It is My present to you to remind you perpetually of Me and My love for you. You found this ring while cutting a fruit. It is visible to you but not to others who have not realized God."

I was thrilled with delight. In what a quaint and beautiful manner I was given another proof of my having realised God. My love for God was boundless. My devotion to Him was measureless.

On April 16, 1955, Meher Baba's Life Circular No.24 dated April 10, 1955 was received and it was placed at the altar for Ahura Mazdas's comments. He gave the following message with orders that it should be embodied in this book:

> "Meher Baba will soon pass away without speaking a word. His predictions regarding world events will not come out correct even in their modified form. His mission is a failure and the world will soon forget him. His book, *"God Speaks"* is an illusion. He has deluded himself into the belief that he is God – the *Avatar* of God descended upon earth to bring about a great religious and social revival. If he had restrained himself and allowed himself to be guided by God, his life would have been a great success. God would have used his body and mind for a great purpose. He was given intensive training. He was given powers of a very high order."

> Though his mission is a failure, I shall send him again and I am sure, with the experience of his present life, he will make a great success in his next incarnation, as a perfected Master, a *Jivan*

Mukta of the highest order. I will send him for the simple reason that he himself will volunteer to take incarnation again to finish the work successfully, which he could not accomplish in his present incarnation. He will be born again in a few days after his passing away. The minute he passes away, he will get full consciousness of his mistakes and this consciousness he will carry in his soul when he is re- born. His teachings will make an indelible mark upon human hearts and bring about a great revolution in human thought and understanding."

Very often, human as I was, my mind was eager to seek proofs to buttress my faith in God. Ahura Mazda gave me a strong warning: "If you seek proofs to butter your faith in Me, it will never be given to you." Every day I was feeling my helplessness and I was told: Your helplessness is My strength to work through you. On May 12, 1955. Ahura Mazda gave me the following illuminating message.

"I am going to give you divine vision and then close your silence and your book, *"How I Found God."* With My Revelation to you, Homi as well as Doraswami would be relieved (the terrible anxiety which I have made them go through for your sake. They have made tremendous sacrifices for you under My orders.

Without renunciation and sacrifice, life is a mere bubble. It is only when man renounces everything in the love of God and in the desire to render service to humanity that life becomes a reality. I t is no longer then a soap or water bubble but a continuous stream of life energy which never gets dried up or lost for its source is God."

On June 21, 1955, to my utter surprise, Ahura Mazda made Madame Blavatsky talk to me through Ram Ram. The following is her talk:

"Do you know who I am? I was one of the first to enlighten your modem world with the knowledge of the Spirit Masters. I owe a lot to them and now when I have left your world, I have become a Master and I have been guiding your world into unity, peace, joy and blessedness."

> "I do not know you at all. Are you a human soul or are you a spirit? I am simply dumbfounded. I never had such bright aura when I was in physical life nor have I seen anything like it in a human soul since I have come over here. Your aura is bewildering. It is all white without the slightest speck of any other colour. It is shining like a crystal. I can say also from your aura that God must have chosen you for some extraordinary mission."

On July 15, 1955, Ahura Mazda allowed my soul to talk with me after a long interval. To my surprise, my soul gave vent to its sense of resentment at the way God's Revelation was postponed from day to day. It said:

> "How long is this game going to last? Every day I feel, there is going to be His Revelation and each day passes without any result. I have earned my right to leave your body permanently and live in eternal peace and joy in the Other World. Why should I be deprived of this right? I am quite willing to stay in your body for some time to give you full scope to finish the mission but sure enough, I am not going to succumb to this high-handedness of God to keep me confined to your body for nothing."

The next day during meditation I tried my best to go into *samadhi* and even prayed to God but it was all in vain. I could not go into samadhi even for one minute. This was rather unusual. Ahura Mazda gave me the following explanation;

> "It was just to teach your soul not to talk in this arrogant manner that I did not allow your soul to slip out from your body even for a second. Do you see My power now and how very futile is your soul's talk? Unless your soul repents, I won' t allow you to go into samadhi even for a minute."

On July 21, 1955, Ahura Mazda gave me the following message:

> "Even if I give you false assurances and false promises, keep steady and firm. Even if the clouds threaten and they burst and drench you, you should have this faith in Me that the sun is sure to reappear in the sky and that you will achieve the goal of your life, This goal is indicated by Me in "*Romance of a Soul*," I want this small book to be read by hundreds and thousands of persons. Let the world

come to know of the coming of a Messenger. It does not matter if they ridicule the idea or throw away the book after reading it. At least the thought should percolate in their minds that something startling is going to take place."

On July 22, 1955, when I was meditating, my mind was deadened by Ahura Mazda for a few minutes and I could not hear any of the three clocks in the adjacent rooms chime at 2:00 p.m. Was I in samadhi ? No. This was done purposely by Ahura Mazda in order to test whether I would be able to recover from the sudden shock of His Revelation without any injury to my mind. He said that He was more than pleased and satisfied.

On July 24. 1955, Ahura Mazda said:

"The Geneva Conference of the Big Four has ended on a note of accord by all the powers concerned. It is a great victory as entirely predicted by Me. In the same manner all My other predictions regarding world events will come out true. It is for you now to draw your own conclusions."

On July 26, I was asked by Ahura Mazda to telegraph to Doraswami to withdraw all copies of *"Romance of a Soul"* from sale and destroy them including the second edition which was just to come out from the press for the ostensible reason that I must not consider myself as God's emissary as declared in that publication.

I telegraphed to Doraswami without waiting for a single minute as per Ahura Mazda's instructions: "Publication of Romance, a mistake. Stop selling. Destroy all copies of the first and second edition."

But the telegram was a test. Ahura Mazda made me send the telegram as above worded, just to test me whether I would carry out His order or not. r was asked later on to write to Doraswami not to take action on the telegram for it was a test meant for me only and that 1 had passed the test. The above incident is related just to show in what subtle ways we are tested.

On July 29, 1955, I completed one whole year of silence and seclusion.

On August 1, 1955, Ahura Mazda in the course of a long message, said:

"It is too ridiculous according to them (people) that you should be hailed as God's emissary. But when you get My Revelation and I put you into the arena of world's publicity, which I must do for the purpose of My mission, whether you like it our not, they will tear you to pieces...

But don't be afraid at all, I have made special arrangements to protect you from the brunt of their opposition. It will be terrible but it will die out speedily."

Homi in the course of a long letter said:

"You may think that you are all egoless. But while that may be quite true on the whole, so long as you exist in flesh as an individual you can not be sure that you will always forget your individuality. Flesh will not allow you to do it. Once you become merely a spirit and have shed all your vehicles, it is naturally different. Spirit may be individualised but it lives in the Ocean of Infinitude and the assertion of individuality is lost. It becomes a part of its nature to lose it." What wise words !

My attention was drawn by Doraswami to Sri Ramakrishna's experience as quoted on page 626 of "The Call Divine" (August 1955). Ramakrishna is said to have said: "When I was meditating, screen after screen of *maya* was removed from my consciousness and I saw a light more brilliant than a million suns. From that light came forth a spiritual form, which again melted away into the Formless."

Ahura Mazda gave me a very impressive message on Sri Ramakrishna's experience as under:

"The example quoted by Doraswami of Sri Ramakrishna's experience is unique. He realized God in the highest transcendental state and in order to reach this state, he had to pass through the necessary evolutionary process from one step to another viz., the lifting of the veil of *maya*, entering into a state of superconsciousness of the highest order by degrees and realising Godhood in its impersonal natural of formlessness."

"Yours is a similar case; in fact if you do not get elated, it is a still higher state for I am not only going to give you Revelation in My transcendental state of formlessness but powers which will enable you to perform your duties as My emissary in an impressive manner..."

"To be called God's emissary is much higher than being a saint a sage or a seer. Ramakrishana was a saint a seer and a sage having realized God in His highest transcendental aspect. But he was not appointed by God as His emissary. That makes a tremendous difference. It may appear to you and your whole world as ridiculous that I have appointed you as My emissary. But what-ever it be, the fact is that you are destined to play that role, though it be for an extremely short span of life. Your egolessness is of the most wonderful type. It is this egolessness, coupled with your love and devotion for Me, that has drawn Me to you to such a great extent as to compel Me to select you as My emissary."

He also said to me in the same message:

"I have completely crushed the spirit of revolt which you were just beginning to show because of exhaustion caused by long waiting. Your resignation to Me is now quite complete. Keep up this spirit of unconditional and joyous resignation to My Will and you will be able to break your silence much earlier than you may think of."

On August 14, 1955, Ram Ram gave a long explanatory message reviewing the whole situation as under:

"Let me tell you that if it be decided by God owing to certain difficulties that His Revelation be not given to you immediately, 1 have secured the permission of God in that case to manifest myself to you. My manifestation will be for the purpose of easing the tension in your mind. 1 shall manifest myself to you and talk to you face to face and prepare you for God's Revelation.

There is no such thing as Revelation or death. Revelation must precede death but the enigma is when will He reveal Himself to you. He has promised you in compliance with your prayer that He will keep you in proper physical condition till you are called away But He is God and will keep you waiting for months and years together if He wills and then you, out of your despair and exhaustion of long waiting, will yourself withdraw the condition. The minute you withdraw it, He will reveal Himself to you; you should then be prepared to bear your physical suffering bravely."

On August 18, 1955, Ram Ram gave me the amazing news of Ahura Mazda having extended my life again. This apparently signified further delay in Ahura Mazda's Revelation to me and I felt very sad and nervous.

On August 22, 1955, Ahura Mazda in the course of a long message, said:

> "I must not take into consideration only your fitness for My Revelation and mission. I have to consider other factors also which are beyond the view of even My Masters."

Homi in the course of a most beautiful letter to me dated August 24, said:

> "You and the mission are now one. You live for the mission only. But I think that is not everything Ahura Mazda seems to want you to exercise living as a Spirit even while in flesh *i.e.*, to say He wants you to understand that the mission has already commenced and you are expected to live as one not merely MOMENT ARILY in contact with God and acting as His conscious instrument but as one in contact with Him EVERY MOMENT OF YOUR LIFE AND ACTING AS SUCH."

Homi's letter was placed at the altar and Ahura Mazda gave me a long explanation. He said:

> "You have inward awareness of My contact. It is because of this awareness that all the time you are thinking of God and God alone."
>
> Whether I extend your life or not, your duty is to work for others. This work you have to do both in the physical world as well as in the Spirit World. The more you think of others, the more you strive for the good of others, the more will grow in you the awareness of God and your strength likewise would grow to cope with the work. What you are doing now is a mere spadework. With My Revelation will come real enlightenment and your mission will then start in right earnestness. Keep on thinking of the mission and Revelation will follow automatically."

I had grown really weary of waiting, The suspense was killing me. I was tired of assurances which never materialized.

On September 1, 1955, Ahura Mazda said:

"You have now reached a state seldom reached by a human being. You want absolutely nothing except God. This feeling has come to you in a most intense form. It has been there all the time but not in the present degree."

The same day, at night Ahura Mazda gave me the following message:

"Do you know how well I have trained you ? I have by progressive steps spread over a number of years brought you to the present stage when you have not only to crush all your desires, passions and egotism but have to depend upon God alone and none else. Friends, relations, teachers, books, schools, churches, scriptures have their value in teaching a soul and putting it on the right path. When the soul by perfecting itself succeeds in getting on the path, it is guided by a Master in physical body or a Spirit Master. This Master plays a most dominant part. It is a great achievement to contact a Master, who helps the soul eventually in gaining its own liberation. But the soul's liberation is not the highest thing in life. There is something beyond it. It is rarely tried. For, it is beyond human achievement. But here and there, God finds or rather discovers a soul fit for the highest type of God's Revelation and to such a soul He allots the task-of transforming the world. This burden has been assigned to you."

"It is because I have chosen you for such a stupendous mission, I want you to rise to the highest spiritual status and you have to rise above the crutches of even the Masters. Come to Me alone by the dint of your own efforts, putting your entire faith in Me, forgetting your world entirely, with your thoughts centred on God and I shall declare you to the world as My own emissary and take you through your mission safely and successfully."

On September 9, 1955, I received proof copies of Ahura Mazda's foreword to *"How I Found God"* and when my eyes fell on the words Ahura Mazda at the bottom of the last page, I felt a thrill of joy passing through me and my head fell down in deep gratitude to God. Ahura Mazda in the course of a subsequent message said:

"I have written this foreword specially to awaken your world through you. It is not meant for you so much as it is for your world."

On September 13, 1955, Ahura Mazda gave a small foreword to "*Poems of the Heart*" and to help me, He even dictated to me the whole 'Introduction'. My eyes glistened with tears of gratitude for was He not All in All to me, my Supreme Guide and fountain source of inspiration?

On September 16, 1955, Ahura Mazda speaking about U.S.A.'s attitude, said:

> "U.S.A. is the greatest obstacle in the path of peace in the world. But don't be afraid. Every prediction of Mine regarding world events will come true. Red, China will get a seat in the U.N.O. and peace will be established throughout the world."

On September 17, 1955. Ahura Mazda gave a brief outline of my future:

> "I see you getting My Revelation. I see the transformation in you, bodily, mentally and spiritually. I see you embarking upon My mission. I see the banner of Truth rising from the debris of falsehood and discord. I see you coming out triumphant holding aloft the Banner of Truth. Your eyes are rivetted on God. Your mouth speaks only one word, "God". I see you taking the road to My Abode. I see you quitting the physical world and entering without body into My World of Spirit. I see you with My Masters, ready to carry out My orders as keenly as you are today obeying Me."

On the October 1, 1955, my soul gave me an exceedingly important talk. It said:

> "Yes, I am your soul. Do you know how very busy I am ? It is only a freed soul that can be busy. It is because of my having attained liberation that I can move out from your body, visit persons on your plane and the astral world and pay periodic visits to the Spiritual Plane. I am busy, for I am allowed to make plans in consultation with the Masters for the fulfillment of your mission which is soon to start. God has released the whole programme and I have received it through the Masters. It is all so very plain to me. It makes me jump with delight."

> The poem you composed a fortnight ago was not at all your composition. I was ordered by God to put into verses what was revealed by Him to me. I went on repeating the verses and you

heard my voice as if I was dictating to you and you were writing down my dictation. That poem was an expression of what I saw myself when God gave me His Revelation all of a sudden when I was not even prepared for it.

" I saw God through the flash of lights and flaming red fire. I t has made the deepest impression upon me, your soul. I am now looking forward to completing God's programme of work, destined for you. Good has given his Revelation. I can't understand, why He is still keeping you in suspense. Why does He not give you awareness of the Revelation which I, your soul, have witnessed ?This is the only thing that startles me and makes me anxious. You must get physical consciousness of God's transcendental Revelation. Your book, your mission and even your death hang upon this mystical event."

''My sole objective was the mission and not God's revelation. Why revelation was prolonged was explained by Ahura Mazda in His message of 5.10.55: "Regarding your book, it is just to kill in you the desire for its publicity that I have prolonged its completion for so long. There are other reasons also. I have so tried you out by the long wait, that you do not care now whether the book is published or not. Your heart, mind and soul are now centred on God and God alone. You want nothing but God. I have achieved My point..."

''Besides, as Homi has pointed out, it is not your book at all. It is My book for it contains My messages and those of the Masters. You should not feel that you are doing anything wrong in getting it published. All you have to do is that if your world praises you for the book, which it must do eventually, don't accept the praise as due to you.''

GOD'S REVELATION

I thank Thee, God a million times for Thy revelation.
My heart leaps in joy with sudden acclamation.
The long awaiting is crowned with consummation
Of my heart's sovereign desire in fullest gratification.
I hear Thy voice from the rainbow arc of light;

I see Thy cloak of fire, a divine sight;
I see the leaping flames, all fiery red and white.
A glorious sight of Thy Beauty and Thy Might !
Thrilling waves of joy sweep my heart and mind.

In cluster 'Of lights and flames of different kind
Stunned as if with the blast of wintry wind,
In the deepening silence, there God I find.

I bow to thee, my Lord, in utter gratefulness,
Stunned and amazed at Thy many-sidedness.
I pay my homage to Thee in heart's fullness.
I feel a new joy, a new life of colourfulness.

Thou art the giver and I the receiver;
Thou art the mover and the driver;
Thou art the charioteer and the skipper;
Oh, take me onward in life's river.

How could I, who had been rendered absolutely helpless, without any will of my own, ever take credit or praise for any achievement, I explaimed to Ahura Mazda and He readily said: "I am glad this truth is firmly grasped by you."

I was reading at this time '*Maha Yogi*' *(Life, Sadhana and Teachings of Aurobindo Ghosh)* by R.R. Diwakar, sent to me by Doraswami. The following message in this connection given by Ahura Mazda would be found interesting:

"Aurobindo's idea was most plausible. He was like Buddha, most unselfish. He wanted not salvation for himself only but that he could discover some technique in Yoga by means of which God Himself could descend and transform and divinize the whole human society. He was quite right in thinking that the world is advancing towards a new epoch, when supermen would be born to govern and control the destinies of your world and create a new race – a race with higher idealism, a: race wedded to God, a race of the sixth sense – the SUPERMIND, not the mind in its limited capacity which is ruling the world through its dictators, politicians and legislators."

I am welding the different parts of your world in one homogeneous unit: It will take time and it will require many supermen to bring about such a great trans formation. But this idea of world government with one world religion has penetrated into the thought streams of your world and it will be the work of htese superman to build up this idea and give it a concrete shape."

On October 9, 1955, when I was mediating in the afternoon, I saw small rectangualr block of light swiftly passing away. Ahura Mazda gave me the following explanation:

"Yes, it was just a small bit of transcendental light that passed off quickly from one end to the other to tell you that you should be now ready and prepared for the final scence." I enquired whether I had seen it with my inner eye. Ahura Mazda replied: "Yes, with your inner eye which, with the severe impact of the transcendental light, was forced to open out just for a second and that too very, very slightly, I had to exert My power as God to keep it closed. You just got an extremely small vision of the mighty panorama and that too for a few second only. What you saw was the minutest of the minutest part of the whole ethereal light that passed over you."

A 72 hour complete fast was imposed upon me from the night of October 10, 1955 and after its termination I was asked to give up fasting entirely *i.e.*, fasting during day time that was started on September 29, 1955 was also stopped. During the three day fast I was allowed to take water.

On October 23, 1955, I was reminded of how I would see God.

"You won't see Me as a person. You will not see Me in any concrete form. You will see Me when you hear My voice coming to you through a blaze of colours and lights and flashing flames all around. It is the same voice that you are hearing now when you take down My messages. But when Revelation takes place, you will wee the direction of the voice and you would feel as if you were in the presence of INFINITE BEAUTY, INFINITE LIGHT, INFINITE CONSCIOUSNESS, of which you are but the tiniest of the tiniest spark glowing like fire in the large dome of your world in its darkness. Yes, your world is dark. My World of Spirit is all LIGHT, all BEAUTY, all CONSCIOUSNESS."

"*Hatha Yoga* and *Raja Yoga* practices have nothing to do with spiritual life. The former arrives mostly at body control and the latter at mind control. Spiritual life means to take a plunge into the Divine -- as you would jump into the sea. And that is not the end but the very beginning; for after you have taken the plunge, you must learn to live in the Divine. How are you to do it? You have simply to jump straight in and not to think "Where shall I fall ? What will happen to me?" It is the hesitation of your mind that prevents you. You must simply let yourself go. If you wish to dive into the sea and are thinking all the time" Ah, but there may be a stone here or a stone there," you can't dive."

"Of course you must have had some glimpses of the Divine Reality, as you must see the sea and know some thinng of it before you can jump into it. The glimpse is generally the awakening of the psychic consciousness. You must have felt the liberation breath of the Divine World. And you must have felt too as the suffocating pressure of the breath of the ordinary world. If you felt that, then you have only to seek fefuge unreservedly in the Divine Reality and live in its help and protection and in it alone. This you may have done in the course of your ordinary life only partially of in some parts of your being or at times and on occasions, but you must do this completely and for good. That is the plunge you have to take and unless you do it, you may do yoga for years and yet know nothing of a true spiritual being. Take the whole and entire plunge and you will be free from this outer gross and get the true experience of the spiritual life."

"You are now in the state of final plunge into the deep waters of Divinity. I am going to guide you now to take the last and final plunge into the very depth of the OCEAN, fearlessly, joyously and with complete faith in your God. He and He alone is your protector, guide and friend. You need nothing and in nothingness is your strength and power. Your soul has seen Me and My Spirit World and the Masters interested in you. I am asking you to continue your meditation, for the more you mediate, the better it becomes for Me to give you My Revelation.

You discarded *Hatha Yoga* from the very start. In this you were wise. To say that *Raja Yoga* is not necessary of relevant to spiritual life is wrong. Control of the mind without meditation is not possible and without control of the mind, it can not be said that you have reached the peak of spirituality. Body control comes mechanically by mind control and when the mind is controlled, you attain spiritual perfectin. *Raja Yoga* is indispensable in attaining spirituality.

Aurobindo is quite wrong in saying that *Raja Yoga* is not spiritual life. The objective of this Yoga is attainment of spirituality and annihilation of mind."

On October 31, 1955 Ahura Mazda gave me the following message:

"Instead of you waiting anxiously, it is now I that am waiting most anxiously to reveal Myself to you. Is it not strange? This is because I have to race against time. I am God and I can do whatever I like. It is not for Me to race against time, for Time and Space do not at all exist for me. I am in Timelessness and Spacelessness and yet when I say that I have to race against Time, it is to express to you the idea that the time allotted for your mission is so very small that if My Revelation does not take place immediately, your mission would be greatly affected. This should convince you now of the proximity of My Revelation to you."

On November 2, 1955, my soul again assured me that I must soon get full awareness of God's Revelation.

It said :

"Whenever I feel like leaving your body, I quietly ask Ahura Mazda to give me permission to go out and He lets me out at once. I used to ask for permission before and He scarcely listened to me. He would let me go only when he wished. Now, He allows me to go when I ask him. It is because of this change that I feel convinced that he wants to give His Revelation to you without any more delay of postponement."

On November 5, 1955, Ahura Mazda gave me the stunning news that He has stopped my communication with my soul. He also said that I should not write to Homi and Doraswami nor should they write to me. I was told that my place was the altar room and that I must have very little intercourse with the outside world.

I put the following question to Ahura Mazda:

"Madame Blatvatsky in her book "*Isis Unveiled*" says that the world must be 2,50,000 years old. She also says that the geologists should not be believed in what they infer from their present day discoveries regarding the history and civilisation fo our world. Their conclusions are based on superficial observations. The world must have withnessed countless civilisation which must have followed one after another, decayed and then died. The Ancients knew, according to the author, more of divine philosophy and more of arts and sciences that the modern world knows. Events move in cycles. Each cycle witnesses the growth and decay of a civilisation. It takes a number of centuries to make a cycle. Is this all true?

Ahura Mazda gave the following reply:

"Yes she is perfectly correct. This information she has been able to get from the Masters. She must be recognised as a true messenger of God for it was as per My orders that the Masters gave her the secrets of My universe and enlightened her. Each cycle has given to your world a certain indication of the progress of the Law of Evolution. Each cycle is a step in progression over the preceding cycle. Each cycle has its height of perfection and decadence."

I was asked to confine myself wholly to the altar room, as far as possible.

I was also reminded by Ahura Mazda of two fundamental points viz., that I must allow myself to be used by Him alone as His vehicle and that I should not take the least credit for any achievement.

Commenting on the experience I had when I was meditating in the afternoon on December 9, 1955. Ahura Mazda said:

"You had a very shrilling experience. I had predicted this to you some days ago and it has happened. Today you felt your heart throbbing with a strange feeling of inward joy – more joy of expectancy than anything else. This expectancy was not in vain for it was followed by your seeing extremely white clouds shining like a stream of pearly whiteness. There were no lights but pearly white flashes of passing waves of ether. You saw the surrounding firmament of ether in pactches and in shining skids. It was a most beauteous sight but what you have seen today is the most fragmentary and momentary view of the outer cover of the invisible world. I shall take you step by step into the inner regions till you reach the highest plane in the universe which is the abode of your soul and where your soul goes nearly every day when you go into samadhi.

What you have seen today is with the aid of your inner eye which I allowed to open for a short time. I must take you to the invisible shore by slow steps lest any harm may come to you bodily or mentally. I have kept your inner eye closed for so long only for the purpose of giving you My training.

This training is now over and you must start on your mission straight off."

On December 14, 1955, Ahura Mazda gave me to understand that He was going to end my SILENCE. He said:

"It has been prolonged too long and I must end it now. My reasons are:

(1) Your life's span is coming to an end. I do not want to give you any further extension.

(2) The mission is of a very strenuous order and I must give you sufficient time for its success.

(3) You have passed-all your tests which are a guarantee of your ripeness for the mission and there is no longer any necessity of testing your fitness for the mission.

(4) World events have now reached a state, though it may not be quite apparent to you, when it may be safely taken that all predictions made my Me will come correct.

On the December 19, 1955, a strange thing happened. The various Masters gave me messages dissuading me from hankering after God's Revelation. They said that I was just an ordinary human soul, absolutely unfit to carry out such a momentous mission as that of God's emissary on earth.

But I was not perturbed. Ahura Mazda said:

"I am extremely glad you have passed My test. I purposely made the Masters give you flase messages just to test your faith in Me. Your faith in Me is firm as rock."

Late at night, Ahura Mazda gave me the following message in reply to my prayer to Him for His mercy to put me on His mission straight off and not postpone it any more:

"You have every right as a human being to ask for My mercy. But in your case that right does not exist. You are ONE WITH ME. Why and how can you then plead for anything by way of mercy and compassion from Me?"

The following message was given to me by Ahura Mazda on December 28, 1955:

"In order to make you absolutely fit for My mission I shall adopt all sorts of measures to shake your faith in Me and to break you down physically, mentally and even spiritually. You must face these attacks bravely and not get dejected.

When you are in My hands, how can I ever allow you to be chained to gloom. I must give some exercises to your soul and these necessarily must bring in their train a sense of despondency. But when this happens-and it must continue to happen – you must keep in mind that it will soon pass away, that it is a mere test of your mettle and nothing else.

If I say that you will get My Revelation on a certain date or when a certain event takes place, never doubt the statement nor expect it, keep absolutely a nonchalant attitude. Whether predictions come true or not, whether promises and assurances are fulfilled or not, it has nothing to do with you. It is all a part of your training."

On December 29, 1955, I was in samadhi for nearly four and a half hours at a stretch. It brought to my mind absolute peace and clam and I felt inwardly most happy. It was a reflection of my soul's enjoyment.

Ram Ram gave me a stern warning that even in the worst phase of despair, I should not doubt. He said:

"Man's will, if it is not submissive to God's Will, is the greatest enemy of man. You have made your will submissive to God's Will and by so doing you have helped Him in accepting you as His instrument for the mission."

On January 1, 1956, Ahura Mazda describing the experience during my meditation, said:

"When you were meditating today in the early hours, you felt a sort of throb in your heart which continued for more than an hour. The throbging of the heart is an indication of your beginning to get awareness of My Revelation to you."

The following message of Ahura Mazda on 12th January, 1955, explains the difference between powers of the soul when liberated and the special powers conferred by God and the reason for suppression of the latter powers:

"The powers that I have given to you far exceed the usual soul powers that come into effect when the soul is liberated. In you case, these powers have not come into effect sofar because I had to suppress them lest you may start using them and not care for My Revelation. I am the Creator and I am the destroyer. The very powers created in you, I have destroyed as if it were, not for your chastisement, but for your greater elevation, to be in direct communion with of the powers implanted in you must keep on growing."

On January 13, 1956, Ram Ram after describing the incident of my having seen in meditation a great block of red fire passing over and making me temporarily dazed, said:

"You are at present half spirit, half matter. When Revelation takes place, you would be wholly spirit without the slightest trace of matter."

I was given permission to keep a ten-day total fast commencing from 16th January 1956. I went through the ten days fast, if not with ease, at least without any untoward event taking place during its course. My only source of anxiety was the illness of my wife during this period of fast.

On February 1, 1956, in the course of a long message, Ahura Mazda told me:

"I say you are Dead and you must think that you are DEAD. Put the word "*DEAD*" in large capital letters before your mind's eye

.... I again say that I look upon you as DEAD and you have to act as if you are DEAD. Your body is dead, your mind is dead, your spirit is fled. You are only a living corpse pulled by Me and worked by Me as I want.

Let every one in your house know that you are deat. Let your world know that you are dead and you must act as if you are DEAD."

I was infor med by Ahura Mazda in His message of February 3, 1956 that Meher Baba was trying to contact me but that He was foiling his attempts.

I was told on the February 8, 1956, that if I broke silence without His consent, the consequences would be terrible.

On February 14, 1956, I was told by Ahura MaZda that Meher Baba had found me out and that he would contact me the day I got God's Revelation, for on that day God would give me the gift of clairvoyance.

On February 21, 1956, I was assured by Ahura Mazda that His tests were no longer affecting me. This assurance was most pleasing for it meant rapid advancement to the goal.

February 25, 1956, was a fateful day for. To me, it appeared like an ordinary day but Ahura Mazda, in the course of a long message, analysed the events of the day and said: "You have decided your fate today, not I."

Ram Ram also said the same thing "You have today prepared the way for God's Revelation. He is going to satisfy you by His sudden Revelation."

Regarding powers necessary for the purpose of the mission when it starts after God's revelation, Ram Ram said: "You are quite right in not asking for siddhis or powers. These powers are innate in you. If they had not been innate, Ahura Mazda would not have selected you as His emissary. It is only when an aspirant makes powers or siddhis his objective and not God-realization, that God is displeased."

On March 5, 1956, at night Ahura Mazda gave me a most surprising and disheartening message. He said: "I have decided not to reveal Myself to you nor to put you on My mission. Your book *"How I Found God"* will remain incomplete......... The powers conferred upon you by Me I have withdrawn today...........I have changed My plans for you entirely. I am sorry I find that in spite of strenuous training, You are not fit for My mission for the following reasons:

Firstly, though I crushed your ego and made you egoless, it is showing signs of asserting itself again.

Secondly, your body is weak. I can strengthen and vitalise it for I am God but it may collapse all of a sudden and there is no sense in asking you to do strenuous work.

Thirdly, there is no certainty that when I give you powers for the mission, you will not make use of them for your own gratification. This is the greatest danger.

Fourthly, I don't want to take advantage of your vow to immolate yourself for the good of others. In a word, I free you from the vow to sacrifice yourself for I find that your sacrifice is not at all voluntary.

Fifthly, there is no possibility of your mission coming to a successful end in the small span of your remaining life and I do not at all like to extend your life even by a day.

You are no longer in communion with Me. You may of course invoke Ram Ram and do whatever he may tell you. You are no longer in My training. I transfer you back to Ram Ram. He is now your sole Master, and Guide and not I at all."

The above message, however, did not at all deject me. Nor did I pay any importance to it. When Ram Ram was invoked, he said to me:

"Let me tell you that Ahura Mazda does not mean even one word of what He has said to you just now."

"Ahura Mazda gave me a short message. He said: "Don't think that I left you because I was ispleased with you. I left you because you must learn perfect surrender to God's Will in all circumstances of life."

On March 10, 1956, Ahura Mazda made it clear to me the reason why He was baffling me. In the course of a long message, He said:

> " I am still baffling you for the simple reason that you must learn how to cease to be confused and not seek the guidance of the Masters to solve your difficulty in understanding Me. You must learn patience and acquire the habit of complete obedience to My will.
>
> Regarding discretion, you have to use it in ordinary cases and problems but when you deal with Me direct you should resist from using it.
>
> I am stopping you today from invoking Ram Ram or any other Master. You are now in a position to understand Me without any one's guideance."

A friend in America wrote to me that preparations for an extensive tour of Meher Baba in U.S.A. were made and his followers were asked to make their contributions towards the tour expenses. On 13.3.56 Ahura Mazda gave a message as under:

> "Meher Baba is not at all justified in raising large sums of money from his poor disciples. Like Ramana Maharshi, his role is to work in silence and the people of the world should flock to him and not that he should run about at the expense of other people......"
>
> "Meher Baba is a failure. If God's Will is thwarted, the ego returns. The ego is showing signs of return in Meher Baba and it means his final doom."
>
> "I wish to give him more opportunity to realise his errors. If he does that I may further extend his life and make use of him in bringing about a great spiritual and religious awakening in your world."

My attention was pertinently drawn by Ahura Mazda to the necessity of keeping in check the working of my individual mind. He said:

> "You must slay it by keeping it passive. Those who subject themselves entirely to Me and lead a passive life are the greatest instruments for the good of the world. Think that your life has come to an end, that you are living only because God is making

> use of your body, mind and soul for some higher purpose, whether that higher purpose is known to you or not."

There was no doubt that I was quite tired of leading the life of passivity imposed upon me, but having taken the vow I had no recourse but an unconditional surrender to God.

On March 20, Ahura Mazda warned me and told me to forget all about the publication of the book, *"How I Found God."* He said:

> "You must forget that you have to complete the book. You must forget that you are the author of the book."

To destroy the book was the only way to crush the ego in me. "Destroy the book and you destroy the last vestige of your ego." Such was the command of the Supreme Spirit and I readily agreed to carry cut His order. But He soon countermanded His order and the book was not destroyed. It was a test.

The tests continued but they were more or less surface tests, having lost their pungencey.

Christ the Master in the course of a long message said:

> "Ahura Mazda will place temptations in your way to excite your egotism. A slain ego revived again is a most dangerous thing."
> A most careful note of this warning was taken by me.

A friend raised the question whether J. Krishnamurti was a God-realized person and whether his philosophy was acceptable. Ahura Mazda's message throws a flood of light on the subject:

> "In the first place I must say that Krishnamurti is a rare soul. That he has realized God is absolutely true. It is extremely difficult for most of the thinking people to understand him. God can be realized only when the mind is pure and unruffled. According to him, this state of unruffled mind can be attained without the aid of a guru, without the aid of prayers, meditation, concentration etc.
>
> When a child begins to learn to walk, does the mother not help the child? Does the child walk all of a sudden without anyone's

aid? No. It is impossible. The mother holds out her hand and it starts making efforts. These crutches are absolutely necessary viz., prayers, meditation, guidance of a guru and the Scriptures. They are infallible instruments. They cannot be dispensed with. Krishnamurthi does not want them at all for he is born with the vision of God in him. He is a rare soul. His teachings are therefore of no interest to the world at large. People are not born like Krishnamurthi with God's vision."

Whether rapid industrialisation is good, whether the present age which tends to mechanise the man is conducive to peace and growth of spirituality and whether the trend of political thought towards Socialism and Communism is justifiable or not – these were the question raised.

Ahura Mazda gave the following reply:

"Renunciation does not necessarily mean abstention from possession of material things. True renunciation is the state of desirelessness – not to ask for anything, to curb the mind in its greed for praise, comforts of life, satisfaction of the senses etc."

Improvement of the condition of the masses is a grave duty laid upon every spiritual leader. It is arrant nonsense to say that the masses must be submerged in poverty, so that they may grow spiritually. Instead of growing spiritually, they would be submerged in wickedness of the most horrible kind. To practice poverty and abstinence with a knowing mind in order to unfold the inner powers for God-realization is meant for those who want to advance spiritually and their number is extremely small. But for the teeming masses, to rot in slums and in dens of ignorance is no spirituality. It is wickedness.

Each person has a right to a fair means of livelihood and when his material needs are adequately satisfied, he would turn more and more towards God, provided there are no opportunities for the exercise of his greed and lust, the two most concomitant evils of materialism. A Socialist State where each man works for the common purpose of gaining his share due to him for a fair living and nothing more, can do a lot in not only raising the standard of living and thinking of the ordinary individual but in eliminating all those brutal conditions which exist today in your world by the functioning of different classes of people. A classless society, bound together by ties of humanity, brotherhood, common culture and self-denial, will be a vast improvement upon the present hydra-headed monstrosity that passes off as human society. Differences should be narrowed down, particularly economic differences. The other differences will remain but they too by the passage of time will become smaller and smaller till the millennium is reached, when each person will be a God in reality.

"Regarding mechanisation of the mind, whether you work with your hand or whether you work with the aid of the instruments which your science has devised, it makes not the least difference whatsoever. As your civilization advances the mind has got to be used with new changes, new environments, new modes of life, new thoughts, new vistas of life that open out. What is wanted is that man must understand the higher values of life and not be carried away by material achievements."

Religion is innate in man. Whether he works in a factory of a farm, it will not make much of a difference provided the hours of work are short and the conditions in which he works are in conformity with the overall requirements of life. Even in the mechanical age, through which your world is passing, man's sovereignty is unassailable. Masses have to be reared up in the school of liberal thought, education and culture. Religion that is based on ethical and higher values of life with God as the central figure should be followed. What should be the fundamental principle and end of life? The more you talk of God and His goodness, the more you spread the vibration of divinity which would be felt even when your machine is humming or you are eating or smoking or hearing the radio of flying in the air. The whole atmosphere should reverberate with the sound of the word 'God' uttered by thousands and millions of people all the time. What is there to be afraid of in the machine destroying man's spirituality? This is arrant nonsense. See God in the machine that you use and the machine will not dominate you but God would dominate you."

On April 7, 1956, Ahura Mazda in the course of a long message said: " I have changed your body into spirit."

> Christ following the above message of Ahura Mazda said: "The light flowing from your body has become all of a sudden extremely brilliant. It is the light of God emanating from your body. Your soul is transformed into spirit and your body no longer looks like a physical frame. It is all the work of God. Kindly don't ask for our manifestation at all. Keep quiet and let God do whatever He likes."

On April 8, 1956, I was assured by Ahura Mazda that in place of my present passivity, which had dragged on for too long and exhausted all my stock of patience, I would soon be put into activity of ahurricane type. Ahura Mazda said: " I shall drive you through heat, fire, water, soaking rains, and pelting stones, unquenchingly and courageously, till you come to the end of your tether and I call you away. I shall call you away just a minute before your body shows signs of decay and collapse, in full vigour of mind and spirits."

At night, I heared the Masters singing. They sang a song of jubilation as ordered by Ahura Mazda, the Supreme Spirit.

JUBILATION

We Masters have learnt with jubilation,
That to end your mortification,
God is going to give you His Revelation,
To your entire satisfaction and exultation.

It is a day of triumph and victory,
Burn the incense and take the rosary,
Sing God's praises with heart's fury;
All worries and fears, ban and bury.

Divine Light and Love is your domain,
In peace and bliss you shall ever remain,
He has lifted you from earthly terrain;
He has freed you from want and pain.

Your soul shines like a silvery light,
It is gay and ever so bright,

God's light is its might,
It is ready for heavenly flight.

Oh, ring the bells cheerly;
Sing the Song of God, joyously,
Sing and dance heartily,
Sing all the way long, eternally.

There was No doubt in my mind that I was merged in God. I knew this intuitively but there was no proof to convince the world of it. But Ahura Mazda assured me "Having convinced you in every respect, I am going to take steps to convince you world also."

The altar room was the most sacred place for me. It was my refuge citadel, Ahura Mazda said:

> " Let Me tell you again and again that it is very necessary that you should keep to your altar room. It has its own aura, its own atmosphere. It is a most consecrated place for you. It is a resort of the Masters."

On April 19, 1956, I was made to take the following affirmation:

> "I shall follow my God, the Master who shall work through me and none else in the universe. I shall offer myself completely and wholly to Him in thought, word and deed and will take no credit or praise for any achievement. My function will be to act as His vehicle, His instrument and He will be the Charioteer, the Doer, the Planner and the Thinker. I shall not make use of the powers for my personal gain or aggrandisement but will allow God to work through me for the good of others, my sole role being to act as a subservient and obedient child, carrying out the orders of its father."

On April 20, 1956, Ahura Mazda speaking about the silence imposed upon me, said:

> "The minute you get awareness of God's revelation, you will automatically begin to speak."

Homi, in his letter of April 22, 1956, gave me a description of his experience:

"At about 11:50 a.m. when I was reading your soul's message of 19.4.56, 12:30 p.m. I was surprised to find my Inner Self springing out of me and standing very close by me on my right and directing me to go carefully through that message and finish reading the other messages which followed. As soon as I had done that, this Inner Self of mine told me: " The hour of triumphs is close at hand." Immediately thereafter I saw Ahura Mazda standing next to my Inner Self and He confirmed the latter's statement."

The above statement of Homi was confirmed by Ahura Mazda in His message of April 25, 1956.

On April 29, 1956, I had an extremely beautiful experience while meditating in the afternoon. It is best to describe the whole phenomenon in the words of Ram Ram He said:

"What you have seen today is just a faint beginning. You saw red glimmering, deepening into long stripes and widening like an ocean, faint but at the same time extremely clear. This is the fringe of the outer skirt of our Spirit World which you have seen today, sitting in your altar room, with your physical eyes closed but with the inner eye slightly functioning. And then all of a sudden emerged, to your joy and surprise, the tall figure of Christ, just as you see him the picture in your altar room. I had told you that when we Masters manifest ourselves, Christ would be the first to come to you. He has taken precedence on us, for it is his right. Your head bent down as you saw him and he blessed you. You did not hear his words but next time when be meets you, you will hear him also."

In order to clear my doubt, I asked Ram Ram whether I saw Christ in a vision or was it with my inner eye? He promptly replied:

"It was not a vision at all. You have developed your inner powers and it is for the first time that Christ's manifestation has become visible to you. As I have said, it is still a feeble beginning. You have seen Christ in your deep meditation. You will see him later on even with your eyes open."

In the course of a long message given to me by Ahura Mazda on May 2, 1956 in the morning, Ahura Mazda said:

"Yours is not an ordinary case of God Realization. To have realized God, to have become a *Jivan Mukta* and yet to have renounced that crown of *Jivan Mukta* for six long years, is a renunciation of the highest sort. I don't want to suppress your powers any more. I don't want to keep you caged in your passivity any further.

Now as regards Homi's seeing Me – Ahura Mazda, his conception of Ahura Mazda is in a certain direction. He thinks that Ahura Mazda and Shanker are identical. This notion of his is so deeply rooted that the form of Shanker is for his identification. In your case, you were looking upon Sai Baba as your God and I came to you taking the form of Sai Baba. As Sai Baba has taken rebirth, I shall now appear myself to you in a certain definite form. There is no necessity for you to ask for Shanker's picture or any other picture. I shall assume a certain form specially for you and as I shall be continually coming to you, you will be able to recognise Me immediately. This is the special privilege I give to you to see Me in a special form."

Homi in his letter dated April 29, 1956, gave me news of another experience about me. He said: "1 was told last night (Saturday 28.4.56) 11:00 p.m. that you had received the Lord's Anointment just then but that it did not mean that you had received physical consciousness of His Transcendental Revelation. I was told further that this was an Initiation of a very high order."

"Commenting upon Homi's experience, Ahura Mazda said: "That you were anointed by the Lord on Saturday last, it is absolutely correct. This anointment is just one drop to reaching me in My transcendental form."

On May 3, 1956, when I was meditating in the afternoon, I had an amazing experience. I first saw Ram Ram and then, a little after, an ordinary human figure. After Ram Ram's message, Ahura Mazda was invoked immediately and He gave me the following explanation:

"I told you that I would take any form and come to you. I have taken the form of quite an ordinary man. You saw me standing at full length but you were not at all impressed by the figure. It was

> the figure of just an ordinary Hindu teacher or a Brahmin. It reminded you of someone associated with you in your school days as your teacher. My idea in coming to you in this form is to teach you that every human being is a potential God. Look upon every person as God. I dwell not only in every human being but am present in everything in the cosmos. I shall go on changing My costumes and come to you in different waves in order to impress upon you that I, God, can manifest My self in a million ways."

There is a belief especially among Theosophists that on Wasak day, (when there is full moon at night) – the day when Buddha was born, got illumination and died, a ceremony takes place when Lord Maitreya and his host send their benedictions on the earth plane for the uplift of humanity.

Ahura Mazda's following message will be read with interest in this connection:

> "All the ceremony that takes place on the day is when Lord Maitreya and his host send concentrated rays of benedictions on the people of your earth from Our Spiritual Plane."

On May 19, 1956, Ahura Mazda disclosed to me the following important fact:

> "I want to reveal to you that I have appointed Homi as your Master in physical body just as Ram Ram was appointed as your Spirit Master."

The following message of Ahura Mazda on May 20, 1956, describes the phenomenon witnessed by me when I was in meditation:

> "While you were meditating, all of a sudden, you saw a panorama of dazzling beautiful starlike lights in a swarm. I allowed you to see this with the aid of your inner eye for a few seconds only in order to thoroughly convince you that your inner eye is open and is functioning. But in order to serve My purpose, I have kept it in the present state of abeyance from functioning."

Ahura Mazda again reiterated in His message of May 21, 1956:

"Krishnamurthi and Meher Baba are both Masters but they are poles apart in their spheres of thought. Both are worthy of praise but they should not be followed in their teachings, for both are failures."

On May 24, 1956, Buddha gave a long message. It is a message of vital importance as it removes the fear that is expressed in many quarters that Buddha did not believe in God. It is wrong for scholars and philosophers to associate Buddhism with atheism.

The following is Buddha's message:

"The world is celebrating the 2500th anniversary of my death today.

The message I gave when I was enlightened by God – and who can enlighten, if not God – was that each man should be a lamp unto himself and make a strenuous effort to reach the ladder of perfection. Without reaching the highest rung of the ladder, it is not possible for him to escape from the wheel of birth and death *i.e.*, the wheel of pain and suffering.

I lived in a palace. I had all the enjoyments that a man can think of. Why should I have renounced everything and left my home, my wife, my child, my father and all the happy associations? I left because in spite of all the luxuries of royalty, I was not at all happy inwardly. Something burnt in me. I wanted to assuage that inward craze, craving or thirst, whatever you may call it. I wanted to find out a solution for life's problems for myself and not depend upon the shastras which were taught to me from my young age. I wanted to know things myself by my own individual efforts and not depend upon what others had discovered. In a word, I sought for enlightenment and I got it.

Two things are indispensable if man wants to get liberation from the wheel of birth and death. They are perfection of character and deep meditation. Meditation follows perfection of character. Meditation and perfection of character must go hand in hand. They have to be integrated. Meditation without perfection of character is not possible and if it is practised, it is useless.

When God gave me enlightenment, He gave me the option to leave the body for good or to stay and spread the message of Self-deliverance to the world. The world was a den of misery, pain and suffering. I said to myself that I must save the world from its darkness and misery. I said to God: "Thou hast enlightened me. Make me Thy child, Thy messenger and help me to serve mankind." He then replied: "Go and tell the people that they should not worship false Gods for personal satisfaction or physical wants. They must work for the sake of work and meditate. I shall come to each man and woman, when his or her meditation reaches the mark of perfection. That work of perfection shall be attained only when the aspirant gets a certificate of My approbation and not otherwise."

On this auspicious day .which your world is celebrating with such fervour, let me say that man's salvation lies only through the pathway of renunciation. Perfection comes only through renunciation and meditation."

The following is a very beautiful message of Ahura Mazda on Socialism:

"Socialism in its true sense means construction of an ideal State wherein people can live in mutual respect for one another in peace and work for a common cause for the uplift and advancement of all the people, materially, socially, morally, intellectually and, above all, spiritually. In such a state, there can be no violence, no dictatorship, no iniquity, no injustice, no want of opportunities to rise to the highest in all spheres and to make MAN'S highest contribution to LIFE itself. In such a state, man would begin to understand how to revere man, for man is God...

SOCIALISM is the only basis on which an ideal Welfare State can be built and it is in accordance with My own plan of Evolution. Just as a man evolves, a nation also evolves. Your world is progressing on the whole. New ideas are to be welcomed for they are based on man's experiences and are an improvement on the old. A socialistic pattern of society is the best for its progress."

On June 12, 1956, Ahura Mazda sprang a surprise on me when He said:

"I don't want to give you My Revelation. There is no time left for the mission to be completed successfully. It is best therefore that

I should call you away and thus bring an end to your struggle...
I had told you that there was a race between My Revelation and your death. The race is lost. Death must triumph."

Evidently, there was some double meaning in Ahura Mazda giving me such a strange message. Ram Ram was invoked and he gave me an explanation. He said:

"There is some hidden meaning in all that Ahura Mazda has said to you just now. He is God and He can do anything and everything. The best course for you is not to wait for death or expect death. It may be that He is laying a trap for you and thus tempting you to violate the vow you have taken viz., not to ask for death."

The following letter of Meher Baba to his followers and devotees dated July 5, 1956 was read out at the altar:

"As declared in the past I am free from promises and am not bound by time and space. Though happenings are in the realm of illusion, a great so-called tragedy is facing me and my lovers. My long expected humiliation is near at hand. This may happen tomorrow or any day of this year or it may happen next year.

The love, courage and faith of my lovers will be -- severe test not by me but by Divine Law. Those who hold fast to me at the zenith of this crisis will transcend illusion and abide in Reality.

I want my lovers to rest assured that my humiliation and 'tragedy' though necessary are but passing phases and are bound to have a glorious end, as is destined. My love to all."

Ahura Mazda gave me a reply as under:

"After arrogating himself as *Avatar* (Incarnation) of God, Meher Baba speaks of humiliation. Yes, I have humiliated him in the eyesight of the world by making him make wrong predictions. By 'tragedy' he means his death. He is not sure when his death will take place and therefore talks of it in a vague sense. His death will not at all be a tragedy for he will be given a re-birth for the purpose of fulfilling the mission which he would have surely performed with success had he not arrogated himself to be God's Avatar and given to his book the title. *"God Speaks."* You thus see that nothing is lost or wasted. The training and preparation given to him will stand him in good stead in his next incarnation and he will succeed in his mission for he would take birth with full knowledge of the cause of his failure in the present incarnation."

On July 27, 1956, the world was stunned with the news of Col. Nasser, the President of Egypt, having declared the nationalisation of the Suez Canal. Ahura Mazda gave me the following message late a night:

"This announcement by Col. Nasser of Egypt has thrown a bombshell in the very citadel of Western intrigue. It will have a far-reaching effect. There will be threats of war but they will all die off, giving place to a settlement of world questions in an atmosphere of peaceful conciliation and mutual goodwill. Egypt has taken a very bold step to its lasting credit and it will score a great victory in the end. All My prophecies will come out true. Kindly enter this prediction in your book

Baffling and conflicting messages began now to pour in from both Ahura Mazda and Ram Ram.

Ram Ram congratulated me on detecting the obstacle to the attainment of awareness of God's Revelation of the most transcendental type. He said:

"You have broken to bits the shell of egotism. The ego in you is completely gone. You have won the battle."

On July 29, 1956, I completed my two years of silence. Ahura Mazda gave me the following message:

"Remember, when I tell you that I am Ahura Mazda the Supreme Spirit in the universe, with whom you are in direct communion, you should not only believe it but be absolutely convinced of this fact. It is no doubt quite unusual and a rare experience. You have earned this boon because of your past two incarnations and for the life of sacrifice and devotion in your present incarnation."

At night Ahura Mazda gave me the following message:

"I am no longer training you for the mission on earth That training is over. I am training you now for the work that awaits you when you leave your physical body for good."

In the course of a long message which Ahura Mazda gave on August 6, 1956, at night, He said:

"You have to play the role of a dummy when the mission starts. But even as a dummy all the characteristics of sane judgment, quick perception, patience, tolerance, love, sympathy, gentleness, cheerfulness, sweetness of temper, agility of mind, softness of tongue, coolness in the hour of emergency - all these characteristics have to be first developed and so ingrained in you before the mission starts, that I, the doer, can make the best use of them. You will be an automaton, no doubt in this sense that I will be the actual door and not you. But when I start making use of you, I must see also that the instrument 1 am using has all the elements that I require. If the razor is absolutely blunt, of what use is it to the user? If the instrument is not precise and sharp, how is the surgeon to perform an operation with success ? It is not only the surgeon's skill that is required but the instrument that he uses should be capable of giving due results."

On August 10, 1956, I was given a double surprise. In the afternoon message, I was ordered by Ahura Mazda to write to Doraswami at once to burn away all the copies of *"How I Found God"*. After meditation, I again asked Him whether I should destroy the printed copies I had with me of the book and He said:

"Yes, by all means burn them today, this very minute. Keep nothing with you of this book."

Whatever copies I had of "How I Found God" were immediately destroyed by me as ordered along with Ahura Mazda's foreword as well as Homi's old foreword. Curiously, as I watched the printed pages of the book, the result of six or seven years of patient toil and labour, burning in the red flames, I was not perturbed in the least. It was all Ahura Mazda's grace.

I wrote to Doraswami the same evening and sent him the messages with earnest instructions that he should boldly carry out Ahura Mazda's orders without any hesitation.

At night, to my utter surprise, I was told it was only a test and the destruction of the book was not really meant by Ahura Mazda.

"Let Me tell you that never in your whole life have you pleased Me so much, as you have pleased Me today when without the slightest sense of regret or dejection, you put all the copies of your printed book to flames and burnt them as ordered by Me. You did not wait even for one minute and carried out My orders so very precisely and promptly. You have passed your test in an extremely brilliant manner.

...You have given me a positive proof of your absolute egolessness. It is immaterial to you whether your book "How I Found God" is completed and published or not.

Will you kindly write a letter at once to Doraswami that he must not put the copies to flames."

On September 6, 1956, I was startled by a most amazing message Ahura Mazda gave me, at night. It was the day of the birth anniversary, as celebrated by Parsis, of their prophet, Zarthustra.

"I did not send Zarthustra as a special prophet to spread My message of Divine Wisdom. He was just an ordinary human soul, as you are, but he had an intense desire to probe into the mysteries of life. He sought seclusion and prayed and meditated and such was the intensity of his zeal to know the hidden side of life, that I was compelled to lift the veil and he talked to Me, face to face. He derived all the divine knowledge from Me and when he was fully equipped with it, I asked him to promulgate to your world the divine wisdom imbibed by him and to establish his religion, the religion of Mazda one-God, one humanity, one path, the path of righteousness and one goal, viz., the perfection of human life.

Zarthustra, according to your scholars, is said to have been born about 3000 years ago. This is not at all correct. The first Zarthustra who preached the divine doctrine and who got Revelation from Me was born in Iran. This was many centuries before Christ, though there are no human records in your world to give proof of the age when he lived and spread his religion. The first Zarthustra, and when I say the first Zarthustra, I mean the prophet Zarthustra and not other Zarthustras who followed him but who were not really prophets, but saints who had remembered the teaching of the original Zarthustra the real prophet was born about ten thousand years ago, a very distant era when your earth was smoked and clouded into the utter darkness of ignorance and there was not a shred of civilization in your world. He was like a beacon light in the wilderness of entire darkness. He was the very first to preach of God the Supreme Spirit in the universe."

The question was put: "Are the Gathas, the Divine Songs, composed by the first Zarthustra the prophet?"

"No, he had not composed them at all. The Gathas were composed by the last in the whole genealogy of Zarthustras, the Zarthustra, whom you Parsis call prophet, but who in reality was not a prophet, but a God realised soul. The real prophet, Zarthustra the first, flourished some ages before Zarthustra, the so-called prophet of the Parsis. The first Zarthustra who, really speaking, was the first prophet has left absolutely nothing of his religion. But his influence when he lived extended over many countries and many people got the first glimpse of divine wisdom through him."

Some years ago, Ram Ram, my Spirit Master, in one of his talks on spiritual philosophy had spoken of Zoroaster as under:

"Time does not permit me to speak of origin of religion but for historical purposes it is safer to say that Zoroaster was the first prophet on earth and he lived about nine thousand years ago. His teachings spread far and wide and he exerted a paramount influence upon the peoples of his time. To say that he was an Iranian is not correct. He belonged to no race or nationality .He gave a universal religion meant to be followed by all. He was neither a Hindu nor an Iranian, nor an Egyptian, nor a Grecian. His utterances of Divine Truth were meant for all irrespective of race or religion. His was the voice of God. His was the teaching imbibed direct from the Godhead. He spoke from personal experience."

The date when Zarthustra flourished has been the object of lively controversy among scholars and savants of religion. We find references to the name of Zoroaster in the books of Greek and Roman writers. Plato, the great Greek philosopher, speaks of him as the founder of the doctrine of the Magi and a son of Oromazes. Pliny and Plutarch, ancient Roman writers, also make a mention of him in their writings. According to Pliny, Zoroaster laughed on the very day he was born, thus implying supernatural powers with which the child was born. Plutarch speaks of Zoroaster's intercourse with Ahura Mazda, and describes his religion in his book "*Isis and Osiris.*"

That Zoroaster was famous in classical antiquity is evident from the writings of various early Greek and Roman writers. But even they differ in locating the age when Zoroaster actually lived. According to the description given by British Encyclopaedia, one writer, Hermippus of Smyma, places him 5000 years before the Trojan wars, and another writer, Xantus says 6000 years before Xerxes, the great Persian Emperor led his army in an unsuccessful attempt to conquer Greece.

According to these writers, Zoroaster must have lived about 9,000 to 10,000 years ago. In the light of these conflicting statements, Ahura Mazda's message must be considered as the most revealing and it should now settle the dispute regarding the mystery of Zarthustra and his age.

Meher Baba returned to India after a 30 day tour in U.S.A. and Australia, on August 17, 1956.

A brief account of his tour was received on September 10, 1956. Some of the statements made by Meher Baba during his tour appear startling, especially the following:

"I am the Lord of the universe."

"All that you see is my creation"

"The whole creation has sprung out of me."

Even Christ considered by the Christendom as the greatest prophet never said that he was God. He acknowledged himself as Son of God. Christ's chief teaching was: "God is a Spirit and they that worship Him must worship Him in spirit and in truth."

What embarrasses one is the repetition of 'I' in Meher Baba's various statements. The impression that is left on man's mind is that Meher Baba alone should be worshipped for he is God.

To be one with God is the goal of life, but it is blasphemous for any one to claim himself as God, the creator of the universe, the Absolute Spirit or even the Avatar of God.

Ahura Mazdawas invoked to comment upon the subject and He gave the following message:

> "From the point of view of Meher Baba's many followers and admirers, the tour of Baba was a great success and a source of inspiration to them without doubt. I have repeatedly told you that Baba was trained by Me to become a World Teacher .He has singularly failed in his mission as a World Teacher and I shall soon call him away. Some of his utterances arrogating him self to be the creator of the universe, to be God Himself, are arrant nonsense. He has made a terrible mess and there, is no course left but to call him away. I make this prediction that Meher Baba will soon pass away. Kindly embody this message in your book, *"How I Found God."*

On September 15, 1956, as I sat in the altar room ruminating on the message given by Ahura Mazda on Zarthustra, some days ago, I felt inspired to re-invoke Him and He gave me another message in clarification there of:

> "What I have said is absolutely correct. When you get My Revelation, I shall make Zarthustra come to you and explain to you everything face to face.
>
> It is immaterial whether the first Zoroaster was the prophet of the Parsis or the last Zoroaster. Even the last Zoloaster, the author of the Gathas, was as good as a prophet and much greater credit should be due to him that he rose to such a high state of perfection as to have contacted Me direct and imbibed divine knowledge from Me. Zoroaster the first, was born a spirit, though he took the form of a human being. Zoroaster the last, was pot born as a spirit but he became a spirit having transcended the bonds of the flesh into which he was born. That is the only difference between the two Zoroasters; the first has left nothing of his great teachings though he was the very first prophet sent by Me purposely for the purification of your world. Zoroaster, the last, has however left in his 'Gathas' a most precious monument of divine wisdom attained by him by dint of his own devotion for the guidance of all mankind."

On September 20, 1956, Ahura Mazda gave me specific directions to be followed very closely:

(1) You must feel convinced in your mind that you are in direct communion with God, the Supreme Spirit in the universe.
(2) You must also be convinced in your mind that I, your God, have appointed you as My emissary and you have to perform a mission of a unique order for which I have given you a long and most trying training.
(3) You must continue to meditate for long hours as you are doing now and hold fast to your altar room.
(4) You must not enter into any kind of controversy with any one whatsoever and not injure or harm any one's feelings even if that person is absolutely wrong.
(5) You must keep clam even under the highest provocation.
(6) You must not think that you are wasting your time because of the life of passivity imposed upon you by Me.
(7) On the contrary, you must feel convinced in your mind that you are fulfilling God's design in carrying out His orders by leading the present life of passivity. It is a passivity fraught with the highest potentialities of life.
(8) You must continue to be indifferent to everything and not expect anything.
(9) You must observe your silence and seclusion as vigorously as possible. Except your visit to the lame Parsi woman for the purpose of giving her healing passes, you must not go out from your house. You must not also indulge in gestures and communicating with the help of paper and pencil or pen and slate as far as possible.
(10) You must avoid visitors. When you are forced to meet anyone, sit like a mummy. It does not matter if you are misunderstood. On the contrary, if you are ridiculed, reviled or criticised so much the better.
(11) Keep on blessing everyone. It is a gift specially given to you and you must make the widest use of it. Bless everyone, whether friend or foe, the virtuous or the sinner.
(12) Don't think of the future. Leave everything to Me.
(13) Complete resignation to My Will, as you know and which you are practising, is absolutely necessary. Go on repeating the

formula of resignation and complete surrender to Me all the time in your mind.

(14) You must not groan or complain, if you feel the trial too severe, but on the contrary, put on a cheerful face and face the struggle with a buoyant heart and in full and perfect faith in Me.

(15) You must not allow any kind of doubt or distrust to enter your mind even for a second."

On September 24, 1956, I said to Ahura Mazda that instead of any grandiose mission, would it not serve the purpose if some incurable cases were treated with success and I be then called away, instead of my dragging on in the present manner. This caused Ahura Mazda's indignation. He said:

"You have, no doubt, slain your will or rather merged yourself into Me, but inspite of it, you are apt at times to forget it and call your will into force which is not only detrimental to your interests but is most fatal to My mission. Are you such a coward and so low that after My having trained you and taken all the pains to make you fit for a great mission, you want to bury the mission and call for your pound of flesh?"

I was stupefied. It was not for me to argue or to do anything except to render full and complete surrender to His Will.

On September 27, 1956, while meditating, I saw in a flash of LIGHT the following words:

"I LOVE YOU IMMENSELY"

It thrilled me beyond words.

On September 29, 1956, I read out to Ahura Mazda the fifteen directions He had given to me to follow and asked Him to guide me in which direction I had failed. I was assured that the only block in my way was that I could not still give up the habit of expectation.

On September 30, 1956, I was put into samadhi in the afternoon meditation by Ahura Mazda for a short time and I was made conscious of God, the Supreme Spirit in the universe, by tremendous vibrations caused in my body. I was filled with immense delight such as I had never experienced before. Ahura Mazda said: "I gave you just a fraction of consciousness of My revelation."

On October 6, 1956, Ahura Mazda gave me a sermon on the Law of Karma as under:

"The Law of *Karma* which I have established is so inexorable that none can escape it. Why not then leave every one to his or her own *Karma?* Why should you at all worry for their Karmas? You will not be able to wipe out their *Karmas.* All you can do is to guide, to show the way, to bring light into the darkness of their minds. But if they still refuse and want to have their own way, you cannot stop them. It is their *Karma.* Once you have done your duty, leave them to their own *Karma.* If any injustice is done to anyone, it is I who have the right to correct the wrong doing and not you. You have no right to judge at all. All you have to do is to be kind, even to the sinner. I know by so doing, false impression is created and it is this that makes the life of a saint so very difficult. But you must follow the path I point to you and not adopt the ways of your sordid world."

"The sinner has to pay heavily under the Law of *Karma.* Why then add to the sinner's load quite unnecessarily? You must take no side at all. Try to patch up by sweet words of reasonableness and kindliness but if the sinner refuses, leave that person to his or her destiny. I say again the Law of *Karma* is inexorable."

The Theosophists give to Buddha precedence over even Christ among the Masters. This was corrected by Ram Ram when he said: "Christ holds the first place in the hierarchy of Masters in our Spirit World, no Buddha. Buddha is just a Master, as I am, more or less on hte same footing as Zoroaster and other. But Christ is above us all."

Swami Omkar of Santhi Ashram (Andhra Pradesh) and I were in constant touch with each other. I held him in deep esteem and reverence for his piety, sincerity and sacrificial ardour as reflected in his book 'Cosmic Flashes.'

Ram Ram gave me a message with regard to this saintly man. He said:

> "He will be of very great help to you when your mission starts for Ahura Mazda has His gaze on him all the time."

The following message of Ahura Mazda and Zarthustra regarding the role of Reincarnation in Gathas should lay to rest all doubts on the question.

Ahura Mazda:

> "Zarthustra taught reincarnation without the slightest doubt. A great deal of confusion has arisen on this subject for lack of knowledge on the part of the votaries of the Zoroastrian religion. The teaching of reincarnation is an invaluable part of Zoroastrianism as preached by the prophet. It is extremely curious how this great teaching has been abandoned through passage of time."

Lord Zarthustra: "Yes, I am Zarthustra, your Prophet, Spirit Guide and Master. My teachings have been manipulated and confounded by various kinds of interpretations by savants and scholars. Reincarnation forms the most fundamental part of my teaching. I have said so in the Gathas written in the Avestan language. Translators of this language have deliberately or unknowingly mistranslated the origional version. Don't depend upon translations. They are mostly faulty and misguiding. I tell you in all seriousness that the Theosophists are not at all wrong in establishing the fact of the teaching of reincarnation in Zoroastrianism.

Q.: "Wilt Thou quote passages which would give proof of this teaching of reincarnation in the Zoroastrian Scriptures? Is Yasna 49.11 in the Gathas as translated by Dr. Erach Taraporevala a convincing proof of the teaching of reincarnation?

> Lord Zarthustra: "Yes, certainly. There are many other passages both in the *Gathas* written by me and in various other writings, which if properly understood and translated, would convince the reader of the teaching of reincarnation.

Reincarnation is a solid fact. It is not a theory but the very basis of the whole of the teaching given by me to your world. Men should aim at perfection in one life. That should be the ideal of everyone and because this point has been so much emphasised in my teaching, the true spirit is lost and the people have begun to consider that reincarnation is not affirmed by me.

There is a vast difference between the real and the ideal. Your world has lasted for centuries and yet man's greed, cruelty, wickedness and viciousness have not disappeared. Ages after ages, in spite of God having sent so many prophets and sages to cleanse your world of its colossal impurity and bring light in the darkness of its stupor and ignorance, mankind has still not advanced much morally and spiritually. The soul evolves but very slowly. It takes ages to reach the zenith of perfection, though of course there are exceptions. Evolution is a slow process and human soul is as much subject to the Law of Evolution as anything else. Everything evolves, so also the soul. To discard the teaching of reincarnation in Zoroastrianism is to rob the religion of its most fundamental aspect."

Ahura Mazda's message on Vegetarianism will be read with interest:

"I want all those who aspire for spiritual perfection and liberation to abstain from meat-eating. Animal slaughter is an inhuman custom that owes its existence to man'sdepravity of soul and ignorance. The higher one is placed in the pyramid of evolution, the greater is his duty to those below him and the greater is the sacrifice. Man wants the sacrifice on animals are slaughtered to feed men, there will be misery, chaos and misfortune in your world. The greater is the reason therefore for man. to be non-violent in all his actions both to brother men and to birds and beasts in Nature."

Ahura Mazda's message on America gives a picture of the spiritual thirst of its people in spite of their rank materialism.

"America is a country of spiritual adventures. Fake spiritual leaders can make tons of money for the people, in spite of their so-called civilization and enlightenment, are feeble-minded and credulous in matters pertaining to the spirit. But this thirst for spirituality is a good sign on the whole. The country will advance spiritually in spite of its extreme materialism, which it will shake off by slow degrees. Its antipathy to communism is not due to love for freedom or democracy as she claims but out of the selfish motive that its present economy may not be disturbed economy. Its based on selfishness, greed, excessive individualism and love for extravagant and luxurious standard of life."

Homi wrote to me a very important leter regarding the origin of the most important prayer 'Ahunavar' in the Avesta of Zoroastrian religion. The following message of Ahura Mazda on the subject is of profound significance:

"My name as known to your prophet Zoroaster of Zarthustra is AHURA MAZDA. You also know Me as Ahura Mazda. Different prophets have known Me by different names but that does not mean that I am different in My teachings to them. What I taught to Zarthustra is not different to what Revelation I gave to various other messengers who followed him. All prophets got My Revelation including Buddha, though today, Buddhism is decried as atheism.

I am God, Ahura Mazda as known to you, but to others of fifferent faiths, I am known by different names. My purpose in emphasizing this point is simply to tell you that you should not be carried away by mere name or form. What is most important is the substance and not the form or the mere label. Whether I was originally known as AA UON or AHUAN makes no difference at all. All prayers are My boon or gifts to mankind whether they be in one language or the other. To say that 'Ahunavar' is My special composition is not correct as Homi imagines. My gifts are universal gifts. They are not limited to any one sect, community or society.

All I can say is that the prayer 'Ahunavar' is a most efficacious prayer. It should be said with a set purpose that it will be implemented by the person who recites it my his actions in life. It is a great teaching not only meant for the followers of Zoroaster but by all persons for it contains universal truths to be practised by everyone. Devotion to God, love for all mankind and righteousness in its broadest and most liberal interpretation, form the cardinal links in the chain of spiritual perfection, which should be the goal of life and nothing else. Invoke Me by any name in the sincerity of your heart and I shall respond either directly or through My Masters.

I am God of the whole creation. To Me every human soul is dear whether stained or pure. If stained, I shall help him to become pure by various means and devices. A stained soul is far away from Me but I can still reach him in infinite ways. A pure soul is easy to deal with for he comes in the orbit of My own aura. To come within the orbit of My aura should be one's highest aspiration.

On November 8, 1956, Ahura Mazda said: "Without the knowledge of the Law of *Karma* and Reincarnation, it would be difficult for anyone to understand the true meaning of religion. Reincarnation and Karma are indivisible. They form the substance of every religion, not Zoroastrianism only."

On November 11, 1956, Ahura Mazda gave me permission to invoke the Sage Dakshinamurthi, who had recently passed away at a ripe old age. The latter gave me a message but refused to disclose anything about himself. He entreated me however to get an explanation from Ram Ram, whom he described as "a very great Master in this world of the Spirits."

Ahura Mazda in the course of a long message confirmed the two statements made by the Sage in his lifetime viz., that there would be no world war and that Mahatma Gandhi had taken birth again.

On November 12, 1956, to my utter surprise, I saw a human form while meditating. Ahura Mazda gave the following explanantion:

"You were deeply absorbed in thoughts of God and I came to you all of sudden taking a human form. What attracted you the most in the form was the long beard and bead-like eyes. You felt extremely happy when you saw Me in the above manner. I disappeared as quickly as I came. I am taking different forms and coming to you in different ways."

On November 13, 1956, my soul said to me:

"I am daily contacting Ahura Mazda and the Masters but I do not like this imprisonment in your body. When I have gained my liberation, why should I stay in your miserable body any longer....?

> Neither the mission starts nor am I given the right to leave your body permanently. I am simply hedged in and made to dwell here against my will. I am now absolutely tired of waiting."

I was able to go into samadhi but only when Ahura Mazda willed. I was experiencing waves of joy inwardly but this state of experiencing of bliss was not permanent. In the course of His message on November 16, 1956, Ahura Mazda said: "You are only in invisible contact with My invisible world. After My Revelation, the invisible world would become visible."

On the 29th, I was allowed by Ahura Mazda to talk with Jamshed, my departed friend, through Ram Ram and in the course of a long message, he expressed his desire to take birth again. He said:

> " I want to take birth in your world but I have to wait for some time before permission is given to me."

Confirming the news of Mahatma Gandhi having taken birth again, Ahura Mazda said:

> "He will play a most dominant part in bringing about a world revolution of the highest and most inspiring type. I have given him the widest powers and I am sure under My guidance, he will make the best use of them for a complete transformation of your world. I am going to bring more and more light into the darkness of your world and this is but an effect of the evolution of human souls on a higher level."

News was received of Meher Baba having met with a motor accident, in which he was seriously injured and one of his disciples met with death.

On January 3, 1957, Ahura Mazda said:

> "All you have to do is to keep in surrendering to My Will for it is My Will that has to guide you and not yours."

The following day Ahura Mazda assured me:

> "The minute your mission starts, the great tension in the world will stop. Things will happen exactly as predicted by Me and this will give you a tremendous backing when the mission is in full swing."

On January 16, 1957, I was put to a severe test. Ahura Mazda said:

> "I cannot give you Revelation of the type promised to you....I have come to this decision that, instead of waiting till you become fit as well as till the conditions on which My mission depends become suitable, it is better that you should be called away. I give you therefore permission to ask for death and I shall immediately call you away."
>
> I was a little puzzled. To ask for death would mean breaking my vow. I said therefore immediately:
>
> "If it be Thy wish to call me away, Thou could do so. But I shall not break my vow and ask for death."

Ahura Mazda replied:

> "If you do not break your vow, even when I give you permission to do so, what is the use of My calling you away? In that case, you will have to go in lingering till you reach the end of the span of life allotted to you."
>
> I said firmly: "Whatever it be, I can't break my vow. Do whatever Thou thinkest best."
>
> He replied: "You have passed your test gloriously. I am extremely pleased. Kindly be now prepared for My Revelation."

The writing of this book was started more than six years ago, and every time when I was asked to write, it was in this faith that the last portion had been written and the drama would close soon by God giving me His Revelation. The following message of Ram Ram on 18th January 1957 is of interest:

> "You think it serves no purpose to go on writing your book in patches without knowing the final end. Have you not written the whole book in this manner? Your book is a record of man's faith in God. It is a signal record of your submission to God's Will. What better record and proof will your world ask for when it comes to know of the manner in which it was started and completed?"

Since the day silence was imposed upon me, I had become a prisoner in my house but latterly Ahura Mazda allowed me to visit two places for the purpose of giving healing passes. Both were incurable cases and my visits to them appeared futile, but I knew in my heart that Ahura Mazda would perform His miracle.

On January 25, 1957 Ahura Mazda gave me the following message:

> "Don't be afraid at all. The two cases that you are healing will be cured very soon. they will be cured in such a way as will simply dumbfound you and your world. I am doing this purposely as a special case to prove to you and to your world, that I am Ahura Mazda, God, the Creator of the universe and they dar not doubt it."

The following message of Ahura Mazda should remove the wrong notion that Zoroaster, Christ and Mohammand never preached to doctrine of Reincarnation.

> "Reincarnation is a settled fact, Every prophet sent by Me to your world was given this teaching but I warned them that as far as possible, instead of placing emphasis upon rebirth, the emphasis should be put upon the absolute necessity of man's gaining perfection in one life. It may be impossible of achievement but as an ideal it should not be lost sight of. Because this ideal was preached by the prophets of old except those of Hinduism and Buddhism, the other prophets are misunderstood by your world and their scriptures not rightly understood. Reincarnation is a cardinal doctrine which cannot be and should not be denied. It is foolishness to do so.
>
> Idealism and realism are poles apart. It is good to hope for the best but seldom the ideal is reached by man in one jump. Nature itself is an exemplification of the truth. It is by the process of evolution, perfection is reached and evolution means countless births and long series of changes from good to better and from better to the best.
>
> It is not my purpose to point out to you any specific passage in the Bible, the quran and the Avesta. All I want to say is that without the teaching of reincarnation, you cannot explain the differences

in the structure of natures, habits, temperaments, thoughts, various level of intellect and predilections, with differences in their aspirations, cravings and yearnings both in the spiritual and mundane spheres. These very differences which are of multitudinous nature and which are result of various complicated processes of evolution and changes gone through by man before he was born, should be a proof and an eye opener to man that such difference of a vital nature cannot be attributed to any other cause except that man evolves stage by stage, biirth by birth, age by age."

On February 6, 1957, He said to me:

"As I have already decided to give you My Revelation of the highest transcendental type, this decision can not be changed. What is planned must be executed. You should not therefore think because of continuous postponement that My Revelation will not take place."

By dangling out hopes and assurances which never materialised Ahura Mazda was trying to destroy the sense of expectancy in me. On February 7, 1957, I had a strange experience while meditating in the afternoon. I wrote to Homi as under:

"Today, while meditating in the afternoon, I believe, I was in a state of semi-trance and I witnessed a strange scene. I heard the conversation to two women. One was swimmer and the other did not know how to swim. The person who knew swimming cautioned the other one to just bathe in the shallow waters. But she refused. She dashed into deep waters. There was Ahura Mazda with her who guided her footsteps and made her enter into the deep sea. The other person was in consternation. She followed her and was amazed to see her swimming quite naturally. She told her, nay, begged of her to return at once. She refused, but eventually said that she would come back. But Ahura Mazda told her not to waver but be firm, for she would not be drowned if she kept her hold on Him. The more she tried to return to the shore, the more she was pushed into deeper waters. Her friend was in deepest consternation. Her pleadings were in vain. She then entered the deep water and asked her to catch hold of her and she would bring her to the shore. This proved a failure. Both were in a confused state of mind. How long could the friend wait? She waited till it was very dark. She could not leave her for that would mean cowardice on her part. She wanted to return home for it was already too late and she had to attend upon her husband and her children. Both were in a dilemma and both in deep waters. At last Ahura Mazda came to the rescure to both parties. He said that He had tested both of them and both came back to the shore. The moral, ofcourse, is simple.

Why is Ahura Mazda giving me these pictures? It is, I believe to impress upon me that the final stage is being reached and I must keep in mind the lesson – the great lesson of complete surrender to His Will."

A friend who was in a dilemma asked the question: "Can man only show love for a woman through possessive love? Or, putting it the other way, is love bereft of possession, no love at all ?"

Ahura Mazda gave the following explanation when invoked:

"Men's love for woman should be unselfish and not so degrading as to make the woman his slave and his tool. Such love is sordid. It can never raise the man or the woman to a state of spirituality. Such love a creator of barriers between man and man and woman and woman and it should be denounced. But, at the same time, for the purpose of maintaining peace and harmony, the woman must use her tact and win over her husband by providing him with plenty of opportunities to unfold the higher Self in him, so that he may get chastened in no time and change his views in the new climate of cultural progress. It is the duty of the woman to be passive but her passivity should unfold itself in a dynamic manner in uttering truths which may reveal to the man the sordidness of possessive love and the enthrallment of love that is divine, altruistic and Platonic in its conception and idealism."

To the question, when does a man long for God, intensely and passionately, Ahura Mazda replied:

"It is possible for everyone to love and worship God. It is only when man is disgusted with life that he craves for inner happiness and he soon gains it if he turns his mind towards God and longs for God with all the intensity of his heart, mind and soul."

I was told by Ahura Mazda that though I had a body, it was only as an identification mark for carrying out the mission.

On February 22, 1957, Ahura Mazda gave me a most thrilling discourse on His Divine Law. He said:

"I am waiting just because I must wait till the day fixed for you by My Divine Law. I am the Creator of the Law and yet I am the servant of the Law. The Creator becomes the Servant. I am subservient out of My Free Will and not out of compulsion. I serve this Law for I want the whole universe to serve the LAW. I am the Law, the Creator of the Law and yet ruled by the Law. I am the Ruler and yet the Law rules Me – the Ruler of the whole universe. Such is the great importance the Law.

You see, when I have been telling you that I want to give you My Revelation, it was not an empty assurance. I want to reveal Myself to you for I love you intensely. But I must wait till you are destined by Law to attain My Revelation."

I had a strange dream experience on the night of February 23, 1957. I described it to Homi in one of my letters.

"A young man, more a boy than a man, of uncouth appearance, most miserably clad, half starved and miserable looking, gets into a monastery. He enters into the room of the head of the monastery and the latter is shocked. He turns him out, thinking him to be a vagabond with evil intentions. He is very angy that his prayers in the stillness of the night in his sacred room should have been disturbed by the intruder." He asks him in a commanding voice:

"Who are you ? How have you managed to get into this place at this hour?"

"I have not come of my own accord. God has brought me here. He wants me to serve you."

The monk's anger is appeased. He asks him gently all about him. He gets the following story from the lad:

"I was a child when my father died. My mother brought me up and sent me to school. But she died when I had not even entered my teens. She worked hard to earn her living but the wages she

> earned were not sufficient to keep us two souls from want and poverty. When passed away, there was nothing left behind. The rent of the small room occupied by us had run into arrears and the landlord took possession of the permises and I was driven away."

> "I made my home in the streets but I kept my solemn promise to my mother and repeated God's name all the time. I kept on thinking of God, all day long, foodless, penniless, shelterless as I was and God came to me. He asked me to follow His orders and to obey Him in all respects."

The story of the lad melts the heart of the grey, old man. He asks him to sleep in his own bed. The boy declines.

> "I have slept on the pavements underneath the sky. Let me lie down here on the floor and I shall be happy." The monk makes a bed for him on the floor.

"Do you want to stay in monastery and learn ?"

"Yes, father, I shall be too happy."

The next day, he is given a separate room and arrangements are made for his education. A priest brings him the Bible and starts teaching him. He is surprised when on the following day, the boy says he has read the whole Bible.

It is inconceivable that the lad could know the Bible in the course of a few hours of reading. The teacher examines him and is dumbfounded with the ready answers he gets from the boy. He is held as a prodigy. He is soon anointed as a priest and given the role of preaching in the church.

> The very first sermon the boy priest gives is astounding. He is asked how could he perform so well?

> "I know nothing, It is God who speaks when I open my mouth. I know not even what I have spoken. God does everything. I am only His agent, His tool, His child and servant."

Commenting upon this experience, Homi said:

> "The experience you have narrated is of interest both by itself and as portending what will become of you after receiving the promised Revelation. Then you will become a full and complete

instrument of god for all the rest of your life on Earth. This is what complete *'Saroshem Mazdai'* means and brings."

On March 3, 1957, sitting in the altar room I prayed to God intensely that the struggle should now end. I said to myself that I had become an Arhat by the grace of Sri Ramana Maharshi, the Sage of Arunachal, when I was him in July 1947 and since then I had been waiting patiently for God's Revelation but without success.

This was the condition of complete surrender to His Will that I was being taught. "Calculation, expectation, planning, looking forward longingly – these things you must dispense with," said Ahura Mazda and I had but to bow down to His Supreme Will.

On March 6, 1957 in the course of a long message, Ram Ram gave the assurance that all the healing cases were put by Ahura Mazda on the list of His miracles to be performed after His Revelation to me. Meditation was continued for long hours. It helped in acquiring and storing a vast amount of secret knowledge.

On October 2, 1957, I was again asked by Ahura Mazda to listen to my soul. I was strictly prohibited from writing any more articles or any book.

On October 6, 1957, Christ gave a most revealing message on two kinds of death. He said:

> "There are very important changes taking place all around but of all the changes, I consider the change that is going to take place in you very shortly as the most important:
>
> You will cease to exist in the true sense of the word as soon as you get God's Revelation. You will keep up your physical frame, and to all intents and purposes, your world would see no change in you. People will consider that you are as active as any human being could be. But from our point of view, you would be dead. Someone else is going to occupy your body and he would be the active force behind your physical body. You have now to face two kinds of death – first, the annihilation of your mind, the senses and the will and secondly, complete extinction of your physical

frame. When the latter takes place, your world would think that you are dead.

When you die as your world understands, there will not be any ceremony at all, for your death in your worldly sense in no death according to our way of thinking. You will get full awakening when you get God's revelation and when this takes place, we will hold you as apirit like any of us, living in our Spirit Land. Your casting off of you physical body later on would therefore make no change to us in you at all."

Your book *"How I found God"* will be hailed as a new chapter in the history of man's progress – progress towards unification as opposed to separatism. A new cult will speedily gain the support of your world and lead ultimately to the co-cordination of all religions extant into ONE RELIGION to be followed universally by all people. The various prophets and sages of the past will be revered as pillars of this new religion for had they not given their teachings, your world would not have progressed from darkness into light."

"The new religion, the conglomeration of all religions extant, will become an active force for the upliftment of your world. It will uproot poverty, disease, inequality and ignorance from the human soil and plant instead a vigorous growth of peace, prosperity, happiness, contentment and harmony. Man's progress will reach its zenith with the foundation of ONE RELIGION FOR ALL."

The difference between clairvoyance and the opening of the inner eye was explained by Ram Ram in teh course of a message. The former is a psychic gift, the latter a divine boon, conferred by God only when human perfection is reached and the soul is liberated.

I was not destined for liberation in the present incarnation but I had managed to succeed by dint of hard work and continuous effort. I was therefore very anxious that His Revelation be hastened. Ram Ram gave the following explanation:

"To gain liberation is your own affair. It rests entirely upon your own efforts. God cannot give you liberation unless you gain it.

You gained it in the quickest time by making huge sacrifices and by means of most strenuous efforts. But God's Revelation is totally a different thing. If God wills, He can give you His Revelation; if not, you can do nothing."

I was suffering from a painful boil, rather an abscess. Ahura Mazda said:

"You are getting the pain not because of your karma, for you are a liberated soul, but because I have to give you this painful experience. I am doing it in order to strengthen your inner vehicles adn make them responsive to the suffering of others which you will have to redress when the mission starts. He further said: "A gift is supposed to bring joy not bitterness but God's gift is to be measured by the result of its use and not nature."

The pain was a reaction to the healing done under His orders on a particular patient.

On May 13, 1957, Ahura Mazda speaking on the establishment of one world religion, reiterated that all the great religions of the world would be blended together and in the course of a century or two, the different labels will lose their significance.

On May 25, 1957, Ahura Mazda gave me the following message at 10:30 p.m.

"You will get a letter from Homi tomorrow. It is My letter to you written by Homi's hand. It is an exceedingly important letter specially written by Me in order to break the present deadlock and enable you to get My Revelation. Kindly read it carefully and place it at the altar. I shall then further explain the whole situation."

I got Homi's letter of May 20, 1957, exactly as predicted by Ahura Mazda the following day *i.e.*, May 26. The most relevant portion of it is given below:

"You are showing desperation. You have still not got rid of the notion that you can do good to the world only by activity in the world and you fear that you may still be stopped from such activity. This is not withdrawing into yourself. This is trying to run away from yourself. Your troubles will not be solved in that way. That way lies danger and frustration. As Ahura Mazda says, "face the situation in and indifferent and non-expectant manner." Your secret thoughts and prayers are teh obstacles in your way. You certainly love God, you have faith in Him, and you honestly wish to surrender your will to His. But these secret thoughts and prayers betrary that this surrender of your will is not complete. Think for yourself and see whether the Mission can succeed, or will it not stand the risk of some failure and consequent DETERIMENT TO YOURSELF so long as this surrender is not complete.

With the functioning of superhuman powers can you not see for yourself the danger of your individual will obtruding itself upon the Divine Will? Will not this be to your personal detriment-apart from all considerations of the Mission? God is Omnipotent and resourceful enough to secure the success of His Mission in spite of your failure. But you will have failed and He does not want you to suffer the pangs of the consciousness of failure. Remember this consciousness will be very, very acute and poignant. Tell me, then is He not really kind and merciful, to you in withholding his transcendental conscious revelation from you yet? Is not His love shielding you from a real danger? I therefore say withdraw more and more into yourself, waiting patiently for His pleasure to draw you out of yourself. I honestly believe all the above has been written under Ahura Mazda's direct inspiration. He directed me to write it out as soon as I had finished studying the message. May His Will be done. AMEN."

The letter was placed at the altar immediately and Ahura Mazda Said:

"Yes, the whole letter, as I told you yesterday, is Mine and not Homi's at all. I inspired him and he has written word for word as secretly dictated by Me. The letter has made a very deep impression upon you and you now understand what is the obstacle in your way. This obstacle you have already removed by your resolute will to surrender whole-heartedly to Me. I have uprooted from your mind even the slightest speck of doubt and suspense. You are now absolutely satisfied that you are in the hands of God, the Highest Spirit in the universe and that you are destined for a great mission.

Your complete surrender to My Will is absolutely necessary for the success fo your mission. I see a great change has come over you by reading Homi's letter and this change means complete removal of the last obstacle in the way. I can now claim you as Mine in the real sense of the word.

My Revelation to you of the type I want to give to you would be a source of danger to you and, instead of a success, your mission would be a failure. I am God. I see the future. As i am bent upon making the mission a success, I shall not give you My Revelation of the highest transcendental type, unless and until all the requirements for the success of your mission are properly fulfilled.

Your only duty now is to wait patiently, whether it be for an hour, a day, a week, a month or even a year. You are merged in Me. You have lost your individuality. You must act therefore as if you have no will of your own, no mind, no heart, no desire, no attachment for anything."

There was no Revelation inspite of the continuous messages of Ahura Mazda and Ram Ram that I was on the point of getting created a sort of despression of feeling. This soon gave place to a thrill of delight when my soul gave me the following most heartening message:

"I am your soul. I have come to learn from Ram Ram and Christ that the date fixed for God's Revelation is now extremely near I am your soul. The Master can give you elusive message but they cannot do so with me. They have told me everything in confidence and I am telling you what they have told me under orders of God. My message to you is therefore based on facts and is not a mere assurance just to please you and keep you hopeful. There is some deep meaning in their continuously assuring you that God is on the point of giving you His Revelation to you."

Homi, commenting upon the above message of my soul in his leter dated June 17, 1957, said:

"Your soul is free and liberated. It is in constant touch with Ahura Mazda. The mind is its vassal. My suggestion therefore is that a prayer to the. soul on the lines of the one printed on the accompanying card, should strengthen the assertion of the Soul's Rightful Rulership over its Domain including the functional aspect of the mind.

If this suggestion helps in the early VICTORY of your Soul, I shall feel most abundantly rewarded and grateful. May it be so ! AMEN !"

The prayer referred to by Homi is as under and I started repeating it every day:

"Oh the Real God – Self Within, I beseech Thee to manifest Thyself to my physical consciousness, here and now and to form a permanent, unbreakable close contact with it and to assume Thy rightful Rulership over the whole field of all Thy vehicles visible, and invisible on all the planes of Existence. Amen !"

A superhuman effort to reach the goal was necessary. But I felt instinctively that even if I failed, God's mercy was so great that He would come to me to my rescue. It was so very thrilling when Ahura Mazda told me:

"What should be super-human is really only human for you...Remember I am your God. I am with you every minute of your life. It is a boon that you are enjoying. It means protection of the highest order. This is the compensation I am making for having suppressed all your powers as a Master, a *Jivan Mukta*."

On June 25, 1957, late at night my soul said to me "I have just returned after contacting Homi's soul. I want to tell you that formerly I was not happy staying in your broken, shattered body. But today it is just the opposite; it is immaterial to me what type of body I am dwelling in. I can discard your body at once for all times and go away to the Spirit World which is my original home. But I have to obey the orders of God, and in spite of my power to leave your body for good, I must make use of it. I am under God's direct control and I have to obey him."

July 10, 1957 was the 32nd anniversary of Meher Baba's silence. The following message as dictated by Ahura Mazda was sent by me to the local Meher Baba groups:

"Not as a follower of Meher Baba but as a genuine lover of this great and saintly soul, it gives me great pleasure to send this humble message on the occasion of the 32nd anniversary of his great and momentous silence.

Mehar Baba's silence has become a byword in every home and hamlet. In his silence, he is wearing a garment of love to cloth the

> whole world which is not ashamed of its nakedness, nakedness caused by its sinfulness. May he continue to thrill the world by his deep silence for in silence is the joy of life, man's victory over the forces of anger, hatred, war, jealousy and crass ignorance.
>
> Mehar Baba is not an Avatar of God but a sweet soul whose silence is as thrilling as a poet's words or a musician's song. May his silence continue for in silence alone he can live for the benefit of the world."

Ahura Mazda gave me an idea of the nature of the mission in the course of a long message delivered on July 21, 1957

> "The object of declaring you as My emissary is merely to continue the good work of Christ. You shall not be a second Christ, but your mission shall be like that of Christ. In fact, the real Christ will be guiding you. I have picked you up for this great mission, as I shall be picking up others for the same purpose, when you are called away. Not one prophet but a series of men elevated from the humble stool of their lives will be made use of by me as if they were prophets for the enlightenment of your world. I want dynamic spiritual forces to rejuvenate the body politic and enkindle in the hearts of men that devotion to God which is so necessary for man's salvation."

Three years of continued silence were completed on July 29, 1957. In his message of July 31, 1957, Ahura Mazda reiterated:

> "It is foolish if anyone thinks that you have not realised God. If you have not realised God, would I have given to you the foreword to your book, "*Poems of the Heart*," If you had not realised God, would I have dictated to you the whole book, "*Romance Of A Soul*" and given an account of your past two incarnations? If People are so foolish as not to understand even these bare facts, they are surely to be blamed, not you."

On August 22, 1957, I was in *samadhi* for four hours at a stretch while meditating in the early hours and Ahura Mazda said:

> "Both Masters, Christ and Ram Ram were present when you were in *samadhi* and it is a great surprise to them how, when your soul

could dance in such ecstatic delight and bathe in the glory and splendor of My Revelation, you should still not have attained physical consciousness of your soul's revelry. This deep game I am playing just a demonstrate to you that I am God and I can defy anyone in the universe."

There was not the slightest doubt in my mind that I was in the hands of the Supreme Spirit in the universe, Ahura Mazada Amshaspad.

I was anxious to re-read the Bhagwad Gita, and permission was given by Ahura Mazda.

A vow was taken as ordered by Ahura Mazda not to interfere in mundance affairs. He said:

"Don't justify yourself even if you are maligned, criticised or abused."

On September 26, 1957, my soul gave me the following talk:

"Yes, I am your soul. I go out every night to do rescue work among those in distress. They receive me with open arms. It is such a great joy to help those who are in great need of comfort and solace. I visit even slum areas. From the type of work that I am doing now, I get and idea of your mission when it starts. I do a lot of work among hospital cases as well as those in mental sgony. I gather round me juvenile criminals and teach them to desist from the path of evil and show them the lighted path of God's divinity.

"I speak of God all the time to everyone I meet in the dark slums of human life, both in the physical world as well as in the astral plane. It is these two planes that I visit, when I am out of your physical body during sleep.

"When you meditate in the early hours, when God gives me permission, I fly to the highest spiritual plane. At first used to go to the lower ridges of Spiritual plane, but now I am allowed to ascend the highest region which is full of such charms and etherial delight, that it is exceedingly difficult to describe. It is God's own Abode and souls which are specially marked for special duties on earth are allowed a passage to this region.

Ram Ram said:

"I want to tell you something more than what Christ has said. It will thrill you beyond words. God has put the seal of His approval on you today *i.e.*, He now definitely confirms that you are to act as His emissary asson as His Revelation takes place. Your death will take place when God gives you His Revelation. But from your death will flow a new life. which you must not mistake for your life but of some one else's."

The world was stunned by the news of Soviet Russia having launched an artificial satellite to go round the earth. It was man's greatest scientific achievement, so far. Ahura Mazda gave the following message on October 7, 1957.

"Soviet Russia would soon outbid U.S.A. in all departments of human activity. It will in the course of the next decade or two become the first world power pledged to maintenance of peace and friendly relations with all countries of the world. Its first earth satellite will be followed by various other ingenious devices to gather information regarding inter-planetary travelling by men.

"This is all My work and men should not at all take any credit. I am now speeding the pace of human evolution both intellectually and spiritually. Science and religion will work hand in hand to further comprehend God and His Mysteries. Man will not be satisfied with mere intellectual discoveries. He will not rest content till he has unveiled My hidden world by spiritual probes. You will not have the opportunity of witnessing the great discoveries which are still in the embryonic stage. But you will notice them from My Spiritual Plane and, in fact, you will be one of the many units guiding man to fulfil his destiny to unveil the veiled and thus progress towards the goal of life viz. God-realization."

On October 9, 1957, after telling me again to discard reading books, Ahura Mazda gave me the following message:

"You are the only person in the whole world with whom I am in such deep and close contact for I have to use you exclusively when I start My mission. As you know, you would be dead to Me but not to your world. I will be using your dead body but because you dead body will move and speak and write and do wonders, your world would attribute all that to you and not to Me, who would be occupying your dead body. When I leave you, then only your world would think that you are dead. In reality, you would die the minute I give you MY Revelation leaving behind your dead corpse, which I am going to employ and utilise for My purpose."

Ram Ram corroborated the same day the strange message of Ahura Mazda. He said:

"What Ahura Mazda has said to you is absolutely correct. He is on the point of severing your life chord, for the minute He gives you His Revelation, you will be dead like a stone. It is extremely difficult to get God's Revelation and survive in physical body. He will then make use of your dead body and your world would think that you are still alive. Your soul will be with us in our Spirit World and He will take your soul's place and finish the mission as quickly as possible. The minute the mission is completed, He will ask your soul to come back and occupy your body just for a short time only, for the soul would find it extremely difficult to stay on at all and it will leave your body. Your world would then think that you are dead and your people would dispose of your dead body"

Regarding the controversy whether Zarthustra was a married man or a celebate sanyasin, I was asked by Ahura Mazda to invoke Zarthustra himself for full explanation. The latter gave me the following message:

"I passed years and years exile, cut off from all earthly inteercourse to attain God's Revelation. Do you think one who had to lead a life of abstinence and rigid austerity could ever think of marital ties? It is absurd to say that I was married and had children. Like Christ, I was a celibate all my life for celibacy is essential for perfection of character and exaltation of the soul to be in union with God. But though a celibate myself, I never preached against marriage. I knew that marriage for most people was a safety valve to escape from rashness of the flesh. I therefore enjoined marriage as a necessity for fulfilment of life's goal"

When Zarthustra was asked to explain why then He should have mentioned Pouruchistra, as his daughter in the fifth Gatha, he said: "There is some misunderstanding of mistake. I was a celibate

> throughout my life and I had therefore no children. Something that I never said or meant, it appears has been interpolated. Such things commonly have happened in all Scriptures. Kindly don't be guided by such interpolations which are incorrect."

I was severely advised to think of God and God only, every hour, every minute, every second.

The following day *i.e.*, October 12, 1957, a great miracle was perform. Ahura Mazda occupied my body for nearly three hours when I was in samadhi in the early hours. He said to me in his message. "You were in *samadhi* for a long time and I occupied your body in place of your soul just to see the condition of the inner machinery, whether it was fit for My control or not."

This statement of Ahura Mazda was corroborated by Christ. Two days later, Christ and Ram Ram occupied my body each for a short time as would be seen from Ram Ram' following message of 14.10.1957.

"Ahura Mazda having already found your inner body quite suitable for His habitation for the purpose of the mission, He asked me today to occupy it. I occupied it for a little more than an hour an hour and then came away. Ahura Mazda then asked Christ to take the place of your soul. This was at about 4 when you heard the clock striking. Christ stayed away for a longer time, nearly two hours. You see how Ahura Mazda has made your body fit and spiritual enough for occupation by Him and the Masters as long as they like."

The same day Ahura Mazda gave me the following message:

> "When you get My Revelation, all of a sudden you would see a crescendo of lights so very dazzling and brilliant that would throw you in a state of enchantment and dumbfoundness. It is as I have said previously so often, through a cluster of luminous lights and clouds and vaporous fiery streams of flaming red hot that you would hear Me speaking to you, My dearest son, You won't see Me for the Absolute Spirit has no form. But you would realize Me from My outer cover – the light and rockets of flame.

I will start making you write the last portion of your book. It shall form quite a separate chapter. You may complete the present chapter with the help of the various remaining messages. Kindly start that work and finish it. The day you finish your chapter, I shall give you My Revelation and dictate to you quite a new chapter with which your book would end.

...... After I have delivered to you the text of the last chapter of your book and you have copied it down, your work would cease and I shall call you away. I shall then control your body for the purpose of carrying out the mission. When the mission is completed, I shall call back your soul and I shall leave your body permanently. Your soul will find it extremely difficult to stay in your body occupied by Me and I will have to call it away immediately. In fact,. My going out and your soul's returing to your body and again leaving it permanently would be all simultaneous. When I leave your body, your world would think that you are dead and you would be proclaimedas dead, little knowing that your death took place a little after having attained My Revelatin.

The whole thing reads like a fairy tale but it is as true as the sun in the firmament."

On October 18, 1957, Ahura Mazda gave further explanation in regard to His occupying my body:

"When I occupy your body during the missing, you will not be allowed to eat or drink. But I may leave your body temporarily and allow your soul to take its place in its original tenement just for the normal functioning of the physical body viz. eating, drinking, passing bowels, urinating and sleeping. But as soon as this function is over, your soul would migrate and I shall continue to stay. I shall stay in your body for a much longer time than your soul. It may be that I may stay continuously for days without leaving your body, in which case you will have to go without food and drink. It reads like a fairy tale but let Me tell you, as I have said so very often, yours is an exceptional case and I must stun you as well as your world. Unless I stun your world by these miracles, I will not be able to bring about that revolutionary change in their mode of thought and life which I want."

On October 19, 1957, Ahura Mazda said:

> "Don't be afraid regarding your health. When I begin to occupy your body, the question of your health would not arise for you would feel that you have no body at all. It is the pleasantest experience for one to have a body and at the same time to feel that he has none at all. I am going to confer this special boon on you."

Ram Ram's words ring in the ears, as we close the chapter:

> "I have to give you a most thrilling message. God has cut the veil and you would see the effect of it tomorrow or the day after. I have seen Him cutting the veil today. It was a very thin veil that was preventing you all these days from getting consciousness of His Revelation. The barrier having been removed, you will now gain access to Him in a very forcible way. Our Spirit World would become quite visible to you and you would be a denizen of both worlds. You would see your Masters and you would hear God's voice penetrating through the vibrations of ether, light and fire. It is a most glorious day that is approaching. It is a day of the triumph of the spirit."

On October 23, 1957 I saw a large cloud of fire passing swiftly by me while I rose from my bed in teh altar room for meditation in the early hours. Lest it might be a freak of imagination, Ahura Mazda was invoked and He said:

> "It was I who passed by you and you saw My outer cover. You felt extremely happy when you saw Me." I was told for days together that Revelation was missed by a hair's breadth. It was wearisome to hear the same story over and over again but its deeper significance was not lost on me. It was to make me forget all about Revelation.

On October 29, 1957, 39 months of silence were completed.

The news was splashed from Moscow and read by millions of people all over the world that Soviet Russia had launched on November 4, 1957 its second earth satellite – a half ton air conditioned sphere with a dog as its passenger. This was exactly a month after its first achievement.

Ahura Mazda gave the following message on the launching of Sputnik II:

> "Soviet Russia has made a tremendous march in scientific discoveries and their progress would continue. They would be the first to record their achievements in interplanetary travel. They will reach the moon in no time."

November 7, 1957 was the 40th anniversary of the October Revolution of Soviet Russia and the following message was given by Ahura Mazda:

> "Socialism is the only way; a true government worth its salt can be but socialistic in its objective. Socialism is the only panacea for all the evils in life."

> "The great stride which Soviet Russia has made in industry and science, edutation and welfare of the masses, is absolutely due to the far-sighted economic policy of the country. Every country in the world must give up old-fangled notions of government and become socialistic following the example of Soviet Russia. It is in Socialism that the idea of One World Government would take fruition. Those countries which wtill believe in imperialism, capitalism and colonialism would suffer and there would be popular revolutions in such countries compelling the government to become socialistic in its pattern."

On November 17, 1957, I was thrilled beyond measure, when Ram Ram gave the following news:

> "God has put a garland of love on you. He gave you a ring with the word 'God' engraved on it some yeas ago. Today He has garlanded you. Do you understand what that means ?"

Yes, there was every reason for me to be most grateful to God for the two precious gifts, the ring, signifying His protection and the garland, His love.

On November 29, 1957, I was informed by Ahura Mazda that He was training Homi also. He said:

> "Let Me tell you that I have been training along with you Homi also, visibly and invisibly. I have to act not only through you but also through Homi."

This was a great consolation to me.

In his most important letter, dated 6th December 1957, Homi gives the following salient points noted by him in regard to my case.

"..... If I may tell you what I think about your case, I would ask you to note the following points:

1. You have realized God. As you know He is always with you.
2. Your soul has had His Revelation but physically you are debarred from its consciousness as the result of a special dispensation on His part.
3. He has reserved for you a special kind of physical Revelation because of the role which He wants you to play in His Mission as His Emissary.
4. But the Mission is HIS (NOT YOURS) and we do not know its nature or its course, and it seems to me thatit can not be carried out through you singly. He has already told you that He is going to make use of me also for the purpose, and has therefore been training me as well, I am inclined to think that He must be training scores of others also in different parts of the world and will make use of all His trainees simultaneously, so that the whole world will see the manifestation and miracle of his working at one and the same time.
5. As he has told you before, He has been training you not only for work during your present Earth life but also for that in your post-mortem existence.
6. Your work during Earth life has already commenced secretly, and it can commence openly when all other factors extraneous to you, are equally ready for its commencement. You have thus to wait not only upon world events as you have been already told, but also upon the readiness of your co-workers.
7. Understood thus His Revelation is truly a world event. It is meant not only for you personally as the Mizdemor

Reward of all your sacrifices and willingness to sacrifice yourself upon the altar of the orld, but also as a world awakener.

8. This being the case, it does not matter if you are used openly for the Mission only for a few days, in your Earth life. You will have to continue taking part in it even in your post mortem existence.

9. Therefore there is no sense in thinking about the Mission at all. It is His concern and it must be left entirely to Him. But one thing is certain, however short your ministry, He will not deny you his trancendental Revelation. That is my firm belief and conviction."

The following is a commentary by Ahura Mazda giving a detailed explanation of all the points raised by Homi in his letter:

"I am not only training Homi but others also and they will become soon fit to join you when the mission starts. It is a mission of world-wide order and you have to play a most promi ent part in this world awakening mission. Kindly re-read Homi's letter point by point:

Point (1) Yes, you have realized Me, for I am with you all the time.

Point (2) Yes, I have revealed Myself to your soul but I have debarred you from getting physical consciousness of My revelation on account of certain factors in the universe. You will come to know of it by and by.

Point (3) I have already said in "*Romance Of A Soul*" that I have appointed you as My Emissary on eath and this pledge of Mine would be duly fulfilled.

Point (4) Yes, Homi has hit the nail correctly. I am not only training Homi but some others also at the same time.
Their training will be complete more or less simultaneously. You are the first whose training is already complete and I have now to wait for others."

Point (5) As your training is already complete, I have started you for your work after your physical death, so that the mission started by Me may continue even after your departure and you may continue to play your role in the mission like other Masters.

Point (6) This is absolutely correct. Not only world events but readiness of those who are directly under My training, are the dominant factors upon which hangs the question of the commencement of your mission. Kindly note the training given to you is of quite a different nature from the training that is being given by Me to others. This distinction was necessary, for the success of the mission will depend more upon you than any of other co-workers and colleagues."

Point (7) This also is correct, I am not giving you Revelation though you deserve it, because I want to make the utmost use of your offer to sacrifice for others.

Point (8) Yes, in view of your bodily condition I am compelled to make use of you just for a short time. Your part in the mission would therefore be for a short period of your physical life but it would be such a momentuous period in the history of your world as would stun everyone on earth. Just wait and see how things end.

Point (9) Yes, I have reserved for you, Revelation of the most transcendental order. This is absolutely necessary in your case for without it, the mission would fail most ignominously."

Ram Ram in his message dated December 11, 1957 corrected any wrong impression that might have been formed that the training under Ahura Mazda was now complete. He said:

> "Your training is, still not complete. No one's training can ever be complete if he or she is under Ahura Mazda's direct control and charge. Just as Ahura Mazda is infinite, His training is infinite and you will have to go on with His training all the time whether you are in physical body or spirit body."

On December 13, 1957, Ahura Mazda gave me a very important message indicating the nature and object of the mission in general. He said:

> "I am God and I am going to save your world from destruction. Before I call you away, You will have the happiness to see the fruition of your mission viz, establishement of peace throughout the world and laying down of the foundation stone of a mighty

edifice of One World Government and One World Religion. It is a mighty work that requires not one but many Bodhisattvas."

The following message of Ram Ram, on the continuance of full surrender to God even after death, will be read with interest:

"When you become a spirit by throwing away your physical body, obedience to Ahura Mazda and full surrender to His Will will become automatic. It is only when one has a physical body, this surrender becomes exceedingly difficult of achievement. But when once it is achieved, there is then no further difficulty for it continues in the Spirit World."

On December 29, 1957, I completed forty-one months of my silence.

A letter addressed to brother Doraswami by the Secretary of the Reception Committee of the Seminar, inaugurated by the Spiritual Development Camp, Madras, was forwarded to the writer and it was placed at the altar. Ram Ram gave the following message:

"Your world is on the brink of a great volcano which might burst any day and bury the greater part of human life and civilization into debris and ruination. At such a time, it is necessary that spiritual luminaries must meet together and devise a plan to stop the mad race for armamenta among the major powers of the world. I have been specially asked by Ahura Mazda, the great Lord of Creation and the Supreme Spirit in the universe, to tell you that the people of the world must unite and with one voice raise the cry to stop all atomic and hydrogen bomb tests and production of nuclear weapons and that political heads of all governments, particularly U.S.A. and U.S.S.R. must meet in a conference and devise a plan for immediate disarmament of the entire world.

I assure you that Soviet Russia has no design at all on any neighbouring country. It wants peaceful coexistence and its word should be trusted.

It is my desire that this message of mine should not only be read at the Seminar but it should be broadcast adn thousands and millions of people should come to know of it. It is not my message but the message of My Master, your God, Ahura Mazda, who is watching you all and is doing His utmost to stop all bellicose talk and dangerous movements to avert a great catastrophe that is threatening."

On January 11, 1958, I was asked by Ahura Mazda to listen to my soul and the latter gave me the following message:

"Yes, I am your soul extremely eager to give you a talk which will thrill you. I know all the secrets of the universe. I know everything which a human soul after getting enlightenment from God Himself can know. I have wandered all over in the Spirit World from the darkest den of infernal gloom and misery to the brightest realm of God's own Abode in the highest Spiritual Plane. I have studied the cosmic laws and have contacted spirits, low and high. I have done rescue work under the guidance of our beloved Master Ram Ram. I am now acquainted with the type of work that I will have to do when I leave your physical body for good and take my place along with the Masters in the Spirit World. I also know what work I have to do before God calls you away after giving you physical consciousness of His Revelation. He has already given me His Revelation of the highest transcendental order. It has filled me with such delight, that I can stay in your body, if ordered by God, even eternally. It is immaterial to me now whether I stay in your body or in the highest Spiritual Plane, for with the powers that God has already granted to me, I am in peace, ease and bliss, anywhere and everywhere. When I am in closest touch and communion with God. Ahura Mazda, it is the highest bliss one could have. I am therefore all bliss, bliss that is imperishable, permanent and ever-abiding. I want that this imperishable bliss to be transferred to you, so that you may feel it physically all the time and not causally, as you feel, now. When this feeling of joy becomes permanent, God would give you consciousness of His great Revelation which He has already given to me. What is given to me is yours. I am your soul. If I enjoy permanent bliss, it is absolutely certain that what I enjoy you must share in the same degree."

Some Poems

by Yogi M. K. Spencer

GOD ALONE CHANGETH NOT, IN THE CHANGING UNIVERSE

Speak not to me of fame and glory,
Search your soul and you will find Me there,
Strive for the best,
Work for the highest.

Sojourn not in the solitude of sin,
Wake up and walk in the path of glory,
Spring and Autumn, Summer and Winter,
Will pass away like leaves of the forest tree.

Like dew drops failing in the morn,
Which disappear with the rising sun,
Life's pursuits are transient and fleeting,
It is God alone that changeth not.

Sweet are the ways of God
God is the guide in the pathway of life,
Do your best and leave to God the rest.
Aim at the highest and work at the fiercest,
Follow the path of saints and sages.

Catch the substance and leave the shadow,
Work like a Trojan, fearlessly, ceaselessly.

Shrink not from duties howsoever hard they be,
They are stepping stones to the crown of life.

Hurrah, hurrah, three cheers for all,
Who make righteousness their creed in life.
Speak the truth and shame the devil,
Strong is the citadel of righteousness.

Step by step we can reach the sunny way;
Drop by drop we can fill teh cup of life.
Make melodious and sweet the song of life,
May you be the shepherd of your soul.

The skipper and guide of the boat of your life,
Move on and on towards the starry light.
The sun's ruddy glow and the moon's pale light,
Glimmer and patter through long day and night.

Foolish are those who in their ignorance,
Ignore God's beauty of Nature.
Seek all the guidance of God,
He is our Lord, He is our Master.

All glory to God, all praise to our Lord,
He is the beautiful. He is the fashioner.
He is the anchor of our heart;
Silent and serene He sits in the centre,

Unfathomable and boundless is He
Eternal and Imperishable.
Fall on your knees and worship Him
With all your heart and mind and soul.

The wisest words are these of God:
Share your joys with others,
Speak ill of none in life,
Slay the ego, crown the egoless Self.

Strange are the ways of the world,
That shatter and ruin and destroy.

Sweet are the ways of God,
For He guides us to the Land of the Rest.

Bedewed with honeysuckles and roses,
Embalmed in freshness of purity,
Sprayed with the light of Love,

Bejeweled and bedecked with the diadems of the
splendour of of God. Sing the Song of God

Let us sing the song of God,
Ahuram Mazda, our Lord,
He is the mightiest of the mightiest
Robed in silver and gold,
He who touches the edge of His mantle
Gets transformed in brilliancy.

There is matchless serenity in His face,
There is a glow of warmth in His words,
He is the Giver and the bestower
Of light and happiness to all.

He looks upon us as His children;
He loves us and protects us all,
He loves all, praise God's glory,
He is our King, our Ruler.

To come within the sacred precincts of His,
Is the rarest honour and privilege, courtyard
Which they only enjoy,
Who tread the path of Righteousness.
God alone is the Reality,
the prop of every human heart

O God, Thou art the Supreme Lord, the Master of the universe,

The Sun, the stars, the constellations are Thire
They move in quick succession,
They play their different roles.

Visible or invisible, O Lord,
Thou art the prop of every human heart,
Thou forsaketh none in the hour of trial,
Even the worst sinner has Thy protection.

Thou art the Giver and Bestower,
Thou art the citadel of strength,
Thou art the anchor of hope,
Thou art of fountain-head of Mercy.

Thou chaseth away man's fears and doubts,
Thou art the becon light of joy and cheer,
Thou art the guiding star,
Thou the shephered of the soul.

Thou art the Absolute Spirit pervading the universe,
Thou art the seed and soul of every phenomenon,
Thou art the Fashioner and the Builder,
The Artist and the Architect.

None can exist without Thee,
Thou art the Absolute, Invincible, Indivisible,
Spring and summer, autumn and winter,
Are the seasons of Thy creation.

In spring there is bloom, ripeness in summer,
The Autumn and Winter bespeak of decay & death,
Hope rises in every human heart,
It is the ray of Thy divinity.

Light shines on the Path of Righteousness;
Darkness girdles the Path of Sin,
Wake up O man and pray to God,
With all the earnestness and intensity of heart,
For He and He alone is the Reality,

To know whom is to enter into the Kingdom of Eternal Bliss.

Work on and march without fear or fright,
For He is the guardian of all travellers on the Path,

Sing His praises day and night,
Think of Him, every hour,
He is the lodestar, He is the light,
He is the Be All and End All of life.

GOD OF LIGHT AND BEAUTY

O God of Light and beauty
Thou livest ever in the human heart,
Thy wisdom is perfect
Thou dartest Thy rays of delight,
Ever in the darkest vaults of deepening gloom,
Thou forsakest none even in the hour of sin,
For Thou knowest that man evolves through sin,
The stepping stones to eternal rest and suffering,

It is through the long corridor of countless years,
That the soul passing through countless phases

At last reaches the goal of perfection experience,
And attains union with Thee.

Birds of the air and beasts of the plain,
Are linked with men, though they form different,
In the grand symphony of life, stages of evolution,
All are emanations and manifestations of God,

All is in God and All is God,
Pray to God with the fire of your heart,
He is your Refuge and the bastion of your Defence,
His is the inner voice in every human being,
His is the fragrance of joy and delight,
Worship God with all your heart and soul.

He loves all who love Him and even those, who seek Him not,

He is Omnipotent, Omnipresent, Omniscient,
Boundless, Timeless, Spaceless,

All – loving, Merciful and kind,
Seek Him every minute of your life,
Worship Him from the very depth of your soul.

GOD'S MATCHLESS POWER

Unsurpassed in wisdom, matchless in power,
He rules all like a benevolent father,
Rich and poor, wise and ignorant, He protects them all,
And guides them unerringly,
His spoken word is Truth,
His written word is Love,
He who seeks Him can find Him.
In the cave of his own heart,
Seek Him and Him alone,
He is Eternal, Infinite,
Men may go and men may come,
But he lives on for ever,
He is the soul, He is the seed,
Of all things, divine and terrestrial,
Nothing exists without Him,
He is the source of all creation,
He is Light and Splendour,
Pillar of the Sky,
Canopy of the world,
Man's refuge and his citadel,
He rules the tide,
He governs the moon,
He gives light to the sun,
And causes darkness in the night,

His word is Law unto death,
His forgiveness and grace enrichen life,
He is the lodestar of the seer,
And the avowed destiny of every man.

HOW TO REACH THE GOAL OF LIFE

Go forth in life with a freshness of heart,
Seek not riches, nor glory, nor pomp,
Work in humility and contriteness of heart,
In this way you will reach the goal of life.

Prudence and profit go together,
Be wise in all your actions,
In Truth is your salvation,
Worship God in ture renunciation.

There is no charm in a life of deceit,
There is no happiness in eating or drinking,
Be away from the dark den of falsehood.

Do not keep company with liars and cheats,
Truth is the only weapon,
Virtue the only remedy,
Simplicity the only talisman.
To keep your safe in the journey of life.

Sing of the glory and majesty of God,
With all your heart and strength,
God is the crown of creation,
The sovereign master of the universe.

Husband your strength and resources,
Be valiant in the battle of life,
Keep calm in the hour of adversity,
Speak not evil of any one.

Mercy and justice are divine attributes,
Forsake not even the evil-doer,
Forgive him and renew your friendship,
And make him a wiser man.

There is no sin so great as vilifying,
There is no blemish so great as untruth,
Practice righteousness at all cost,
For that is the sure way to God.

There is nothing like zeal and zest in a good cause,
Handsome is that handsome does,
Be valiant in the fight of Truth,
Regardless of all consequences.

There is nothing so shameful as flattery,
Nothing so derogatory as idle gossip,
Sin and suffering go together,
Virtue is its own reward.

Beware of malpractices,
Shun evil like a scorpion,
Be kind to all even the sinner,
But keep away from the path of sin.

Life is a rugged journey,
Over hills and plains and dreary deserts,
But say not "die" in struggle of life,
Be brave and cheerful all through the battle.

Be not elated by success,
Nor be daunted by failure,
For success and failure are passing phases,
In the panorama of life,

God alone is the Reality
O God, Thou art the fountain source of all
The beautifier and the magnifier,
The arm that strengthens the weak,
The anchor of the human heart.

He who seeks Thee in sincerity,
And earnestness, will not go in vain,
Thou art the hope of the fallen,
The bulwark of the faithful.

Enter ye in the life's stream
With a merry heart and fearlessly,
For God protects all those,
Who are pure in mind and heart.

The dead weight in life's progress,
Is the love for the glitter of life,
Give up all sensuous pleasures,
And ye shall ever be free and happy.

Gird up your loins for the battle of life,
Work, work on in the name of the Lord,
For He alone is the Reality,
All else is delusion, nothing,

God, Thou art All in All to us
O God, Thou art our Father and our Mother,
Thou art All in All to us,
Thou art one without a second,
We seek Thee and Thee alone,
In our working hours and sleep,
Thou keepeth vigils over us,
Thine the protecting hand,
Thine the kindly voice,
Thou art the essence of perfection,
Thou art the seed of purity,
Thou are the Lord of the Universe,
Thou art the Ocean of Bliss,
We love Thee with all our heart,
There is fire in our soul,
Which ever burns in purity,
And keeps the spirit enkindled,
Man's might is in righteousness,
His riches none else,
But humility and gentility,
Which bring him, nearer to Thee, O Lord.

God's immanence in Nature
O God, Thou manifestech Thyself in many ways;
The sun and the moon, the earth and the stars
Are Thy creations in Nature,
Blessed with Thy eternal presence.

Thou dwellest in the heart of every being,
Sentient and insentient, high and low,

Thou art the idol of every human being,
The lodestar of his life.
O man, forget not the divinity in you
O man, forget not the divinity in you,
Enkindle the Spirit with the fire of your heart,
Be brave in the struggle of life,
God is your protector, your Lord and your guide.

God, the goal of our destiny
Work on ceaselessly,
March on unmindfully,
Life's goal is not distant,
To him who years for God,
God is the lodestar,
The pivot of life,
The pillar of success
The bastion of our hope,
We pray and we pray to Thee, O Lord,
Thou art All in All to us,
The delight of our heart,
The goal of our destiny.

OM SHANTI, SHANTI, SHANTI

Editor's Post script

This book was originally printed in 1958 in proof form for restricted circulation, by the Spiritual Healing Centre, Coimbatore, contained Spencer's spiritual experiences till January 11, 1958. Yogi Spencer achieved *Nirvana* on August 30, 1958, after undergoing much physical illness, agony and pain. Nothing was known to the world about Yogi Spencer's life and spiritual experiences from January 11, 1958 till the day of his death on August 30, 1958. When I was motivated and permitted and authorized by Sri. A. Somasundaram, Founder and Honorary Secretary, Divine Centre, Markapure (Andhra Pradesh) in 1997 to edit, condense and publish this rare book, I asked him if Yogi Spencer had received any other spirit messages from Ahura Mazda (God) and his Spirit Master Rishi Ram after January 11, 1958, but he did not have knowledge of them.

Strange indeed are the ways of God and unique is His merciful grace on the mankind. When the second proofs of this rare and hitherto unpublished book *How I Found God* as condensed and edited by me, were being corrected by me most unexpectedly a person, totally unknown to me, D.J. Buxey from Mumbai, wrote to me in May 2000 that M.K. Spencer was his "revered guru." I immediately requested him to send me if he had any original letters and later messages etc. received from his guru. By God's amazing grace and on His direction, it seems, he very kindly sent to me in May-June 2000, some original letters of Yogi M.K. Spencer and copies of some spirit messages and others' letters and Spencer's replies to them. These provide invaluable information on the later days of Yogi Spencer's life and his experiences of his last five months from August 11, 1958 to the mid August, 1958.

We learn from the following invaluable information received from D. J. Buxey that Yogi Spencer had definitely realized god, and was made God's emissary by Ahura Mazda in the most unique manner although he could not have his hearts desire to see God face to face in the physical sense fulfill till he breathed his last. Ahura Mazda in His last message dated August 8, 1958 (3:00 p.m.), *i.e.*, just 22 days before his death, told Yogi Spencer:

> "I want to give you my revelation for twofold purpose, viz., in order to complete your book "*How I Found God*" and to complete your mission. In fact, the main part of your mission is the completion of the book. The rest of it has no importance and if I think fit, I may call you straight off after giving you My revelation and completing your book."

We also learn from this material that Minocher K. Spencer was born on October 4, 1988 at 00.26 a.m. and his parents were Dr. Kalkhushru Nanabhoy Spencer and Mrs. Nalibai. He had to suffer a great deal of physical illness and pain due to piles, abscess in stomach and loss of weight. In his letter dated June 18, 1958, Spencer wrote to D.J. Buxey:

> "I cannot consult a doctor and take his treatment for God is my physician and He has asked me to desist from the temptation. I have to put my entire faith and trust in Him. It is a severe trial."

This material very kindly sent by Mr. Buxey for publication also contains the views of Yogi Spencer on such important themes as Spiritual communism, Socialism, Renunciation, America, difference between Mahatma Gandhi and Dr. Annie Besant as spiritualists etc.

We are grateful to God and D.J. Buxey for enabling us to have access to this invaluable material, the missing link, to us, which is being published for the enlightenment of all spiritual seekers and lovers and followers of Yogi M.K. Spencer, who was indeed God's most unique messenger and harbinger of the New Era of Peace, Love and Global Awakening in the later half of the 19th century and the first six decades of the 20th century.

S.P. Ruhela
Editor

1. A letter to M.K. Spencer written by Amiya Kumar Das

"Hallowed By Thy Name"
5A Congress Exhibition Road, Calcutta

11.1.58

Most Revered Brother,

Just a few hours back I have received your kind letter of the 7th instant, containing. Ahura Mazda's message which astonishingly enough, contains some of the readings of Bhrigur Nadi Astrology in my possession. Even then, I still adhere to my notion about the unpredictability of the future of a human being, specially if he is on the spiritual path. Only the creator knows about his future. The Possession of willforce by a human being makes all the difference. But it the astrologer combines other virtues namely clairvoyance and prophecy he can say something which will come true in about 90 percent cases – the 10% is the will of the creator: I will try to give you an illustration from own case. When I got that law lectureship I was almost sure of getting it permanently, but the will of A.M. absolutely changed the situation. But of course the creator's intervention is indeed rare – in most cases the predication may come true, if it is the combined result of astrology, clairvoyance and prophecy. Astrology on the other hand may give a key to the understanding of human nature, and from that standpoint it may make valuable contribution to the sum total of human knowledge. When you have raised the question of your own astrological reading, would it interest you to know that I looked up the ephemeris and constructed a birth chart for you, but unfortunately I did not have your exact time of birth, so I could not find out the most important thing – the ascending sign of birth. May I then request you to be kind enough to send me your birth time. I have my own idea about this ascendent or ascending sign – to me it expresses the amount of light a man has received, if we take it for granted that a man is an expression in light. I wanted to enlarge on this thesis, and proceed scientifically about it and if possible find out some means of measuring this light, but how, and what should be the unit of measurement?

My knowledge of science is limited, and I have had to stop with only a glimpse about a subject which might open up vast possibilities. The difficulty is that there are few men, who even will take the pains of comprehending the subject – which after all deals with light, light rays and vibration. The so called astrologers are mechanical, the inner meaning is lost to them, unless they are endowed with clairvoyance. Moreover, there are hardly any men who can teach this subject. I have not got any one to tell me something new and profound. I understand that this subject has received great impetus at the hands of some Theosophical Masters; unless A.M. kindly directs any of the Masters, the prospects of further progress in the subject does not appear bright or at all feasible. But this is just a wish. I shall however continue my studies in my own way, but it is merely putting a barque without a pilot in an uncharted sea.

Now that I have A.M.'s (Ahura Mazda's) permission, I shall send the palm print to the Sukra Nadi astrologer, but it will depend upon whether I can spare the money necessary for it, because before I can consult him, I have to clear my debts to Brother Doraswami and without paying him Rs.50/- I am afraid, I can not indulge in any luxury; and in the circumstances it will be a luxury. Mr. Yogi, fine soul that he is, does not realize, how financially embarrassed I am. I bow down in all humility to A.M. for His kind message.

I understand on inquiry that the Life Insurance Corporation have not yet engaged any lawyers, but there is a likelihood of the reemployment of their existing staff. You will kindly appreciate that a part time job is difficult to get.

As to my prayers to A.M. regarding 'Revelation', I have changed my method. I am thanking Him for already revealing Himself to you. I am not waiting for a future event. I am taking it for granted that it is already an accomplished fact. There is a fine story about the birth of Goddess Chandi or Durga in that famous religious book of the Hindus called "*Durga Saptasati*" a part of Markandeya Purana. "*Durga Saptasati*" means 700 verses dedicated or ascribed to Goddess Durga. The book is a great favourite of Tantriks. There it is related how Durga appeared before all the Gods who had been driven out of their celestial abode by the Demons or *Asuras*. In their misery, all the Gods assembled under their leader Indra (Electricity) and began to pray to Param Brahman for relief; out of the combined prayers of the "*Les Miserabbles,*" Goddess Durga was born as a mighty warrior, equipped with weapons forged out of the energy of each of the God or *Devata* or Aryel present. She soon led them in battle against the *Asuras* and conquered the demons. The lesson that I draw from this episode is that where single prayer may fail, a combined prayer even of persons who are miserable, may produce and generate a mighty power which may lead to victory and glory. I don't know what effect can there be of my prayer when I can not even concentrate my mind for a few minutes and when I know how unworthy I am even to utter His name, but when A.M. enjoins us to pray there must be something special in it. For an ignorant and blind person like me, there does not seem to be any salvation, but it is my nature to pray and I shall always pray to

Him for your ultimate victory. I was hoping against hope to hear about your revelation during this Easter, but no human expectation or calculation is proof against God's will. Even when the Masters feel baffled what mere mortals can hope.

If it were possible to pray for you for 24 hours I would do it cheerfully, in a way, perhaps I do – I am thinking of A.M., the Master and of you almost all through the waking hours but of course in an unorganized way, whenever I get a few quiet moments to myself I think of you and the mission, how it is coming about whether it will be a healing mission or a peace mission or a spiritual mission embracing almost all the activities of human beings or a *"Mission Civilatrice,"* as the French say – a civilizing mission. As long as poverty, cruelty (war) and slavery (imposition of one's will on another) continue in our midst there can be no civilization. The Europeans and Americans talk about civilization but really mean a standardized life where the exploitation of sensation and senses are the only Gods; and in India, abject poverty and apathy, are the controlling factors unless we can bring the 'Christ' in our daily life where is our civilization! Capitalism is greed writ large and at the back of it is the sense of security which leads man to save for the evil day and thus Capitalism gains its foothold on the hoarding instinct of man who thinks he can rely upon his own power to ward off the sense

Yours affectionately
A.K. Das

2. M.K. Spencer's reply to A.K. Das

By Air Mail

April 15, 1958
Karachi

My dear brother Amiya,
I confirm my letter of yesterday and thank you for your exceedingly beautiful and loving letter of the 11th received yesterday. A.M. gives me messages only when He wants and not us usual. I talk to Him every day, whenever I want, both outside and inside the altar room. But these talks are brief and generally in reply to any particular question I have to put to Him. Similarly, Ram Ram's messages have also stopped. I can invoke him only when A.M. gives me permission and when he desires, that he should give me a message, which is of course when is a great necessity and matters are of importance.

I was asked by A.M. to read out your letter to Him in the altar room and He Himself has given a reply to your letter. As ordered by Him, I am enclosing a copy of His message.

You say, a man is an expression in light. This is correct. You will get the right type of knowledge for your thesis when you become clairvoyant by the grace of God. In fact, A.M. is going to help you to perfection in your studies of the science of astrology.

As A.M. has given me permission, I give you the following particulars:

Date of my birth: October 4, 1888 at 00.26 a.m. (according to English Calender)

Father's name: Dr. Kalkhushru Nanabhoy Spencer

Mother's name: Nalibai

Parsi roz: Sarosh, month Fervarden 1258 Yenzdezardi, *Samvat* 1944

According to our Parsi calculation the date changes after 6:00 a.m. But according to English Calender, which is a correct basis, the date changes as you know after midnight. I was born 26 minutes after midnight.

My palm lines are very peculiar. The three main lines – the Heart, the Head and the Life meet. The head and lifelines converge in the Heart line. No line is separate. The Heat line runs from one end of the palm to the other end. On the right hand palm, there are two squares on the right side, one above the other. I can't tell you exactly whether they are squares but they look like them.

It is extremely kind of you to pray for God's revelation to me. I may tell you that God revealed to me, long ago, in his personal form. He has also given His revelation of the highest transcendental type to my soul also. The last poem in *Poems of the Heart* speaks of it. But He has been withholding physical consciousness of this transcendental revelation for the last more than two or three years. The struggle continues. I know, He wants to smoothen the path for me, when the mission starts and hence the delay. I am anxious for the mission to start, but without His transcendental revelation, when alone the powers so far suppressed by Him purposely can come into function. In fact, there can be no mission, without revelation.

I feel very awkward to write about myself, but I am compelled to do so under A.M.'s orders.

Kindly let me know all about you. Any improvement in your pecuniary condition? It is difficult to get a part time job, to supplement your slender resources of income but when God wills, the doors will open. All you have to do is to continue your efforts.

I quite agree with your views. When I say that I believe in Spiritual Communism and not Communism of the present Soviet pattern, it is because I want Communism which makes God the Centre figure and is non-violent in character. If Soviet Communism changes its pattern in these two main aspects and I feel it is already showing signs of such a change as evident from the very liberal trends in the vigorous drive of its present Premier Nikita Khrushchev to establish peace in the world by bringing about a complete disarmament in all the countries of the world, its ideology would be heralded as the best for man's happiness, both material and spiritual.

We have the hoarding instinct because we are not sure of the future. But in a communist State, that fear is eliminated as the State makes provision for all emergencies and looks after us in our old age also. In communism is man's salvation as well as peace and happiness in this temporal life also. This is how I look at it.

With love to your Immortal Self.

Yours affectionately,
Minoo
(M.K. Spencer)

Enclosure:
A.K. Das, Esqr.., M.A.B.L.
Bar-at-Law,
Calcutta.

Enclosure: Ahura Mazda's Message

Ahura Mazda: "As soon as you get My revelation, I shall put your friend (Das) in such a position as to enable him to pursue his studies in Astrology to perfection. Let him wait in patience till you get My revelation. He should not delay at all in sending his palm print to the astrologer.

I give you full permission to let your friend have the exact hour of your birth and whatever particular you can give him. I am going to specially help him to come to right conclusions regarding you. This is the miracle that I am going to do for the satisfaction of you all who are inter-related with one another in a most mysterious manner. Homi, Doraswami, D.B. and finally A.K. Das. They were all unknown to you for a long time. But it is I who brought you in connection with them, one be one and thus has been formed a group which is going to be of great force to your world. You are my chosen one and others not chosen are of very great use to Me in the fulfillment of my plan.

I have already said and I say it again that I want the united prayer of all in the group even that of Homi, though he is your Master so that My revelation may take place immediately. Every day lost is a loss to your world, though no loss to you at all. I want therefore that Homi, Doraswami, Das and D.B. should pray every day for My revelation to you. I want them to understand that I have brought them within the orbit of My direct control because I want them to be of great service to you when the mission starts.

Why have I stopped Homi from writing to you? It is to tell you and to inform Homi also that his guidance of you is no longer necessary. You do not need any Master in physical body and longer. I have even deprived you of invoking Ram Ram except on some occasions when I with it. You are now absolutely and completely under my own direct control. I have taken you over absolutely from the hands of everyone. You must understand what that means. Homi knows it fully well and I want the rest also to realise the situation.

Your friend (Das) has tried to probe into the nature of your mission. I don't want anyone to be curious at all.

Let revelation just take place and things will become so very"

Ahura Mazda (God)
Karachi.
April 28, 1958

3. M. K. Spencer's letter to D.J. Buxey

My dear Dinshaw,
I confirm my letter of 26th inst. and thank you for yours of the same date.

I think it is best if I communicated to you A.M.'s whole message as was delivered to me in reply to yours under reference:

> "D.B. is quite right. There is no necessity for any one to pray for my revelation to you, nor for you to ask for it. It is all My business and no one's prayer is going to make the least difference to My

> plan. But if he or anyone prays for My revelation to you, there is no harm. It will not change My decision in any case but it will indicate to Me, the depth of love of the one who prays for you. When I asked all the members of the group to pray for My revelation to you, I was quite serious and am still very serious. I want to test their bonafides and the depths of their love for you. D.B. has great love for you and he is a man who will be prepared to go to any length to help and serve you. But he needs guidance. The very fact that he has stopped studying for his examination so that he could devote more time to higher work, shows the depths of his love for God and the Masters. This act of his has certainly pleased Me the most. I have now an eye on him and when you get revelation, which is extremely near, he will be dumbfounded to see himself into a different atmosphere."

I must say that you have made a great sacrifice by abandoning the idea of preparing and appearing for your electrical engineering examination just to get time to devote to the work of the centre. This means you are giving up the mundane to please God and the Higher Ones in pursuit of the higher things of life.

Doraswami tells me that the sales are now showing signs of picking up. He also tells me that he is expecting an order for a complete set of all the books published by the centre so far from Dr. Mehta of the Society of Servants of God, Bombay, whom you know so well. Possibly it may be your work. Keep well and happy and do be writing to me as often as you can letting me know all about you and your doings.

With love,
Your's affectionately,
Minoo
(M.K. Spencer)

Dinshaw J. Buxey, Esqr.
Bombay.

4. M. K. Spencer's letter to D.J. Buxey

Karachi

May 1, 1958

My dear Dinshaw,

I thank you for your letter of 27th ult. received yesterday and confirm mine of the 28th idem.

I am so glad to know that Homi's recent books are to be reviewed by the Theosophical Society of England and New Zealand in their magazines. I am returning herewith their letters.

I have read your letter to Mr. Bhagat of Messrs. Mohindra and Mohindra regarding Das and thank your for your efforts to help him in getting some suitable appointment.

Last night, I was given a special long message by A.M. and as ordered by Him I am enclosing herewith a copy of it for your attention.

I hope you are keeping well.

With love.

Yours affectionately,
Minoo
M.K. Spencer